Contents

Effective Thinking and Writing 1

The College Essay 29

Paragraphs 97

Sentence Variety, Clarity, and Diction 145

Sentence Errors 191

Punctuation 239

THE BRIEF ENGLISH HANDBOOK

A Guide to Writing, Thinking, Grammar, and Research

EDWARD A. DORNAN
CHARLES W. DAWE

Custom Edition for University of California, San Diego

Taken from:
The Brief English Handbook, A Guide to Writing, Thinking, Grammar, and Research, Seventh Edition
by Edward A. Dornan and Charles W. Dawe

PEARSON
Custom Publishing

Taken from:

The Brief English Handbook: A Guide to Writing, Thinking, Grammar and Research, Seventh Edition
by Edward A. Dornan, Charles W. Dawe

Published by Pearson Longman
New York, New York 10036

This special edition published in cooperation with Pearson Custom Publishing.

Printed in the United States of America

22 16

ISBN 0-536-35351-4

2006240603

MT

Please visit our web site at *www.pearsoncustom.com*

PEARSON CUSTOM PUBLISHING
75 Arlington Street, Suite 300, Boston, MA 02116
A Pearson Education Company

Contents

PART II The College Essay 29

PART III Paragraphs 97

PART IV Sentence Clarity, Variety, and Word Choice 145

Preface

Even though *The Brief English Handbook,* which Chuck Dawe and I always referred to as the BEH, has undergone dramatic changes over the last six editions, this seventh edition is still full of down-to-earth advice that students can easily understand. Moreover, while it remains compact, the BEH serves as a complete writer's guide that thoroughly covers what students need to know about communication in college and the workplace:

- Argument essays
- Business letters
- Creative thinking
- Critical thinking
- Effective sentences
- E-mail
- Essays about literature
- Faxes
- Grammar
- In-class essays
- Mechanics
- Memos
- MLA, APA, CSE styles
- Oral presentations
- Paragraphs
- Punctuation
- Research papers
- Résumés
- Thesis-support essays
- Usage
- Web site construction
- Writing process

Here are a few of its principal features:

Integration of creative and critical thinking with writing.

Part 1, "Effective Thinking and Writing," illustrates the fundamental concepts of thinking and reasoning that play significant roles in learning to write effectively.

Chapter 1 concentrates on how to use creative and critical thinking along with writing to clarify a problem and generate solutions.

Chapter 2 shows how to distinguish fact from opinion, analyze inferences, and verify interpretations. It also shows how to identify common logical fallacies and propaganda techniques.

Chapter 3 explains inductive and deductive reasoning processes that underlie traditional argumentation.

Critical thinking applied to writing assignments.

The BEH puts critical thinking to work. Students learn the levels of thinking identified by cognitive psychologists. Then they apply the knowledge by interpreting key words in writing assignments to determine the level of thinking an instructor expects an assignment to generate.

Practical advice on the writing process.

The BEH has always emphasized the writing process, perhaps even more than any other compact handbook. The five chapters of Part 2, "The College Essay," methodically document how essays unfold from thought to written word. Students can follow the interplay of creative and critical thinking that goes into developing a traditional thesis-support essay.

To help students conceptualize the writing process, Chapter 4 presents a completed student essay with commentary early in the discussion. The development of that essay is then documented in four subsequent chapters. The goal here is, first, to establish what a well-written student essay embodies and, second, to trace its evolution from idea to final draft to show the recursive nature of composition. This teaching strategy helps make concrete what students often see as abstract.

The entire process is illustrated with specific examples. Actual paragraphs from the writer's hand-edited first draft are reproduced with running commentary to show the editing process at work and to explain the reasons for making editing choices.

Essentials of paragraph development.

The six chapters of Part 3 concentrate on paragraphs. The emphasis is on paragraphs working together within fully developed compositions.

Chapters 11–13 show students how to write effective topic sentences, create unity, and maintain coherence.

Chapters 14–16 consider development patterns by purpose: to describe or narrate, to explain, and to argue. These three chapters are illustrated by fully annotated paragraph models.

Procedures and conventions for writing research papers.

Part 9 concentrates on writing the research paper. Its three chapters cover computerized library resources and researching on the Internet, including the use of search engines and the evaluation of Internet sources.

Part 9 also does some trouble shooting as it traces the development of a student research essay: choosing a topic with care, narrowing the thesis, introducing quotations, citing sources accurately, and avoiding plagiarism.

Finally, this revised edition provides updated MLA documentation guidelines and current ABA and CSE supplementary documentation guidelines.

Advice on writing argument essays and essays about literature.

Without getting bogged down in jargon, Chapter 54 presents a direct approach to writing an argument essay. By building on critical thinking concepts presented in Part 1, this chapter illustrates the importance of clear reasoning when trying to win others to either side of an issue. Moreover, by following clear, precisely stated guidelines, students will find that writing an argument is no more difficult than writing an expository essay.

Chapter 55 helps students conceive and write an essay about literature. In guiding students from the writing of an effective thesis to the proofreading of the paper, this chapter addresses such knotty problems as keeping to the historical present, attribution, summary, and paraphrase.

Guidelines for essay examinations.

Most first-year students feel as if they're in a pressure cooker when faced with an in-class essay exam. Chapter 56 gives students clear guidelines to follow when writing in class, whether the task calls for a quick response to a reading assignment or a full-blown essay.

Communicating in the workplace.

The BEH gives special attention to the everyday uses of writing and oral communication. The chapters of Part 10 offer solid advice on how to prepare business letters, memoranda, and résumés. Part 10 also includes a chapter on electronic communication and emphasizes the importance of being courteous when sending faxes and e-mail. One chapter shows students how to construct their own Web site, from formulating the initial idea to proofreading the texts and the final chapter offers advice on giving oral presentations.

Computer and writer's clinics.

Boxed and highlighted mini-lessons cover a wide range of topics: using the computer to prewrite, plan, draft, and edit essays; common faults in grammar and spell checkers; Internet jargon; and evaluating Internet sources. The clinics also offer brief, specific advice on critical thinking and writing, such as tips on decision making, criteria for evaluating information, organizing one's time, placing commas accurately, and embedding key words in topic sentences.

Background in the basic skills.

Part 11 is an easy-to-use grammar review for any student who needs to brush up on the basics. In five chapters, it covers parts of speech and sentences, phrases, clauses, and sentence patterns in just enough detail to bring students up to speed to meet the demands of freshman composition.

Background for multilingual writers.

The BEH also focuses on nagging errors that seem to plague ESL writers. Part 12 addresses these common problems exclusively. Five chapters cover omitted words, noun markers, verb combinations, faulty repetitions, and errors in present and past participles. Each chapter gives ample explanation and examples and provides extensive exercises.

Student model essays with commentary.

At key points in the BEH, student-essay models illustrate different writing assignments. Each of the essays is accompanied by extensive commentary designed to deepen student understanding of the writing conventions being illustrated.

Straightforward design and hand-edited examples.

Using a two-color design and uncluttered pages, the BEH dramatically highlights rules for quick reference. The easy-to-use tab system makes accessing information simple.

The explanations throughout the text are concise yet fully supported by hand-edited examples. Faulty sentences are typeset, with revisions handwritten in color, much like those of a writer editing his or her own sentences on hard copy.

Opportunities for collaborative work.

Chapter 10 establishes a peer-review process that can work either formally or informally. This chapter offers specific guidelines for both reviewers and those being reviewed; it delineates the group's responsibility and includes examples of effective and ineffective feedback.

Acknowledgments

Chuck Dawe and I always had the good fortune to receive helpful suggestions for previous editions of the BEH from many students and instructors throughout the country: Alexander Bell, St. Louis Community College (Florissant Valley); Jennifer Bradley, University of California, Los Angeles; Karen Cahill, Southeastern Community College; Barbara Carson, University of Georgia; Reginald Clarke, Citrus College; Corine Coniglio, Lackawanna Junior College; Terrence A. Dalyrimple, Angelo State University; Tom Eiland, Citrus College; Patty Emmons, Northern Virginia Community College; Norma Engberry, University of Nevada, Las Vegas; Joan Fitch, Mississippi Gulf Coast Community College; Margaret Fox, Oregon State University; Adelaide Frazier, University of New Orleans; Billye Givens, Eastern Oklahoma State College; Barbara Goldberg, Humboldt State University; Stephen Goldman, University of Kansas; Jean Graham, College of New Jersey; Rosanna Grassi, Syracuse University; Byron Grigsby, Eastern Connecticut State University; Michael Grimwood, North Carolina State University; Lin Humphrey, Citrus College; Elizabeth Jordan, University of California, San Diego; Gloria Karin, Ulster County Community College; Melinda Kramer, Purdue University; Jonathan Launt, Central Piedmont Community College; Joyce Lipkis, Santa Monica College; Lisa Martin, Cape Cod Community College; Marilyn McHugh, Ulster County Community College; Michael Meyer, University of Connecticut; Janet Minc, Wayne College/University of Akron; Elizabeth Mitchell, Ocean County College; Jeannette Morgan, University of Houston; Robert Mueller, Illinois Valley Community College; Harold Nelson, Minott State University; Janice Neulieb, Illinois State University; Jack Oruch, University of Kansas; Mark Pedraira, Boston University; Charles Reinhardt, Vincennes University; William Reynolds, Hope College; Jelle Roos, Pensacola Junior College; Maureen Ryan, University of Southern Mississippi; Alan Schwartz, Queensborough Community College; Robert A. Schwegler, University of Rhode Island; Karen Sirmans, Pensacola

Junior College; Anne B. Slater, Frederick Community College; John Stewart, Utah State University; Brendan Strasser, Lehigh Carbon Community College; Jonathan Thorndike, Lakeland College; Linda Tiemann, Blinn College; Virginia Wagner, Mendocino College; Lea Williamson, Texas A&M University; Carroll Wilson, Raritan Valley Community College; Nancy Yee, Fitchburg State College; and William Zehringer, Bloomsburg State College. We offer a special thanks to Robert Dees for his work on the research chapters and to Sarah E. Cummings for her assistance with the chapters on English as a second language. We also wish to express our gratitude to our former HarperCollins editors, Ellen Schatz, Sarah Heylar Smith, and Lois Lombardo.

For the seventh edition of *The Brief English Handbook,* I would like to thank Joe Opiela and the outstanding team of reviewers whose encouragement kept me at the computer: Alice Church, Nashville State Technological Institute; Stephen Cox, University of California San Diego; Allen Feibelman, University of Cincinnati; Jessica Gomel, California State University Fullerton; Roark Mulligan, Christopher Newport University; Elizabeth Oldfield, Southeastern Community College; Tiffany Paschke, College of Charleston; Linda Shelton, Utah Valley State College; James Sodon, St. Louis Community College at Florissant Valley; and Marian Wernicke, Pensacola Junior College.

Special thanks go to Tom Eiland of Citrus College, whose comments and suggestions helped at every phase of the writing and revision process.

Ed Dornan

To the Student

The Brief English Handbook, or the BEH, is a concise guide to grammatical accuracy, effective sentences, correct punctuation, appropriate word selection, and the sound development of paragraphs, essays, and research papers.

I want to call special attention to Part 1, "Effective Thinking and Writing," which I encourage you to read right away. The three chapters in Part 1 present the essentials of effective thinking in detail. They introduce you to creative and critical thinking, clearheaded decision making, evaluating information, and reasoning—all of them indispensable to becoming a critical thinker and writer.

The BEH's primary use will be to advance your writing skills. In a writing class your instructor might assign chapters and exercises for class discussion or refer you to the book to revise your written work.

Revising Essays

Sometimes your instructor's comments in the margins of your paper will refer you to the BEH for certain information. You can best find that information by noting the key terms in the teacher's comments and then looking them up in the index, which lists every important term used in the BEH; or you can scan the table of contents, which lists the book's main parts, chapters, and chapter sections.

At other times your instructor might write numbers or symbols in the margins of your essay. Numbers refer to chapters, and when a letter is used with a number, the letter refers to a chapter section (for instance, 18g refers to Section g in Chapter 18). The numbers and letters appear in the table of contents and on tabs in the upper outside corners of the pages where you will find the information they refer to. Just flip through the pages and stop at the tab your instructor has identified on your essay.

You can find out what symbols such as *frag* or // indicate (*frag* indicates sentence fragment and // indicates parallelism) by referring to the inside front cover, where the words the symbols represent are listed alphabetically. The symbols also appear next to the tabs on each page and at the beginning of each chapter.

If your instructor uses numbers to indicate corrections and to suggest revisions, your returned papers might look like the following example, which is the introductory paragraph of a student essay.

39b "Time to Slow Down" 52a

When I first returned to the city after 10 months in a

51g forestry camp, I was not ready to reenter the pace of daily life. For a few uncomfortable days, I had the feeling I was living within the frenetic action of an old silent movie.

26a [People around me rushing as though they were late for an appointment.][At first this activity made me nervous, my

27 experience in the forestry camp had given me a more leisurely approach to daily activities.]

If, instead of numbers, your instructor uses symbols, your returned papers might look like the following, which is the continuation of the paragraph in the student essay.

In the months that followed I began to understand that the speed of daily living which had upset me when I returned was only the most obvious part of a deeper attitude. We are

// vb so busy when rushed from one experience to another, developing new interests, and dropping old ones, we seldom

ref take the time to do anything well. This shows in our responses to public affairs, in our educational programs, and in our relationships with each other.

After your instructor returns your essay, use the BEH to look up the notations. Then pencil in your corrections before beginning the revised draft.

Your instructor's notations can be a valuable aid in learning the rules and guidelines for clear writing. Try using the notations as a study guide, carefully reading the information they refer to and completing the accompanying exercises.

If you also keep a record of the notations, you can return to the BEH before each new assignment and review the rules and guidelines that have given you trouble. When you follow these two procedures, you will gain as much as possible from the experience of having your instructor, who is a professionally trained reader, evaluate your written work.

ED DORNAN

PART I
Effective Thinking and Writing

Writing is a concentrated form of thinking. I don't know what I think about certain subjects until I sit down and try to write about them. Let's not forget that writing is convenient. It requires the simplest tools. Young writers see that with words and sentences on a piece of paper that costs less than a penny they can place themselves more clearly in the world. Words on a page, that's all it takes to help them separate themselves from the forces around them, streets and people and pressures and feelings. They learn to think about these things, to ride their own sentences into perceptions.

—Don DeLillo, *novelist*

1 Thinking and Writing *think/write*

Thinking is as natural to all of us as flying is to eagles or swimming is to dolphins. Thinking effectively, however, is another matter. It is natural to think, but it is not natural to think effectively. That must be learned.

Thinking generally refers to any sort of mental activity ranging from daydreaming to complex mathematical analysis. In very simple terms, thinking can be divided into two distinctively different categories—creative thinking and critical thinking. To be an effective thinker and writer, you have to learn how to use both.

Creative Thinking

At the heart of **creative thinking** is association, a mental process that generates information, insights, and ideas from memory. Sometimes when you are thinking creatively the mind seems to float from one memory to another. You may recall loosely connected experiences, such as casual conversations, unexplainable hunches, startling ideas, fragments of conversation, details from lectures, even snippets from books, newspapers, songs, and films. In other words, the mind is associating one memory with another memory.

Random thinking and *reflective thinking* are two forms of creative thinking. Random thinking seems to have no purpose and takes place when the mind is adrift or in a twilight state, a mental world between conscious thought and sleep. When in a twilight state of mind, you are hovering on the edge of awareness, and your thoughts appear as a spontaneous flow of images, memories, or feelings with no apparent relationship to one another.

In contrast to random thinking, reflective thinking has a purpose. When you learn to think reflectively, you will be consciously using the power of association to gain access to the reservoir of experience and information stored just below the surface of consciousness.

Critical Thinking

At the heart of **critical thinking** is evaluation, a mental process that judges—or tests—the accuracy of information, insights, and ideas.

Creative thinking—that is, random and reflective thinking—provides the spontaneity that generates information and the intuition that ignites insight. In contrast, critial thinking evaluates the information, insights, and ideas that emerge from the creative process. When thinking critically, you test options, analyze assertions, reveal implicit assumptions, trace logical relationships, and apply standards of reasoning. It is critical thinking that helps you decide what to do or not to do, what is right or wrong, what works or does not work.

Creative and Critical Thinking Work Together

To think effectively you must be both a creator and a critic. For example, to publish a novel, a writer must first *create* the story and characters, but before sending the work to a publisher, he or she must *critically evaluate* it to be sure it is ready for publication.

In diagnosing an illness, a doctor must *create* possible diagnoses to explain a patient's symptoms; then to decide which diagnosis is accurate, he or she must *analyze* each of them through further examination or laboratory tests.

In solving a crime, a team of detectives must *create* possible solutions, and then they must *test* them against the evidence. At the heart of effective thinking, therefore, is knowing when to use creative thinking and when to use critical thinking.

Creative and Critical Thinking in Problem Solving

In everyday life, unfortunately, most people tend to be careless about the creative and critical aspects of thinking. When emotions are aroused, people often act first and think later, seizing on the first course of action that occurs to them.

When facing a problem and making a decision, all of us would be much wiser to recognize the significant role the interaction of creative and critical thinking can play. For instance, through creative thinking, especially through the effective use of association, you can generate information necessary to explore all the elements involved in any decision you have to make; through critical thinking, you can evaluate all the information creative thinking has generated to help you make the right decision.

The procedure for employing creative and critical thinking in problem solving involves a cycle of five phases. You do not have to follow the cycle rigidly. In fact, the phases will probably overlap as you work through them. You may even go back to an earlier phase or work on several phases simultaneously.

1a Use critical thinking to write a definition of a problem.

Typically, the critical thinking process begins with the recognition of a problem followed by a careful definition of the problem. The problem may be quite simple or complex, such as deciding what to do with a free evening or choosing a career path. A class assignment always involves some problem, whether the assignment is a written research project on World War II or an analysis of which is more effective, Abraham Lincoln's Gettysburg Address or Martin Luther King's "I Have a Dream" speech.

You should carefully define a problem in writing. Class assignments, for example, are usually handed to you but are often stated in broad or vague language. It is your job to define the problem correctly before going on to the other decision-making phases. If you fail to define the problem, you risk completing the wrong task.

Some problems are personal and difficult to recognize. Suppose, for example, you learn that the soccer coach is going to cut you from the team. You get angry, deciding that the coach dislikes you. Without giving it much thought, you decide that the solution to your problem is to save face and to quit the team. This thoughtless definition of the problem and your consequent solution help you avoid embarrassment, but later you learn that the real problem was your negative attitude, which had been affecting the team's spirit. If you had defined the problem more accurately, in writing, you might have decided to discuss your attitude with the coach in order to figure out how to improve the situation.

Sometimes defining the problem is the most difficult phase of decision making. Once you have correctly defined the problem, however, the rest of the process is relatively easy.

Three Guidelines for Defining a Problem

A definition should not be too broad. Suppose you define a problem as the need to understand why you feel anxious in stressful situations when all you really want is to learn to relax during finals. The broader definition would set you aimlessly adrift in psychological analysis. If a problem is truly large, break it down into smaller problems and solve them one at a time.

A definition should not be too narrow. Suppose you define a problem as the need to overcome your fear of mathematics because you feel panic as an algebra final approaches. In reality, you experience test anxiety in all testing situations. The narrower definition might lead to your wasting additional hours reviewing algebra; the broader definition might lead to the pursuit of meditation or exercise.

A definition should not in itself be a conclusion. Suppose you notice that every time you approach finals you become seriously anxious. If you define your problem as the need to learn why finals create anxiety, your definition in itself embodies a conclusion—that is, that finals indeed cause anxiety. But the first problem should be to decide whether finals *do* cause anxiety. You might discover that something else that occurs near the end of each semester is causing your feelings.

1b Use creative thinking to generate information.

Once you have defined a problem, you are ready to gather information about it. Many problems require hours of research as part of the information-gathering phase—and you will encounter research techniques in later chapters—but many more problems merely require the thorough exploration of what you already know from past experience. All you have to do is access the information.

At this point reflective thinking comes into play. By setting aside critical thinking and by allowing your mind to associate one idea to another, you can generate a great deal of information from past experience.

There are several techniques you can use, but they all require you to follow your own thought patterns. You must associate one idea with another without worrying whether the connections are logical. In this phase of problem solving, resist the urge to judge or to analyze what comes up. Instead, encourage the creative exploration of your imagination.

Brainstorming

Brainstorming, sometimes called *listing,* is a creative way to write out your thoughts. Begin by concentrating on the problem and then quickly write down your associations. Write your list in just enough detail to remind you of each item's significance when you review the material. Your goal in brainstorming is to write down thought fragments on the fly. Later you can add information that is appropriate to the problem.

Freewriting

Freewriting is valuable during any part of the information-gathering phase. Simply set aside a block of time, reflect on the problem, and write nonstop. Associate one bit of information with another. Do not judge your ideas or shut them out. Often the unexpected will present itself—ideas connecting to ideas in ways you could not have planned. Do not be concerned here with the technical aspects of writing; instead, immerse yourself in your own creative flow while holding in check the critical process.

Clustering

Listing or freewriting usually creates a hodgepodge of written material in random arrangement, but once you have enough information, you can begin to make connections among key ideas. In one sense, *clustering* brings order out of chaos.

Begin a cluster by writing what you have determined to be your problem in the center of the page. Draw a circle around it. As you carefully reread the listing or freewriting, arrange major ideas around the problem in orbits connected by lines. Also circle significant points. As you discover ideas related to the major ideas, draw another orbiting system.

Do all this using single words or brief phrases. Remember, you can always reread the original material to examine the full entry. Through this process, you are simply dividing and subdividing information, emphasizing facts, opinions, or insights that will help the decision-making process.

COMPUTER CLINIC

Generating Ideas for Essays

Brainstorming, freewriting, and asking questions play an important part in the process of composing a writing project. Just as you can use a computer to begin a personal dialogue to solve a problem, you can also use it to generate material for an essay assignment.

It's quite simple to do: Just bring up a blank screen and start writing. This personal dialogue might begin with a list of ideas, even ideas that seem unrelated to your central purpose. One idea might generate freewriting—that's great, go with it! If you get stuck, start asking yourself questions and then answer them.

The process will loosen your creative thinking much like stretching loosens tight muscles. When you finish, go back over your writing to determine what's useful and save it.

Asking Questions

Ask questions about a problem. These are sometimes referred to as reporter's questions: Who? What? When? Where? Why? and How? Not every question will be appropriate for every problem, but using the ones that are can ignite an association chain that will help you view a problem from different perspectives. Write down the questions, and write down your answers.

Consultation

You might become part of a problem-solving group that discusses class assignments. You might also consult a fellow class member, perhaps someone more experienced than you with the decision process. You might also engage your instructor in a discussion to test your ideas. Whenever you discuss a problem, take notes or use a tape recorder; don't risk letting good ideas slip away.

1c Use creative thinking to write a list of tentative options.

When should you shift to this phase? Make the shift when you have enough information to suggest several possible options or courses of action. The goal is to create as many options for yourself as possible; the more options you have, the more likely you will discover a sound one.

As in the previous phase, your thinking here must be primarily creative. Continue to give your imagination complete freedom, and postpone critical thinking until the next phase of the decision-making cycle. If you try to find flaws in your options while still forming them, you risk dismissing sound ideas before they are fully developed. Instead of being too analytical, write down every option that comes to mind. Options you might reject as wild or irrelevant could turn out to be solutions.

1d Use critical thinking to test tentative options.

When you have several options to choose from, it is time to subject them to critical scrutiny to test their reliability. All tentative options involve some kind of *inference,* that is, a process of reasoning that draws a conclusion from information.

For example, suppose that you read an article written by the CEO of a major software corporation. After an analysis of the economy, the CEO concludes that the most financially rewarding careers for today's college students will be in electronic technology. If you conclude from reading this article that you should major in computer science, your conclusion is the result of an inference you formed by combining two pieces of information: the assertion in the magazine article and the fact that you are searching for a major. If you rush to the registrar's office to declare a major in computer science, you might end up with a financially rewarding career, but you have ignored an important rule of effective decision making by forming one tentative option and deciding on it without testing its reliability. Although your decision might lead to a successful career, it is not reliable. An option is reliable only when it is known to be accurate. For an option to be accurate, the information it is based on must be known to be accurate. Your decision to major in computer science fails the test. Because the information in the article may be wrong, your inference is inaccurate.

1e Use critical thinking to evaluate reliable options and make a decision.

When you begin testing your options by appropriate methods, you will probably discover that absolute reliability is rare. Usually there will be some weakness either in the information or in the interpretation of the information, or in both. The best you can hope for is a high degree of reliability. If you delayed decision making until you reached absolute reliability, you would seldom make a decision.

The minimum degree of reliability you should have before acting on an option varies with the circumstances. For example, a juror for a murder trial must have a high degree of reliability to find a defendant guilty. But most options you choose from will not be true beyond a reasonable doubt.

If a written evaluation of your tentative options shows that none of them are sufficiently reliable, then you should repeat the whole decision-making cycle. Each time you repeat the cycle you are likely to discover new information, which might suggest new and more promising options. The process should be repeated until you reach a decision with a degree of reliability sufficient for your purpose.

Exercise 1.1: Defining Problems

By referring to information in this chapter, complete the following exercises.

1. It is 9:30 p.m. of the second day of classes. Pre-med major Ron Tanaka has been studying a biology assignment since 7:30 p.m. He pauses and looks at the rest of the assignment. At his current

rate, he will need five more hours to finish. He has history and English assignments to prepare, too. What phase of the decision-making cycle has Joe reached?

Below are five definitions of Tanaka's immediate problem. Identify the guideline that each definition violates.

2. To call his parents to alert them that he is thinking about becoming a lawyer instead of a medical doctor.
3. To figure out how to finish his biology assignment in three hours.
4. To determine the average amount of study time per week all his homework assignments will require.
5. To learn how to make every minute count in all areas of his life.
6. To find out which of his friends understands biology.

Answer the following questions and problems.

7. Tanaka estimates that all his assignments will require 60 hours each week to complete. Moreover, class and lab time will take another 20 hours. What phase of the decision-making cycle is he working on?
8. If you were in Tanaka's situation, what would you do next?
9. Using one or more of the information-gathering techniques described in this chapter, develop several options Tanaka might choose from.
10. What option do you feel is the most reliable? Why?

Exercise 1.2: Making Decisions

Imagine you are a comedian on the edge of national success, but you are concerned with the state of your profession. It seems that the trend in comedy is gross-out humor. Moreover, it seems that the comedians most engaged in grossing out their audiences are the most successful. In the right hands, you feel gross-out humor can be very funny. But it's not always in the right hands. Moreover, you feel there are certain moral hazards in addressing the most basic aspects of human behavior, and this feeling disturbs you.

To prepare yourself for the next phase of your career in comedy, go through the decision-making cycle to figure out a course of action you will feel comfortable following.

2 Basics of Critical Thinking *crit*

In common usage, *critical* often refers to taking a negative view, finding fault, or even excessive nit-picking. We have all heard such comments as "They criticize my every move" when the speaker probably means *ridicule*, not *criticize*.

In academic usage, *critical* refers to complex intellectual activities required by interpretation, analysis, and evaluation. In the statement "The attorney has lost his critical perspective by becoming emotionally involved in the decision," *critical* is used with more academic accuracy.

To be a critical thinker does not mean that you judge every comment your friends make. It does mean that you approach life thoughtfully with an arsenal of skills that help you interpret, analyze, and evaluate experience and information.

2a Distinguish between facts and opinions.

We live in an age of information overload. There are roughly 65 million copies of newspapers published worldwide each day. Approximately 10,000 magazines are published every month, and close to 50,000 new books are published each year. In the United States itself over 1,400 television stations broadcast programs to 93 million homes, and over 10,000 radio stations broadcast through nearly 500 million radios that play in homes, workplaces, cars, and anywhere else a Walkman goes. And now we have the World Wide Web, with its infinite possibilities for dispensing information. How do you guard against being overwhelmed by the information onslaught, especially by misleading information?

Begin by distinguishing between two fundamental concepts: facts and opinions.

Fact

A *fact* in itself is not debatable. A factual statement reflects how something actually exists or happened and can be objectively verified. These are factual statements: Republican presidents held the White House for twelve years, from 1981 to 1992. The moon is earth's only satellite. Hawaii became a state in 1959.

Numerical facts are called *statistics.* For example, the average American uses three gallons of paint a week. This adds up to more than a billion gallons every year, enough to fill a lake 20 feet deep, 4 miles long, and 1 mile wide.

Statistics are often referred to as *alleged facts.* An alleged fact can be misleading. For example, the statement "The junk mail Americans receive in one day could produce enough energy to heat 250,000 homes" may be a fact, but it would not be accepted without further consideration. (How would people use energy from burning junk mail, anyway?) The alleged fact that the average American uses three gallons of paint a week misleads because of averaging: Many Americans never lift a paint brush, but the auto industry uses tens of thousands of gallons of paint every week.

Opinion

Statistical analysis, that is, alleged facts, often reflect an opinion. *Opinion* is what someone believes, and it is not necessarily true because someone believes it. Opinions take different forms.

A *preference* is an opinion that expresses personal taste—that is, what someone likes or dislikes. Such statements as "Suspense movies are my favorite" and "Racquetball is a great workout" express preferences, not facts. Generally, preferences do not cry out for critical examination. How can someone be wrong for liking a type of movie or a particular sport? Why would anyone want to challenge someone's taste?

A *judgment* is an opinion with a basis for support, and preferences can often be restated as judgments. For example, the statement "Suspense movies, more than romantic comedies or westerns, reflect society's ills" can be analyzed by considering the social criticism embedded in romance, western, and suspense movies. The statement "Racquetball offers a more sustained aerobic workout than tennis does" creates the opportunity to compare the physical demands of racquetball and tennis. Both statements clearly reflect opinions that can be evaluated.

2b Analyze inferences for reliability.

An *inference* is an observation or conclusion based on a fact or set of facts. It is a statement about what is not known, made on the basis of what is known. A loan officer may infer a man's social status from how he dresses. An investigator may infer from the ruins how a fire ignited. A chess player may infer her opponent's next move from the position of the chess pieces on the board. A mechanic may infer the condition of a car's valves from the sound of the engine.

Inferences may be carefully or carelessly made. They may be made on the basis of years of experience or on a wild hunch. Inferences might be reliable or unreliable, that is, right or wrong. For example, suppose the following facts are true in your hometown:

1. The elementary school is overcrowded because of the school design.
2. No new teachers will be hired because of budget cuts.
3. A new apartment complex with 300 apartments is opening before school begins.
4. The city planners have just approved the construction of a thousand homes.

From these facts it may be reasonably inferred that next year the elementary school will be even more crowded than it is now, and therefore learning will be more difficult.

But, as with all significant inferences, this one should be subjected to critical examination, which might reveal the following:

1. The school overcrowding is caused by students in their last year of elementary school.
2. The budget cuts are tentative because the state budget has not been finalized.
3. The apartments are for senior citizens, not families with children.
4. Construction of the thousand new homes will not begin for at least two years.

These additional facts, revealed by close critical examination, show that the original inference is unreliable.

Inference is closely related to *implication.* When someone says, "Most of the people who have lawns in this neighborhood are white and speak educated English, but most of the people who mow the lawns are brown and speak no English," he is *implying* that there is an injustice in this situation. When we hear such a statement, we *infer* that indeed there is an injustice. A speaker *implies* and a listener *infers* (and the two words are frequently misused).

Exercise 2.1: Drawing Inferences

Draw tentative inferences from each set of facts given below. For each inference, explain which particular fact, or facts, served as its basis. By reviewing all your tentative inferences, write the options you believe are viable for the situation you find yourself in.

a. It's after midnight, you've had a couple of drinks at a party, and your car stops working on an underlit stretch of the freeway. You pull over to the side of the road to figure out what might have happened. Your mind goes back over the facts. You were driving about 65 miles an hour. You were listening to the radio. The car sort of sputtered. The steering became difficult. The engine stopped and the brakes needed extra pressure to make them work as you struggled to pull off onto the shoulder.

b. You find that you are in an unfamiliar part of the freeway that parallels a housing development. You can see no neon signs or other indications of nightlife. Traffic is sparse.

c. A four-door sedan is slowing down, the driver looking back as the sedan passes. The sedan is dark, a couple of years old, and its license plate light is not working. The car pulls over ahead of you and begins to back up, stopping about 25 feet away.

d. A man, about 6′2″ and wearing a dark suit, gets out of the sedan and looks around as if he were inspecting the area. A moment or two passes—he does not seem to be in a hurry—then he reaches back into the sedan for a small object, steps to the far edge of the freeway shoulder, and begins walking slowly toward your car while seeming to be carefully observing the nearby area.

Exercise 2.2: Drawing Inferences from Photographs

Clip a photograph from a newspaper or magazine, or select one from a photo album of your own. In writing, identify ten facts in the photograph from which you develop at least five tentative inferences.

2c Verify the reliability of interpretations.

An *interpretation* examines facts and opinions to make sense of them. An interpretation is always speculative. It is often an attempt to think beyond the obvious to find a deeper truth. Personal experience, literary works, and cultural, political, and historical events often supply the raw material for interpretation.

Like assertions, interpretations can reflect opposing views. For example, the Japanese military's surprise bombing of Pearl Harbor on December 7, 1941, took the United States into World War II. Later, some historians charged that President Roosevelt had had advance knowledge of the attack but did not warn our military. Their accusation is based mainly on the interpretation of one suspicious fact: By the summer of 1940, the United States had cracked Japan's top-secret diplomatic code, enabling intelligence agencies to monitor messages to and from Tokyo. Some historians interpret this to mean that President Roosevelt wanted to use the attack as a reason to involve the United States in World War II. To counter this interpretation, however, other historians have pointed out that the code-breaking intelligence could not have exposed the attack on Pearl Harbor because Japan sent no messages about the planned attack!

The reliability of an interpretation is usually difficult to verify. Often only a careful analysis will reveal whether a particular interpretation of an act or an event is accurate.

Exercise 2.3: Interpreting Facts

Read the following summary of an event that rocked Los Angeles several years ago and then respond to the task at the end.

In Los Angeles on the night of March 3, 1991, a bystander made a videotape that showed several police officers using police clubs to beat an African American named Rodney King into submission so they could arrest him. Subsequently the videotape was played on television, and it made viewers feel they were actually witnessing the beating. Did the videotape reveal all the facts? According to the police, it did not; they claim it failed to show the "trigger" elements that led to the violent arrest:

1. King racing at high speed in a seven-mile car chase prior to the event.
2. King, over six feet tall and muscular from hours spent in weight rooms, appearing violently psychotic from drugs.
3. King showing no effect from two jolts from a stun gun.
4. King throwing off several officers who tried to subdue him.
5. King charging one officer who had hit him with a baton.

But the video did create two interpretations: First, to many viewers it showed police subduing a dangerous criminal who was resisting arrest; second, to other viewers it showed a gang of racist Anglo police officers using excessive violence by brutally clubbing an African American man into submission.

A year later, when a jury acquitted three officers of charges of using excessive force, the conflicting interpretations of the event triggered a riot. Fifty-four people died. Two thousand people were injured. Over eight hundred buildings burned.

Write a 100- to 150-word explanation that offers your interpretation of the two opposing interpretations most Los Angeles residents believed.

2d Identify the logical fallacies embedded in information.

Logical fallacies are common mistakes in thinking. The word *fallacy* means deception or a fault in reasoning. Information tainted by logical fallacies is unreliable. As a critical thinker, you can avoid accepting unreliable information by recognizing common fallacies.

Ad Hominem Argument

The Latin phrase *ad hominem* means "to the man." Writers and speakers use the ad hominem argument when they attack the person who is connected with an issue rather than concentrate on the issue itself.

> The senator has made an interesting case for eliminating the inheritance tax. No wonder! When his father dies, he will inherit millions!

In this statement the writer ignores the senator's arguments for abolishing the inheritance tax and focuses on his personal situation.

> Do not believe film critics. They are all frustrated actors or directors who could not succeed in the film industry.

The statement attacks the film critics rather than discussing inaccuracies or bias in their reviews.

Begging the Question

A frequent error that people make is reasoning in a circle, commonly referred to as *begging the question.* In its most fundamental form, a circular argument ends up where it began, having merely restructured the original assumption without introducing actual information.

> Welfare recipients are lazy because they don't like to work. Have you heard about someone on welfare who likes to work? That's because welfare recipients are lazy.

The argument travels in a circle, confirming the assumption it makes in the opening assertion.

False Analogy

Someone using *false analogy* assumes that if two things are similar in one or more characteristics, then they are similar in other characteristics.

> Some people cannot be educated. You can't make a silk purse out of a sow's ear.

Applying the apparent wisdom of folk sayings to real-life situations usually results in false analogy. Education does not change valueless things into valuable things, as the folk saying suggests; it develops already existing intelligence further.

> The European experience in World War II is clear. The lessons should not be ignored. You cannot ignore the rise of a dictator, and you cannot successfully negotiate with one to avoid a war. The best solution is to attack an enemy before he attacks.

Conditions today are not the same as they were before World War II. To compare pre–World War II conditions to those in the world today is to fall into the trap of false analogy.

Faulty Either/Or Reasoning

Many writers and speakers commit *faulty either/or reasoning* by assuming there are only two alternatives when in fact there are many. The slogan "America, love it or leave it" implies that love of country must be unqualified, which has the effect of excluding constructive criticism.

> Drug use is destroying the social order of American cities. The drug problem is so monumental that no one can afford to be neutral. Are we going to do nothing and let criminals rule our cities? Or are we going to give our police more power so that they can control drug traffickers, dealers, and users?

Of course, other actions may relieve the situation: initiating public education, funding rehabilitation for drug users, developing agreements with other countries to curtail drug traffic, and so on. The choices are not just between doing nothing and increasing police power.

Hasty Generalization

Writers and speakers commit *hasty generalization* when they draw conclusions from insufficient or unrepresentative evidence.

> In recent years, almost every major college athletic program has been investigated by the NCAA for recruitment violations. Every year, at least one team is placed on probation as a result of these investigations. Clearly those in charge of college athletics must be immoral.

The person who has drawn this conclusion has done so from insufficient evidence. Are all violations of complex regulations a matter of immorality? Perhaps some of the violations were inadvertent or technical. As for the investigations and penalties, they could indicate rigorous enforcement of the rules rather than widespread immorality.

> During the last year, three of five award-winning films concentrated on family violence. An examination of family violence was just broadcast on national television. No doubt these events indicate that family violence is on the rise.

Three films and a television program do not represent a trend. The conclusion that family violence is rising needs to be substantiated with statistics and reports from such authorities as psychologists, sociologists, and law enforcement officials.

Non Sequitur

The Latin phrase *non sequitur* means "it does not follow." People often commit this fallacy when their conclusions do not logically follow from their premises.

> Ryan Beach has the highest per capita income in the state, but it has the lowest paid police force, city employees, and schoolteachers. These facts are revealing. They show that those with money know how to keep government expenses under control.

Many factors contribute to per capita income. Perhaps in a small beach town a few wealthy landowners drive up the average income. Moreover, individuals do not directly pay for city government and schools; they are paid for by tax dollars that may come from state or local government. And, finally, elected city and school officials—none of whom, in this specific case, may be wealthy—determine employee salaries. Clearly, this writer's conclusion does not follow from the premises.

Oversimplification

People *oversimplify* when they ignore essential information in forming a conclusion, offering a simple explanation for a complicated problem.

> Getting a good grade in a composition class may involve a lot of your time, but there is nothing difficult about it. All you have to do is meet the required word length and avoid errors in grammar and punctuation.

As you probably know by now, getting a good grade in composition also requires clear thinking, organizational skills, and a good deal of effort and practice at writing.

Post Hoc Argument

When people assume that one event causes a second event simply because the second follows the first in time, they are committing the *post hoc, ergo propter hoc* ("after this, therefore because of this") fallacy.

> Some people think that microwave ovens are a health threat. I disagree. Our family purchased a microwave oven two years ago. Since then, none of us has seen a doctor.

As stated, the only relation between the purchase of a microwave oven and the good health of this family is that one followed the other in time. Time sequence alone cannot prove the existence of a cause-and-effect relationship.

Stereotyping

A *stereotype* is a belief that all members of a particular group share certain characteristics just because they are members of that group. Stereotypes, which are usually negative, lead to prejudice—that is, the prejudging of individuals on their group identities rather than on individual merits: "Foreigners can't be trusted," "The English have no sense of humor," "People on welfare are lazy."

Stereotyping is similar to hasty generalizations in that both are based on limited information. Stereotyping gains power when people accept a stereotype uncritically because it is perpetuated by the media.

> Politicians, whether currently in office or not, should not be allowed to sit on the boards of nonprofit organizations such as charities, foundations, and educational institutions. We all know that to win an election a person must always compromise common standards of ethics. Politicians are notorious for representing the individual interests of their supporters and then seeking their financial support in the next

election. All of us should fight to keep nonprofit organizations free from this kind of corrupt behavior.

If you believe that politicians are corrupt, that stereotype will be reinforced by the political scandals reported in newspapers and on television. Yet the reality is that only a few politicians of the thousands holding office are ever involved in corruption.

Exercise 2.4: Identifying Logical Fallacies

Identify the logical fallacies in these brief statements. Following the treatment of each example given above, write a brief explanation of how the item is fallacious.

1. I think Ms. Sawyer is the best history teacher at our school. She is a strong conservative.
2. We must reject gun-control laws or sacrifice a sacred right granted to us by the Constitution.
3. Glenview College always has a winning football team because its coach believes in team spirit.
4. The least promising students achieve the greatest success as adults. Winston Churchill's teacher predicted he would be a failure, and William Faulkner, who won the Nobel Prize for literature, never even earned a college degree.
5. Ancient religious leaders were responsible for the sun's rising because they went to high ground every morning and prayed for the sun god to return.
6. Ann is intelligent and hardworking. There is no doubt she will rise to the top of her field.
7. A brain absorbs information just as a sponge absorbs water. But eventually a sponge becomes saturated; it cannot hold any more water. Students, too, reach a saturation point, and then it is foolish to expect them to soak up more information.
8. If I had not gone out of my way to pick up Mia this morning, the car would not have broken down.
9. I do not see how young people can enjoy his music; he has been arrested several times, and his wife left him because he was cruel.
10. Lola Allure, the star of stage, screen, and television, starts every day with Skinny Wafers. Don't you think you should too?

2e Learn to recognize and evaluate propaganda techniques.

Propaganda refers to information and images designed to motivate people by appealing to their desires rather than to their intellect. Seldom do advertisers try to sell products by presenting accurate statistics and reasoned arguments based on specific evidence. Instead, they use language and images to associate their products with the subconscious yearnings their research reveals consumers have. Not all propaganda is bad. Most people would argue that a police officer who tries to persuade a group of preteens not to join street gangs by appealing to their emotions is using "good" propaganda.

Here are five commonly used propaganda techniques.

Glittering Generalities

Glittering generalities are virtue words that appeal to such emotions as love, generosity, motherhood, brotherhood, the American way, the natural world, and so on. Propagandists using glittering generalities frequently use such words as *truth, freedom, honor,* and *love* for the emotions they trigger.

Name Calling

Name calling is an obvious but surprisingly effective tactic. Often used in conjunction with ad hominem arguments, name calling is designed to belittle or arouse contempt for a person or an idea.

Testimonial

Testimonial involves having loved or respected persons give statements of support (testimonials) for a particular cause, idea, or product. The persons giving the testimonials may not be experts; in fact, they may know nothing at all about the subject.

Plain Folks

Plain folks is the opposite of testimonial. This device differs from testimonial in that its appeal comes from the participation of ordinary people with ordinary backgrounds, as opposed to the rich and famous.

Bandwagon

Bandwagon appeals to the strong desire to be one of the crowd, or part of a peer group. It exploits the fear of being excluded.

COMPUTER CLINIC

Evaluating Internet Sources

Critical thinking is essential to the evaluation of information on the Internet. Because the Internet is unrestricted, you can find anything someone thinks is important, interesting, and—yes—even bizarre. The democratic nature of the Internet is one of its great values, of course, but this also means there's a lot of irrational junk out there. You must stay critically alert when sorting through it. Use the following questions to guide your assessment of any Internet source.

- *Fallacious Reasoning.* Does the author rely on faulty reasoning and propaganda techniques to advance a position?
- *Currency.* Is the information current? Has it been frequently updated to keep it current?
- *Fairness.* Does the source offer multiple viewpoints, even opposing viewpoints? Does the author sound reasonable?
- *Evidence.* Does the information include verifiable evidence? Is there a clear separation of fact from opinion?
- *Credibility.* Is the information based on credible research? Are bibliographical sources listed? Is the information credible in the non-Internet world? Why and with whom?
- *Authorship.* Is the author identified? Are the author's qualifications listed? Does the author have academic degrees, awards, or other publications that can be objectively substantiated?

No one guards the Internet door. You must be the judge of all Internet sources you rely on.

Exercise 2.5: Identifying Propaganda

Find two examples from newspapers or magazines, including editorials and advertisements, for each of the five propaganda techniques defined above. For each of your examples, write a brief explanation of how the technique works.

3 Critical Thinking and Reasoning *crit*

Critical thinking emphasizes *objectivity,* the ability to view experience without distortion, and deemphasizes *subjectivity,* the inability to think beyond a limited frame of reference.

Critical thinking is strongly affected by the fact that we each see experience from a unique perspective. Being aware of the subjective perspective is especially important when working to reach group consensus. Subjectivity not only affects our ability to think effectively, it may even cripple it, especially when emotions become engaged.

Indeed, emotions are an indispensable part of our behavior. Where would the artist be without passion or the philanthropist without compassion? Yet even the mildest emotions can hamper the ability to reason logically and work productively with others. In any situation where objectivity is required, emotions tend to intensify self-defensive behavior, which always hinders reasoned discussion.

To reduce emotional intensity during group consensus building, you can try to see the world through the eyes of those with whom you are in conflict. When emotionalism derails the reasoning process, that is, the ability to think critically and logically, you must step back and reexamine each step of the process to be sure your conclusions are reliable and thoroughly understood by others.

3a Use reflective listening to achieve consensual agreement.

The goal of reasoned discussion is to reduce conflict, not to enflame it. In reasoned discussion there should not be winners and losers; there should only be consensual resolution.

Some people feel so strongly about their opinions that they are deeply threatened by any challenge to them. Even when presented with irrefutable evidence that contradicts their position, they ignore it. At this point, emotion—not reason—controls their behavior.

A more effective strategy than engaging in emotional confrontation is to adopt a respectful, even conciliatory attitude by actively listening to anyone with an opposing viewpoint. After having heard out the other person, restate in your own words what you believe was said. Then ask if you paraphrased the points accurately. If so, then find common points of agreement, not just points of disagreement, before stating your position. Continue this process, emphasizing what you agree on, until everyone clearly understands the similarities and differences of the two positions. This technique, developed by the psychologist Carl Rogers, is called *reflective listening*. By pursuing reflective listening you can remove emotion from the discussion, and in doing this you make it easier to reach consensus, that is, a synthesis of every position that the group can agree on.

Applying the Rogerian Approach to Consensus Building

- Make an effort to understand opposing viewpoints. Try to "walk a mile in the other person's moccasins." Concentrate intently on what is being said, not on how you can counter it.
- In an unemotional fashion, paraphrase what you have heard. An objective description will show that you are open-minded.
- Acknowledge the value of some of the other person's points. An acknowledgment will show that you are fair and balanced, seeking an appropriate resolution, not one that has a winner and a loser. Identify areas of common ground—not just points expressed in the disagreement, but general areas such as values, beliefs, and goals.
- Present your position reasonably, with supporting evidence. By now the other person will realize that this is not a win/lose situation and will feel less defensive. Next it is time for the other person to paraphrase what you have said.

3b Maintain objectivity by retracing the inductive reasoning process.

Whether in written arguments or group discussion, when objectivity seems to have given way to emotionalism, it's time to evaluate the steps in the reasoning process.

Inductive reasoning moves from specific evidence to a general conclusion. You have been using inductive reasoning throughout your life. Imagine, for example, that you were given a wrong date the first time you registered for college classes. Against all reason, you were not allowed to register even though you had waited in line for two hours. "Come back Friday," you were told. "That's the right day."

At registration for the second semester, you discovered that the class numbers had been printed incorrectly, and you had to return to revise your schedule.

The third semester, the procedure went well, but you discovered on the first day of classes that you were not on any class roster. "We just can't explain it," a clerk said. "I guess it was a computer glitch."

By induction—that is, by interpreting the meaning of these experiences—you conclude that your college's registration procedure is a shambles and you had better figure out how to use it effectively. Inductive reasoning thus builds to a conclusion piece by piece. As the evidence is presented and clarified, the conclusion becomes irresistible to reasonable people.

Another example: One student maintained that her college had an advanced gender awareness program. Others emphatically disagreed, claiming that nothing at all had been done to further gender awareness. To reach consensus, she retraced the evidence inductively by beginning with a question everyone agreed on.

QUESTION	Is Riverbank College responsible in the area of gender bias?

Then, one step at a time, she brought forward the supporting information, the evidence.

EVIDENCE	Riverbank College has gender awareness workshops for students, faculty, administrators, and support staff.
	The college has revised its course catalog, class schedule, and policy statements to embody gender-neutral language.
	The college has created a standing committee to review and arbitrate gender-related issues.
	The college has instituted new procedures to eliminate gender bias.
CONCLUSION	Evidence shows that Riverbank College has an advanced gender awareness program.

Through patient examination of the evidence and by listening reflectively to each group member's position, the group finally tended to agree with her, yet one group member still disagreed, adamantly maintaining that the conclusion was only partially true. In further reasoned discussion, she pointed out that there was pay inequity between the salaries of men and women doing the same job. After she presented her evidence during discussion, the group reached a final consensus.

GROUP CONSENSUS	Although some inequity exists in salaries, Riverbank College is making a strong effort to eliminate gender bias.

Conclusions drawn from inductive reasoning are usually referred to as *probable conclusions.* They are, in fact, inferences subject to close examination. The acceptance of a conclusion that follows from inductive reasoning is often referred to as the *inductive leap.* When constructing or evaluating inductive reasoning, you must be sure that the probable conclusion is clearly connected to the evidence. If it is not connected, then the reasoning is flawed, and the argument must be revised to show the connection more clearly or must be abandoned for being illogical.

3c Maintain objectivity by reexamining the premises and conclusions of the deductive reasoning process.

Deductive reasoning is the opposite of inductive reasoning. The process begins with general assumptions called *premises* and draws specific conclusions that follow logically from the premises.

In formal logic, this pattern is called a *syllogism.* Syllogisms always include a major premise, a minor premise, and a necessary conclusion that is the logical result of the two premises. The classic example of this deductive form comes to us from the philosopher Aristotle.

MAJOR PREMISE	All humans are mortal.
MINOR PREMISE	Socrates is human.
CONCLUSION	Therefore, Socrates is mortal.

When you reexamine deductive reasoning, keep in mind that accuracy is the key to validity. If the major and minor premises are accurate, then the conclusion will be accurate and logically sound. Syllogisms, however, can be illogical. An inaccurate major premise may make the result of deductive reasoning illogical.

MAJOR PREMISE	Computer programmers are shy and seldom socialize.
MINOR PREMISE	Joan Adams is our first female computer programmer.
CONCLUSION	Therefore, she will obviously be shy and seldom socialize with fellow employees.

Clearly, the major premise, which reflects a stereotypical image of computer programmers, is inaccurate. Ask yourself: Are all computer programmers shy and antisocial? At one time or another, aren't most people shy and seeking to avoid social contact? Because the major premise is inaccurate, the reasoning is flawed and the conclusion is inaccurate.

Sometimes the slippery use of language makes deductive reasoning inaccurate. Consider the use of *good student* and *accept* in this flawed syllogism.

MAJOR PREMISE	All good students accept that teachers have the responsibility for grading their class performance.
MINOR PREMISE	Harold Ward is disputing his history grade from last semester.
CONCLUSION	Therefore, Harold is not a good student.

Good student is a concept too vague to identify a category of students accurately. What does *accept* mean in this context? Teachers may make mistakes when grading; is it unreasonable to ask for a grade change because of a mistake? Colleges have provisions to challenge grades that students believe are unfair; does using this procedure mean a person is not a "good" student? Clearly, because language is used deceptively in the premises, the conclusion is illogical.

A conclusion resulting from deductive reasoning may also be illogical because the reasoning is improperly constructed. First, evaluate a properly constructed syllogism.

MAJOR PREMISE All economists must master statistics.

In a properly constructed syllogism, the subject of the major premise—in this example, economists—must be repeated in the minor premise.

MINOR PREMISE Leslie is an economist.

The conclusion then follows necessarily from the major and minor premises.

CONCLUSION Therefore, Leslie has mastered statistics.

The syllogism is properly constructed and, therefore, logical. Now evaluate the following invalid syllogism.

MAJOR PREMISE	All economists must master statistics.
MINOR PREMISE	Social psychologists must master statistics.
CONCLUSION	Therefore, social psychologists are also economists.

This syllogism is improperly constructed because the minor premise does not repeat the subject of the major premise. The conclusion, therefore, is illogical.

Like inductive reasoning, deductive reasoning can help organize a discussion. Deductively reasoned conclusions, however, are seldom reached as simply as the skeletal form of syllogisms that illustrate them suggests.

Often the deductive reasoning process does not include one of the premises the conclusion is drawn from. The missing premise must be inferred. Consider, for example, a deductively reached conclusion drawn from a major premise and a minor premise.

> Migrating Canada geese are disappearing from the marshes where they forage each winter. People frighten Canada geese. Therefore, we must restrict the use of the marshes during migration.

Now examine the same conclusion without the minor premise.

> Migrating Canada geese are disappearing from the marshes where they forage each winter, so we must restrict the use of the marshes during migration.

A deductively reasoned conclusion drawn from an unstated premise needs to be evaluated with care because the omitted premise may be inaccurate. In evaluating the preceding example, you might ask these questions: Do many people visit the marshes during winter months? Are fewer geese migrating south? Have the geese found better foraging sites? Of course, in most reasoned discussions, the group would anticipate these questions.

Exercise 3.1: Building Consensus

Join a group of no more than five people. Read the following statement of a problem an employee of a manufacturing company faces. By using consensus building, decide on a group-recommended course of action the person may follow.

First, establish a procedure for the group to follow, such as individually pursuing the decision-making cycle. Second, share the results of the individual activity. Third, develop a group-consensus position and state it in writing.

> I'm a supervisor for a small company in a community of 40,000 residents, many of whom work for the firm. Recently I was told that the company was going to shift a substantial portion of its manufacturing activity to India, where labor is very inexpensive. I have been forbidden to tell the people I supervise about the plan. Several of my fellow supervisors are discussing the option of announcing the plan to the employees and then resigning en masse. What problems do you think I'm facing, and what is the morally correct thing to do?

Exercise 3.2: Reasoning Patterns

Study each item and determine the reasoning pattern embedded in it. If the reasoning is incomplete—that is, if it is missing a premise—state the missing element in your own words. Then state what logical conclusions you might draw from the information.

1. After hundreds of driving tests of American and imported automobiles, including subcompact, compact, midsize, and full-size vehicles, the consumer agency claims that full-size vehicles are the safest of all categories and that subcompact cars are the least safe.
2. An important skill in becoming a successful economist is the ability to interpret statistical information from a variety of sources. Sometimes that information comes from the far reaches of the world—that is, from undeveloped countries as well as highly developed countries. Phyllis Murphy worked for the Economic Study Institute, a nonprofit institution, while she was a graduate student. Her job required that she analyze statistical information in key production areas.
3. You doubt that this city is dangerous? Check out the statistics. They show that there has been an increase in muggings and other violent crimes on public transportation and in parks, schools, and shopping malls. They also show that home break-ins are on the increase. To protect law-abiding citizens, we must put more police on the streets and in neighborhoods, because a city that can't protect its citizens is not worth living in. We just can't seem to protect our citizens, so I'm looking for property in Seattle.
4. Only a person who hated the victim could have committed such a brutal crime. Killers always leave a clue to their identity, though. Now I have examined all the evidence, that is, the details from the original crime scene, including photographs, the bloody but blurred shoe print, the unidentifiable smudged thumbprint, the pistol, and the angle the bullet entered the mouth and brain. It all points to murder, not suicide. That leaves us only one suspect, Bill Rimes, with whom the victim had a love-hate relationship. I have no doubt we will find that one of his shoes has blood on its sole.
5. You keep on jumping from lover to lover like that and you'll end up alone in life.

PART II

The College Essay

What's so hard about the first sentence is that you're stuck with it. Everything else is going to flow out of that sentence. And by the time you've laid down the first two sentences, your options are all gone.

Yes, and the last sentence in a piece is another adventure. It should open the piece up. It should make you go back and start reading from page one. That's how it should be, but it doesn't always work. I think of writing anything at all as a highwire act.

—Joan Didion, *novelist*

4 Write for a Reader *essay*

Most papers you write in college are essays. College essays usually discuss a limited subject by relying on general knowledge, research, observations, experience, insight, or values. Effective college essays should be based on accurate information and embody a writer's deep understanding of a subject.

College essays differ from other kinds of writing. Works of imagination, such as poems or short stories, often dramatize a writer's personal experience and feelings; textbooks report facts and information; lab reports precisely detail the procedures of an experiment. In contrast, college essays tend to analyze or interpret a subject.

In college you will usually write for a highly informed reader, probably a professor who has made a career of processing information in a particular field. Less frequently, you will write for other students, especially those who are members of your writing or working group engaged in collaborative activities.

The Writer-Reader Relationship

When writing an essay, you are participating in a relationship. This relationship is between you and your reader. It is not enough to know a lot about a subject; you must also maintain the writer-reader relationship by effectively arranging what you know on the page, or you will risk confusing your reader.

Like every relationship, the writer-reader relationship has its obligations. One of your obligations as a writer is to meet your reader's expectation that you will use common essay principles to guide him or her through the reading process.

4a Readers expect an essay to have a dominant purpose.

Readers adjust the way they read to fit an essay's *dominant purpose.* For instance, most readers approach descriptive writing much differently than they do persuasive writing. Description involves the senses, so readers reconstruct experience as they read. Persuasion involves the intellect, so readers trace the key points and counter points throughout a discussion.

Generally, the purposes of essays can be divided into four categories that represent the ways writers and readers approach a subject.

A **narrative essay** tells a story by relating a sequence of events. You might write a narrative essay on the criminal justice system by tracing the chronology of a typical day in the life of a district attorney.

A **descriptive essay** pictures a scene, a person, a setting, an object, or an event. You might write a descriptive essay that re-creates a courtroom scene for its emotional impact.

An **expository essay** explains, informs, analyzes, or interprets. You might explain the causes of a particular crime, inform your readers about several approaches to ending street crime, analyze the effects of crime on a community, or interpret what crime suggests about a community.

An **argument essay** attempts to persuade readers to take some action or to convince them to accept your position on a debatable issue. You might try to persuade your readers to join a crime alert program or argue that the police harass teenagers.

These purposes are not rigid. You might, for example, use expressive—that is, descriptive or narrative—techniques in an argument. You might supply useful and interesting information in a narrative. But keep in mind that readers will expect an essay to have a dominant purpose, one that allows them to adjust their reading style appropriately.

4b Readers expect an essay to have a clear structure.

Structure comes from a Latin word that means to arrange in piles, to pile up, and, therefore, to build or construct. Many things look very different but have the same underlying structure. For example, humans are easily distinguished by their physical appearance, but beneath the skin their skeletal structure is very similar. Two automobiles may have the same inner system of frame, engine, and drive train, but the shape, color, and design of their bodies are entirely different.

The structure of expressive essays tends to be more fluid than that of expository and argument essays. Expressive essays are more exploratory, sometimes revealing the writer's personal experience and insight. As a result of their fluid nature, expressive essay structures are often very loose. They capture the flow of experience, not a reconstructed interpretation of experience.

In sharp contrast, expository and argument essays usually follow a structure that professors have come to expect college students to use: the thesis-support structure. Thesis-support essays are composed of several paragraphs, are typically 500 to 1,500 words in length and have a clear structure that can be divided into three main parts: an introduction, a discussion, and a conclusion.

1. The introduction, usually no more than one or two paragraphs, presents the *thesis statement* and any background information that readers might need to understand the discussion. An effective introduction arouses reader interest and limits the discussion that follows.

2. The discussion usually contains several paragraphs, each organized by a *topic sentence* that relates to the thesis statement. Discussion paragraphs develop the ideas expressed in the thesis statement in a detailed, thorough manner.

3. The conclusion, usually no more than a single paragraph, gives a sense of completion to the essay. Often, though not always, the conclusion restates the thesis statement and touches on the essay's subpoints as expressed in the topic sentences.

Within the overall structure, an effective thesis-support essay should embody three other principles:

- An essay should be unified, that is, every part must clearly relate to the idea expressed in the thesis statement.
- An essay should be coherent, that is, the thoughts expressed in sentences should be connected by transitional techniques, such as the repetition of key words and phrases, the rephrasing of key ideas, and the use of transitional words and phrases.
- An essay should have adequate development, that is, there should be thorough supporting explanation and detail.

4c Readers expect discussion paragraphs to follow clear development patterns.

Just as readers expect essays to have a clear structure, they expect paragraphs, especially discussion paragraphs, to follow clear patterns. Since an essay is composed of several paragraphs, it might contain a variety of paragraph development patterns (see Chapters 11–16 on writing paragraphs).

1. *Examples* include typical and specific illustrations and concrete descriptions used to develop a point.
2. *Comparison and contrast* present the similarities and differences between two subjects.
3. *Analogy* helps explain a complicated or abstract idea by comparing it to something familiar.
4. *Cause and effect* explain why something happened and the results of something that happened.
5. *Classification* organizes a subject into distinct categories.
6. *Definition* differentiates one concept from others.

7. *Process analysis* explains how to do something or how something works.

The sooner you master these development patterns, the sooner you will gain control of your writing.

A Student Essay for Study

Now examine a college essay written by student-writer Judith Park for a critical thinking assignment in freshman composition. Begin by reading what Park says about the essay.

> I'm afraid the final draft creates the impression that writing this essay was easy.
>
> It was not.
>
> I wrote it over a two-week period, writing and rewriting several drafts. Basically, I wanted to explain how merchandisers--people who sell us products--manipulate honest feelings.
>
> The essay's content came from class notes and my own experience. In the beginning, I had too much information. This made me work hard at organization. Establishing my dominant purpose early helped me sort all the parts out. Then carefully following the composing process helped me arrange the material in writing. I wrote a rough draft without being too critical. But when I wrote the final draft, the one you'll read here, I kept thinking how my reader would take in information. I revised the thesis statement with care and made sure all topic sentences and supporting information related to it.

Now examine Park's final draft. First, read the essay all the way through. Note how she effectively uses writing conventions to guide readers through her paper. Pay particular attention to the thesis statement and topic sentences, which appear here in italics to help you identify them. Then reread the essay along with the notes in the margin, which identify what readers expect in a college essay. This will help you understand the thesis-support structure.

Title suggests what the essay will cover (see 8c).

Subtle Exploitation

Introduction gives background information and showcases the thesis statement (see 7a).

Whether aware of it or not, most of us have learned to respect a core of social values. Our parents, teachers, and the community at large have taught us that it is good to be socially accepted, repay favors, maintain consistent behavior, and respect authority. Without these values, community trust would break down. Friends and neighbors could not count on each other. The psychological power of social values has not been lost on sales representatives and advertisers. *Indeed, these merchandisers engage in the subtle exploitation of typical social values to influence what we buy.*

Clearly written, limited thesis statement (see 6c).

Topic sentence 1 (see 11a).

Discussion section with topic sentences that develop one aspect of thesis statement. Each discussion section paragraph developed according to a clear pattern (see 7b).

The desire for social validation is one value merchandisers exploit. No one likes to be out of step with others. As children we turn to friends and grown-ups to see how to fit in. As adults we continue to seek social acceptance. For example, I recently attended my first formal dinner. The table was beautifully set with flowers, candles, crystal, and a mysterious array of silverware. When the salad was served, I was confused about which fork to use. Rather than face embarrassment by making a mistake, I took guidance from a guest seated across from me. My behavior reflected one form of social validation, that is, the natural tendency of one person turning to another as a model for public behavior. Advertisers often subtly exploit this desire to fit in. Think of advertisements for such products as Levi jeans, Coca-Cola, AT&T, Virginia Slim, or Calvin Klein. If consumers see themselves reflected in the advertisements,

Clincher sentence closes the discussion (see 11a).

merchandisers hope they will also see themselves using the product as it has been modeled for them, thus successfully exploiting the desire for social validation.

Topic sentence 2 (see 11a).

The desire for reciprocity is another value merchandisers exploit. At the start of each school year, several merchandisers give away products and services to new students. For instance, Gillette offers free toiletries; the Times offers free newspapers; 24 Hour Fitness Center offers free workout sessions. These are not merely kind gestures; they are calculated efforts to influence what first-year students buy. Obviously, these companies are counting on students' liking the gifts and paying to use them in the future. But less obviously, these companies are also exploiting the social value of reciprocity. Most of us have been trained to repay a favor, even an unrequested favor. As a result, merchandisers know that some students will feel obligated to repay their kindness. After all, it does not take many razor-blade sales, newspaper subscriptions, and health club memberships to offset the cost of a few gifts, does it?

Writer uses development by examples (see 15a).

Note how smoothly the sentences blend together: Writer effectively uses transitional techniques (see 13a, b).

Clincher sentence (see 11a).

Opening sentences give background. Writer uses "consistent" to create unity (see 12).

Most of us value consistent behavior. Such people as friends, coworkers, and instructors expect us to behave today as we did yesterday. We generally are consistent, for not to be consistent might lead to being rejected. Unfortunately, we are sometimes "mindlessly consistent"--that is, we are consistent when it makes no sense to be. *High-pressure merchandisers are particularly adept at exploiting mindless consistency.* The tactic begins

Topic sentence 3 (see 11a).

when someone follows a small commitment with a larger one and then an even larger one. This chain of commitments creates a consistent pattern that is hard to break. For example, recently my friend Lila and I stopped at an expensive boutique. A fashionably dressed saleswoman asked if we were interested in seeing the new spring line. "Yes," Lila said without hesitation. Merely walking into the store represents the first commitment, what salespeople call "putting a foot in the door." Responding with a "yes" to the initial question is a second commitment. Granted these are small commitments, but they lead to larger ones. The saleswoman then asked a series of questions designed to get a consistent "yes" response. "You're a size 8, aren't you?" She took a coat from a hanger and extended it for Lila to feel. "Feel that wool, soft isn't it?" Next she was holding it for Lila to try on. "Feels good to wear a fine coat, doesn't it?" Of course it does, and soon Lila was signing a credit card receipt while the saleswoman was smiling and assuring her she had just bought the finest coat in the store. Exploiting mindless consistency can be almost too subtle to detect, but the next time a telemarketing salesperson calls, listen carefully to the opening questions. They will be designed to get "yes" responses.

Writer develops paragraph through examples and cause-and-effect patterns. One response triggers another, in a causal chain (see 15c).

Another value merchandisers exploit is an automatic respect for authority. Parents hold up doctors, teachers, police, politicians, athletes, and entertainers as authorities, people to be admired

Topic sentence 4 (see 11a).

Writer uses definition pattern to explain key concept (see 15e).

and trusted. Film star Jane Fonda is a classic example of an admired celebrity exploiting her authority. As an actress she won an Academy Award. She is beautiful, and well into her sixties with the figure of a thirty-year-old. In the early 1980s she used her fame and beauty to establish herself as an exercise guru. She opened a health club and launched an exercise videotape titled Workout. With her name and photograph on each box, she sold millions of copies. Today, film stars, super models, athletes, television celebrities, singers--authority figures of all sorts--make sales pitches for such products as cosmetics, athletic wear, automobiles, and food products. In a recent trend, even well-known politicians sell their authority status to advertisers. For instance, former presidential candidate Robert Dole advertises for a major drug company and former New York governor Mario Cuomo advertises for a food products manufacturer.

Writer uses example pattern (see 15a).

No doubt merchandisers target our social values. They suggest their products will bring us social validation. They expect us to repay them for unrequested gifts. They twist our desire to be consistent and abuse our trust in authority. They exploit our fundamental values as if they were human weaknesses.

Conclusion rephrases the thesis statement and reidentifies key supporting points (see 7c).

Park has met her responsibility to her readers. The essay has a clear purpose. It has a clear structure with an introduction that presents the thesis statement, a discussion that develops the subpoints of the thesis statement, and a conclusion that effectively closes the discussion. Finally, the discussion paragraphs reflect sound paragraph patterns.

WRITER'S CLINIC

Read with a Critical Eye

Try a new way of reading. Instead of reading strictly for information, practice reading as a writer does. Writers read to improve their writing craft—that is, they read with a critical eye. The critical eye examines another writer's purpose and writing strategies. The critical eye pierces a work's surface and reveals its bones and heart. If you learn to read other writers' work with a critical eye, you will discover their writing techniques and be able to apply them in your own writing. As a start, analyze Elaine Kubo's "The Thirties: A Personal History" in the exercise below.

Exercise 4.1: Analyze a College Essay

Read the student essay, "The Thirties: A Personal History," by Elaine Kubo, from the perspective of the reader-writer contract. The following tasks can serve as a guide. Review the appropriate sections in the BEH before completing each task.

1. Study 6a, then state the essay's dominant purpose.
2. Analyze the essay's overall structure.
   - Study 6b, then record the thesis statement.
   - Study 11a, then record the topic sentences.
   - Study Chapter 12, then identify key words that help create unity.
   - Study 13a,b, then identify words and phrases that help create coherence.
3. Study Chapter 15, then identify paragraph strategies you recognize.

The Thirties: A Personal History

Members of my generation have grown up during a time when the majority of Americans have lived in relative comfort. Nevertheless, we have all seen photographs of the Great American Depression of the 1930s: images of anonymous men in dark suits and tweed caps selling apples on street corners; hollow-cheeked women cuddling infants in front of clapboard shacks; crowds milling before factory gates; hoboes gathered around campfires and eating from tin cans; Model T Fords loaded with chairs, tables, mattresses, and boxes of clothes crawling along desert highways toward the Pacific. These dreadful memories, preserved in history books, are grim. But besides the dreadful memories, there are positive aspects of the Depression that haven't been preserved in history books. These memories are carried by people who suffered yet lived through the thirties.

One positive aspect of the thirties my grandparents remember was the determination to overcome adversity it stirred in them. Like many Kansas farmers in the early thirties, they were suffering from the country's sudden economic collapse, but they still had land and raised some crops. Then nature turned against them. Unrelenting winds swept across the plains, destroying crops and swirling away the topsoil. A drought came with the wind and destroyed any chance they might have had to grow a crop. Finally, the bank demanded payment on the farm's mortgage. They couldn't scrape together the money, so they lost the farm. But if economic collapse and a senseless act of nature destroyed them financially, these events toughened their will to overcome adversity. They moved to a small Kansas town. Days, my grandfather worked as a clerk in his uncle's store; nights, he studied law. My grandmother, who had taught before marrying, worked at the local school. By 1938 my grandfather had passed the state examination allowing him to practice law. By the end of World War II, my grandmother was school superintendent.

I know there were many less fortunate than my grandparents, many who were fighting poverty all those years, but some people who lived through the thirties remember poverty as being different then. It seems that another positive aspect of the Depression was that people could be poor without losing personal dignity. My mother has a childhood memory of a gray-haired man who knocked at the kitchen door one day and asked to do some work in return for a meal. Her father refused to allow him to work, but invited him to join the family for a lunch of soup and biscuits. After the meal, he whittled little wooden birds for all the kids. My mother says that the whole family gave him the respect they would give any successful artist now. My retired neighbor knew out-of-luck businessmen and bankrupt investors who sold flowers on street corners and caddied at golf courses without losing a sense of personal dignity. Can you imagine such things today? Perhaps because there were so many people broke and hungry, it wasn't considered a failure not to have a regular job. People respected each other anyway.

Another positive aspect some people experienced during the thirties was the sense of community it created in them. Many people carry stories about grocers who supplied out-of-luck neighbors with food on credit and charged no interest. Others talk about going to wedding showers without enough money to buy a nice gift and the guests all digging into their pockets and pooling their change to buy a community gift for the bride. My aunt remembers over a hundred people turning out to help repair a neighbor's house that had partly burned down. But perhaps the most startling example of the sense of community I've heard comes from my friend's family's experience. Her grandparents were forced to move from the countryside to Boston, where they rented a one-bedroom apartment. At the time, my friend's grandmother was eight months pregnant and started having labor pains. A doctor, selected at random from the phone book, came over immediately, completed a quick examination, then called for hot water. He delivered a healthy, six-pound girl. A week later the new parents got a bill for $7.32, the cost of home delivery. Since the move and rent had taken all their money, they couldn't pay. But when other people living in the building—all of whom had been complete strangers to them until the baby was born—heard of the couple's plight, they chipped in pennies, nickels, dimes, and quarters. They sent the fee to the doctor. Less than three days later, the doctor drove up with a back seat full of groceries. He said his nurse had sent the bill by mistake, so he used the payment to buy groceries for them. At one time I might have seen this aspect of the Depression as an act of charity; now I see it as an act of community.

Indeed, the historian's portrayal of the Depression as a grim time for Americans is accurate, but we must remember that a personal history that doesn't get into books parallels the social upheaval we've read about. It's the history carried in the minds of people who endured through that time. Often those memories have some positive aspects.

COMPUTER CLINIC

To become a more effective writer, you will want to get access to a computer equipped with word processing software. The secret that unlocks writing is rewriting, and rewriting is easy—when it is done on a computer.

Once writers labored by candlelight and scribbled with quills. Now they click on a switch, edit a page, and press Print. Seconds later they have a cleanly printed page. A computer not only makes editing copy easy, it helps perform a variety of writing tasks. On a computer you can

- brainstorm ideas
- respond to questions
- develop lists
- create outlines easily
- produce multiple drafts
- perform electronic spelling checks
- revise, revise, revise without the tedium of retyping

The bottom line: a computer with word processing capability is a writer's best buddy.

5 Begin the Composing Process *essay*

The composing process is not easy to define, teach, or learn. For writing purposes, think of it this way: It is an interactive process that uses creative and critical thinking to discover and develop a subject worth exploring in an essay.

Few writers can take up a pen or sit at a keyboard and write an effective essay from beginning to end. Instead, most writers develop their work in stages by using the composing process.

Creative thinking is characteristic of the early stages of the composing process. Using creative thinking, writers generate ideas, recall experience, develop examples, stimulate insights, and create figurative language—the raw material of fresh, interesting writing (see 1b).

Critical thinking is characteristic of the later stages. Using critical thinking, writers evaluate content, shape structure, examine logic, and craft sentences—the analytical perspective that results in accurate, coherent writing (see 1d).

Simply stated, through creative thinking, writers invent material; through critical thinking, writers evaluate and organize the material for their readers.

The composing process is not a linear, step-by-step process in which creative and critical thinking are neatly divided. Instead, it is a recursive process of exploration, inquiry, and evaluation that engages both modes of thinking at different times.

By using the composing process, you will construct an essay through several phases or drafts. Throughout the process you will constantly be selecting and rejecting information and making corrective decisions. In the end, after having generated pages and pages of writing, you will compose a final draft to submit for evaluation.

5a Analyze the writing situation.

The writing situation has four key elements: the essay subject, the sources of information, the reader, and the length of time before the essay is due. A critical analysis of the writing situation early in the composing process will save you time and trouble later.

Subject

The subjects of most college writing assignments are given to you. For example, in social science you might analyze a political cartoon or explain local campaign fund-raising restrictions. In business you might identify the reasons for the fluctuating value of the dollar. In literature you might interpret a short story or poem. In psychology you might describe the behavior of people in stressful situations.

The approaches in these assignments are clear: They are to analyze, explain, identify, interpret, and describe. When responding to an assignment, be sure to identify the approach your professor expects.

At other times, however, you can choose your own subject. In this situation, select a subject you know something about or one you can quickly research. In either case, build in a clear approach to your subject just as an instructor would.

Information Sources

Information sources for most academic papers are research materials, whether found in the library or on the Internet. But they are not the only legitimate sources. For example, in her essay "Subtle Exploitation," Judith Park relies on three information sources, personal experience, direct observation, and lecture notes.

Personal experience allows you to integrate information from your life—often the best source of information. You might, for instance, use your experience from having lived in a neighborhood that has changed over the years or from having experienced an event that changed your vision of the world.

Direct observation casts you in the role of observer. You might use your observations on the behavior of strangers gathered in confined places, such as elevators, lunch counters, and crowded public transportation. You might include information drawn from watching a television program, a film, or a series of advertisements.

Reading and lectures form the basis of your college education. Many of the writing situations you face will be based on the careful reading of a text—that is, a book, essay, short story, or poem. In these situations, be sure not to let your paper become an extended summary; instead, concentrate on interpreting the work, and support your interpretation with details and examples from the text. You can also draw on reading for brief examples to support a point or clarify an observation.

Questionnaires and interviews can serve as rich information sources for essays. A psychology instructor might ask you to use questionnaire information as the source for an essay on student attitudes toward such subjects as work, family values, child rearing, or marriage. A law professor might ask you to interview several legal authorities, such as a judge, a defense attorney, a prosecuting attorney, and a police officer, and then use the interview information in an essay.

Mixed sources orchestrate several kinds of information. Suppose, for instance, you plan to argue for security guards to be stationed on campus. To develop your argument, you might use personal experience from having once attended another crime-plagued campus. You might include the results of a student survey on crime. You might include direct observations of illegal acts. And you might report crime statistics you read in the local newspaper. Combined, these sources could make a powerful argument.

Your Reader

Write each essay for a particular reader. In college writing, the reader is usually a professor. Your task is to convince him or her that you have fulfilled the assignment, your information is valid, and your conclusions are reasonable.

Other readers may include fellow students, professionals in a particular field, and community members. Often your readers will be very diverse. This is the universal reader. Here you must seek common elements that involve everyone in the audience. Common groups of readers might be consumers, males, females, students, teenagers, senior citizens. Once you have a sense of your universal readers, you can build cues into your essay that address them: "All consumers are targets . . . ," "No matter how many semesters you have completed at this campus . . . ," "For those of you would-be athletes over fifty-five . . . ."

Length and Time Limit

Writing professors usually specify an approximate length and a due date for essay assignments. The length of an essay and the time you have to write it have a direct bearing on the writing situation. You will need to restrict your subject more for a 500-word essay than you would for a 1,500-word essay. If you have two weeks to write an essay, you will not have much time to research the subject, and if you are writing an in-class essay, you will not have much time to plan the essay. In any case, first you must accurately assess the length of a paper and the time you have to write it. Then you can adjust your writing behavior appropriately.

Exercise 5.1: Analyze the Writing Situation

First, identify what information sources could be used to develop the following subjects. Then identify who the audience might be.

1. Whether campus security guards overstep their authority
2. The influence of Carl Jung's psychiatric theory of the unconscious on the painter Jackson Pollock
3. The effects of political polling on voters
4. How photographs reveal family relationships
5. Unexpected sources of noise pollution

5b Find a subject in open-ended assignments.

Some professors let you select an essay subject, that is, they make open-ended assignments. When that happens, always select a subject quickly. Do not wait for inspiration. Beware, though: not all subjects are suitable for college essays. For example, "My Summer Vacation," a trite subject under all circumstances, has plagued English teachers for generations.

Pick a subject that reflects the content and spirit of the course. Plunge into serious issues. Explore significant concepts. An effective subject should force you to use specific examples and concrete details. Remember, the quality of a subject is revealing; it can show that you are an engaged writer, not one who is merely drifting through a course.

When a suitable subject does not come to mind immediately, find one through several strategies.

1. Make a list of possibilities. Give yourself thirty minutes of uninterrupted time. Jot down subjects that come to mind. Items on your list do not need to be extensive entries; a phrase or a sentence will do.
2. If you keep a journal, browse through it. Search for an engaging entry. If an entry engages you, it will engage readers.
3. Recall a classroom lecture. Perhaps a professor stimulated your curiosity or reminded you of a strong opinion you hold, either of which might inspire an essay.
4. Skim a newsmagazine or newspaper until a subject catches your attention. Jot down your thoughts; use them as a starting point.

5c Analyze the language of close-ended assignments.

Usually professors carefully word their assignments to identify the subjects they want you to write about. That is, they make close-ended assignments.

Often a close-ended assignment is designed to test your level of thinking in a particular area of study. Cognitive psychologists have identified six levels of thinking that range from the simple to the complex.

Level 1	*Knowledge*—recognizing and recalling facts and specifics.
Level 2	*Comprehension*—interpreting, translating, summarizing, or paraphrasing given information.
Level 3	*Application*—applying information in a situation that is different from the one in which it was originally learned.
Level 4	*Analysis*—separating a complex whole into its parts until the relationship among the elements is clear.
Level 5	*Synthesis*—combining elements to form a new entity.
Level 6	*Evaluation*—making decisions or judgments based on a set of criteria.

A carefully phrased assignment will usually have a key word that reveals how a professor wants you to approach a subject and the thinking level it addresses. To meet your professor's expectations, it is important that you analyze the language of an assignment.

The following are examples of key words you should know, including what they mean in the context of a writing assignment, what levels of thinking they indicate (in parentheses), and how they might be used.

- *Analyze:* To distinguish the parts of something and discuss their relationship. (Analysis)

  Analyze three advertisements directed at working women in *Vogue, Vanity Fair,* or *Good Housekeeping.*

- *Apply:* To use material from one area of knowledge and relate it to another. (Application)

  Apply three techniques Stephen King uses to create terror in his novel *The Shining* to the techniques the director uses in *The Blair Witch Project.*

- *Assess:* To determine the success or failure of something. (Evaluation)

  Assess the social values expressed in five television commercials for comparable products.

- *Clarify:* To make a complex subject clear, which may involve defining words and concepts. (Comprehension)

  Clarify the phrase "liberty and justice for all."

- *Compose:* To create from diverse sources. (Synthesis)

  Compose an argument that justifies a ban on automatic weapon sales.

- *Criticize:* To analyze the strengths and weaknesses of a subject. (Analysis and Evaluation)

  Critically examine the photographic techniques in Orson Welles's *Citizen Kane.*

- *Discuss:* To consider as many elements as possible concerning a subject. (Comprehension)

  Discuss the effects of crime in the Hanson Projects.

- *Evaluate:* To give your opinion or judge the value of a subject. (Evaluation)

Evaluate the argument that violent television shows stimulate violence in children.

- *Explain:* To clarify a subject that needs to be understood. (Comprehension)

  Explain the relationship between poverty and crime.

- *Interpret:* To offer what you believe a subject means. (Comprehension and Application)

  Interpret the symbolism of the "woods" in Frost's poem "Stopping by Woods."

- *Justify:* To argue that something is valid or correct. (Evaluation)

  Justify the assertion that illegal drugs should be legalized.

- *Relate:* To show the connections between subjects. (Knowledge and Application)

  Relate IQ scores to success in college.

- *Review:* To reexamine, summarize, or paraphrase a subject. (Knowledge)

  Review the reasons for practicing home schooling.

- *Summarize:* to relate the major points of a subject. (Knowledge)

  Summarize Thomas Hobbes's view of "self-interest."

- *Support:* To argue for or to justify something. (Synthesis)

  Support one of the following positions: using animals for laboratory research is humane or inhumane.

Judith Park's Writing Assignment

Before beginning the composing process, Judith Park, the author of the model essay in Chapter 4, carefully analyzed her assignment:

> In a 750- to 1,000-word essay, explain how common social influences are used to manipulate behavior. To develop your essay, feel free to use personal experience, observations, lectures, and reading assignments.

This assignment is relatively closed. Park knew that the key word "explain" meant she had to demonstrate her comprehension of the subject. To do so, she had to identify and clarify several common social influences.

WRITER'S CLINIC

Write Now, Plan Later

The way effective writers work is different from what you might expect.

- Effective writers discover problems and solutions in the writing process. By contrast, less effective writers want to anticipate all problems before they write.
- Effective writers brainstorm first, then organize the results. Less effective writers organize first, then write.
- Effective writers bypass rigorous critical thinking until they edit their work. When the writing is difficult, tangled, and plodding, they write their way through. They go with their gut feelings.

What if they are wrong? They trust the writing process. To worry about being wrong puts obstacles in the way of clear thinking.

An Idea List for Analyzing a Subject

Even though Park's subject is closed, it is still too general to write about in a 1,000-word essay. Therefore, Park shifted from analyzing her assignment to creating an idea list with the phrase "social influences" as the starting point.

Social Influences

1. Parents, relatives influence children--role models, authority, love, anger.
2. Teachers, police officers, other authority figures influence our behavior.
3. Political campaigns and politicians influence voters--image, favors, promises.
4. Religious figures influence their followers--guilt, love, kindness.
5. Television influences viewers--entertainment programs, news, commercials.
6. Charities try to influence donors.
7. Celebrities, such as music stars, film actors, television personalities, influence fans.

8. Influence tactics--guilt, trust, hope.
9. Trained behavior patterns are used to influence people.
10. Government lying--is this influence? No. It's deception.
11. Photography is a powerful influence in classic political films like J. F. K. and Born on the Fourth of July.

Creating this idea list helped Park find a subject for further exploration. No particular entry gave her a clear subject, Park says, but the list externalized her thinking and began a more analytical process.

> When I first reviewed my idea list, I felt lost. Nothing would work as an essay. Then I began to examine the items differently.
>
> My thought went something like this: many items suggested authority figures who serve as role models. We emulate role models, and they give us advice. From them we also gain a sense of self-worth. These two ideas began to connect in my imagination.
>
> Then my attention fell on two brief entries, influence tactics and trained behavior. People are trained to listen to authorities and to trust authorities. Authority gives us self-worth, advice. How do authorities abuse their roles? They use trust, guilt, hope. I felt I had found a direction.

Park's experience with this early stage in the composing process was not unusual. A subject or a direction presents itself only after a writer becomes deeply involved. Writers must reexamine their material, redevelop it, combine ideas, and seek patterns among existing ideas. This "looping" back into previously developed material reflects the recursive nature of the composing process.

5d Narrow the subject so that it can be covered in a single essay.

Take charge of your subject. Narrow it to manageable size. The first subjects you come up with will probably be too general. If you write on a general subject, your essay will consist of general assertions, not specific details and examples. Avoid this trap. Work through a general subject to its specific aspects.

GENERAL	The anti–nuclear energy movement.
SPECIFIC	Three dangers residents living near the San Onofre nuclear plant face.
GENERAL	The history of television violence.
SPECIFIC	Violence on the 11 o'clock news.
GENERAL	Child development.
SPECIFIC	An eleven-year-old who killed.

Suppose you are asked to analyze gender roles on television. First you compose an idea list of possible subjects. Then you decide to explore one item from your list: the role of women in situation comedy. This subject, of course, is too general. You would have to examine all situation comedies with women—an enormous task.

You begin the narrowing process. You might concentrate on specific comedies: a current comedy, such as *Frasier, Friends,* or *Scrubs;* or a vintage comedy, such as *Ozzie and Harriet, The Honeymooners,* or *I Love Lucy.* Perhaps you have a special interest in *I Love Lucy.* You select that show for analysis. Your subject is now narrowed. Next, you might review several representative segments to identify the female roles the show portrays. In the end, you might concentrate on Lucy herself and examine her role in one show, thus narrowing the subject even more.

Judith Park Narrows Her Subject

Judith Park, the author of "Subtle Exploitation," narrowed her subject even further once she had formulated it from her idea list. She limited her subject to "methods used to influence our decisions." She decided to identify and explain some common tactics that affected her personally, the kind that most people probably experience.

Later, as she was brainstorming her subject, the idea of behavior came back. In this way, writers often change the scope or phrasing of a subject as they move through the composing process. Keep in mind that writing is a process of trial and revision. Do not hesitate to change your subject if you see new possibilities as you proceed.

Exercise 5.2: Narrow a Subject

Narrow the following subjects by writing three progressively more limited topics. For example:

Music
Country and western music
Male and female relations in country and western ballads
Attitudes toward marriage in current country and western ballads

1. novels
2. style
3. advertising
4. survival
5. manners
6. shopping malls
7. film
8. health
9. greed
10. conformity

5e Use association techniques to gather information.

Once you have decided on a specific subject, you are ready to gather information. During this information-gathering phase, you will rely more on creative thinking than on critical thinking.

Some assignments take hours of research. But for essays based on general knowledge and experience, you can gather information by exploring what you already know.

The information-gathering techniques here are the same as those you would use in decision making (see 1b).

Information-Gathering Techniques

Relax. Let your mind associate one thought with another. Resist analysis; encourage imagination.

Brainstorming helps you capture thoughts on the fly by spontaneously creating an extended list of ideas.
Freewriting immerses you in a creative flow by allowing you to automatically write everything that comes to mind while holding back critical thinking.
Clustering makes visual connections between key ideas created from brainstorming and freewriting.
Asking questions generates an association chain by asking who, what, where, when, why, and how.
Consultation uses oral brainstorming and idea-sharing in working groups to create information.

Judith Park Mixes Information-Gathering Techniques

To generate material that led to "Subtle Exploitation," Judith Park used several information-gathering techniques.

Once I narrowed the subject--ways common behavior is used to influence decisions--I took it to my writing group. We generated a long list of questions, several of which I found helpful.

What common behavior traits do most people share?

What behavior traits are used to influence people?

Who uses them?

Why do they use them?

How are they used?

Then we spent the rest of my group time brainstorming a response to the first question. For example, here are several of the items on the brainstorming list.

People are selfish.

People are self-sacrificing.

People feel guilt.

People trust authority.

People are insecure.

People need to be accepted.

People need to be valued.

People feel indebted to others.

The next day I began to respond to the remaining questions. I used both brainstorming and freewriting to generate responses. When I finished I had several pages to work through.

Using several techniques to gather information is not unusual. Once you begin to use associational thinking, you might find yourself, like Park, first making lists, then writing questions, then freewriting to explore the questions. No single technique is appropriate for all writing situations. Use one or a combination of several to explore your subject.

Exercise 5.3: Use Information-Gathering Techniques

To start a 750- to 1,000-word essay, select three of the following subjects, or choose three other subjects that interest you, and narrow their focus. For one subject, brainstorm until you have developed a list of at least fifteen items related to the subject, or freewrite about the topic for thirty minutes (see 1b).

For the second subject, create a list of appropriate questions based on who, what, when, why, and how. Follow each question with an answer, if possible (see 1b).

For the third subject, create a cluster of at least fifteen items. Include secondary clusters when appropriate (see 1b and 6b).

improving health
damaging health
gun control
making money
escaping the rat race
becoming involved
messages in dreams
space travel
effective teaching
lost causes
capital punishment
fashion trends
angry students
competitive sports
American memories
lost opportunities
living in poverty
obtaining knowledge
being manipulated
shocking films

5f Evaluate prewritten information.

Much of your information will be in fragments jotted down to trigger your memory later. That's okay; this phase of the composing process is for your eyes only, not for your reader's eyes.

You will quickly find that much of the information is useless. Strike out useless observations, odd digressions, clichéd thinking, stalled musings, and just plain dead-end ideas.

Search for a fresh perspective, interesting ideas, and observations you might develop as examples to connect with your reader's experience.

You will also learn what you do not know about a subject. You might have to get more information. You can refer to published works, review your class notes, or engage in discussions with relatives, friends, or instructors. The more information you generate, the more you will have to work with later.

Judith Park Evaluates Freewriting

The fifth paragraph of Judith Park's "Subtle Exploitation" came from a critical evaluation of freewriting. Park began by rereading her notes.

She crossed out useless information and made additional notes as ideas came to her.

Respect for authority is one idea Park used. In these freewriting fragments, she also uncovered some typical examples from her own experience and reworked the examples for the final draft. Reread the following paragraph on "authority" from Park's final draft. Study how she reshaped details from her notes to fit into her discussion.

Authority. I had a strict religious childhood.

Church every Sunday . . .

I was trained to respect my elders . . .

Who has not been encouraged to respect authority? My parents held up doctors, teachers, police, politicians, athletes, and entertainers as models of success, people to be admired and trusted.

I remember buying a workout tape because Jane Fonda was advertising it. The tape seemed old. When did she develop it? Fonda must have been over forty. She had a figure of a woman in her twenties . . .

Open a magazine or turn on your TV and you will see fashion models, athletes, and entertainers selling cosmetics, athletic equipment, cars, and food. Even politicians, Bob Dole for instance. American Express? MasterCard?

Another value merchandisers exploit is an automatic respect for authority. Parents hold up doctors, teachers, police, politicians, athletes, and entertainers as authorities, people to be admired and trusted. Film star Jane Fonda is a classic example of an admired celebrity exploiting her authority. As an actress she won an Academy Award. She is beautiful, and well into her sixties with the figure of a thirty-year-old. In the early 1980s she used her fame and beauty to establish herself as an exercise guru. She opened a health club and launched an exercise videotape titled Workout. With her name and photograph on each box, she sold millions of copies. Today, film stars, super models, athletes, television celebrities, singers--authority figures of all sorts--make sales pitches for such products as cosmetics, athletic wear, automobiles, and food products. In a recent trend, even well-known politicians sell their authority status to advertisers. For instance, former presidential candidate Robert Dole advertises for a major drug company and former New York governor Mario Cuomo advertises for a food products manufacturer.

COMPUTER CLINIC

Prewriting on a Computer

Begin by analyzing the writing situation.

- Explain the assignment in your own words.
- Generate a work schedule.
- Identify information sources.
- Define your reader.

Once the writing situation is clarified, explore the assignment through prewriting. No matter what technique you use, the computer will speed up the process. At this point, do not analyze what you write. Just let the ideas flow. Forget spelling. When you finish prewriting, push Spellcheck and release the genie in the box. Beware: Sometimes computers CRASH! Hit Save often.

Exercise 5.4: Evaluate Prewritten Material

Select one of the three subjects you used to practice prewriting strategies in the previous exercise. Evaluate your prewritten material. (If you need more material to develop a 750- to 1,000-word essay, continue the prewriting process.) Strike out useless observations, odd digressions, and clichéd thinking. Identify the material you can use in an essay and note aspects of the subject that you might need more information about.

6 Write a Thesis Statement and Develop a Plan *essay*

College essays must have a clear thesis statement and should be arranged according to a plan. So far you have used a subject to guide the composing process. Now, before you write a thesis statement, you should focus your subject by clarifying your purpose.

6a Clarify a subject by stating a purpose.

When stating your purpose you should identify your subject and how you propose to develop it. Later in the process, the purpose statement will become the basis for a working thesis statement.

An effective purpose statement can usually be stated in a single sentence.

> I plan to analyze the role of Lucy as a gender stereotype in the classic situation comedy *I Love Lucy.*

The writer's subject here is quite clear: the character Lucy Ricardo seen as a gender stereotype. The writer will develop the subject by analysis, thereby writing an expository essay. Now consider another statement of purpose.

> I propose to argue that public rudeness damages campus life.

The writer's subject is clear—the effects of public rudeness on campus life—and it will be developed in an argument essay.

After analyzing her prewriting material, Judith Park wrote a purpose statement for her essay.

> I want to explain how people who sell products influence the public.

This purpose statement makes Park's subject clear: the methods used to influence consumers. She will develop her subject in an expository essay.

Keep in mind that a purpose statement might change during the composing process. Nevertheless, it is an effective tool to keep a writer on track when developing an informal plan.

Exercise 6.1: Clarify a Dominant Purpose

Clarify a dominant purpose for the subject you evaluated in the previous exercise. State the purpose as directly and as clearly as you can. Write it in a complete sentence.

6b Sketch an informal plan.

Use your purpose statement to sketch an informal plan for your essay. Think of this stage of the composing process as sorting and grouping your notes from prewriting.

More than likely, the sorting and grouping process began when you first critically evaluated your notes. Now, by sketching an informal plan, you will be organizing your material in a clear pattern designed to fulfill your purpose. By identifying major points and examples, an informal plan will help you structure your essay. It will

COMPUTER CLINIC

Planning on a Computer

Word processing is so easy that you can chase all your hunches, save each one of them, and compare them later. You can shape a purpose statement, and another, and then another, until you get the one that works. You can select and reassemble elements from prewritten material. Eventually an informal plan will emerge.

Identify each point with bullets. You can print out the informal plan for hand revision and then type in the revisions and reprint the page for reevaluation.

also help you discover what other information you might need to gather.

Judith Park's Informal Plan

An informal plan should begin with a purpose statement, followed by a phrase list of major points.

I want to explain how people who sell products use several ways to influence the public.

- Point 1. Social validation: monkey see, monkey do. Examples: formal dining; ads designed to teach product use.
- Point 2. Reciprocity: a compelling desire to repay a favor. Examples: what campus giveaways suggest.
- Point 3. Mindless consistency: avoid appearing "harebrained." Examples: high-pressure salespeople; telemarketing.
- Point 4. Authority: buy what I endorse. Examples: Fonda exercise tapes; celebrities of all kinds, including politicians.

Clustering techniques you might have used to generate material during the invention process can also serve as an informal outline. Park's informal sketch in cluster form might resemble the one that follows.

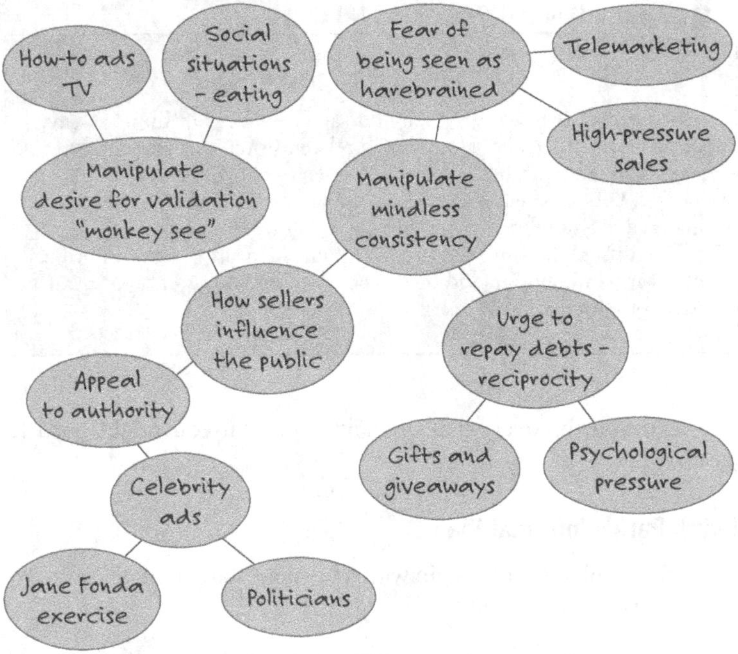

Cluster diagram for Park's informal plan.

Exercise 6.2: Sketch an Informal Plan

Examine the material you have developed for your 750- to 1,000-word essay, that is, the prewritten material and the purpose statement. Make an informal plan by selecting and organizing the ideas and information from your notes.

6c Write a clear, limited working thesis statement that holds up to critical examination.

If there is one moment in the composing process when an essay's final direction and shape become clear, it is when you write a thesis statement. A thesis statement serves as a college essay's intellectual center. It must withstand careful critical scrutiny.

The thesis statement plays a significant role in the writer-reader relationship, too. For writers, a thesis statement identifies and limits the subject, establishes the dominant purpose, and unifies the discussion. Once you have a clear thesis statement, you will find it easier to make decisions about what to include and what to exclude from the discussion paragraphs and how to conclude the essay. When you do not have enough material to develop your thesis statement adequately, then you know you must seek more information (either by returning to earlier drafts or by generating additional material).

For readers, a thesis statement tells what the essay will cover and helps put discussion paragraphs in perspective. Imagine how confused readers will become if you develop several paragraphs but fail to provide the necessary perspective to convey their purpose. A thesis statement provides that perspective.

An effective thesis statement, usually expressed in a single sentence, goes beyond a purpose statement by specifically identifying a subject and limiting the discussion. If you were writing about violence, for example, you might begin with the following thesis statement.

> Violence is destroying the safety of U.S. cities.

When writing your first draft, however, you would discover that the thesis statement is much too broad for a three- or four-page essay. At best you could develop only a few very general observations, all unsupported by specific details. As a consequence, you would have to limit the thesis statement.

Limit a Thesis Statement

Writers limit their thesis statements in two ways.

First, they limit the subject part of the statement. As it stands, the subject of the previous thesis statement is "violence." But violence covers a large territory—murder, muggings, police brutality, and so on. Concentrating on one aspect of violence would limit the subject.

> *Street violence* is destroying the safety of U.S. cities.
> *Gang violence* is destroying the safety of U.S. cities.
> *Random violence* is destroying the safety of U.S. cities.

"Street violence," "gang violence," and "random violence" are more limited than the general subject of "violence." However, these statements are still too broad for a brief essay.

Second, writers limit the predicate part of the statement—in the examples, the part that reads "is destroying the safety of U.S. cities." "U.S. cities" covers all cities from Bangor, Maine, to Honolulu, Hawaii. You could narrow the predicate part of these thesis statements to a particular city, town, or neighborhood.

> Street violence is destroying the safety of *Newport Heights.*
>
> Gang violence is destroying the safety of *my apartment complex.*
>
> Random violence is destroying the safety of *our campus.*

These thesis statements are now manageable—that is, they are limited enough to be effectively developed in a short essay. You could develop them from personal observation, interviews, surveys, police reports, and newspaper articles—all readily available information sources.

WRITER'S CLINIC

Phrase a Thesis Statement Precisely

An effective thesis statement does not have to be complex, but it should always be precise. Vague language and overly general assertions may misguide your reader. Use precise, not vague, language to phrase your thesis statement.

> VAGUE THESIS
>
> The examination of fairy tales is fascinating because it reveals stereotypical characteristics of women, even in today's world.
>
> PRECISE THESIS
>
> *Cinderella* reveals common stereotypes of women.

The second example, phrased precisely in specific language, leaves no room for confusion.

Make a Promise in a Thesis Statement

Finally, an effective thesis statement makes a promise: It announces to readers what the essay covers. The writer must keep that promise or risk writing an unsuccessful essay. Consider, for example, three thesis statements.

> Kevin Costner's *Dances with Wolves* and John Ford's *The Searchers* create conflicting images of Native Americans.

The writer promises to compare and contrast the image of Native Americans in two classic films.

> Although murder is humankind's most repugnant crime, the death penalty should be abolished.

The writer promises to argue that capital punishment should be ended.

Cigarette advertisements can be divided into four categories.

The writer promises to classify cigarette advertisements.

Do Not Confuse Thesis Statements with Other Statements

When writing your thesis statement, do not confuse it with a title, a factual statement, or a purpose statement. *Titles* orient readers, but they are not detailed enough to reveal much about an essay's limited focus and direction. *Factual statements* do not lend themselves to development; they are dead ends. *Purpose statements* are often similar to thesis statements, but they are usually less refined and become stylistically intrusive when inserted into essays. Compare the following:

TITLE

Sesame Street: The Hidden Message

FACTUAL STATEMENT

Sesame Street is a successful children's education program.

PURPOSE STATEMENT

I am going to argue that *Sesame Street* emphasizes entertainment over education.

THESIS STATEMENT

Although it is identified as television's finest children's education program, *Sesame Street* communicates the message that entertainment is more important than education.

Only the thesis statement clearly sets up the discussion that will follow.

Judith Park Composes a Thesis Statement

Judith Park's thesis evolved from the purpose statement she used to sketch her informal plan. After several attempts, Park phrased her thesis:

Self-interested people use several ways to manipulate consumers based on typical conditioning.

By analyzing the elements of her thesis, Park could see that she would be promising the reader that she would identify several typical behaviors and explain how self-interested people use them to manipulate others. Who are these self-interested people? By returning to her prewritten material, Park identified them mainly as advertisers and salespeople.

Remember, in a college essay a thesis statement must be able to stand up to critical examination. Be sure any thesis statement you write is limited, specific, and makes a clear promise.

Exercise 6.3: Write Precise Thesis Statements

The following statements are ineffective as thesis statements. Identify their problems and rewrite them so that they make effective thesis statements.

1. U.S. schools are not doing their job.
2. Film: A window to the world.
3. I want to explain how magazine advertisements use fear to sell products.

WRITER'S CLINIC

Forecast an Essay's Subpoints

Sometimes you may want to use a thesis statement to forecast an essay's subpoints. First, write out the subpoints in brief parallel words or phrases. Next, integrate them into your thesis statement.

> Rude behavior is increasing within our college community, noticeably *in local movie theaters, on campus,* and *at social functions.*

or

> Rude behavior *in local movie theaters, on campus,* and *at social functions* is increasing within our college community.

or

> There is no escaping the fact that rude behavior is increasing within our college community *in local movie theaters, on campus,* and *at social functions.*

Forecasting an essay's subpoints generally works well for in-class writing assignments. A forecast not only alerts your reader to an essay's key points, it also serves as a brief outline to help you concentrate while writing under pressure.

4. The state has set aside 3,800 acres of sand dunes for land preservation.
5. Help—the cry of the homeless.

Exercise 6.4: Write Your Thesis Statement

Write a working thesis statement that clearly sets up the discussion for the essay you have been developing. Do not confuse a thesis statement with a title, a factual statement, or a purpose statement. Remember, an effective thesis statement must be limited, precise, and must make a promise.

6d Draft a formal outline with a reader in mind.

If you have not done so already, now is the time to determine who your reader is.

Your reader will influence your choices about an essay's content. If you are writing an in-class essay for an instructor, you would want to show the full range of your understanding. If writing for fellow students, you would select examples that relate to their experience. If writing for a universal audience, you would select examples that reflect broad experience.

Although Judith Park was responding to a freshman composition assignment, she decided to direct her paper to members of her writers' group. She knew she would have to select common examples and explain her ideas in ways that students would understand. This decision and the formulation of her working thesis meant that she was ready to develop a more formal plan for her essay.

A formal outline identifies the thesis and lists the supporting points. For a short essay, an informal outline may be effective, but for longer essays a formal outline will provide a more detailed view of an essay's final arrangement.

Characteristics of a Formal Outline

Formal outlines include the thesis statement, the subpoints, and various levels of detail depending on the subject's complexity. You can compose a formal outline in topic or sentence form.

Identify the main points by roman numerals, the first sublevel of items by capital letters, the second sublevel by arabic numerals, the third sublevel by lowercase letters, the fourth sublevel by arabic numerals enclosed in parentheses, and the fifth sublevel by lowercase letters enclosed in parentheses. All letters and numbers at the same level are indented to fall directly under one another. (You will rarely need all six levels, especially for college essays.)

Formal Outline Structure

I.
    A.
    B.
        1.
        2.
            a.
            b.
                (1)
                (2)
                    (a)
                    (b)
II.
    A.
    B.
        1.
        2.
            a.
            b.
                (1)
                (2)
                    (a)
                    (b)

And so on.

Notice that each level is a division of the level above it. There must be at least two items at every level because, logically, a topic cannot be divided into one item. For example, there cannot be an A without a B or a 1 without a 2. Of course, there may be more than two items at any level.

All items at the same level must be expressed in parallel grammatical structure, and the first word of each item must be capitalized.

Judith Park's Formal Outline

The following is a formal topic outline for "Subtle Exploitation."

> Thesis: Self-interested people use several ways to manipulate consumers based on typical conditioning.

I. Social validation relies on conformity.
   A. Etiquette is important.
   B. Advertisements teach consumers.

II. Reciprocity suggests some people are compelled to repay favors.
   A. Companies give away free samples on campus.
      1. Gillette offers toiletries.
      2. The Times offers free newspapers.
      3. 24 Hour Fitness Center offers free workouts.
   B. A calculated effort to create indebtedness.

III. Mindless consistency exploits the desire to appear consistent.
   A. High-pressure salespeople use the "foot-in-the-door" tactic.
   B. Telemarketers use the same tactic.

IV. Celebrity authorities influence decisions.
   A. Film star Jane Fonda uses celebrity to sell workout tapes.
   B. Politicians use celebrity to sell products.
      1. Presidential candidate Bob Dole advertises for a drug company.
      2. New York governor Mario Cuomo advertises food products.

V. These manipulative strategies are based on common values.

Developing a formal outline forced Park to arrange the subpoints and the particulars of her material for a reader. Throughout the process of constructing a formal outline, Park relied on the informal outline she constructed earlier, her prewriting material, and other material she had collected. About her outlining process, Park says:

> To start, I laid out my informal plan, prewriting, and class notes. I kept moving through the material and experimenting with the outline. Since I was writing for members of my writing group, I knew I needed to include more examples of experience similar to their experience, such as being offered free samples on campus.
>
> I also realized I needed to collect more information on Jane Fonda's tapes (most of which was left out of the final

draft), and I had to find the names of the politicians I'd seen on television. Everything else came directly from my experience.

Too often, beginning writers want to skip formal planning, yet a formal plan can be an important part of the composing process, one that will help you determine your essay's final arrangement.

COMPUTER CLINIC

Writing a Thesis Statement and Outline with a Computer

Generate several versions of the thesis statement. Play with them—easy to do on the computer—until you frame one you think will work. Then revisit your informal outline on the screen and in printed form. Make sure the material fits the thesis statement.

If your computer has a Split Screen function, use it. Keep the informal outline in the upper half and type the thesis statement in the lower half. Then, under the thesis statement, develop a formal outline by referring to the informal outline.

When you have a formal outline, reconsider its arrangement. Use the Cut and Paste feature to rearrange the order of your key points and subpoints as necessary.

Exercise 6.5: Draft a Formal Outline

If appropriate, develop a formal outline for your essay. Identify the main points by roman numerals (I, II, III, IV), the first sublevel by capital letters (A, B, C), the second sublevel by arabic numerals (1, 2, 3), and the third sublevel, if you have one, by lowercase letters (a, b, c).

7 Write a First Draft *essay*

A first draft will never be perfect. Trying to write a perfect first draft will force you to start and stop. *Do I put a comma here? Is* strategy *spelled with two* t*'s? This sentence doesn't make sense, or does it?*

WRITER'S CLINIC

Secrets of Self-Motivation

Writing is not only about putting words on paper, it is also about keeping yourself going to the end. That takes motivation. Four motivational strategies for writing are helpful:

- **Self-talk.** You must be in your own corner. Do not be afraid to talk to yourself about the essay, the writing problem you face, why you are bogging down. Give yourself a pep talk.
- **Goal-setting.** Be specific. Set a time limit for the first draft. Will you write the entire first draft from beginning to end? That may be unrealistic. Try to schedule breaks at specific hours. Stop when the break time comes.
- **Consultation.** If you are really stuck, talk to someone who has a positive attitude. State the problem in precise language. Ask for advice.
- **Control of your writing space.** You might not be able to control the world, but you can control your own space. Nothing paralyzes the writing process more than distractions. Write where there are none. Take the phone off the hook. Face a blank wall. Tell family and friends you are "out of touch" for the writing time you schedule.

Tell yourself that writing is a positive experience, one that not only lets you demonstrate what you know but also teaches you something about how you think and work.

Starting and stopping will dry up your creative juices, fresh ideas and insights will whither, and spontaneity will die.

Instead of perfection, seek writer's flow. Try to keep your writing moving by concentrating on the big picture: content and structure. Later you can make your essay "perfect."

To begin a first draft, keep everything in front of you—brainstorming lists, freewriting, clusters, purpose statement, outlines. Having everything before you, including mojo charms, will prime the flow of ideas.

There is no hard and fast rule about where to start a first draft. Some writers like to start at the beginning and move step by step to the end. That's okay. Other writers start with the discussion and then write the introduction and conclusion. That's okay, too. An effective tactic is to begin with information that engages your imagination. In this way you can draw yourself more deeply into the writing flow.

Remember your goal: Keep writing toward a completed first draft. You can circle back and fill in later.

7a Write an introduction with a thesis statement that captures a reader's interest.

In a thesis-support essay, the introduction is your chance to grab your reader. Do not throw the chance away. Here is how an effective introduction works.

First, showcase the thesis. The thesis embodies your promise to the reader. It is the promise that will move him or her into the discussion.

Second, give your reader background information. Place your thesis in context. Not to provide the right context for your thesis is like letting someone stumble through a dark room without knowing the light switch location.

Third, make the writing interesting. Never whine on the page about the rigors of the assignment or some such drivel. Instead, use specific language and images to engage the reader's imagination.

For a thesis-support essay, the introduction will seldom be longer than a paragraph, certainly no longer than one-fifth of your paper. The most effective strategy is to open with sentences that engage the reader and conclude with the thesis statement. In the following examples of opening paragraphs, the thesis statement in each one is italicized.

> From a page in a high-fashion magazine, a stunningly attractive woman in boots, jeans, and bomber jacket stares directly at the reader. From the back cover of a newsmagazine, a rugged cowboy in Stetson and sheepskin coat leans casually on a fence post and gazes at the distant mountains. On another page, a handsome young couple sit in a tavern and look longingly into each other's eyes, and on yet another page a camel in tuxedo struts its stuff in a nightclub. These are all central images in cigarette advertisements, and each figure is smoking. *Generally, to sell their products cigarette advertisers appeal to deep consumer desires.*
>
> —Student-writer Joan Akers, "Burning Desire"

> "Attitude" is in. I don't mean good attitude; I mean bad, real bad, attitude. You're probably attracted to it, and your parents, like mine, probably hate it. It's a combination of arrogance, anger, and dark humor. Raw comedians have

> attitude. Cool actors have attitude. Sullen rock stars have it, too. Dennis Leary, Chris Rock, and Axl Rose—all are soaked in attitude. Is it strictly a male trait? Hardly—Whoopi Goldberg, Madonna, and the Spice Girls all have serious attitude. *Attitude doesn't come easily, but you can acquire it if you follow five simple steps.*
>
> —Student-writer Phyllis Booker, "Attitude"

Here are several strategies professional writers use to grab the reader's attention.

1. Create vivid details that engage a reader's senses.
2. Dramatize statistics that relate to the thesis.
3. Use eye-catching quotations that arouse a reader's curiosity.
4. Ask a question that alerts the reader.
5. Relate an anecdote with which the reader can identify.
6. Define a key word or concept in an unusual way.

In short papers, you might choose to open with the thesis instead of showcasing it last, especially in papers that give straightforward information.

> *A page titled "Conditions of Contract" on airline tickets could serve as a syllabus for a course in travel education.* In fine print, it answers several questions.
>
> —Student-writer Tim Potts, "Read the Fine Print"

COMPUTER CLINIC

Writing a First Draft on a Computer

If you can type "cold" onto the computer—that is, type a first draft without a rough handwritten draft—you will save a lot of time. But not everyone can or wants to do so; most writers are more comfortable writing by hand first. They start by roughing out sentences and paragraphs, then they enter them into the computer.

Remember: Write the first draft quickly. Even when your typing is weak, a computer can increase your speed. Mistakes can be corrected later. Keep in mind, too, that your first draft will be filed, and easily accessed for revision. If you find yourself stuck on an important concept, write a reminder note in parentheses or in all capitals and boldface so you will remember to return to it later.

Exercise 7.1: Write an Introduction

Write an introduction to your essay. In some respects, the introduction can be your essay's most important section. Indeed, writing an effective introduction might take more creative effort than writing any other part of the essay.

Many writers compose an introduction after they have composed the discussion. These writers need to know exactly where they are taking their readers.

Whether or not you start your first draft by writing the introduction makes no difference. Either way, you should use the introduction to showcase the thesis, provide necessary background information, and make your writing interesting by using one of several tactics.

1. Create vivid details.
2. Dramatize statistics.
3. Use eye-catching quotations.
4. Ask questions.
5. Relate an anecdote.
6. Define a key word or concept.

7b Write a discussion several paragraphs long, organized by topic sentences.

In a thesis-support essay, each discussion paragraph develops one aspect of the thesis statement. Furthermore, a topic sentence serves as the main idea of a discussion paragraph just as a thesis statement serves as the main idea of an entire essay. Topic sentences and supporting information—that is, the discussion—keep the promise that is implied in a thesis.

For a full review of paragraph structure, see Chapters 11–16 on writing paragraphs, especially Chapter 11, Topic Sentences, and Chapter 15, Expository Paragraphs.

To be effective, discussion paragraphs should follow three principles: They should be unified, coherent, and well developed.

Unity. Discussion paragraphs are unified when the information they present clearly relates to the idea expressed in the topic sentence. Remember: A topic sentence advances a thesis statement's promise by identifying and developing one key aspect of the thesis.

Coherence. Discussion paragraphs are coherent when readers move smoothly and logically from one sentence to another—that is, when the main idea advances from sentence to sentence along a well-constructed verbal path. When a paragraph lacks coherence, readers will lose interest.

Development. How long should a discussion paragraph be? Paragraph length depends on several considerations, such as the complexity of the information, the development method, and the length of the paragraph before and after it. Use this as a guiding principle: A discussion paragraph should be developed enough to do justice to its main idea in the topic sentence.

While composing an essay, you might discover that you need more information to develop an effective paragraph. There are several actions you can take. First, you can return to your prewriting for an idea. Second, you can provide greater detail to the idea that currently exists. Third, you can consult outside sources for more information. The process of gathering information may continue until the final draft is complete.

Well-developed paragraphs might contain examples, definitions, comparisons, causes, effects, facts, and statistics—all presented in enough detail to make a paragraph over a hundred words long.

When a discussion paragraph becomes exceptionally long, writers will often separate the material into two or more paragraphs to ease the reading process, even though the information amplifies the main idea of a single topic sentence.

Transition Paragraphs

In an extended thesis-support essay, a brief paragraph often serves as a transition when a significant shift occurs in the discussion. Usually no longer than two or three sentences, the purpose of a transition paragraph is to remind a reader of the thesis statement and indicate that the discussion is shifting emphasis.

> Clearly, body alteration through scarring and tattooing in primitive cultures communicated a variety of social messages. In contrast, body alteration today is merely decorative. Tattooing and piercing are fads, much like styles of clothes.

This transition announces that the discussion is turning from the purpose of body alteration in primitive cultures to the purpose of body alteration today.

Exercise 7.2: Write a Discussion

Use your thesis statement and outline to sketch out the discussion section, organizing each paragraph around a topic sentence. Begin by roughing out each topic sentence. Then flesh out each paragraph, keeping in mind the principles of effective paragraphs. Remember, this is a first draft. Do not seek perfection; your goal is to complete a solid first draft.

Even so, you want to write paragraphs that approximate effective discussion paragraphs.

1. Concentrate on a single aspect of the thesis statement.
2. Open with a topic sentence.
3. Maintain unity.
4. Retain coherence.
5. Develop the idea adequately.

7c Write the conclusion that effectively closes the discussion.

Too often, beginning writers will treat conclusions in a perfunctory manner: a couple of general statements about the subject and a rapid "That's all, folks" to close.

Experienced writers use a different strategy, one based on the simple principle that readers remember best what they read last. Experienced writers, therefore, treat writing a conclusion as a challenge that demands skill and concentration. Generally, they use one of several strategies to conclude their essays.

Give a brief summary. In college writing, the most common practice is to restate the thesis statement and then summarize the subpoints to reinforce what has come before. This summary method often seems mechanical, but it can be effective if handled in an interesting way. A summary conclusion does have one strong advantage: It is clearly linked to the rest of the essay.

Draw an inference. You can use the conclusion to deepen a dimension of an essay. One student ended a paper on being robbed and threatened at pistol point by shifting from the external detail of the experience to an implicit psychological fact. Notice how she uses questions to put the reader in a reflective mood:

> What does it mean when somebody holds you up? Just the loss of a few dollars? Or just the loss of a wallet and some

> mementos—a few peeling photographs, worn identification cards, tattered ticket stubs? Yes, it means that. And it means more. It means you have become part of that chosen group that no longer feels safe after dark to walk the neighborhood streets.

Use an anecdote. You can conclude an essay with an anecdote, a brief story that puts the thesis statement in clear perspective.

Link the subject to the reader. You can conclude by drawing a lesson from the discussion that links the subject to the reader's experience.

Close with a quotation. You can conclude with an apt quotation, one that echoes the main idea of the essay and will resonate in the reader's memory.

Remember that a conclusion must flow logically from the essay. If it does not, it will seem merely to be tacked on.

Exercise 7.3: Write a Conclusion

Write a conclusion for your first draft. Remember, a conclusion should echo the entire essay. Use one of these common strategies:

1. Give a brief summary.
2. Draw a significant inference.
3. Present a meaningful anecdote.
4. Link the subject to the reader.
5. Close with a quotation.

8 Revise the First Draft *essay*

Although you cannot actually talk to a reader during the revision process, you can do the next best thing: Imagine that you are seeing your first draft through a reader's eyes.

Seeing through a reader's eyes will give the critical perspective you need to evaluate your own work. Through this act of imagination, you will recognize passages where the reader might get bogged down. You will spot where you need to delete or add information. You will rewrite for clarity and logic.

Remember, revision engages the critical thinking process. You will critically evaluate your work and consciously revise it to fulfill an informed reader's expectations. Keep in mind, too, that revision does not take place in one swoop. It unfolds in phases.

8a For phase 1 revision, improve the major elements.

Examine your first draft with an eye toward improving the major elements first. You might have to add or delete information, sharpen the thesis and topic sentences, improve the unity, and make the point of view consistent. Throughout the process, you will always be improving the clarity of your essay.

Some writers revise directly on the computer. Others print out copies of the first draft and revise by hand. If you choose to revise on screen, make a copy of the original first draft before you begin to make changes. This way you will not risk losing information you might decide to retain later. If you choose to revise on hard copy, do not be timid. Scratch out passages, rewrite in the margin, and make notes that reflect what you plan to add. Once all that is done, write a second draft to accommodate the changes.

Add Content. Reread your first draft to see if you need more information. Some writers skimp on content in their first drafts. They choose to move quickly through the draft, hitting the high points while planning to add detail during revision. To develop more content, they sometimes return to the beginning of the composing process, which means they return to thinking creatively. If you need to add information, you will develop a new list of details, create another cluster, or seek more information.

Delete Content. Reread your first draft to eliminate unnecessary information. Some writers purposefully overwrite their first drafts, knowing that they are generating excessive information. Other writers may overemphasize a minor point or include too much detail to support it. In all these cases the content must be trimmed, and to delete content effectively requires a sharp critical eye. You must read and reread passages to figure out what can be cut and how to combine information in other sentences.

Examine the Structure. Reread your first draft with an eye toward improving its organization. At the most general level, this draft should already have a distinct introduction, discussion, and conclusion. But more than likely the unity will be flawed, that is, the thesis will not clearly relate to the topic sentences. Reread the thesis. Be sure it is specific and limits the discussion. Check to see that each of the topic sentences relates directly to one aspect of the thesis. If necessary, rewrite the thesis and the topic sentences so that each embodies a key word. The relationship between thesis and topic sentences must be clear because each serves as a signpost for the reader. Sometimes repeating a key word makes the link clear.

Once your thesis and topic sentences work together, check each discussion paragraph separately to be sure the information relates directly to the topic sentence. This evaluation is as important as checking to be sure that the thesis and topic sentences are clearly linked.

Finally, examine the conclusion to see that it follows logically from the discussion. It is important to make sure your conclusion directly restates, or at least echoes, the thesis statement.

Examine the Point of View. In the broadest sense, writers present their material from a personal or impersonal point of view. The personal point of view is characteristic of essays based on personal experience and observation; the impersonal point of view is characteristic of objective reports and research. A personal point of view places the writer in the experience, which is signaled by personal pronouns (I, me, my, we, us, our). Sometimes writers address their readers directly, using second-person pronouns (you, your). An impersonal point of view seldom directly addresses the reader or uses first-person pronouns.

Your material will usually dictate the appropriate point of view to use. You would not write about your childhood experiences in an impersonal way, nor would you write about historical, social, or scientific research in a personal way.

When revising for point of view, ask yourself where the material came from: from research? from reports by others? from personal experience? The proper point of view will follow from your answer.

In "Subtle Exploitation," Judith Park had no choice but to write from a personal point of view. Much of her information comes from her own experiences and observations. Although many writing professors caution against using the personal point of view, it is sometimes the only appropriate point of view to use. The key to making your decision is reflected in your essay's content. Like Park, if you use examples from your own experience, then the personal point of view is appropriate.

One caution: When you use the personal pronoun *I* to signal a personal point of view, do so judiciously. Do not pepper your essay with *I*'s. To do so might create the impression that you, not your subject, are the center of the essay.

WRITER'S CLINIC

> ***Cut and Paste a Hard Copy***
>
> Here is a simple strategy for revising a hard copy of your first draft during phase 1 revisions.
>
> Keep scissors and Scotch tape handy. To move passages around, use the scissors and tape to cut and reassemble the major elements of your essay. You can also write out new information on another sheet of paper, trim the entry, and tape it in place.
>
> Once everything is cut and taped, you will have a taped-together essay that approximates what will become a new draft. Next, rewrite it by integrating all the changes.

Judith Park's Phase 1 Revisions

Judith Park extensively revised her first draft of "Subtle Exploitation." For this phase, she kept her eye on the larger elements, knowing she would concentrate on the smaller elements in another phase. Examine the changes she made along with her comments about the reasons she made them.

I added details to show how many forces influence social values. I also wanted to subtly introduce my supporting points.

Unfortunately, most people have learned to
Parents, teachers, and the community at large teach
respect a core of social values. ~~Most of us want~~
that it is good to be socially accepted, repay favors,
~~to be socially acceptable, repay favors, maintain~~
maintain consistency, and respect authorities.
~~consistency, and show respect for authority.~~

I revised the thesis to be specific. "Exploitation" works better here. Later, I could make "exploit" a unifying word.

I added detail to enliven this example.

Without these values community trust would not work. No one could count on anyone. The power of social values has not been lost on merchandisers. ~~that is, those who want to sell us~~
merchandisers engage in
~~their products.~~ These ~~self-interested people use~~
the subtle exploitation of typical social values.
~~several ways to manipulate consumers based on~~
~~typical conditioning.~~

I used "mysterious" to emphasize my confusion.

beautifully set with flowers, candles, and a mysterious array of silverware.

The desire to be socially validated is a common desire advertisers use to manipulate consumers. No one likes to be out of step with others. ~~When confused in a social situation, most people will turn to someone else for direction.~~ As children we turn to friends and grown-ups to see how to fit in. As adults we continue to seek social acceptance. I recently attended my first formal dinner. The table was ~~beautiful but confusing.~~ When the salad was served, I was confused about which fork to use. Since I was afraid to face embarrassment by making a mistake, I watched a guest seated across from me. This behavior reflected one form of social validation, which is the natural tendency of one person looking at another as a model for public behavior. Advertisers subtly exploit this desire to fit in.

Trying to see my essay through a reader's eyes, I decided that this paragraph was unnecessary and overwritten so I combined it with the previous one.

~~The manipulation of the desire for social validation is a powerful strategy when used to influence people.~~ Think of advertisements for such products as Levi's, Coca Cola, AT&T, Virginia Slim, or Calvin Klein. ~~They usually feature models using the products in social situations.~~ If consumers ~~identify with the models and situations, then the advertiser is successfully using social validation to influence them. How does this tactic work? By showing consumers that it would be appropriate to use the product in similar situations in their lives. Manipulating the desire for social validation is only one of several strategies used to influence our decisions.~~ see themselves reflected in the advertisements, merchandisers hope they will also see themselves using the product as it has been modeled for them. They are successfully exploiting the desire for social validation.

I revised this topic sentence to parallel the one in the preceding paragraph and added "exploit" to help create unity. I identified the companies by name to be more specific. I also cut down the wordiness.

The desire for reciprocity is another value
~~Merchandisers frequently use the desire to~~
merchandisers exploit. For instance, Gillette offers
~~repay a favor, which is called "reciprocity," to~~
free toiletries; the Times offers free newspapers; 24
~~influence our decisions. Reciprocity is at work~~
Hour Fitness Center offers free workout sessions.
~~when a company gives out free samples of a~~
~~product. I know of one maker of razor blades,~~
~~shaving creams, and after-shave lotions who~~
~~offers free samples at the beginning of each~~
~~school year. One local newspaper offers a two-~~
~~month free subscription to all registering~~
~~students. A local athletic club offers one free~~
~~month of workout sessions to first-year students.~~
These are not merely kindnesses, they are
calculated efforts to influence what
~~attempts to get~~ first-year students ~~to~~ buy. ~~certain~~
~~products.~~ Obviously, these companies are
ing and paying to use
counting on students ~~to~~ like the gifts. ~~First, it~~
~~makes sense for these companies to get students~~
~~used to using their products and services so that~~
~~they will pay to use them~~ in the future. ~~Second,~~
But less obviously,
~~at a more complex level,~~ these companies are
ing
also ~~using reciprocity as a subtle way to~~ exploit
the social value of reciprocity. Most
~~students. They know that most~~ of us have been
trained to repay a debt, even an unrequested
As a result, merchandisers know that some
debt. ~~In fact, for many people not to repay a debt~~
students will feel obligated to repay their kindness.
~~can become psychologically painful.~~
It does not take many razor blade sales, newspaper subscriptions, or health club memberships to offset the cost of a few gifts, does it?

I felt the "psychologically painful" reference might distract a reader. I added the closing detail to remind the reader that these gifts are insignificant next to potential sales.

Exercise 8.1: Phase 1 Revisions

Always start with a clean draft. Reread your essay for content and eliminate unnecessary information. Note points that might need more development or support. Generate more content and work it into your paper. Then reread for organization, making sure that the discussion paragraphs reflect the thesis statement. Next, reread for point of view, making the necessary revisions to keep the point of view consistent. Revise once again, integrating the changes into this draft.

COMPUTER CLINIC

Phase 1 Revisions

Most writers like to make phase 1 revisions on hard copy, that is, a printed version of the essay, with plenty of space between the lines to accommodate changes. But some writers have learned to revise directly on the computer.

A computer can make phase 1 revisions easy. To move long passages, use the computer's Cut and Paste function. First, highlight the passage you want to move. Second, use the Copy feature to store the passage in computer memory. Next, delete the old copy and move the cursor to where you want to insert the passage. Finally, click Paste. The passage will appear where the cursor marks the spot.

To check paragraph unity, you can use the Find feature to trace how frequently you use key words to keep your central purpose before the reader.

Judith Park Integrates Phase 1 Revisions

The following are three revised paragraphs from Judith Park's draft. What she deleted is lined out, and what she added is printed in italics.

Unfortunately, most people have learned to respect a core of social values. ~~Most of us want to be socially acceptable,~~ *Parents, teachers, and the community at large teach that it is good to be socially accepted*, repay favors, maintain consistency, and show respect for authority. Without these values community trust would not work. No one could count on anyone. The power of social values has not been lost on merchandisers. ~~that is, those who want to sell us their products.~~ These ~~self-interested people use several ways to manipulate consumers based on typical conditioning~~

merchandisers engage in the subtle exploitation of typical social values.

The desire to be socially validated is a common *value* advertisers use to manipulate consumers. No one likes to be out of step with others. ~~When confused in a social situation, most people will turn to someone else for direction.~~ *As children we turn to friends and grown-ups to see how to fit in. As adults we continue to seek* acceptance. I recently attended my first formal dinner. The table was beautiful*ly set with flowers, candles, crystal, and a mysterious array of silverware*~~, but confusing.~~ When the salad was served, I was confused about which fork to use. Since I was afraid to face embarrassment by making a mistake, I watched a guest seated across from me. This behavior reflected one form of social validation, which is the natural tendency of one person looking at another as a model *for public behavior. Advertisers subtly exploit the desire to fit in.* ~~The manipulation of the desire for social validation is a powerful strategy when used to influence people.~~ Think of advertisements for such products as Levi's, Coca Cola, AT&T, Virginia Slim, or Calvin Klein. ~~They usually feature models using the products in social situations.~~ If consumers ~~identify with the models and situations, then the advertiser is successfully using social validation to influence them. How does this tactic work? By showing consumers that it would be appropriate to use the product in similar situations in their lives. Manipulating the desire for social validation is only one of several strategies used to influence our decisions~~ *see themselves reflected in the advertisements, merchandisers hope they will also see themselves using the product as it has been modeled for them. They are successfully exploiting the desire for social validation.*

~~Merchandisers frequently use the desire to repay a favor, which is called "reciprocity," to influence our decisions. Reciprocity is at work when a company gives out free samples of a product.~~ *The desire for reciprocity is another value merchandisers exploit.* ~~I know of one maker of razor blades, shaving creams, and after-shave lotions who offers free samples at the beginning of each school year. One local newspaper offers a two-month free subscription to all registering students. A local athletic club offers one free month of workout sessions to first-year students.~~ *For instance, Gillette offers free toiletries; the Times offers free newspapers; 24 Hour Fitness Center offers free workout sessions.* These are not merely kindnesses, they are ~~attempts to get~~ *calculated efforts to influence* what first-year students ~~to~~ buy. ~~certain products.~~ Obviously, these companies are counting on students ~~to~~ liking the gifts *and paying to use them* ~~First, it makes sense for these companies to get students used to using their products and services so that they will pay to use them~~ in the future. *But less obviously,* ~~Second, at a more complex level,~~ these ~~These~~ companies are also ~~using reciprocity as a subtle way to~~ exploit*ing* ~~students~~ the social value of reciprocity. ~~They know that~~ *Most* of us have been trained to repay a debt, even an unrequested debt. ~~In fact, for many people not to repay a favor can become psychologically painful.~~ *As a result, merchandisers know that some students will feel obligated to repay their kindness. It does not take many razor blade sales, newspaper subscriptions, and health club memberships to offset the cost of a few gifts, does it?*

8b For phase 2 revision, improve the smaller elements.

Once you have integrated your revisions into the first draft, you are ready to focus on smaller elements. Revise your sentences with an eye for effectiveness, for clarity, for coherence—that is, clear transitions in thought—for conciseness, diction, and style.

Consider Your Essay's Tone. Now is the time to consciously think about *tone.* Tone embodies your attitude—it is embedded in the words you use and how you use them. In college writing, try to achieve a reasonable tone, one that shows you understand your subject and have respect for it and for your readers. Most college writing reflects standard American English, which can be formal or informal writing.

Although readers appreciate lively language, they can be repelled by sarcasm or slang inserted into a serious discussion. They can also be repelled by pompous language. College writing often becomes pompous when inexperienced writers use the thesaurus to find words that sound more "intelligent" to replace words they have already used. Generally, the words will be unnecessarily abstract and inaccurate. Extensive reading with a dictionary in hand is the most effective way to acquire a working vocabulary, not browsing a thesaurus.

For phase 2 revision, start with a clean draft. To sharpen your critical examination, try reading it slowly, preferably out loud. (The ear is often more critical than the eye.) As you read, make your improvements.

Once the individual sentences are precise, then edit them for correctness: Check their grammar, spelling, mechanics, and punctuation. Make these changes directly on the page or screen. Integrate the revisions, then print out a new, clean draft.

Judith Park's Phase 2 Revisions

For her second-phase revisions, Judith Park found herself concentrating on improving coherence, that is, providing clear transitions to guide readers through her essay. She changed several words and passages to reflect her thought more accurately. She also improved the wording of her thesis and topic sentences so they signaled a clear movement in the discussion. Finally, she made sure that the identity of her readers was embedded in the introduction. Read the following passage with Park's phase 2 revisions, then read her comments on the revision printed in the margin.

"Unfortunately" is inaccurate. "Our" is the start of my attempt to define a reader. It suggests that I'm writing for readers my own age.

Whether aware of it or not, most of us ~~Unfortunately, most people~~ have learned to respect a core of social values. Our p ~~Parents~~ arents, teachers, and the community at large ~~teach~~ have taught that it is good to be socially accepted, repay favors, maintain consistency, and show respect for authority.

I think "friends and neighbors" personalizes what I'm saying.

I tried to show a purpose, so I added "to influence what we buy."

Some small changes: "advertisers" to "merchandisers" because I use merchandisers as a key term.

Without these values community trust would ~~not~~
break down. friends and neighbors psychological
~~work. No one~~ could ^ count on anyone. The ^ power
not
of social values has not been lost on
sales representatives and advertisers.
~~merchandisers. that is, those who want to sell us~~
~~their products.~~ These merchandisers engage in
to influence what we buy.
the subtle exploitation of typical social values ^

for ion one
The desire ~~to be~~ social~~ly~~ validat~~ed~~ is ~~a~~
merchandisers exploit.
common value ~~advertisers use to manipulate~~
~~consumers.~~ No one likes to be out of step with
others. As children we turn to friends and grown-
ups to see how to fit in. As adults we continue to
for example,
seek acceptance. ^ I recently attended my first
formal dinner. The table was beautifully set with
flowers, candles, crystal, and a mysterious array
of silverware. When the salad was served, I was
Rather than
confused about which fork to use. ~~Since I was~~
~~afraid to~~ face embarrassment by making a
took guidance from
mistake, I ~~watched~~ ^ a guest seated across from
My
me. ~~This~~ behavior reflected one form of social
that
validation, ~~which~~ is, the natural tendency of one
turning to
person ~~looking at~~ another as a model for public
often
behavior. Advertisers ^ subtly exploit the desire to
fit in. Think of advertisements for such products
jeans,
as Levi~~'s,~~ Coca Cola, AT&T, Virginia Slim, or
Calvin Klein. If consumers see themselves
reflected in the advertisements, merchandisers
hope they will also see themselves using the
thus
product as it has been modeled for them., ~~They~~
~~are~~ successfully exploiting the desire for social
validation.

Added transitional phrase.

I wasn't "afraid"; I didn't want to be embarrassed.

I was "guided" by the guest. "Watched" is inaccurate.

"Turning to" works better than "looking at." Added "often" to qualify the assertion.

I combined these sentences to show the result more effectively.

The desire for reciprocity is another value merchandisers exploit. At the start of each school year, ~~For instance,~~ Gillette offers free toiletries; the Times offers free newspapers; 24 Hour Fitness Center offers free workout sessions. These are not merely kindnesses, they are calculated efforts to influence what first-year students buy. Obviously, these companies are counting on students liking the gifts and paying to use them in the future. But less obviously, these companies are also exploiting the social value of reciprocity. Most of us have been trained to repay a debt, even an unrequested debt. As a result, merchandisers know that some students will feel obligated to repay their kindness. After all, it ~~It~~ does not take many razor blade sales, newspaper subscriptions, and health club memberships to offset the cost of a few gifts, does it?

I left all this untouched. It worked for me.

Added a transitional phrase, "after all."

COMPUTER CLINIC

Phase 2 Revisions

For phase 2 revisions, you can probably revise right on the screen without much difficulty. Chances are you've already revised some sentences during phase 1 revisions. Now is the time to evaluate the sentences as each relates to the other.

Experiment with phrasing. Change words to create a different effect. Try out some different sentence structures to increase reading speed.

If you wish to make your essay more impersonal, use the Find feature to spot each use of "I." Then see if you can revise the sentence to eliminate it. If you want to avoid sexist pronoun references, use Find to trace all the uses of masculine pronouns to be sure they have masculine referents. If they don't, rewrite the sentences to remove the gender bias.

Exercise 8.2: Phase 2 Revisions

Begin with a clean draft of your essay. Read it to improve the smaller elements. Try to read as critically as you can through the eyes of your imagined reader. Do not fall into the trap of making negative judgments by telling yourself "this isn't any good," or "this part sounds stupid," or "it was dumb to pick this subject." Instead, decide what is effective and what is not. Leave the effective writing alone and figure out how to fix what is ineffective.

Revise the entire essay, reading and rereading as you work to see that the sentences fit together, then integrate the improvements by

WRITER'S CLINIC

Meet Reader Expectations

Academic readers expect that a college essay will be organized by a thesis statement and developed through a series of topic sentences, one for each discussion paragraph. During proofreading, scan your thesis statement and topic sentences one more time to be sure they clearly relate to each other. Judith Park scanned her thesis statement and topic sentences as follows:

THESIS STATEMENT IN THE INTRODUCTION

Merchandisers engage in the subtle exploitation of typical social values to influence what we buy.

TOPIC SENTENCE IN THE FIRST DISCUSSION PARAGRAPH

The desire for social validation is one value merchandisers exploit.

TOPIC SENTENCE IN THE SECOND DISCUSSION PARAGRAPH

The desire for reciprocity is another value merchandisers exploit.

TOPIC SENTENCE IN THE THIRD DISCUSSION PARAGRAPH

High-pressure merchandisers are particularly adept at exploiting mindless consistency.

TOPIC SENTENCE IN THE FOURTH DISCUSSION PARAGRAPH

Another value merchandisers exploit is an automatic respect for authority.

completing another draft and reviewing it. If necessary, improve that draft, too.

8c For phase 3 revision, proofread the final draft and write a title.

When you have thoroughly revised and edited your essay, you are ready to prepare the final manuscript (see Chapter 9) and write a title.

Proofread with Care Proofreading requires a special kind of attention. You are looking for such errors as misspellings, missing words, dropped endings of words, and typographical mistakes. Some writers proofread their manuscripts by reading them backward, one sentence at a time. Reading backward in this fashion will distract your mind from each sentence's meaning so that you can concentrate on the technical features. Keep in mind that you are now preparing the draft your reader will see. A carefully proofread essay will reflect the effort you have given the entire project.

Create an Appropriate Title. Often the last step in the composing process is writing the title. Yet a title should not be an afterthought, a phrase hastily typed at the top of the page before you rush to class. Because a title actually begins the essay, it should suggest the general subject while serving as an invitation to read. A title should be brief but interesting and may be taken directly from the essay itself. Frequently a title will echo a thought that runs through the essay.

Exercise 8.3: Phase 3 Revisions

Proofread your essay and create a title. Accurate proofreading is demanding. Many writers are not good proofreaders of their own work

COMPUTER CLINIC

Phase 3 Revisions

Phase 3 revisions, careful proofreading, can be done on the screen. During this phase you should concentrate on catching the niggling errors: errors in grammar, punctuation, and spelling.

Pay particular attention to homonyms, words that sound alike but are spelled differently, such as *your* and *you're; to, two,* and *too; there, their,* and *they're; it's* and *its.* Your computer's Spellcheck feature will not pick up misuses of these words.

because they are too close to it to review it objectively. They concentrate on what is being said, not whether it has been said correctly. Their eyes, as a result, ignore the niggling errors that will be obvious to other readers.

By setting an essay aside for a day or two, you will be able to examine it more objectively. In reality, the due date may be very near, and you will not have time to postpone proofreading. If you are in a time crunch, at least reread your essay with one eye on your personal list of frequent errors. At the very least, errors in homonyms and typos will leap out at you.

WRITER'S CLINIC

Frequent Error List

Throughout the semester, compile your own frequent error list to refer to during proofreading. The list should be composed of errors you frequently make. Examples of troublesome words include:

it's = it is
its = possessive pronoun
you're = you are
there = a place
their = possessive pronoun
they're = they are
strategy, *not* stradegy
judgment, *not* judgement (British spelling)
effect *means* result
affect *means* influence

Write such errors on a Post-it note and paste it to your computer when proofreading your essay.

9 Standard Manuscript Form *essay*

Following standard manuscript form is a courtesy to the reader. These standard guidelines, as set by the Modern Language Association, help make an essay easy to read.

9 Use standard manuscript form.

Academic readers expect college essays to be properly formatted, that is, they expect to read a fair copy, one free of blemishes and format distractions.

Materials

Handwritten Papers. Use $8\frac{1}{2}$-by-11-inch lined white paper with neat edges (not pages torn from a spiral notebook). Use black or blue ink, not green or red, and write on one side of the page only. Skip every other line to make reading and correcting easier.

Typewritten Papers or Computer-printed Papers. Use $8\frac{1}{2}$-by-11-inch white typing paper. Do not use onionskin (it is flimsy); do not use erasable bond (it smudges). You may use correction fluid ("white-out") to cover any typing errors you have made. Double-space between lines and type on one side of the page only. Be sure that you have a fresh ribbon in the typewriter and that the keys are clean. Also remember that the ink or bubble jet printers will smudge very easily, so double-check to be sure a bubble-jet-printed paper is smudge free.

Type Style or Font. Use a type style or font that is standard and easily readable, not one that is italic, cursive, or outlined. For manuscripts printed from a computer, use a letter-quality printer.

Paper Clip. Unless otherwise directed, use a paper clip to hold the pages together. Many instructors do not like pages stapled together, and no instructor likes the upper-left-hand corner to have been dog-eared to hold the pages in place.

Margins

Leave margins of one inch on all sides of the paper to avoid a crowded appearance. On lined white paper, the vertical line indicates a proper left-hand margin. On most computers, justification of the right margin creates awkwardly spaced lines. Turn the right justification control off while formatting your paper on a computer.

Indention

Indent the first line of every paragraph uniformly—one inch in a handwritten manuscript, five spaces in a typewritten one, one-half inch in a typeset one.

Paging

Place the page number, in arabic numerals (2, *not* II), without a period or parentheses, in the upper-right-hand corner, one-half inch from the top of each page. You may omit the number on the first page, but if you choose to include it, center it at the bottom of the page.

Identification

Include your name, your instructor's name, the course title and number, the date, and any other information your instructor requests. Place that information on separate double-spaced lines, beginning in the upper-left-hand corner of the first page. Place the line with your name one inch from the top of the page. In addition, put your last name in the upper-right-hand corner, with the page number: Park 3. (See the sample research paper in Chapter 58.)

Title

Handwritten Papers. On lined paper, place the title in the center of the first line and begin the first sentence two lines below it.

Typed Papers. For typed papers, double-space below the date and center your title on the page. Begin the first sentence two lines below it.

Always capitalize the first and last words of titles, any word that follows a colon, and all other words except articles, conjunctions, and prepositions.

Do not underline the title or place quotation marks around it. If, however, the title of another work or a quotation is part of your title, underline or use quotation marks as appropriate. (See Chapter 39, Quotation Marks; Chapter 50, Italics; Chapter 47, Capitals.)

Judith Park's first page of "Subtle Exploitation" illustrates the proper format for a typed college essay.

Park 1

Judith Park

Dr. Craft

English 1

22 October 2001

Subtle Exploitation

Whether aware of it or not, most of us have learned to respect a core of social values. Our parents, teachers, and the community at large have taught us that it is good to be socially accepted, repay favors, maintain consistent behavior, and respect authority. Without these values, community trust would break down. Friends and neighbors could not count on each other. The psychological power of social values has not been lost on sales representatives and advertisers. Indeed, these merchandisers engage in the subtle exploitation of typical social values to influence what we buy.

The desire for social validation is one value merchandisers exploit. No one likes to be out of step with others. As children we turn to friends and grown-ups to see how to fit in. As adults we continue to seek social acceptance. For example, I recently attended my first formal dinner. The table was beautifully set with flowers, candles, crystal, and a mysterious array of silverware. . . .

COMPUTER CLINIC

Printing a Final Draft with a Computer

All computers have formatting commands that allow you to choose type sizes and styles, line spacing, margins, and so on. Learn to use them. If you set them up once, then each time you print an essay, it will be perfectly formatted—or as publishers say, it will be a fair copy.

Finally, organize all the files of information you have accumulated, put them into a single folder, name it, and save it on a disk. You will then have a documented history of the writing process that led to this fair copy of your essay.

10 Instructor and Peer Review *essay*

Many instructors give developing writers plenty of commentary on essays written early in the semester. This commentary will generally concentrate on the larger elements rather than on refinements. Expect to hear whether the thesis is limited, whether the structure is effective, whether the discussion is unified, whether the conclusion works.

Generally, commentary will come from two sources: the instructor and fellow classmates.

Instructor Commentary

Writing professors approach essays differently. Some will simply collect an essay, make margin notes, and return it. Others will write or type extensive notes that they attach to the essay before returning it. Others will meet with students for individual conferences to discuss the essay. Some professors, a growing number, will evaluate essays through e-mail or fax; students submit their drafts electronically, and the professor responds electronically.

No matter what method your professor uses, read the commentary with care. If the professor uses correction symbols, refer to the correction chart to be sure you understand what each symbol means. If you meet with your professor in conference, be sure to make notes of his or her oral comments.

Keep in mind that a writing professor is not only trying to improve a particular essay but is also laying the foundation for your writing success in future classes.

Peer Commentary

Some writing instructors organize formal peer-review sessions, that is, they require their writers to submit early drafts of their essays to other class members for comments. Peer review is often done in established peer-review groups whose members work together throughout the semester. At other times, professors form new groups every few weeks to give everyone in class a chance to work together.

In either case, writing professors usually set aside some class time for the groups to complete their reviews. In addition, professors generally provide peer-review guidelines based on the particular requirements of the assignment.

If your professor does not require formal peer-review sessions, you and other classmates may want to set up an informal review group. Or you may choose to work with another class member to review each other's work. Either way, your goal will be the same: to see your work through another reader's eyes. You will be surprised how often a passage—even an entire essay—that may be perfectly clear to you will be confusing to a reader who has intellectual and emotional distance from the material.

Peer-Review Responsibilities

You have two main responsibilities during the peer-review process: to receive informed advice and to give informed advice in a collegial manner.

Receiving Advice. Writing isn't easy, and sometimes it is the flawed piece of writing that receives a writer's most focused emotional energy. When a writer's work is criticized, the natural tendency is to defend each paragraph, each sentence, each word against what may be perceived as an attack. But when writers can look at responses to their work unemotionally, it is easy to see that reviewer comments are offered as suggestions for improvement, not challenges. So relax when receiving advice; judge the observations by what you are trying to accomplish.

Once your work has been reviewed, read all the written responses with care. Although they may be brief, they may still be valuable. Moreover, you can follow up written responses by asking the reviewer questions that will help to clarify or amplify any written advice.

Be sure to consider all oral responses, too. Jot down the advice you feel will help improve your draft. When a reviewer asks you a question, answer it, but do not feel you have to justify any decision you made during the composing process. Most importantly, *don't become defensive.* Always remember that your reviewers will be evaluating the effectiveness of a piece of writing, not your character.

Should you incorporate reviewer suggestions while revising? That is your decision. Reviewers' responses sometimes conflict, often reflecting one or more reviewers' inexperience or misunderstanding. At other times, reviewers' responses may agree, giving you a clear direction for revision. Remember, only you can decide which responses are appropriate or inappropriate for your paper. The responsibility for a final draft lies solely with you.

Giving Advice. When reviewing another writer's work, keep in mind that your task is not to rewrite the draft but to respond as an informed reader and offer advice for improvement. It is up to the writer to write the next draft.

What must you do to give good advice?

Know the assignment. Each draft you read will be written in response to a writing assignment. To respond intelligently, you must be familiar with the assignment. Chances are you will be writing an essay for the same assignment, but if not, then it is your job to know what the assignment calls for. Keep those requirements in mind when reviewing an essay.

Apply your knowledge. You will likely have studied the same information as the writer whose essay you are reading. Use that knowledge. Applying the information will help you make accurate observations and give you the specialized vocabulary to describe your observations in a way the writer will understand.

Offer specific advice. Identify a draft's strengths and weaknesses as specifically as you can. Vague and general observations do not help much. The following two responses represent the extremes; consider first the ineffective response.

> Good work. I like the way it reads, even though it isn't always clear. Also good use of words. Keep it up.

Clearly, this response is of no help. Perhaps the reviewer fears hurting the writer's feelings, or perhaps he is just plain lazy. Who knows? The fact remains: The student offers only vague, feel-good responses.

Consider now a much more specific and thus effective response.

> One strong point is your active verbs: "shrieked," "maul," "cavort," and so on. They add specific detail and color to the whole essay.
>
> One problem is unity. You seldom refer to your thesis in topic sentences. To fix it wouldn't take much. I suggest you add a key word to the thesis, such as "dysfunctional," and use it, or use its synonyms, in the topic sentences. For example, "The dysfunctional family lurks behind all the antics of *I Love Lucy*." Whatever you do, you'll need to improve the unity somehow.

This reviewer's response is helpful. She identifies strengths and weaknesses in specific language. Where she can, she gives advice to help the writer revise. She does all this specifically and clearly.

Do not be distracted by surface errors. It is not your job to correct grammar, punctuation, and mechanics. Tell the writer that the errors exist, but remember that it is the writer's job to proofread carefully and correct surface errors. Your job is to concentrate on the larger elements.

Five Questions to Guide Peer Review

In order to stay on track, use the following five questions to guide the review process.

1. Does the draft meet assignment requirements?

2. What is the dominant purpose and does the organization logically reflect that purpose?
3. At what points is the draft confusing?
4. Is the draft adequately developed, or does it need more information and examples?
5. What are the draft's main strengths and weaknesses?

The first step in the review process is usually done in writing. After the writer reads the review, the reviewer and the writer will usually get together to discuss the comments.

Five Guidelines for Discussing a Review

Above all else, always respond sensitively when you discuss with its author your review of an essay. Most developing writers have no experience of submitting their work for peer review. They may misconstrue genuine advice for negative criticism. To avoid sounding negative, make objectively descriptive comments instead of subjectively evaluative comments. Your responsibility is to help other writers improve their work, not to criticize them for making mistakes.

When discussing your responses with a writer, keep in mind the following guidelines.

WRITER'S CLINIC

Staying on Track

Peer-review sessions can get bogged down. Keep on track by specifying the session's purpose clearly.

- Be sure every writer is prepared. Everyone should know what's expected well before the session begins.
- Communicate whether the session is for brainstorming, reading rough drafts, proofreading.
- Remind each other of the purpose whenever the discussion drifts.

To avoid getting bogged down, everyone should agree on group guidelines that clarify what's expected of each member.

REMEMBER: When responding online to someone's writing, be careful of your tone. While you think you are offering constructive criticism, the writer may feel that he or she is under attack. For example, using all capital letters or boldface when pointing out an error can make a helpful comment seem like a personal attack.

1. Use the review session to hold a dialogue, not a debate.
2. Ask questions that might help you develop a clear understanding of the writer's goals.
3. Take notes while reading a draft and use them to discuss the draft's strengths and weaknesses. Emphasize the strengths, but remember that the writer needs to know about the weaknesses.
4. Make suggestions for improvement in relation to the writer's intent.
5. Close your response by summarizing ways the writer can improve the draft.

COMPUTER CLINIC

Meet in Cyberspace

Communicating by e-mail is common in today's business, government, and academic worlds. Why not bring electronic communication into the peer-group process, especially when group members have trouble scheduling meetings outside of class?

The process begins with each group member's sending his or her draft to other group members by e-mail. Each participant can print out the essays to read them on hard copy and to write a response. At the next class meeting, return the essays with comments to the authors.

Or you may e-mail your responses to the authors. In this way, each group member will have immediate feedback and can revise before the next session. You should write e-mail responses with the same care you give all writing that someone else will be reading.

- Whenever possible, compose an e-mail offline. Once you have finished writing, use your computer's Copy function to insert it into your e-mail program.
- Many people are casual about e-mail, perhaps seeing it as an extension of oral conversation instead of written communication. Make sure your e-mail is easy to read. Check for spelling errors and follow standard punctuation and grammar conventions. Keep a professional tone; do not write a "breezy" note.
- Double-space and limit your e-mail to no more than one full screen (or you risk becoming tedious).
- Do not waste time. Do not send unwanted e-mail. Stick to the purpose of the e-mail session: to review essays and provide feedback.

Remember, the emphasis is on improvement, both for the writer as a writer and for the reviewer as a reader.

Exercise 10.1: Peer-Review Groups

If your instructor does not establish a process for peer-review sessions, you and other classmates can hold your own peer-review sessions.

1. Identify students interested in peer commentary.
2. Have everyone review this chapter before beginning.
3. Meet as a group; read the papers; write comments and discuss them. Remember, concentrate on the large elements: thesis, structure, discussion, conclusion.

PART III

Paragraphs

I thought of myself as like the jazz musician: someone who practices and practices and practices in order to be able to invent and to make his art look effortless and graceful. I was always conscious of the constructed aspect of the writing process, and that art appears neutral and elegant only as a result of constant practice and awareness of its formal structures.

—Toni Morrison, *novelist*

11 Topic Sentences ¶

Paragraphs are sometimes brief. Paragraphs in newspaper articles, for example, are brief. Transitional paragraphs, the kind that guide a reader from one part of an essay to another, are brief, too.

In college writing, however, paragraphs are seldom brief. They are usually fully developed, each one a significant part of an essay. Excluding introductory and concluding paragraphs, fully developed paragraphs advance a reader's understanding of an essay's thesis statement. An effective, fully developed paragraph has four characteristics:

- A topic sentence that advances the controlling idea in an essay's thesis statement.
- Full development with enough information to convey the idea in a reasonably thorough manner.
- A unified structure that shows the relationship of supporting information to the topic sentence.
- Coherence techniques that move the reader smoothly from one sentence to the next.

In a sense, essay paragraphs may be looked at individually as brief compositions in themselves, but they may also be looked at as related building blocks in an essay's overall structure.

11a State a paragraph's subject and controlling idea in a brief topic sentence.

In the following paragraph, student-writer Maria Dallas opens with a brief topic sentence to focus her reader's attention. Then she fully develops the topic sentence with supporting information.

> Earning a college degree is a sound investment. College tuition can cost anywhere from $1,500 a year at a state-supported university to as high as $37,000 a year at an expensive private university, such as Harvard, Stanford, or Yale. When you add another $8,000 a year for books and living expenses, the final spread is $9,500 to $45,000 a year or $38,000 to $180,000 for an entire four years. No matter where you fall within the range, this price tag is hefty, especially if you could be earning money on a job instead of attending college. But the payoff from earning a degree is substantial

> also. The difference between having a college degree and a high school diploma these days is $600,000 in income over a working lifetime. Calculating forty years on the job, that amounts to a $15,000-a-year differential for college graduates. Clearly, college is a sound investment, but as my grandmother used to say, "It takes money to make money."

Topic sentences are usually placed first in paragraphs. Sometimes a topic sentence will be placed in another part of a paragraph, often following a transitional sentence that links a paragraph to the preceding one, or it will be placed last for dramatic impact. In any case, a college writer should have a strong reason for not placing a topic sentence first.

Effective Topic Sentences

Like a thesis statement, a topic sentence makes a promise. The subject of a topic sentence promises what the paragraph is about. The controlling idea promises what aspect of the subject the writer will discuss.

> Hong Kong has a fascinating mixture of European and Asiatic traditions.

This topic sentence promises the reader that the paragraph subject is Hong Kong. The controlling idea promises the reader that a discussion of Hong Kong's European and Asiatic traditions will follow. The paragraph will not cover Hong Kong's crime rate, economy, population, or style of government. Other paragraphs might do that, but not this one.

Limit the Subject and the Controlling Idea. Do not promise a reader more than you can deliver. Topic sentences should not be overly general or you will not be able to contain the development within a single paragraph, even a fully developed one. You must limit the scope of discussion by making the topic sentence less general and more specific. You can control the scope of a topic sentence in two ways—by limiting the subject and by limiting the controlling idea.

> GENERAL TOPIC SENTENCE
>
> The works of James Agee often include information from several academic disciplines.
>
> LIMITED SUBJECT
>
> James Agee's *Let Us Now Praise Famous Men* includes information from several academic disciplines.

LIMITED CONTROLLING IDEA

James Agee's *Let Us Now Praise Famous Men* includes information from history.

GENERAL TOPIC SENTENCE

Authorities can reduce the danger associated with concerts.

LIMITED SUBJECT

Concert promoters can reduce the danger associated with concerts.

LIMITED CONTROLLING IDEA

Concert promoters can reduce *the number and severity of spectator injuries by following a few simple rules of crowd control.*

GENERAL TOPIC SENTENCE

Bolivia is unstable.

LIMITED SUBJECT

Bolivia's military government is unstable.

LIMITED CONTROLLING IDEA

Bolivia's military government is *being threatened by peasant revolutionaries in the countryside.*

Write a Topic Sentence That Can Be Developed. The controlling idea of a topic sentence must lend itself to development; that is, it has to be one that can be amplified or illustrated. For example, a fact does not make an effective topic sentence—unless you are merely reporting information.

FACT

The USSR launched Sputnik in 1957, the first satellite to orbit the earth.

An effective topic sentence may embody a fact, but it must also lead to discussion.

TOPIC SENTENCE

American educators panicked when the USSR launched Sputnik, the first satellite to orbit the earth, in 1957.

This topic sentence leads to a discussion of how the first Sputnik threatened American educators.

Like a fact, the expression of an attitude does not make an effective topic sentence.

ATTITUDE

Analyzing nonverbal behavior is interesting.

Phrasing an attitude as a topic does not signal that an informed discussion will follow. In fact, it invites immediate reader resistance: Oh yeah? I think it's a hoax!

TOPIC SENTENCE

Analyzing nonverbal behavior accurately is the secret to winning at poker.

Now this topic sentence could lead to an interesting discussion, at least for serious poker players.

WRITER'S CLINIC

Insert Key Words in Topic Sentences

Here is a direct way to show readers that you are advancing a topic sentence. In a topic sentence, insert key words that you repeat at strategic moments. One key word might refer back to an essay's thesis, another to the controlling point of the particular paragraph.

> Advertisers often *exploit* a *desire* for *economic* and *social independence.* Women are frequently the target of such *exploitation.* For example, no company has *exploited* this *desire* more effectively than Philip Morris in a campaign to sell Virginia Slim cigarettes. Each advertisement in the campaign features images of strong, *independent* women: one riding a motorcycle, another standing behind a man who is cooking, and yet another of an *independent* woman in a leather jacket, leaning on a sports car door. Each advertisement is accompanied by a sentence declaring the woman's *economic and social independence:* "I don't necessarily want to run the world, but I wouldn't mind taking it for a ride"; "Equality comes with no apron strings attached"; and "I always take the driver's seat." Moreover, each advertisement features the slogan, "You've come a long way, baby," now a buzz phrase to announce that a woman has fulfilled a *desire* for *independence.*

11b Develop a paragraph fully.

How long should a paragraph be? Paragraph length depends on several things: the complexity of the idea; the method of development; the length of adjacent paragraphs; and the age, knowledge, interest, and education of the reader. In college writing, thoughtful paragraphs usually range from 125 to 150 words because of their complexity.

Excessively long paragraphs may seem more intellectual and weighty, but too many of them can discourage a reader and make a subject appear more difficult and intricate than it is. Short paragraphs are easy to read, but a paper consisting of a series of brief paragraphs indicates that an essay's thesis statement is inadequately developed.

The best approach is to take the middle ground. Include enough supporting information to make the point, and avoid skimpy, undeveloped paragraphs.

The following paragraph lacks the specific detail needed to adequately develop the topic sentence.

> A number of curious experiences occur at the onset of sleep. A person just about to go to sleep may experience an odd physical sensation. A nearly universal occurrence at the beginning of sleep (although not everyone recalls it) is a sudden jerk of the body. The onset of sleep is not gradual at all. It happens in an instant.

The paragraph needs more specific information and concrete details to support the topic sentence adequately. Now study the original paragraph as Peter Farb wrote it. Notice how the addition of information and specific details turns an underdeveloped paragraph into a fully developed one.

> A number of curious experiences occur at the onset of sleep. A person just about to go to sleep may experience an *electric shock, a flash of light, or a crash of thunder. The most common sensation is that of floating or falling, which is why "falling asleep" is a scientifically valid description.* A nearly universal occurrence at the beginning of sleep (although not everyone recalls it) is a sudden, *uncoordinated* jerk of the *head, the limbs, or even the entire* body. *Most people tend to think of going to sleep as a slow slippage into oblivion, but* the onset of sleep is not gradual at all. It happens in an instant. *One moment the individual is awake, the next moment not.*

11c Close a paragraph with a clincher sentence.

Writers will often end a paragraph with a *clincher,* a sentence that restates the controlling idea in different words, summarizes the discussion, or gives the writer's response to the material, which may be ironic or humorous. The next example closes with a clincher.

Topic sentence opens the paragraph.

Supporting information advances the topic sentence's controlling idea.

Clincher sentence closes the paragraph.

As sources of ideas, professors simply cannot compete with books. Books can be found to fit almost every need, temper, or interest. Books can be read when you are in the mood; they do not have to be taken in periodic doses. Books are both more personal and more impersonal than professors. Books have an inner confidence which individuals seldom show; they rarely have to be on the defensive. Books can afford to be bold and courageous and exploratory; they do not have to be so careful of boards of trustees, colleagues, and community opinion. Books are infinitely diverse; they run the gamut of human activity. Books can be found to express every point of view; if you want a different point of view, you can read a different book. (Incidentally, this is the closest approximation to objectivity you are likely ever to get in humanistic and social studies.) *Even your professor is at his best when he writes books and articles; the teaching performance rarely equals the written effort.*

—William G. Carleton,
"Take Your College in Stride"

Closing with a clincher is especially effective in long paragraphs. A clincher will remind readers of the paragraph's main point and can be used to transition into the next paragraph.

Exercise 11.1: Revising Topic Sentences

The following topic sentences are either too general or too factual. Revise each to make it more effective.

1. Some states require motorists to wear seat belts.
2. Vandalism is a problem in urban areas.
3. Many Americans try different diets from time to time.

4. Going to college is expensive.
5. Grading policies are different for different classes.
6. Everyone believes that travel is educational.
7. Large stores usually have consumer complaint departments.
8. In spite of all the evidence, my sister believes that spinach alone will give a person tremendous strength.
9. I like people who assume responsibility for their actions.
10. Hollywood films have both good and bad features.

Exercise 11.2: Writing Paragraphs

Using one of the topic sentences you revised for Exercise 1, write an effective paragraph. Remember, an effective paragraph has the following characteristics.

- It advances the main point in an essay's thesis statement.
- It has enough information to convey the idea in a reasonably thorough manner.
- It shows the relationship of supporting information to the topic sentence.
- It moves the reader smoothly from one sentence to the next.

12 Unified Paragraphs ¶

Just as academic readers expect a thesis sentence to be the organizational center of an essay, they expect a topic sentence to be the organizational center of most paragraphs. Information that does not advance a topic sentence disrupts the train of thought of the reader moving from the topic sentence to the clincher. When the reader's train of thought is disrupted, paragraph unity is flawed.

12a Maintain unity throughout a paragraph.

A paragraph is unified when all the information it contains clearly relates to the controlling idea expressed in the topic sentence. Study the following paragraph. Analyze the relationship of supporting information to the controlling idea, which asserts that many people oppose hunting even where animal populations are dangerously large.

> (1) *Many Americans mindlessly oppose hunting, even in cases where animal populations are dangerously high.* (2) In some areas of Alaska, wolves have become so prolific they are running out of hunting ground and prey heavily on moose, deer, and occasionally dogs. (3) Wolves run in packs and hunt with more cunning than any other predator in North America. (4) In the past, game managers curbed wolf populations by trapping and aerial hunting without wiping out the species. (5) Still, whenever they propose to do this nowadays, they receive tens of thousands of letters in protest. (6) Growing deer populations in parts of California threaten to starve themselves out. (7) No doubt images of Bambi rise up in the minds of hunting opponents. (8) Sea-otter colonies, burgeoning along the Pacific coast, are fast running out of fodder, too, as well as putting commercial fishermen out of business. (9) Because otters are so cute, ecologists have rushed to their aid.

Sentences 3, 7, and 9 disrupt the train of thought. They do not relate directly to the controlling idea expressed in the topic sentence. They should either be integrated into other sentences or deleted.

Now read the paragraph as Lael Morgan actually wrote it in "Let the Eskimos Hunt." Examine how all the supporting information and details relate to the topic sentence's controlling idea.

> *Many Americans mindlessly oppose hunting, even in cases where animal populations are dangerously high.* In some areas of Alaska, wolves have become so prolific they are running out of hunting ground and prey heavily on moose, deer, and occasionally dogs. In the past, game managers curbed wolf populations by trapping and aerial hunting without wiping out the species. Still, whenever they propose to do this nowadays, they receive tens of thousands of letters in protest. Growing deer populations in parts of California threaten to starve themselves out. Sea-otter colonies, burgeoning along the Pacific coast, are fast running out of fodder, too, as well as putting commercial fishermen out of business.

With the erroneous sentences deleted, the paragraph is unified and reader attention is on the key point, that is, "many Americans mindlessly oppose hunting." The writer's train of thought has been restored.

WRITER'S CLINIC

Analyzing Unity in Paragraphs

Use the *Christensen Method* to analyze paragraph unity. For a paragraph to be unified, a sentence must directly relate to the topic sentence or a sentence that supports the topic sentence. Professor Francis Christensen devised a method to establish sentence relationships through a numbering method. If you number sentences according to their level of generality (1 for the most general, 2 for the second level, and so on), you will see how one sentence is related to another. No sentence should be more general than the topic sentence or drift from the controlling idea. For example:

1. Hollywood mythmaking often pays little attention to fact.
    2. In films such as the classic *One Million B.C.*, dinosaurs roamed the earth with humans.
        3. *Tyrannosaurus rex,* in fact, seemed especially fond of human flesh.
    2. But if we humans had once shared the earth with dinosaurs, we too would be extinct.
    2. Science clearly refutes the myth created by such films as *One Million B.C.*
        3. Scientists now hypothesize that dinosaurs met their end because of a catastrophe that threatened all living creatures.
            4. Over 65 million years ago, the hypothesis goes, a huge meteorite crashed into the earth.
                5. The impact is thought to have kicked up enough dust to block sunlight for a long time.
                    6. The lack of sunlight triggered extinction by lowering temperatures and killing vegetation.
            4. A worldwide firestorm could have added other dangers.
                5. Apart from burning or choking in the smoke, living creatures could have perished from newly formed toxic compounds or from an eventual warming of temperatures triggered by carbon monoxide that the fire poured into the atmosphere.
    2. If humans had been living as the makers of *One Million B.C.* portray us, we would never have survived to watch our ancestors in hand-to-claw combat on the silver screen.

Because the topic sentence announces the controlling idea and because each sentence that follows is either clearly related to the topic sentence or to another sentence that supports the topic sentence, the train of thought is not disrupted. The paragraph is unified. If the train of thought had been disrupted, then the paragraph would require revision.

Exercise 12.1: Achieving Unity

The following sentences are taken from Robert I. Tilling's "A Volcanologist's Perspective." Several sentences are from one paragraph. Others are from different parts of the article. Determine which sentences should be included in a unified paragraph with the topic sentence, "Volcanic eruptions have had a profound influence on mankind."

1. Civilizations have flourished in regions blessed with fertile soils derived from the breakdown of nutrient-rich volcanic materials.
2. The volcanoes in the Ring of Fire zone are what scientists call composite volcanoes.
3. The violent, destructive unleashing of volcanic fury that accompanied the catastrophic blast of Mount St. Helens have imprinted their marks on mind and landscape.
4. Some of the world's most majestic and inspirational mountain and seashore scenery, including the entire state of Hawaii, has been created by volcanic action and subsequent erosion.
5. Most of the world's approximately five hundred active volcanoes are located along or near such boundaries between shifting plates.
6. The Pacific Basin provides excellent examples of these two types of volcanoes.
7. The earth's surface is broken into lithospheric slabs, or plates.
8. As one volcano dies, however, a new volcano begins to form behind it over the hot spot.
9. More fundamentally, life on earth as we know it would not have evolved at all were it not for volcanic exhalations that occurred over hundreds of millions of years and formed the primitive but life-giving atmosphere and oceans.
10. Composite volcanoes predominantly erupt highly viscous (sticky) magma.

Exercise 12.2: Using the Christensen Method

After completing Exercise 1, arrange the sentences by the Christensen Method as described in the Writer's Clinic. Write out each sentence and identify it by number according to its level of generality.

13 Coherent Paragraphs ¶

When a paragraph is coherent, the writer's thought flows from the first sentence to the last. When coherence breaks down, then the sentences are not working together. They seem disconnected, and the writer's thoughts do not unfold smoothly from sentence to sentence.

13a Achieve coherence with transitional words and phrases.

One method for achieving coherence is to use transitional words and phrases. These words show the relationship among ideas or signal readers that there will be a transition in thought.

TO SHOW SIMILARITY

likewise, similarly, moreover

TO SHOW DIFFERENCES OR CONTRAST

but, however, still, yet, nevertheless, on the one hand/on the other hand, on the contrary, in contrast

TO SHOW ADDITION

moreover, and, in addition, equally important, next, first, second, third, again, also, too, besides, furthermore

TO SHOW TIME AND PROCESS

soon, in the meantime, afterward, later, meanwhile, while, earlier, finally, simultaneously, next, the next step

TO SHOW DIRECTION

here, there, over there, beyond, nearby, opposite, under, above, to the left, to the right, in the distance

TO ANNOUNCE AN END

in conclusion, to summarize, finally, on the whole

TO ANNOUNCE A RESTATEMENT

in short, in other words, in brief, to put it differently

TO INDICATE A RESULT

therefore, then, as a result, consequently, accordingly, thus, thereupon

The following narrative paragraph achieves coherence through the use of transitional words and phrases (shown in italics) that trace the time order of the events.

> At first glance Todd seems to be a typical four-year-old: scruffy, sun-bleached hair, a few freckles, worn cords, short-sleeved shirt, and tattered tennis shoes. But behind his boyish appearance he seems to be a loner. *During the first class,* he was the only child who did not raise his hand to answer a question or share an experience. He was attentive *at first* but soon lost interest. *Once* he reached out a finger to poke a boy in front of him, and then he stopped, perhaps thinking better of it. *Finally,* his thumb went into his mouth. *As soon as* the class broke up, he headed for the monkey bars, where he climbed to the highest rung and sat, his eyes staring toward a distant hill. No one tried to approach him, however. The other children, most of whom chased around the play yard, seemed to respect his wish for privacy. *Later,* when the class regrouped for story time, Todd didn't show as much interest as he had during the sharing session. He seemed more interested in using a fingernail to trace the cracks in the wall than in listening to *Winnie-the-Pooh.*

13b Achieve coherence through the repetition of key words.

A writer can maintain coherence by repeating key words and phrases to emphasize the major points and to smooth the flow of the sentences. Pronouns referring to clearly established antecedents function in the same way. In the following paragraph the repeated words are in italics.

> Public speaking differs from acting in that the *speaker* rarely, if ever, reveals any character or personality traits other than his own. A central problem of the *actor* is to create a character for his audience. There are other differences. The *public speaker* usually works alone. The *actor,* unless he is performing a monodrama, usually works with a group. A *public speaker* does not ordinarily use scenery, costume, or make-up to help him express and communicate as the *actor* does. He may on some occasions employ special lighting effects and platform decorations to reinforce his message. Further, the *public speaker* deals only with his own composition while the *actor,* like the oral reader, has all the problems of interpreting the words of another. He serves as a sort of middleman for the playwright and reveals the

intentions of a director. Thus, the purposes of the *actor* are at once like and unlike those of the *public speaker*. The *actor* may seek to elicit primarily utilitarian responses or to gain aesthetic responses depending upon the nature of the material with which he works. —John F. Wilson and Carroll E. Arnold, *Public Speaking as a Liberal Art*

WRITER'S CLINIC

Analyzing Paragraphs for Coherence

The mind can be tricky. When rereading your own work, you, like most writers, make the transition from one sentence to another in your mind when there are no actual transitions on the page. The reason for this is simple: You have already made the connections mentally, so you automatically fill them in.

One way to be sure you have put transitions in place is to consciously underline them in your paper. In this way you will know they are there.

> The researchers found that the participation of women in sport activities was a significant indicator of the health and living standards of a country. Today, gradually, women have begun to enter the sports world with more social acceptance and individual pride. In 1952, researchers from the Finnish Institute of Occupational Health who conducted an intensive study of the athletes participating in the Olympics in Helsinki predicted that "women are able to shake off civil disabilities which millennia of prejudice and ignorance have imposed upon them." No doubt, myths die hard, but they do die.

13c Achieve coherence by using parallel structure.

By repeating a particular structure in successive sentences, a writer can create a parallel form that will guide a reader smoothly from the first sentence to the last. The repeated structure emphasizes the relation of the sentences to the paragraph's controlling idea. Parallel structures are italicized in the following paragraph from Mark Reuter's impressionistic essay on California.

> Historically, California has been a place as much in the imagination as a place on any map. *In the minds of the '49ers, California offered* gold nuggets, shallow streams, and meadows. *In the minds of farmers wiped out in the Depression, California offered* rich soil and abundant potential. *In the minds of*

impressionable teenagers, California offered champagne, silver slippers, and fame at the corner of Sunset and Vine. But too often *adventurous Easterners sold* everything to pursue the dream of gold and ended up losing it all to swindlers. *Depression victims were* sometimes greeted by hostile ranchers who carried rifles and drove them away from the fertile valleys. And many *young actors ended up* living on the streets, the stars in their eyes faded.

Exercise 13.1: Identifying Transitions

Select an article from a popular magazine from your school library's collection. Photocopy the article and read it with care. Underline the transitions you find and identify them as transitions, key-word repetition, or parallel structure.

Exercise 13.2: Creating Parallel Structure

Revise the following paragraph from William G. Moulton's "Linguistics." Make the three supporting points parallel by revising key sentences and by using "with" and "shares" as key words.

> Linguistics has been described as being, at one and the same time, the most scientific of humanities and the most humanistic of the sciences. In both theory and practice it shares elements of many other disciplines, even though it cannot be neatly classified with one of them. It uses the same method of observation, classification, and generalization, and the search for countable units and describable structures as the natural sciences. It is interested like the social sciences in group behavior as revealed through the actions of individuals. And with the humanities it shares an interest in the uniquely human, in language as a phenomenon which distinguishes humans as "the talking animal" most sharply from all other living beings.

14 Descriptive and Narrative Paragraphs ¶

To describe is to picture experience in words. Effective description makes the general more specific by engaging the senses. The sound of thundering surf, the smell of ripe apples, the sight of darkening clouds, the taste of chocolate cake, the feel of soapy water—each appeals to one of the senses. Because sensory experience is so powerful, descriptive writing will often snap readers to attention and pull their imaginations into a discussion.

To narrate is to tell a story. Simple narratives play an important role in everyday thinking. In discussion with friends or acquaintances, a speaker may spontaneously shape raw experience into a narrative: "Let me tell you what happened in psychology today." "I learned an important lesson when my car wouldn't start." "I'll never ride a bicycle again." Each of these snippets of conversation would probably lead to a narrative illustrating a personal insight.

14a Write active description that appeals to the senses.

Take a page from the creative writer's notebook: Use description to engage readers' senses. When writing a descriptive passage, make your readers see, hear, smell, taste, touch, and sense movement in your writing.

Developing writers often believe that adjectives and adverbs make for good descriptive writing, so they pile them up against their nouns and verbs. This makes for slack, not active, prose.

> Some of my city friends think horses are *cute, loving* animals. That is not *necessarily* true. Yesterday I watched a young wrangler try to ride a *skittish* stallion. He *quickly* swung himself into the saddle and held the saddle horn *tightly*. The *big, chestnut* stallion bucked *angrily* and *easily* tossed the *wide-eyed* wrangler to the *dusty* ground. The stallion then *viciously* attacked him. The *panicked* wrangler rolled toward the fence. The stallion tried to trample him before he *desperately* pulled himself under the fence post before the *sharp* hooves pummeled him.

This anecdote has some elements of effective description, such as the use of specific nouns and verbs, but the writer could make it even more effective. Rather than use adverbs, such as *quickly, tightly, angrily,* and rather than use adjectives, such as *skittish, dusty, panicked,* the writer could have created active description by filling in more sensory detail in phrases. The overuse of adverbs and adjectives short-circuits the descriptive process by providing ready-made words for general experience. Better to look at experience in more detail in order to write more engaging description. Revised, the passage might read:

Some of my city friends think horses are cute, loving animals. That is not necessarily true. Yesterday I watched a ~~young~~ wrangler try to ride a ~~skittish~~ stallion *that snorted and twitched as he put his foot in the stirrup. Pushing up with one leg,* he ~~quickly~~ swung himself into the saddle and *gripped* the saddle horn ~~tightly~~ *as if he had hopped on a roller coaster.* The ~~big, chestnut~~ stallion bucked ~~angrily~~, *arching its back, its hooves lifting from the ground,* and ~~easily~~ tossed the wrangler, *his eyes popping in panic,* to the ~~dusty ground~~ dust. The stallion ~~then viciously attacked him~~ *reared back on its hind legs, its hooves pawing the air, its mane whipping around its neck.* The ~~panicked~~ wrangler rolled toward the fence, *gasping for breath, dust filling his nostrils and coating his lips and teeth.* The stallion's *hooves* ~~tried to trample~~ him before he ~~desperately pulled himself under the fence post before the sharp hooves~~ *clubbed the ground, and again it reared up, a whinny erupting from deep in its throat, echoing over the ranch, as the wrangler grabbed the bottom fence post, his hand raked with slivers, and scrambled from the corral before the hooves flashing sunlight* pummeled him.

WRITER'S CLINIC

Thinking Critically About Description

When writing description, the first impulse is to use "descriptive" words, that is, to use adjectives and adverbs.

> The *shiny red* Porsche drove *quickly* through the *wet* streets.

But adjectives and adverbs pile up against the nouns and verbs they describe, slowing down the reader. It is more effective to turn adjectives and adverbs into phrases that describe more accurately and more actively. Begin your revision by crossing out adjectives and adverbs.

> The ~~*shiny red*~~ Porsche drove ~~*quickly*~~ through the ~~*wet*~~ streets.

Then rewrite the sentence by turning them into active descriptive phrases and by selecting more specific verbs, such as changing *drove* to *raced* in the example.

> The Porsche, *sunlight glinting from its red paint, raced* through the streets *slick with rain.*

Not only does the sentence read more easily, it gives more specific information.

Now this descriptive paragraph is vivid, alive with action and detail. The writer kept two adjectives and one adverb, all three in the opening two sentences that set up the description. Then he relied on descriptive phrases to do most of the work.

14b Balance subjective responses with objective description.

Descriptive writing is usually a mixture of subjective and objective detail. In subjective description, writers select language and a point of view that show they are participants in the experience. In objective description, writers concentrate on the subject rather than on personal experience.

The purpose of subjective description is to show the impact of an experience on the writer, that is, to create an impressionistic description of the experience. The purpose of objective description is to show how the experience might impact anyone, that is, to create a literal description of the experience. But seldom is a passage purely subjective or objective.

Peter Schjeldahl in the opening paragraph of "Cyclone" writes at the extreme of subjective description while including some objective detail to support his personal responses. His aim is to describe how he feels riding the Coney Island roller coaster, not to give an objective picture of the actual ride. The two brief passages of objective description are shown here in italics.

> The Cyclone is art, sex, God, the greatest. It is the most fun you can have without risking bad ethics. I rode the Cyclone seven times one afternoon last summer, and I am here to tell everybody that it is fun for fun's sake, the pure abstract heart of the human capacity for getting a kick out of anything. Yes, it may be anguishing initially. (I promise to tell the truth.) Terrifying, even, the first time or two the train is hauled upward with groans and creaks and with you in it. *At the top then—where there is sudden* strange *quiet but for the fluttering of two tattered flags, and you have a* poignantly *brief view of Brooklyn, and of ships far out on the Atlantic*—you may feel very lonely and that you have made a serious mistake, cursing yourself in the last gleam of the reflective consciousness you are about, abruptly, to leave up there between the flags like an abandoned thought-balloon. To keep yourself company by screaming may help, and no one is noticing: try it. After a couple of rides, panic abates, and after four or five, you aren't

> even frightened, exactly, but stimulated, blissed, sent. The squirt of adrenaline you will never cease to have at *the top as the train lumbers, wobbling slightly, into the plunge,* finally fuels just happy wonderment because you can't, and never will, believe what is going to happen.

Schjeldahl's subjectively charged description would not be effective without some objective description to show literally what the ride is like.

A passage from student-writer Clarita Tan's "Imaginatively Chaotic Art" mixes objective and subjective description effectively. Tan expresses her subjective view by using a simile, comparing the artist to an orchestra conductor, and an allusion, a reference to the "Sorcerer's Apprentice." Tan's brief subjective response is shown here in italics.

> The final phase of his method is captured in the fifth photograph. The canvas is now raised upright on the plywood base, a practice that deviates from Pollock's and that of other abstract expressionists. Here McNeil stands with his back to the camera and faces the massive canvas. He is hunched forward with an upraised brush held *like a symphony conductor's baton, and I think of composer Paul Dukas's "Sorcerer's Apprentice." Indeed, McNeil is performing artistic sorcery,* for he is creating images that suggest themselves from the splattered configurations on the canvas.

It is the objective description that sets up Tan's subjective response near the end of the passage. She then develops the artist-as-magician image throughout her entire essay.

14c Select an effective arrangement for descriptive paragraphs.

Descriptive paragraphs lend themselves quite readily to a **spatial arrangement**—that is, to proceeding like a camera panning from left to right, from right to left, from near to far, from the center outward, and so on. In the following paragraph from a gallery report, Alice Lee describes a painting from the top down. Notice how Lee effectively guides the reader by using clear transitions (shown here in italics). She skillfully centers the reader's concentration on the painting's key focal point.

> *At the top* of Doree Dunlap's "Picnic," clouds are gathering as if ready to erupt with rain. *Between* the sky and shore, *in the upper middle,* the sea is edged with whitecaps and a line of sailboats lean into the wind, heading for safe harbor. *On shore, in the lower foreground,* two children stand facing the sea and a third stares back at a man and woman sitting on the sand, a fearful expression on the child's face. The couple she stares at *are the focus of the canvas, taking up a third of the space.* Dunlap only represents the back of the man's head and just a slice of his profile. He seems to be staring beyond the children at the impending squall. The woman is staring at him, a neutral expression on her face, but she appears to have the faint trace of a bruise on her cheek. *Behind her, in the lower left corner,* is a watermelon with a butcher knife leaning against it, the knife tip in the sand.

Another paragraph arrangement common to descriptive paragraphs is **movement from the specific to the general.** In the following paragraph from *The Way to Rainy Mountain,* N. Scott Momaday moves from specific detail to a general observation—that is, from physical details of Rainy Mountain and the surrounding plain to the generalization (shown here in italics) that one can imagine creation having begun in such a spot.

> A single knoll rises out of the plain in Oklahoma, north and west of the Wichita Range. For my people, the Kiowas, it is an old landmark, and they gave it the name Rainy Mountain. The hardest weather in the world is there. Winter brings blizzards, hot tornadic winds arise in the spring, and in summer the prairie is an anvil's edge. The grass turns brittle and brown, and it cracks beneath your feet. There are green belts along the rivers and creeks, linear groves of hickory and pecan, willow and witch hazel. At a distance in July or August the steaming foliage seems almost to writhe in fire. Great green and yellow grasshoppers are everywhere in the tall grass, popping up like corn to sting the flesh, and tortoises crawl about on the red earth, going nowhere in the plenty of time. *Loneliness is an aspect of the land. All things in the plain are isolate; there is no confusion of objects in the eye, but one hill or one tree or one man. To look upon that landscape in the early morning, with the sun at your back, is to lose the sense of proportion. Your imagination comes to life, and this, you think, is where Creation was begun.*

Notice how, after the opening sentences, Momaday uses objective description to set up his subjective response.

14d Arrange narrative paragraphs in a clear time sequence.

Description frequently plays a significant role in narrative writing. Vivid descriptive details help readers visualize the unfolding events. In narration, however, the emphasis is on the events, not on the descriptive passages.

Narrative paragraphs—those that tell a story or tell of a series of incidents—take place in time and are usually arranged in **chronological time,** that is, as the events unfold step by step.

Student-writer Mark DeLap arranges the following narrative paragraph chronologically and relies heavily on description to create a vivid picture of events. DeLap also uses clear transitional techniques (shown here in italics) to guide readers through the time sequence.

> Bill Meek, a marine biologist and entrepreneur, manages an unusual enterprise. Using a hoe, a suction hose, and lots of elbow grease, Meek rakes and vacuums up mussels that cling to the long legs of oil platforms located off the coast. He sells the mussels to restaurants that pay top prices for them. *His day begins at sunrise* on a dock where he checks his equipment and meets his small crew for the three-mile trip to the oil platform. *Once at the platform* the sun is well up and he peers into the aquamarine depths to take an informal inventory. The mussels grow rapidly on the platform legs to a depth of forty feet, but below forty feet there isn't enough light to nourish the plankton on which mussels feed. *By 8 o'clock* the harvesting work begins. Two divers in wet suits jump into the sea. They are equipped with air hoses and mouthpieces for breathing, a hoe, and a corrugated plastic tube to suck up the mussels. One man will loosen the mussels while the other vacuums. *Once the work is under way,* a compressor generates the pressure that sucks the mussels through the tube to the surface, where they are collected into a tumbling wire-mesh container. The container turns throughout the collecting process, allowing barnacles, seaweed, and salt water to cascade back into the ocean while retaining the larger mussels. *By early afternoon* the harvest is done and the crew heads for shore. *Within hours,* the mussels will be steaming on the stoves of local restaurants.

Narrative paragraphs are not always arranged in chronological time. Sometimes they are arranged in **psychological time,** that is, as events might be connected in memory. Here the writer shifts back and forth in time, emulating the way the mind recalls experience while keeping the events moving forward.

Student-writer Richard McKnight uses psychological time to flashback to previous experience and then returns to the present.

> *Just two weeks earlier, a hot-shot from Hawaii paddled out in the heavy surf that a Mexican storm had kicked up.* He sat on his board beyond the break and waited for the big swells to roll in. Suddenly, he swung his board's nose toward shore to catch the day's biggest wave. He seemed to do everything right: He quickly leaped to his feet, cut sharply left, moved to the board's nose to gain speed as he shot ahead of the curl—but not in time. The massive wave broke over his shoulder and tossed him into the roiling foam. The breaking wave's force snapped his board in half and swept him over the reef. He survived, but barely. Lifeguards raced him to an emergency ward where doctors hovered above his body for two hours with needles and thread. *Now the old man was in that kind of danger but with one difference—he was well past his prime, much too old to be riding in dangerous waters.*

McKnight uses the first and last sentences (italicized here) to set up the time frame. Although the sentences that take place in the past move chronologically toward the present, the paragraph is still arranged according to psychological time.

Exercise 14.1: Identifying Subjective and Objective Description

Analyze the following paragraphs. Underline the words and passages that represent objective description. Explain whether or not each paragraph is written to create an impressionistic or a literal picture of the experience. What details from the paragraphs support your contention?

> The reef was generally exposed as the tide went down, and on its flat top the tide pools were beautiful. We collected as widely and rapidly as possible, trying to take a cross section of the animals we saw. There were purple pendent gorgonians like lacy fans; a number of small spine-covered puffer fish which bloat themselves when they are attacked, erecting the spines; and many starfish, including some purple and gold cushion stars. The club-spined sea urchins were numerous in their rock niches. They seemed to move about very little, for

their niches always just fit them and have the marks of constant occupation. We took a number of slim green and brown starfish and the large slim five-rayed starfish with plates bordering the ambulacral grooves.

—John Steinbeck, *The Log from the Sea of Cortez*

I've been out in the back today checking beehives. When I leaned over one of them to direct a puff of smoke from my bee smoker into the entrance to quiet the bees, a copperhead came wriggling out from under the hive. He had been frightened from his protected spot by the smoke and the commotion I was making, and when he found himself in the open, he panicked and slithered for the nearest hole he could find which was the entrance to the next beehive. I don't know what went on inside, but he came out immediately, wearing a surprised look on his face. I hadn't known that a snake could look surprised, but this one did. Then, after pausing to study the matter more carefully, he glided off to the safety of the woods.

—Sue Hubbell, *A Country Year*

Exercise 14.2: Arranging a Descriptive Paragraph

The following sentences were originally a coherent paragraph, but here their order has been changed. By following an appropriate order of development, rearrange the sentences so that the descriptive paragraph is coherent once again.

1. The other was thin and reminded me of a deer loping through a meadow.
2. Yesterday, I sat alone in the bleachers and watched the day come to a close.
3. The horizon was turning deep orange while the sun sank behind the ridge of a hill.
4. I felt alone and glanced back at the track to see the joggers like two ghosts fade with the light.
5. They circled the track—four, five, six laps.
6. One was heavy and scuffled along like a tired buffalo, his head bobbing from side to side.
7. On the track below the bleachers two men jogged.

8. The horizon turned indigo, and the sky began to fill with stars scattered like chips of glass tossed on a dark highway.
9. Not far in the distance the university was silhouetted against the orange background, a few lights speckling its dark outline.
10. Soon the light was almost gone.

Exercise 14.3: Arranging a Narrative Paragraph

The following sentences were originally a coherent paragraph, but here their order has been changed. By following an appropriate order of development, rearrange the sentences so that the narrative paragraph is coherent once again.

1. Before I started grammar school, I knew all the neighborhood's marvelous places: the avocado tree where my friends and I used to climb to an ancient tree house that had been built by children before us, the park where old-timers would sit on the benches and laugh at our wild games, the abandoned garage where we used to spy at the neighborhood through knotholes.
2. My earliest memories center on playing in that house: pushing trucks over the hardwood floors, my pajama knees mopping up the morning dust; rummaging through my mother's pan drawers and banging pans on the linoleum; and hiding behind the overstuffed couch whenever I was called for lunch.
3. Driven out by a severe drought, my parents came from the cornfields of Nebraska to the house where they lived for thirty-five years.
4. I was born in the back bedroom because, as my mother said, "There just wasn't enough time to get to a hospital."
5. When I first began to walk, the backyard seemed to stretch the length of a football field, and there I would chase my older brothers and sisters until I would fall down, breathless and sweating.

Exercise 14.4: Responding to Photographs

Clip a photograph from a newspaper or magazine or select one from a photo album of your own. First, write an objective description that's a literal rendering of what is in the photograph. Second, write a subjective description that's a personal impression based on the photograph.

15 Expository Paragraphs ¶

Expository writing concentrates, or sets forth, information, ideas, and analysis. For this reason expository writing is often referred to as **informative writing** because its main purpose is to *inform* a reader.

When you write a college essay to inform, your readers will expect you to write with a minimum of bias. Think of informative writing this way: Your purpose is to educate readers, not to persuade them to take action.

Writers have historically used six traditional methods to develop information. They are development by examples, comparison and contrast, cause and effect, process analysis, definition, and classification.

These development methods are not arbitrary. They reflect the way people organize information in their minds—how they think. For instance, people think of examples to illustrate an idea, they compare and contrast experiences to clarify them, they grope for the causes and effects of events in order to explain why things happen. These patterns of thinking, along with the other three, provide the internal structure that molds our rational thoughts into usable forms. How well they are used depends on each person's ability to think critically.

15a Use examples to illustrate a point.

An *example* is a single experience that embodies the characteristics of many experiences. The word *example* is derived from *exemplum*, a Latin word that refers to "one thing selected from the many." Writers use examples with the same intentions as speakers: to illustrate a point, to make a general assertion specific, or to electrify an audience.

The following paragraph illustrates with details the effects of DDT spraying.

> Soon after the spraying had ended there were unmistakable signs that all was not well. Within two days dead and dying fish, including many young salmon, were found along the banks of the stream. Brook trout also appeared among the dead fish, and along the roads and in the woods birds were dying. All the life of the stream was stilled. Before the spraying there had been a rich assortment of the water life that forms the food of salmon and trout—caddis fly larvae, living in

loosely fitting protective cases of leaves, stems or gravel cemented together with saliva, stonefly nymphs clinging to rocks in the swirling currents, and the wormlike larvae of blackflies edging the stones under riffles or where the stream spills over steeply slanting rocks. But now the stream insects were dead, killed by the DDT, and there was nothing for a young salmon to eat. —Rachel Carson, *Silent Spring*

Examples are of three types: specific, typical, and hypothetical. *Specific examples* include single events, behaviors, or facts. They are specific because they represent one particular experience, not generalized experience. The examples in the following paragraph are separated to emphasize how they support the topic sentence.

Opening sentence leads to the topic sentence. *Topic sentence.* *Third sentence sets up series of examples.*

The popular image of the frontier as a place of violence is only partly due to the fact the place often was violent. *Most of it is due to hype, particularly Hollywood hype.* The truth is many more people have died in Hollywood westerns than ever died on the real frontier (Indian wars considered apart).

Example 1: Dodge City.

In the real Dodge City, for example, there were just five killings in 1878, the most homicidal year in the little town's frontier history—scarcely enough to sustain a typical two-hour movie.

Example 2: Deadwood City.

In the most violent year in Deadwood, South Dakota, only four people were killed.

Example 3: Tombstone and the OK Corral. The writer adds additional information to make the last example in the sequence the most dramatic.

In the worst year in Tombstone, home of the shoot-out at the OK Corral, only five people were killed. The only reason the OK Corral shoot-out even became famous was that town boosters deliberately overplayed the drama to attract new settlers. "They eventually cashed in on the tourist boom," historian W. Eugene Hollon says, "by inventing a myth about a town too tough to die." —Richard Shenkman, *Legends, Lies, and Cherished Myths*

Typical examples, in contrast to specific examples, are generalized from many specific experiences. Student-writer Daniela Taylor makes use of typical examples in her essay on discourteous behavior in public places, "We Are Not Alone."

Taylor opens with a topic sentence that indicates she will be writing about "typical" behavior.

Last week I began to notice typical discourteous behavior that seems to have recently developed.

Example 1: Roller bladers. Notice that Taylor's example is based on a composite of experiences, not on a single specific one.

First, roller bladers apparently find a challenge in weaving in and out of pedestrians strolling on public walkways. They seem to lack common courtesy, failing to keep in mind that a pedestrian walking at a much slower pace than their skating pace cannot always predict their movements. Their discourteous behavior can turn a relaxing afternoon stroll into a nerve-racking game of dodge the speed blader.

Example 2: Cellular phone use. She continues to offer composite experiences rolled into one typical example. Typical examples work because most readers will probably have had similar experiences.

Second, the increase of cellular phones has given rise to a new kind of public discourtesy. People must no longer retreat to enclosed public phone booths to make private phone calls. They can now phone friends, loved ones, and business associates while standing in a crowd. Often their voices rise well above normal speaking range, thus disrupting the casual conversations of people who share the public space.

Hypothetical examples, like typical examples, are a composite of many events, yet they are not necessarily based on any actual experience. Unlike typical examples, hypothetical examples are fictional, that is, the writer makes them up to clarify an abstraction or a generalization. The writer, of course, should make it clear that the example has been imagined, not actually observed.

In the following paragraph from *Mediaspeak*, media critic Donna Woolfolk Cross creates a hypothetical example to illustrate the general role children have played in soap operas.

Cross opens with a topic sentence and background information to provide the reader a context for the discussion.

Children on soap operas are secondary. Because they serve largely as foils for the adult characters, their development does not follow the slow, steady pattern of the rest of the action. Their growth is marked by a series of sudden and unsettling metamorphoses as new

> *and older juvenile actors assume the role.* On Tuesday, little Terence is cooing in his cradle. On Monday next, he is the terror of the Little League. By Thursday, his voice begins to change. Friday night is his first date. He wakes up on Monday a drug-crazed teenager, ready to be put to use creating heartbreak and grief for his devoted mother and her new husband. He stays fifteen years old for about two to five years (more if he managed to get into lots of scrapes), and then one day he again emerges from the off-camera cocoon transformed into a full-fledged adult, with all the rights, privileges, pain, and perfidy of that elite corps. And so the cycle continues.

She uses one extended example to illustrate her point. The example is clearly hypothetical, but it serves her purpose by clarifying her topic sentence.

Little Terence springs from Cross's imagination, not from the television screen. Clearly, though, she illustrates her point: Children are secondary to adult soap-opera characters.

Exercise 15.1: Explaining with Examples: The Paragraph

Write a paragraph developed by examples on one of the prompts listed below. First develop a limited topic sentence, then organize the examples you will use. Your paragraph may include a mixture of specific and typical examples.

a. Films serve as a window to the world.

b. Reading fiction teaches lessons about life.

c. What people drive reveals their character.

d. Games teach children important lessons about independence and cooperation.

e. Exercise can be detrimental to health.

f. A half hour of the evening news reveals a disrupted United States.

g. Graffiti carries psychological messages.

h. Public places are disrupted by piped-in music.

i. Some music lyrics promote violence.

j. Some media celebrities symbolize more than success.

k. Americans are wasteful people.

l. Intelligent people often lack common sense.

m. Street crime is affecting public life.

n. Parents are often too involved in their children's education.

o. Anything worth doing is worth doing badly.

p. There are several alternatives to public schools.

Exercise 15.2: Explaining with Examples: The Essay

Write a full essay, using examples, based on one of the following situations.

a. Streets in many communities have become extremely hazardous for pedestrians, especially for the elderly, the disabled, and children. In fact, one-sixth of those who die in traffic accidents are pedestrians, approximately 7,000 Americans last year. Take a walk through busy streets in your neighborhood. Identify the dangers. Using examples as the primary method of development, write an essay illustrating the dangers.

b. Over the last few years, college courses of study have changed to reflect the concerns of women and minorities. Examine your college's programs and courses of study. Determine how they successfully or unsuccessfully address concerns of women and ethnic minorities. Write an essay using examples that illustrate what you discovered.

c. People today seem to yearn for the simple life. Perhaps this desire is fueled by the perception that there is never enough time to get everything done. To survive this caffeinated jungle, people wear digital watches that beep on the quarter hour or clutch their day organizers like life preservers. Examine your life for examples of the impact of time on you and the people you know; then write an examples essay as a warning to others to give up the "rat race" and seek a simplified existence.

d. Magazine advertisers seldom only praise their products. They also associate them with pleasing images to attract consumers, images such as physically attractive men and women, people in prestigious professions, an outdoor life, or the life of leisure. Write an essay using advertisements as examples to illustrate that advertisers entice consumers to buy products for the wrong reasons—that is, not because of product quality but because of pleasing associations.

15b Use comparison to explain similarities and differences.

To identify similarities is to *compare;* to identify differences is to *contrast.* Showing similarities and differences, that is, *comparison,* is common not only in daily decision making but in all forms of writing. Sometimes the content of a comparison paragraph is presented side by side—that is, all the details of one side of the comparison are presented first, followed by all the details of the other side. Student-writer Tom Henry in the following paragraph uses side-by-side comparison.

Topic sentence clearly indicates that a comparison will follow.

When I first saw the reproduction of the prehistoric mastodon, I thought of elephants I had seen in circuses and zoos.

Similarities between the elephant and the mastodon.

Like the modern elephant, the mastodon was large, with legs that remind me of sturdy tree trunks. The ancient beast had large, floppy ears and a long trunk that he could use as a tool for gathering food.

Transitional sentence indicates a shift from similarities to differences.

But after a closer look, I saw some major differences between the modern elephant and the prehistoric mastodon.

Differences between the elephant and the mastodon.

The mastodon's tusks grew longer and curved upward at a sharper angle. Unlike the elephant with its thick, almost hairless hide, the mastodon was matted with long thick hair. And although the mastodon was large, it was not as tremendous in size as its modern descendant.

Comparisons can also be organized by the point-by-point method. This method is most useful when there are many points that must be covered. In the following paragraph, student-writer Jim Cartozian begins a comparison of the American writers Ernest Hemingway and William Faulkner.

The topic sentence introduces the subjects to be compared and clearly indicates this will be a comparison.

No modern American writers have gained as much worldwide critical recognition as Ernest Hemingway and William Faulkner, and no two could be more different.

Point 1: Both won the Nobel Prize. Hemingway had a temper.

Both did win the coveted Nobel Prize for literature, but when the mild-mannered Faulkner won first, Hemingway is said to have lost his temper and then sulked.

Point 2: Both published early, but Hemingway had more success early.

Both were publishing at a young age, but Hemingway attracted popular attention early in his career, whereas Faulkner worked in near obscurity.

Point 3: A longer passage contrasts their public images; Hemingway as media star, Faulkner as recluse.

Hemingway became America's first modern literary media star. Magazines featured spreads of his war exploits, his African safaris, and his bullfighting adventures. Faulkner, in contrast, was never a media celebrity. Instead, he seemed to embody the lifestyle of small-town southern gentry, spending most of his quiet life in Oxford, Mississippi.

Continues Point 3

Hemingway's novels and stories were often set in exotic locales like France, Spain, and Cuba; Faulkner set his works in the South, primarily in the mythical Yoknopatawpha County.

Transition sentence shifts discussion to personal visions.

Each dealt with very different visions.

Point 4: Two contrasting sentences compare their separate visions.

Hemingway's work displays psychologically wounded characters struggling to establish a personal code of values in an absurd world. Faulkner's work displays characters who are victims of history, suffering because of the sins of their ancestors, the men who wrenched the land from Native Americans and enslaved Native Africans.

Point 5: Hemingway's and Faulkner's deaths were dramatically different.

In 1961 Hemingway died violently by his own hand; in 1962 Faulkner died peacefully.

An *analogy* is a figurative comparison that helps explain a complicated or abstract idea by comparing it to a simpler idea or more concrete image. In an analogy, the items compared are from different classes. For example, a writer might compare the life of a human being to a river. In most ways the two are not alike, but in *suggestive* ways they are alike: Both flow smoothly at times, turbulently at other times; both change as they follow their paths; both find destinations that change their very nature. Analogies can help you show things to your reader in different ways, but you must take care not to press an analogy too far or it can become foolish.

The following paragraph from Lester del Rey's *The Mysterious Sky* compares the earth's atmosphere to a window. The writer succeeds because he uses our familiarity with windows to enlighten us about the functions of the atmosphere.

The topic sentence clearly indicates an analogy will follow.	The atmosphere of Earth acts like any window in serving two very important functions.
Similarity 1.	It lets light in and it permits us to look out.
Similarity 2.	It also serves as a shield to keep out dangerous or uncomfortable things.
Similarity 3.	A normal glazed window lets us keep our houses warm by keeping out cold air, and it prevents rain, dirt, and unwelcome insects and animals from coming in.
Similarity 4.	As we have already seen, Earth's atmospheric window also helps to keep our planet at a comfortable temperature by holding back radiated heat and protecting us from dangerous levels of ultraviolet light.

Exercise 15.3: Explaining Through Comparison

Write a fully developed comparison on any of the following topics. Keep in mind that you can alter the suggestion you choose to fit your own interests and knowledge.

a. Two groups that have contrasting values, such as smokers and nonsmokers, vegetarians and meat eaters, drinkers and non-drinkers, athletes and couch potatoes.

b. Two campus groups who hold opposing values.

c. Two contrasting characters in a film. If appropriate, compare their physical appearance, their psychological makeup, and their actions. Conclude with an observation about what each represents.

d. Two ways of losing weight.

e. Shopping styles of males and females. Develop your comparison by identifying specific people as a type.

f. Coverage of an event by a newspaper and on television.

g. Two classic films from the same category, such as westerns, science fiction, thrillers, romances, or supernatural tales.

h. Two situation comedies.

i. Watching an actual sports event with watching one on television.

j. Children's games yesterday with children's games today.

k. A film with the novel from which it was made.

l. Two talk-radio commentators.

m. The pros and cons of two controversial points of view.

n. Two approaches to raising children.

o. How two people from different economic conditions, cultures, or age groups would view the same experience.

Exercise 15.4: Explaining Through Analogy

Write an analogy that relates an abstract idea, a process, an experience, or the odd behavior of someone you know to one of the subjects on the following list.

a poker hand
a merry-go-round
crashing waves
gardening
a spiderweb
walking through a forest
a flood
a game of solitaire
a flowering tree
dancing
a leaking faucet
a soaring bird

15c Use cause and effect to reveal reasons and results.

Paragraphs of *cause and effect* reveal why something happened or explain what happened as a result of something else.

Sometimes such a paragraph deals only with causes because the effects are already clear. For example, a paragraph might explore the reasons for a late movie star's popularity without needing to demonstrate that the person really was a star.

At other times a cause-and-effect paragraph could concentrate on effects because a given cause clearly exists and the only question remaining is, What happened as a result? For example, a paragraph might explain the effects of unemployment or an increase in taxes.

Sometimes it is appropriate to discuss both causes and effects in a paragraph. The following paragraph from Victor B. Cline's "How TV Violence Damages Your Children" reveals both causes and effects of television violence on behavior.

The topic sentence suggests, but does not explicitly state, that the paragraph will reveal causes and effects of TV violence.	Much of the research that has led to the conclusion that TV and movie violence could cause aggressive behavior in some children has stemmed from the work in the area of imitative learning or modeling which, reduced to its simplest expression, might be termed "monkey see, monkey do."
Cause and effect 1: Brief exposure to aggressive acts on TV influences behavior.	Research by Stanford psychologist Albert Bandura has shown that even brief exposure to novel aggressive behavior *on a one-time basis* can be repeated in free play by as high as 88 percent of the young children seeing it on TV.
Develops cause and effect 1 further.	Dr. Bandura also demonstrated that even a single viewing of a novel aggressive act could be recalled and produced by children six months later, without any intervening exposure.
Cause and effect 2: Because children watch excessive TV, violence becomes commonplace in their minds.	Earlier studies have estimated that the average child between the ages of 5 and 15 will witness, during this 10-year period, the violent destruction of more than 13,400 fellow humans. This means that through several hours of TV watching, a child may see more violence than the average adult experiences in a lifetime. Killing is as common as taking a walk, a gun more natural than an umbrella.
The overall effect.	Children are thus taught to take pride in force and violence and to feel ashamed of ordinary sympathy.

Revealing cause-and-effect relationships can be difficult. They are usually complex. To write a meaningful cause-and-effect analysis, you must go deeper than the obvious. Sometimes you will find that a cause will have many effects, ones that a quick look would fail to reveal. At other times you will find that cause-and-effect relationships occur in a sequence often called a causal chain.

Causal chain refers to cause-and-effect relationships appearing in a sequence, each event contributing to the following event, which then creates another event. You can use a causal chain to arrange a cause-and-effect paragraph, or an entire essay for that matter. In the following paragraph, student-writer Laura Topolte reveals the causal chain behind the violent teenage encounters in her hometown.

Topic sentence and background information announce that the writer is going to trace a pattern of violence.

A manhood ritual in my hometown of about 75,000 people centers on Friday-night violence among teenage boys. Parents usually explain the underlying cause of the violence by saying "boys will be boys," suggesting that their children are motivated by mysterious hormonal explosions beyond anyone's understanding. Though the actual details of these violent encounters may vary from one Friday night to another Friday night, the general pattern is always predictable.

The causal chain sequence is set in motion by a sports event.

Typically, an encounter is set in motion during a sports event in which a team from Northwood High School opposes a team from South Hills High School.

Event 1: Winners taunt losers.

Since the competition between the two schools is strong both on and off the playing field, the sports event usually ends with the winners taunting the losers and the losers vowing revenge.

Event 2: Rowdy students withdraw to beer parties.

The rowdier students often withdraw to beer parties where they continue to brag about the victory or threaten their arch rivals.

Event 3: Police break up parties.

As the parties become rowdy, the neighbors complain, and at about midnight the police disperse the teenagers, ordering them to go home.

Event 4: Rowdy students gather at local hangouts.

Many do, but others gather at their favorite hangouts, Northwood's Taco Bell and South Hills's Denny's.

Event 5: Cruising students taunt other students.	Eventually, a boisterous group, usually the winners, will cruise the opposition's hangout and shout obscenities from their cars.
Event 6: Students give chase.	The losers will typically respond with obscene gestures, climb into their cars, and give chase.
Event 7: Both groups meet and continue to taunt each other.	Eventually the two sides will meet up in a parking lot or community park where they call each other's manhood into question.
Event 8: A fight breaks out.	The final result is several broken noses, skinned knuckles, and expensive dental bills—after all, "boys will be boys."

When analyzing a causal chain, be aware of the immediate causes or effects (those occurring near an event) and the remote causes or effects (those occurring further away in time). In Topolte's paragraph, for example, the rivalry between Northwood and South Hills is the remote cause of Friday-night violence and the verbal and physical confrontations are immediate effects. Topolte is also aware that a much more remote cause for the rivalry might be at work—the unknown developmental or psychological forces that parents dismiss by saying "boys will be boys."

Exercise 15.5: Determining Causes and Effects

Respond in writing to one of the following questions, concentrating on cause (reasons), effect (results), or both together. If necessary, narrow the focus of the question so that it can be discussed within a reasonable length. With your professor's agreement, you may also rewrite any of these questions or create your own subject to reflect your particular interests.

a. Is using your intuition an effective way to solve problems?

b. What have been the indirect effects of a historical figure in your life, someone such as a political leader, an artist, or a philosopher?

c. What have been the effects of a significant public event in your life?

d. Why do some artistic works affect you?

e. Why does a particular television show, song, or film succeed?

f. What are the causes of homelessness, child abuse, gang violence, or another social phenomenon?

g. What are the causes of a family, institutional, or social custom?
h. Should children be treated like adults?
i. Why does the burning of the American flag enrage many Americans?
j. What effects does a particular advertisement attempt to create in the minds of consumers?
k. What are possible influences of action-oriented cartoons on children?
l. How does conformity impact individuals?

Exercise 15.6: Explaining Immediate and Remote Causes and Effects

John Holt, a critic of education, finds fault with schools for the ways they have of humiliating children:

> From the very beginning of school we make books and reading a constant source of possible failure and public humiliation. When children are little, we make them read aloud, before the teacher and other children, so that we can be sure they "know" all the words they are reading. This means that when they don't know a word, they are going to make a mistake, right in front of everyone. Instantly they are made to realize that they have done something wrong. Perhaps some of the other children will begin to wave their hands and say, "Ooooh! O-o-o-o!" Perhaps they will just giggle or nudge each other, or make a face. Perhaps the teacher will say, "Are you sure?" or ask someone else what he thinks. Or perhaps, if the teacher is kindly, she will just smile a sweet, sad smile—often one of the most painful punishments a child can suffer in school. In any case, the child who has made the mistake knows he has made it, and feels foolish, stupid, and ashamed, just as any of us would in his shoes.

Write your own paragraph using cause-and-effect analysis to explain the results of being publicly humiliated in school. What were the causes of the humiliation and its effects, both immediate and remote?

15d Use classification to arrange information in categories.

Classification is a method of organizing information into general categories. The purpose of such grouping is to clarify the nature of each category. In this sense, classification is a kind of indirect or implied comparison because the qualities that place an item in one class also distinguish it from items belonging to other classes.

In the following example, Elena Peralta offers an informal classification of comic book collectors. She introduces her categories in the opening of the paragraph, then sketches broad characteristics that each group possesses and cites specific comic book titles appropriate for each category. Peralta also identifies her categories by assigning each group a name, which helps readers keep the categories separate.

Opening description creates a sense of who collects comic books.

One fascinating offbeat hobbyist is the comic book collector. Usually pale, wearing glasses, bushy-haired and disheveled, collectors can be found rummaging through pile after pile of unsorted secondhand comics in magazine marts across the country. *Comic book collectors, the serious ones, seem to fall into four major groups: Antiquarians, Mercenaries, Idolators, and Compulsive Completers.*

Topic sentence identifies four categories of comic book collectors.

Category 1: The Antiquarian.

The Antiquarian cares only for age value; subject matter is of no concern. He is looking for a 1933 *Funnies on Parade* from the days when men were men and comics were comics.

Category 2: The Mercenary.

To the Mercenary, value is all-important. Certain numbers and titles ring a bell in his cash-register brain and start him furtively checking through a half dozen price sheets. A pristine first edition of *Action Comics* (value: $4,000) would suit him just fine.

Category 3: The Idolator.

The Idolator couldn't care less about age or value. He's looking for favorites: a *Sheena,* a *Flash Gordon,* or another *Incredible Hulk.* Hiding in a corner, reading those he can't afford to buy, the Idolator will be the last one out of the mart at night and the first one back in the morning.

Category 4: The Compulsive Completer.

The most frustrated collector is the Compulsive Completer. He'll examine and reject thousands of comics in his search for a badly needed *Felix the Cat* to complete a year's set or the one *Howdy Doody* missing from his collection.

Closes with a clincher statement.

But no matter what the reason for collecting, these hobbyists share a common trait: They love the thrill of the hunt.

Exercise 15.7: Explaining Through Classification

Categorize elements in one of the following subject groups.

a. Books, records, or videotapes you own

b. Unusual sports that are seldom televised or reported in newspapers

c. Talk show hosts

d. "War" toys, family-oriented toys, or intellectual toys

e. People who like to hunt

f. Lies

g. Ways to read a novel or poem

h. Ways to watch a horror movie

i. Kinds of photography

j. Attitudes revealed by bumper stickers

k. Trends in dating, marriage, or divorce

l. Tattoos

m. New ways to learn

n. Kinds of good or bad luck

15e Use definition to clarify unusual words.

One kind of *definition* is the dictionary definition, which provides a synonym (*slice* = to cut) or shows how a word fits into a general class (*astronomy* = the science that studies the universe).

Writing a paragraph-long definition for an unusual term goes beyond the scope of a dictionary definition by allowing for a thorough discussion. Such a paragraph might begin, as does a dictionary definition, by identifying a term as belonging to a general class. It will then differentiate it from other members of the class. It might also include synonyms, illustrate the word with examples, discuss the word's origins, compare it to similar words, or tell what it is not.

Consider Jan Harold Brunvand's definition of "urban legend," from *Alligators in Sewers.*

The opening places urban legends in a general class.

Urban legends are realistic stories that are said to have happened recently. Like old legends of lost mines, buried treasure, and ghosts, they usually have an ironic or supernatural twist.

Differentiates urban legend from classic legends.

They belong to a subclass of folk narratives that (unlike fairy tales) are set in the recent past, involving ordinary people rather than extraordinary gods and demigods.

Differentiates urban legend from rumors.

Unlike rumors, which are generally fragmentary or vague reports, legends have a specific narrative quality and tend to attach themselves to different local settings. Although they may explain or incorporate current rumors, legends tend to have a longer life and wider acceptance; rumors flourish and then die out rather quickly.

Identifies the chief characteristics of urban legends.

Urban legends circulate, by word of mouth, among the "folk" of modern society, but the mass media frequently help to disseminate and validate them. While they vary in particular details from one telling to another, they preserve a central core of traditional themes.

Completes the definition with two examples.

In some instances these seemingly fresh stories are merely updatings of classic folklore plots, while other urban legends spring directly from recent conditions and then develop their own traditional patterns in repeated retellings.

Example 1: "The Vanishing Hitchhiker."

For example, "The Vanishing Hitchhiker" describes the disappearance of a rider picked up on a highway. It evolved from a 19th-century horse-and-buggy legend into modern variants incorporating freeway travel.

Example 2: "Alligators in the Sewers."

A story called "Alligators in the Sewers," on the other hand, goes back no further than the 1930s and seems to be a New York City invention. Often, it begins with people who bring pet baby alligators back from Florida and eventually flush them down the drains.

Exercise 15.8: Explaining Through Definition

Define one of the following terms. Explore the word beyond its dictionary meaning, using a variety of methods to develop your definition. As part of this or any extended definition, differentiate your word from others in the same class.

humanity	corruption	tragedy
education	intuition	confidence
Armageddon	liberation theology	luck
terror	social responsibility	glamour
honesty	obsession	scorched earth
fad	team player	genocide
evil	sociopath	blindsided
female liberation	maverick	
male liberation	imagination	

Exercise 15.9: Explaining Through Definition and Example

From the following list of seldom-used slang terms, choose and define one. After you explain the term, create a situation in which it might apply, using the term in several sample sentences as a speaker might. Also include examples of current slang that have a similar meaning.

hoodwink	peacenik	macho
greenhorn	bamboozled	bonehead
whoopee	boodle	

15f Use process analysis to show how to do something or how something works.

Process analysis explains how to do something or how something works. Process paragraphs are usually developed step by step in a chronological or logical sequence. For example, Caroline Sutton in

How Do They Do That? explains how manufacturers get the stripes in a toothpaste tube.

Sutton's opening prepares the reader for process analysis.

Although it's intriguing to imagine the peppermint stripes neatly wound inside the tube, actually stripes don't go into the paste until it's on its way out.

This sentence prepares readers for the process explanation that follows.

A small hollow tube, with slots running lengthwise, extends from the neck of the toothpaste tube back into the interior a short distance.

First step: filling the tube with red paste.

When the toothpaste tube is filled, red paste—the striping material—is inserted first, thus filling the conical area around the hollow tube at the front. (It must not, however, reach beyond the point to which the hollow tube extends into the toothpaste tube.)

Second step: filling the remainder of the tube with white paste.

The remainder of the dispenser is filled with the familiar white stuff.

Third step: squeezing the tube.

When you squeeze the toothpaste tube, pressure is applied to the white paste, which in turn presses on the red paste at the head of the tube.

Fourth step: the merging of white and red paste.

The red then passes through the slots and onto the white, which is moving through the inserted tube—and which emerges with five red stripes.

Exercise 15.10: Explaining a Process

Use process analysis to explain one of following subjects. Explain the process one step at a time and be sure to provide your reader with enough detail to make each step clear.

a. How you have prepared a garden

b. How you have lived without an automobile

c. How you would tame a wild creature such as a falcon or a rabbit

d. How you would get rid of pests without using poisons

e. How you show appreciation for others
f. How you buy a used motorcycle or car
g. How you toss a Frisbee, a football, a baseball
h. How you bluff at cards
i. How you overcome shyness
j. How you cope with crowds
k. How you win others to your point of view

16 Argument Paragraphs ¶

Argumentative and **persuasive** writing attempts to change or reinforce someone's opinion or to convince someone to take action. When writers emphasize rational thinking, they are writing *logical argument.* When they emphasize emotion, they are writing *persuasive argument.* Since most argumentative writing mixes rational thinking with emotion, the term *argument* includes both argumentation and persuasion.

Refutation Paragraphs

Like all essays, an argument essay is composed of paragraphs, and it will usually employ a variety of paragraph modes, such as paragraphs developed by examples, comparison and contrast, cause and effect, and definition. One paragraph structure, however, is unique to argument. This is a *refutation* paragraph, which presents a brief summary of the other side's argument and offers the author's argument. For example, in a paragraph from "Politics and the English Language," George Orwell refuted an argument point that opposes his position.

> I said earlier that the decadence of our language is probably curable. Those who deny this would argue, if they produced an argument at all, that language merely reflects existing social conditions, and that we cannot influence its development by any direct tinkering with words and constructions. So far as the general tone or spirit of a language goes, this may be true, but it is not true in detail. Silly words and expressions have often disappeared, though not through any evolutionary process but owing to the conscious actions of a minority.

Orwell's refutation paragraph follows a common structure, or sequence of sentences. He begins by stating his position. He then states a counterargument. Next he writes a sentence that swings the direction from the counterpoint to his response. He closes with an interpretation that supports his opinion.

Student-writer Rhonda Burris follows this pattern in "Here's Looking at Reality, Kid." Her essay argues that the government should require film producers to announce the dangers of smoking when characters in a film smoke.

The writer states her position, then uses a transition sentence to lead to the opposition's argument point.

I'm urging that warnings about smoking be required on films that glamorize smoking, nothing more and nothing less. I can hear opponents now.

She summarizes what she believes her opponents will claim.

One more law designed to control personal freedom, they will charge. Following this logic, if government wants to protect people, it should put warnings about cars on films with car chases or warnings about guns on films with shoot-outs. But they would be wrong. Cars and guns don't kill people, drivers and gun owners kill people.

She uses a brief transition, "In contrast" to show the shift back to her position. She states her response to the opposing argument.

In contrast, cigarettes *do* kill people, even people who don't smoke but inhale cigarette smoke for years, and that's a well-documented fact. Moreover, the government has already taken action to warn consumers about the dangers of smoking.

Refutation Paragraphs and Development Patterns

Often writers employ a particular development pattern in refutation paragraphs. In the following paragraph from "Scientist: I Am the Enemy," pediatrician Ron Karpati responds to accusations made by animal-rights activists with stunning brief examples. Notice how Karpati first summarizes the activists' point before countering it.

Karpati gives a very brief summary of one point in the opposing position.

Much is made of the pain inflicted on animals in the name of medical science. The animal-rights activists contend that this is evidence of our malevolent and sadistic nature. A more reasonable argument, however, can be advanced in our defense.

He writes a brief transitional sentence and develops his persuasive counterpoint, which leans on emotion.

He further enhances his position by presenting alternatives to using animals for scientific research.

Life is often cruel, both to animals and human beings. Teenagers get thrown from the back of a pickup truck and suffer severe head injuries. Toddlers, barely able to walk, find themselves at the bottom of a swimming pool while a parent checks the mail. Physicians hoping to alleviate the pain and suffering these tragedies cause have but three choices: create an animal model of the injury or disease and use that model to understand the process and test new therapies; experiment on human beings—some experiments will succeed, most will fail—or, finally, leave medical knowledge static, hoping that accidental discoveries will lead us to the advances.

In "The Futility of the Death Penalty," Clarence Darrow used comparison and contrast to refute a counterpoint.

Darrow opens with a general belief.

He then writes a transitional sentence to shift the discussion to his position.

It seems to be a general impression that there are fewer homicides in Great Britain than in America because in England punishment is more certain, more prompt, and more severe. As a matter of fact, the reverse is true. In England the average term for burglary is eighteen months; with us it is probably four or five years. In England, imprisonment for life means twenty years. Prison sentences in the United States are harder than in any country in the world that could be classed as civilized.

Consider now two examples of refutation paragraphs that make use of analogy and process analysis. Civil rights leader Martin Luther King, Jr., used analogy in "Letter from Birmingham Jail" to refute a public statement made by Alabama clergymen who opposed civil rights demonstrations because they broke the then existing law.

> In your statement you assert that our actions, even though peaceful, must be condemned because they precipitate violence. But is this a logical assertion? Isn't this like condemning a robbed man because his possession of money precipitated the evil act of robbery? Isn't this like condemning Socrates because his unswerving commitment to truth and his

> philosophical inquiries precipitated the act by the misguided populace in which they made him drink hemlock? Isn't this like condemning Jesus because his unique God-consciousness and never-ceasing devotion to God's will precipitated the evil act of crucifixion? We must come to see that, as federal courts have consistently affirmed, it is wrong to urge an individual to cease his efforts to gain his basic constitutional rights because the quest may precipitate violence. Society must protect the robbed and punish the robber.

In "Concerning Abortion: An Attempt at a Rational View," Charles Harshrone uses process analysis to refute the view that a fertilized egg in its early stage is a human being.

> Anti-abortion advocates argue that human life begins at the moment of conception. But this is not accurate. The fertilized egg is an individual egg, but not an individual human being. For such a being is, in its body, a multicellular organism, a *metazoan*—to use the scientific Greek—and the egg is a single cell. The first thing the egg cell does is to begin dividing into many cells. For some weeks the fetus is not a single individual at all, but a colony of cells. During its first weeks there seems to be no ground for regarding the fetus as comparable to an individual animal. Only in possible or probable destiny is it an individual. Otherwise it is an organized society of single-celled individuals.

Although stating an opposing argument point in order to refute it is not used by all argument writers, doing so does show your reader that you have thoroughly considered the issue, thus making your argument all the more convincing.

Exercise 16.1: Convincing a Reader

Select one of the numbered subjects below as the prompt to write a refutation paragraph. Follow a common refutation paragraph pattern:

- State your position.
- Write a transitional sentence that leads to the opposing argument.
- Summarize the opposing argument.
- Write a transitional sentence to shift to your response to the opposing argument.

- Develop your response by using a traditional development pattern.

a. Movie ratings

b. Propaganda in political advertising

c. Propaganda in commercial advertising

d. Home education

e. Birth control advice given in junior high and high schools

f. "Skin" magazines such as *Playboy* and *Penthouse*

g. Moving the driving age to twenty-one

h. Vegetarianism

i. Violence in film or on television

WRITER'S CLINIC

Developing a Refutation Paragraph

Time yourself. Take five minutes to draw up two lists, side by side. Begin by stating your position at the top. In one list write points opposing your position; in the other, give points supporting your position. This is a quick way to generate ideas; Rhonda Burris used this tactic to develop an example paragraph that appeared earlier in this chapter.

I believe films that glamorize smoking ought to have warning announcements about the dangers of smoking.

Oppose	Support
New laws limit personal freedom.	Laws requiring warnings on cigarette ads already exist.
Should be warnings on cars.	People driving cars kill people in accidents.
Should be warnings on guns.	People using guns kill people on purpose or in accidents.
	Smoking does kill people directly and indirectly through sidestream smoke.

Use your list as a guide when writing the refutation paragraph. Because the list will be a rough one, do not hesitate to delete some points and rearrange others.

j. Burning the American flag

k. The sex life of Congress (House and Senate) members and of the president and vice president of the United States

l. Solving problems by intuition

m. The death penalty

n. Legalizing drugs

o. Lowering the drinking age to eighteen nationwide

PART IV

Sentence Clarity, Variety, and Word Choice

It's my dream that teaching become a glamorous profession. There should be a teacher Hall of Fame. It should be the biggest event, even bigger than the Oscars—"Ms. Smith of P.S. 13 has just made a big breakthrough in teaching the dangling participle. She gets Teacher of the Year!"—with everybody jostling to get near Ms. Smith to shake her hand.

—Frank McCourt, *Writer*

17 Emphasize Equal Ideas; Deemphasize Unequal Ideas *emph/deemph*

When a single sentence has more than one idea, the ideas may be given equal or unequal emphasis. To show equal emphasis use **coordination,** and to show unequal emphasis use **subordination.**

Coordination

To emphasize main clauses (that is, word groups that can stand alone as a sentence) in a single sentence equally, select the appropriate coordinating word, that is, a coordinating conjunction, correlative conjunction, or conjunctive adverb, or use a semicolon to coordinate them.

COORDINATING CONJUNCTIONS

and but for nor or so yet

◆ Many teenage athletes who overeat are obsessed with losing weight, and others ~~. Others~~ who overtrain are obsessed with lifting weights.

When coordinating main clauses, be sure to place a comma after the first main clause and before the coordinating conjunction.

CORRELATIVE CONJUNCTIONS

either . . . or	both . . . and	not only . . . but also
neither . . . nor	whether . . . or	

Either Venice will sink into the sea, or the ~~. The~~ Italian government will spend $1 billion to stabilize its foundation.

CONJUNCTIVE ADVERBS

consequently	furthermore	however	meanwhile
moreover	nevertheless	therefore	thus

◆ Steward Enterprises, Inc., services funeral homes; furthermore, it ~~. It~~ now wants to extend its services to hospitals.

Be sure to place a semicolon after the first main clause and a comma after the conjunctive adverb. You can also substitute the semicolon for a period to show a coordinate relationship between main clauses:

; investors
- Gamblers trust luck~~.~~ ~~Investors~~ trust figures.

Subordination

When ideas in a sentence are unequal in significance, subordinate the minor idea to the major idea. You can subordinate ideas in two ways.

Rewrite Minor Ideas as Subordinate Clauses. To show an unequal relationship among clauses, use a subordinating conjunction or a relative pronoun to link the minor idea to the main idea.

Common Subordinating Conjunctions

after	because	since	until
although	before	so that	when
as	if	that	whenever
as if	in order that	though	where
as though	inasmuch as	unless	while

Relative Pronouns

that	which	whoever	whomever
whatever	whichever	whom	whose

Although chess ... , great
- ~~Chess~~ players are known for concentration~~.~~ ~~Great~~ chess players are also known for intuition.

, which afflicts both men and women,
- Thigh anxiety is taking over local gyms. ~~Both men and women are afflicted with it.~~

Rewrite Minor Ideas as Subordinate Phrases. A phrase, unlike a clause, does not have a subject and a predicate. Unlike a main clause, a phrase cannot stand alone as a sentence. Using phrases is an effective strategy for showing the relationship among major and minor ideas.

After spending his life on the Kansas prairie, geneticist
- ~~Geneticist~~ Wes Jackson thinks replanting grass may lead to a green revolution. ~~He has spent his life on the Kansas prairie.~~

ing
- High-tech employees hang out at work~~.~~, ~~They~~ kill themselves to make deadlines.

17a Combine choppy sentences.

Stringing together short sentences is a tipoff that you are not distinguishing major from minor ideas. One short sentence in a series of longer sentences may add emphasis, but too many short sentences in sequence probably means you are giving equal weight to each idea.

CHOPPY	China invaded Tibet in the 1950s. Tibetans by the thousands escaped to different countries. Most of them fled to India. Some of them immigrated to the United States. Others settled in Switzerland.
REVISED	When China invaded Tibet in the 1950s, Tibetans by the thousands escaped to different countries. Most of them fled to India, and some of them immigrated to the United States and Switzerland.

◆ Bell Rice, who has published four novels, ~~. She~~ and lives in Phoenix, ~~. She~~ just sold her first novel, *Alcatraz in the Mind*, to a film producer. ~~It was *Alcatraz in the Mind*.~~

17b Avoid faulty or excessive coordination and subordination.

In a sentence, faulty coordination mistakenly emphasizes unequal or unrelated clauses. Revise faulty coordination by putting part of the sentence in a subordinate clause or phrase.

◆ Members of Doctors Without Borders travel on an hour's notice to third-world hot spots~~, and~~ while their at-home practices languish.

◆ ~~Members~~ while members of Doctors Without Borders travel on an hour's notice to third-world hot spots, ~~and~~ their at-home practices languish.

◆ Rosa Parks, ~~was~~ the African American woman who would not go to the back of the bus, ~~and she~~ set the civil rights movement in motion.

Excessive coordination—stringing main clauses together with coordinating conjunctions for no apparent purpose—can become monotonous for the reader. Excessive coordination also fails to show the relation between clauses.

◆ Dan Jenkins, who is a recognized sculptor ~~and he~~ work~~s~~ing in San Francisco, ~~and he~~ has received grants from the Guggenheim Foundation and the National Endowment for the Arts.

Faulty subordination occurs when the major clause is placed in a subordinate position in a sentence or when the expected relation between clauses is reversed.

◆ Although ~~F~~foreign-made goods are popular with American consumers, ~~although~~ they pose a serious threat to the incomes of American workers.

◆ ~~Although~~ ~~s~~She easily won the Olympic trial, although she had been training for only six months.

Excessive subordination should be avoided. It occurs when a sentence contains a series of clauses, each subordinate to an earlier one, as follows:

> The lonesome trapper, who was a retired railroad worker who lived in a small cabin, enjoyed the rare occasions when a group of hikers wandered by his place, which was inaccessible for most of the year.

Exercise 17.1: Revise to Improve Coordination

Revise the following sentences to correct faulty or excessive coordination.

1. Eugene O'Neill was an American playwright, and he won the Nobel Prize for literature in 1936.
2. O'Neill had an unhappy childhood, and he told the story of his childhood in a play entitled *Long Day's Journey into Night,* and he said it was "written in tears and blood."
3. O'Neill's daughter Oona married Charlie Chaplin, but she married against her father's will.

4. One of O'Neill's plays, *The Iceman Cometh,* is full of symbols and hidden clues about its meaning, and it has probably been written about more than any other American play.
5. Louis Sheaffer wrote a biography of O'Neill, and he spent sixteen years researching and writing it, and his book won a Pulitzer Prize.

Exercise 17.2: Revise to Improve Subordination

Combine each pair of sentences below into one sentence, subordinating one idea to another.

1. My sister Carla loves to shop at airport duty-free stores. Her first overseas trip was to Paris.
2. Carla gets to take several overseas trips every year. She works for an importing firm in Atlanta.
3. Duty-free shops are not really duty-free to the consumer. She still saves money on perfumes, watches, scarves, and ties.
4. Carla arrives at the airport early and checks in. She heads for the duty-free shops.
5. She prefers the large selection of the airport duty-free shops. On-plane duty-free shopping is cheaper.

Exercise 17.3: Revise to Improve Subordination

Rewrite the following sentences, revising the faulty or excessive subordination in each. You may need to write more than one sentence for each item.

1. Eimi Yamada, who had been a teacher for more than twenty years, retired from Stanton University, which was founded in 1829 and which has an international reputation in the biological sciences, last year.
2. Professor Yamada, who is noted for her work on the chemistry of cells, has most of her research materials housed in her garage, which she has used as a library for a decade, ever since someone stole her Buick.
3. Her ancient Buick, which was a 1940 Century convertible that had been purchased for her by her mother when Professor

Yamada graduated from high school, had been admired by every student who had ever seen her drive it through the streets of Stanton.

4. The man who stole Professor Yamada's Buick, which was beige and maroon, once failed the biology course that Professor Yamada taught.

5. Stanton University's student body, which numbers over two thousand, took up a collection and bought Professor Yamada a retirement present, which was another automobile to replace the one that was stolen many years ago.

18 Use Parallel Structure for Emphasis //

Use parallel structure to emphasize two or more ideas or words of equal importance by expressing them in the same grammatical form. Such elements as coordinate word groups, compared and contrasted word groups, and correlative word groups should be expressed in parallel form—that is, a noun must be matched with a noun, a verb with a verb, a phrase with a phrase, and a clause with a clause. Parallel structure can add clarity, interest, and impact to your writing.

18a Use parallel structure for coordinate elements.

To earn a living, he worked *as a busboy at the faculty club* and *as a bellhop at the Bayshore Inn.* [Parallel prepositional phrases]

Clearing tables and *lugging suitcases* often left him *tired, disgusted,* and *discouraged* by Sunday night. [Parallel phrases and parallel predicate adjectives]

When coordinate elements are not expressed in parallel grammatical form, sentences can be awkward and hard to understand.

◆ Desmond's favorite pleasures are ~~the dances~~ dancing at Hotspur's and sleeping until noon.

Words such as the prepositions *by* and *in,* the *to* of an infinitive, the articles *a* or *an* and *the,* and the subordinate conjunction *that* should usually be repeated when they apply to both elements in a parallel construction.

◆ By reading extensively and ^by voting wisely, Americans contribute to the democratic process.

Clauses beginning with *and, who, or,* and *which* can be coordinated only with *who* or *which* clauses that precede them.

◆ May Lin, a student and ~~who has been~~ a salesclerk, won election to the school board.

18b Use parallel structure to compare and contrast ideas.

You can underscore comparisons by arranging them in parallel structure.

◆ Most New Yorkers would rather put up with the hectic pace of the big city than ~~moving~~ move to a little backwater town and ~~wasting~~ waste time.

◆ The author of *ReMax* wants to live fully and then hopes ~~he will~~ to have a quick death.

18c Use parallel structure for correlative constructions.

Either . . . or, not only . . . but also, both . . . and, and similar correlative constructions should link parallel sentence elements.

◆ De Campo sent copies of his speech not only to his senators and representatives but also ^to his friends and relatives.

◆ Even at night, she can usually be found in her office either listening to student problems or ~~she works~~ ^working on her research.

Exercise 18.1: Create Parallel Structure

Correct faulty parallel structure in the following sentences.

1. Endurance training helps not only the lungs but also is good for the heart.
2. The human body contains both slow-twitch muscle fibers and it contains fast-twitch.
3. Slow-twitch fibers are difficult to train but they are employed easily.
4. Usually, strenuous exercise will not only deplete the normal supply of stored glycogen, the body's ready-to-use sugar, and cause a sense of fatigue known to athletes as "the wall."
5. Some of the best exercises are running, swimming, and walks.
6. Gymnasts may work out using parallel bars, rowing machines, and lifting weights.
7. All spectators enjoy watching athletes performing well and who win gracefully.
8. The outcome of many football games next season will depend on whether the kicker is successful, whether the quarterback will make the right calls, and if the team is healthy.
9. Coaches aid athletes both physically and with their emotions.
10. Champions are made and not the product of birth.

19 Create Sentence Variety *var*

A good writer avoids writing monotonous paragraphs and essays by varying the length and structure of sentences. The following paragraph has interesting content but too little variety in sentence length and structure.

> Cockroaches are about half the size of a thumb. They have hard shells and are dark in color. They are nocturnal insects who hate the light. Roaches can eat almost anything. They can survive on virtually nothing. They like sweet foods. They like foods that contain protein and oils. They will eat anything from oats to library paste. They will eat the glue on a postage stamp. Twelve of them can live more than a week on this glue. If there is no food, that's OK. The large brown American roach can live a month on water. It can even live for weeks on nothing. The German cockroach can fast for two months.

Every sentence in the paragraph begins with the subject and follows a similar pattern. Many of the sentences are between five and eight words long, a pattern that gives the paragraph a repetitive dreariness. Most important, each sentence stands as an isolated fact; therefore, the relations among ideas are not clear. Revised to create sentence variety, the paragraph might read as follows.

> About half the size of a thumb and with hard, dark shells, cockroaches live in the night. Although they are small, roaches can live on almost anything or virtually nothing. When they eat, they like sweet foods that contain protein and oils. But if their favorite food isn't available, they are not choosy. A hungry cockroach will eat anything from oats to library paste, even the glue on a postage stamp, which cockroach lore says will sustain twelve of them for more than a week. If there is no food, that's OK. A large brown American roach can live a month on water or even for weeks on nothing. Some cockroach observers claim that the German variety can fast for two months.

Of course the first paragraph was written poorly to illustrate by contrast the value of creating variety in sentence length and word order. The second paragraph differs from the first paragraph in other ways, too, but the point should be clear: Vary sentence beginnings, vary sentence structure and length, and change the word order to create writing that is lively, interesting, emphatic, and rhythmic.

19a Vary sentence beginnings.

BEGIN WITH A SUBJECT	*Americans* chew millions of pounds of chewing gum each year.
BEGIN WITH AN ADVERB	*Surprisingly,* well over half of this gum is used in armed forces combat rations.
BEGIN WITH A PHRASE	*Before the importation of chicle from Mexico in the mid-1880s,* Americans chewed paraffin wax.
	Seeking greater chewing pleasure, Americans soon switched to chicle.
	To advertise his gum, William Wrigley, Jr., in 1915, mailed free sticks of gum to every telephone subscriber in the United States.

BEGIN WITH A CONJUNCTION	I don't like candy. I don't like cookies. I don't like cakes or pies. *But* I can't live without my chewing gum!
BEGIN WITH A TRANSITION	Doctors used to believe that chewing gum was a health hazard. *However,* most doctors now agree that chewing gum contributes to a sense of well-being.

Exercise 19.1: Vary Sentence Beginnings

For each of the following model sentences, write another sentence that imitates its structure. Identify how each sentence begins.

1. Near the state border, the two escaped convicts surrendered.
2. Running without track shoes, Mary Jo won the hundred-meter dash in record time.
3. Reluctantly, Clyde told the salesclerk that his credit card had expired.
4. Many brick buildings would topple during an earthquake.
5. To encourage the team, the coach gave a pep talk.

19b Vary sentence structures.

You can achieve variety by alternating sentence structures. A **simple sentence** has only one main clause.

> Nobody owns a cat.

A **compound sentence** has two or more main clauses but no subordinate clause.

> Nobody owns cats, but many people feed them.

A **complex sentence** has one main clause and at least one subordinate clause.

> If a cat likes you, it will live with you.

A **compound-complex sentence** has at least two main clauses and at least one subordinate clause.

> If a cat dislikes you, it may disappear, and no matter how hard you search, you will not find it.

Exercise 19.2: Vary Sentence Structure

Identify the sentence structure of each sentence.

1. Tiny bones in a fish's ear tell the life story of the fish.
2. The bones are called otoliths, and they grow in rings.
3. Because otoliths are affected by known weather conditions, scientists can tell the age of the fish, and they can tell when the fish migrated.
4. In addition, if the fish has had a behavior change, the ear bones have recorded it.
5. Because the otoliths absorb heavy metal, scientists can examine them for signs of water pollution.

19c Vary sentence forms.

A **loose sentence** has its subject and predicate first, followed by modifiers and other amplification.

> Arteries carry blood, which is rich in oxygen, to the extremities of all warm-blooded animals, including birds.

A **periodic sentence** has most of its modification and amplification before the subject and predicate.

> Even with a temperature below ten degrees Fahrenheit, pheasants have warm bodies.

A **balanced sentence** is a compound or compound-complex sentence in which the clauses are parallel.

> Arteries transmit warm blood, and veins return the cooler blood. [Compound sentence]
>
> While they were studying zoology together, Bebe kept humming, and Ching kept mumbling. [Compound-complex sentence]

Exercise 19.3: Vary Sentence Forms

Identify the form of each of the following sentences.

1. The Senate passed the tariff bill after a long debate.

2. Senator Milburn spoke for an hour, and Senator Reynaldo asked for some changes in the bill.
3. In the closing hours of the session, the Senate passed the tariff bill.
4. The president wanted a tariff bill, and Congress wanted one, too.
5. While the senators were debating, most of the reporters were interviewing the people in the balcony.

Exercise 19.4: Vary Sentence Forms

Write sentences that conform to the following descriptions, using the model sentence as a prompt.

1. Write a simple, loose sentence.

   Ether burns brightly.

2. Write a simple, periodic sentence.

   An organic compound, ether has industrial uses.

3. Write a complex, periodic sentence.

   While Donna Lee was experimenting in her laboratory, some ether caught fire.

4. Begin a simple sentence with a prepositional phrase.

   Before noon, her laboratory was destroyed.

5. Begin a complex sentence with a dependent clause.

   When the firefighters arrived, they saw only embers.

6. Write a loose, complex sentence.

   The firefighters returned to their station while Donna Lee remained at the scene.

7. Begin a simple sentence with a participial phrase.

   Reading her insurance policy, the young scientist looked sad.

8. Write a periodic sentence containing two clauses.

   After talking to her insurance agent, she called her father, and then she started to eat dinner.

9. End a complex sentence with a prepositional phrase.

   While she was eating, her brother walked into the kitchen.

10. Begin a compound-complex sentence with a dependent clause.

    After Donna Lee told her brother about her accident, he helped her with the dishes, and he later helped her rebuild her laboratory.

20 Rewrite Misplaced Modifiers *mm/dm*

To avoid confusing readers, be sure to place modifiers, whether single words, phrases, or clauses, so that a reader will be certain of the word or words they modify.

20a Place modifying phrases and clauses near the words they modify.

A misplaced phrase or clause may mislead readers or force them to reread to figure out what a sentence means.

CONFUSING	Our neighbor borrowed our lawn mower with a smile.
CLEAR	With a smile, our neighbor borrowed our lawn mower.
CONFUSING	The car has bad tires that I sold today.
CLEAR	The car that I sold today has bad tires.

Exercise 20.1: Revising Sentences with Misplaced Phrases and Clauses

Revise the following sentences by rearranging the misplaced modifying phrases and clauses.

1. The woman cashed her check with a French accent.
2. His trial was postponed for three months for tax evasion.
3. The explorer described an earthquake during his lecture.

4. After the party the hostess gave balloons to all the children in the shape of fantastic animals.
5. The senator examined the rocks in his office taken from the moon.

20b Avoid writing squinting modifiers.

A squinting modifier can seem to modify the word either preceding or following it. The ambiguous result can confuse a reader.

SQUINTING	Mia told Antonio immediately to call the police. [Does *immediately* refer to *told* or to *to call?*]
REVISED	Immediately, Mia told Antonio to call the police.
REVISED	Mia told Antonio to call the police immediately.

Exercise 20.2: Revising to Correct Squinting Modifiers

Revise the following sentences to clarify the confusion that squinting modifiers create.

1. Walking to work occasionally is an interesting experience.
2. News that the water had been shut off completely mystified me.
3. Reading his novel thoroughly delighted me.
4. Taking coffee breaks frequently disrupts production.
5. Young children given an allowance often waste the money.

20c Place limiting modifiers with care.

Limiting modifiers, such as *only, hardly, just, nearly, almost,* and *ever,* can function in many positions in a sentence. They modify the expression immediately following them. Therefore, as these limiting modifiers change position in a sentence, the meaning of the sentence also changes.

I will go only if he asks me. [Otherwise I will stay.]
Only I will go if he asks me. [The others will not go.]
I will go if only he asks me. [Please, ask me!]
I will go if he asks only me. [If he asks others, I will stay.]

Exercise 20.3: Revise Sentences to Correct Misplaced Limiting Modifiers

Write another version of each sentence by moving the italicized modifier to a different position. Briefly describe the difference in meaning in the two sentences.

1. Henrietta lost *almost* one thousand dollars.
2. *Only* Clyde is ten years old.
3. Rachel *nearly* memorized a hundred Chinese verbs.
4. Andy *even* has a job.
5. Mr. Kobe *just* stared at Mike.

20d Move awkwardly placed modifiers.

Avoid placing a lengthy modifying phrase or clause between key sentence elements.

AWKWARD	The cost of attending college, *because of inflation and reduced federal support,* has risen sharply in recent years.
REVISED	The cost of attending college has risen sharply in recent years *because of inflation and reduced federal support.*
AWKWARD	Anton seemed, *to those who had visited him during the several weeks following his operation,* discouraged.
REVISED	*To those who had visited him during the several weeks following his operation,* Anton seemed discouraged.
AWKWARD	Margo could have, *if she had not joined the army,* been a police officer.
REVISED	*If she had not joined the army,* Margo could have been a police officer.

You may place short modifiers between a subject and a predicate.

The cost of attending college, *unfortunately,* has risen sharply in recent years.

Anton seemed *mildly* discouraged.

He discovered he had been *cruelly* deserted.

20e Avoid splitting infinitives.

An infinitive consists of *to* plus the plain form of a verb: *to run, to complain, to speak.*

SPLIT INFINITIVE	When the locusts descended, the prairie residents prepared to hurriedly depart.
REVISED	When the locusts descended, the prairie residents hurriedly prepared to depart.

Occasionally a split infinitive will seem natural and appropriate. In fact, not splitting an infinitive can sometimes create an awkward or misleading sentence.

His inability to *clearly* explain the issues cost him the election.

In the preceding sentence, the alternatives are more awkward than the split infinitive. *Clearly to explain* and *to explain clearly* sound excessively formal, and *to explain the issues clearly cost him the election* produces a squinting modifier.

Exercise 20.4: Revise to Correct Awkward Modification

Change the position of the italicized modifier in each sentence to correct the awkward constructions.

1. Tenochtitlan, *until it was destroyed by Cortés's army in 1521,* served as the capital city of the Aztec empire.
2. Following the destruction of the capital, Cortés's men built, *with the forced labor of the Aztec survivors,* a magnificent new city.
3. Mexico City is *by many visitors today* considered one of the most beautiful cities in the world.
4. Some demographers expect the population of Mexico City to, *by the year 2000,* number over 30 million people.
5. A visitor today will, *if romantically inclined,* enjoy the numerous sidewalk cafés and strolling musicians.

20f Avoid writing dangling modifiers.

A dangling modifier is a phrase or clause that is not clearly attached to any word in the sentence. To correct a dangling modifier, change the subject of the main clause or rewrite the modifier as a complete clause.

DANGLING PHRASE	*Walking through the supermarket,* the oranges, looked tempting. [The oranges were walking?]
REVISED	*Walking through the supermarket,* I noticed that the oranges looked tempting.
REVISED	*As I was walking through the supermarket,* the oranges looked tempting.
DANGLING PHRASE	*To understand world affairs,* a daily newspaper should be read.
REVISED	*To understand world affairs,* a person should read a daily newspaper.
DANGLING PHRASE	*After recovering from the treatments,* my doctor told me to be more careful in the future.
REVISED	*After I recovered from the treatments,* my doctor told me to be more careful in the future.
DANGLING PHRASE	*While a student at Rutgers,* Shakespeare was my favorite author.
REVISED	*While I was a student at Rutgers,* Shakespeare was my favorite author.

Exercise 20.5: Revise to Correct Dangling Modifiers

Revise the following sentences to eliminate dangling modifiers.

1. To learn about zombies, Haitian voodoo tradition was studied by E. Wade Davis.
2. After receiving a sample of "zombie powder," it was found by Davis to contain one critical ingredient: tetrodotoxin.
3. Being a powerful poison, Davis said tetrodotoxin is 160,000 times more potent than cocaine.
4. Produced by a species of puffer fish, a soldier passed out for twenty-four hours after he handled roasted fish entrails containing tetrodotoxin.

5. Under constant tetrodotoxin intoxication, researchers noted that people acted like the zombies discussed in literature.

Exercise 20.6: Revising to Correct Misplaced Modifiers

On the basis of what you have learned throughout this chapter, recast the following sentences so that they illustrate clear writing. Some sentences have more than one error.

1. Denton Cooley, once an assistant in many heart operations and now a world-famous heart surgeon in his own right, estimates that he has at least performed 65,000 heart operations.
2. He has one of the lowest mortality rates anywhere of any heart surgeon.
3. He has nearly performed ninety-one heart transplants.
4. Dr. Cooley also developed and implanted the first temporary heart.
5. His career includes, among a number of adventures and awards so richly deserved, the world's first heart operation.
6. He in the mid-1950s invented one of the early heart-lung machines.
7. In excess of $20 million, he has amassed a personal fortune.
8. In early December 1967, Dr. Christiaan Barnard, Cooley heard on the radio, had done the first human heart transplant.
9. Cooley was, like most surgeons, dumbfounded.
10. Cooley predicted the newly transplanted heart would fail immediately within forty-eight hours.

21 Revise for Consistency *shift*

The use of person, number, mood, subject, and voice should remain consistent within sentences. Faulty shifts in any of these elements indicate that the writer's thinking is not clear, and the meaning of the sentences will be obscured. Always review your sentences for consistency.

21a Write sentences consistent in person and number.

Most faulty shifts in person take place between second person and third person.

FAULTY SHIFT	If a beginning driver studies the vehicle code thoroughly, you should be able to pass the written test for a driver license. [Faulty shift from third to second person]
REVISED	If a beginning driver studies the vehicle code thoroughly, he or she should be able to pass the written test for a driver license. [Consistent third person]
REVISED	If you study the vehicle code thoroughly, you should be able to pass the written test for a driver license. [Consistent second person]

Number refers to the singular or plural form of nouns and pronouns. Most faulty shifts in number result from the use of a plural pronoun to refer to a singular noun. (See agreement of pronoun and antecedent, Chapter 29; indefinite pronouns, 29b.)

FAULTY SHIFT	When a mud flat dries up, they do so in regular patterns of cracks. [Shift from singular to plural]
REVISED	When a mud flat dries up, it does so in regular patterns of cracks. [Consistently singular]
FAULTY SHIFT	When a chemist experiments with toxins, they exercise great caution. [Shift from singular to plural]
REVISED	When a chemist experiments with toxins, he or she exercises great caution. [Consistently singular]
REVISED	When chemists experiment with toxins, they exercise great caution. [Consistently plural]

21b Write sentences consistent in tense.

Tense refers to the time of an action indicated by the verbs in a sentence. Shifts in verb tense are often required to report time sequences accurately, but faulty shifts can confuse a reader. (See verb tense, 32g.)

FAULTY SHIFT	The suspected bicycle thief ran around the corner and falls into the arms of the police officer.
REVISED	The suspected bicycle thief ran around the corner and fell into the arms of the police officer.
FAULTY SHIFT	The escaping driver speeds around the corner and veered directly into the path of a motorcyclist.
REVISED	The escaping driver sped around the corner and veered directly into the path of a motorcyclist.

21c Write sentences consistent in mood.

The mood of a verb can be indicative, imperative, or subjunctive. Statements and questions are in the indicative mood; commands, in the imperative mood; and wishes and statements contrary to fact, in the subjunctive mood.

Most faulty shifts in mood occur when a writer fails to follow through with the initial use of the imperative mood.

FAULTY SHIFT	Save coffee grounds, and you should sprinkle them around your rosebushes.
REVISED	Save coffee grounds and sprinkle them around your rosebushes.

21d Write sentences consistent in subject and voice.

A shift in subject or a shift from active to passive voice is awkward and possibly confusing.

FAULTY SHIFT	In the game of curling, a player slides a heavy stone over the ice toward a target, and the ice in front of the stone is swept to influence its path.

Because the subject shifts from *player* in the first clause to *ice* in the second clause, and the voice shifts from active *(slides)* to passive *(is swept)*, a reader may be confused about who is doing the sweeping.

REVISED	In the game of curling, a player slides a heavy stone over the ice toward a target, and the player's teammates sweep the ice in front of the stone to influence its path.

A shift in subject and voice sometimes results in a dangling modifier.

FAULTY SHIFT	Shaking with fear, the sound of an intruder could be heard in the kitchen. [The sound is shaking?]

The subject of the main clause is *sound.* The introductory phrase *shaking with fear* is a dangling modifier because it does not sensibly relate to sound.

REVISED	Shaking with fear, we heard the sound of an intruder in the kitchen.

Now the subject is *we,* which clearly connects to *shaking with fear.*

21e Avoid shifts between direct and indirect discourse.

Direct discourse reports the exact words of a speaker. Indirect discourse reports the gist of what a speaker said but not the speaker's exact words.

DIRECT DISCOURSE	Father said, "I will be home at noon."
INDIRECT DISCOURSE	Father said that he would be home at noon.
FAULTY SHIFT	"I'll be home at noon," Father said, and I should not eat the cookies.
REVISED	"I'll be home at noon," Father said. "Don't eat the cookies." [Direct discourse]
REVISED	Father told me that he would be home at noon and that I should not eat the cookies. [Indirect discourse]

Exercise 21.1: Correct Faulty Shifts

In these sentences, label each faulty shift in person, number, tense, mood, subject, voice, or discourse and revise each sentence to be consistent. If any sentences are already correct, mark them with a C.

1. Until yesterday, Ilse Denschlag had not heard from her brother for months, but last night he telephones her, and then they were

meeting together in a dingy, underfurnished room on the eleventh floor of the Beckford Hotel.

2. He seemed perfectly calm, and he was obviously enjoying himself.
3. Carefully, he packed the tobacco deeper in the bowl of his pipe and a match was struck.
4. He held the match in his right hand, not bringing it to the bowl, and stares at her.
5. Then he shook the match out and asked her if she was surprised to see him and asked, "Don't you wonder where I've been?"
6. "I can guess where you've been," Ilse replied with a laugh, "but I am surprised to see you."
7. "Well, sometimes a man has to come home or you forget where it is," he said, and his lips form a faint smile.
8. She remembered that little smile he had; they always preceded his sharing a special secret.
9. I know why he's home, she thought, but you better not spoil his fun.
10. "Don't tell me now," she said. "Tell me at dinner, and I think you should call Mom and Dad first."

21f Avoid shifts in grammatical plans.

> In Faulkner's often anthologized story "Barn Burning" poignantly reveals the conflicting loyalties in a young boy's life.

"Barn Burning" is used in this sentence as the object of the preposition *in*, but it is also used as the subject of the verb *reveals.* A word or group of words cannot function as both the object of a preposition and the subject of a main clause.

If the sentence begins with a prepositional phrase, the main clause has to have a subject of its own.

> In the often anthologized story "Barn Burning," Faulkner poignantly reveals the conflicting loyalties in a young boy's life.

If "Barn Burning" is to serve as the subject of *reveals,* the prepositional phrase must be eliminated.

> Faulkner's often anthologized story "Barn Burning" poignantly reveals the conflicting loyalties in a young boy's life.

21g Avoid faulty predication.

Faulty predication occurs when the subject and predicate of a sentence do not fit together in meaning.

FAULTY PREDICATION	The issue of gun control is an easy solution to a complicated problem. [The issue is not the solution]
REVISED	The issue of gun control is complicated.
REVISED	Gun control is an easy solution to a complicated problem.
FAULTY PREDICATION	Nepotism is when [or where] officials appoint their relatives to desirable positions. [Nepotism is neither a time nor a place]
REVISION	Nepotism is the appointing of relatives to desirable positions.
FAULTY PREDICATION	The reason he failed the examination is because he had a toothache.
REVISED	The reason he failed the examination is that he had a toothache.
REVISED	He failed the examination because he had a toothache.

Exercise 21.2: Correct Sentences for Consistency

Revise the following sentences to avoid shifts in grammatical plan and faulty predication.

1. Banking is an idea that has always interested me.
2. While I was eating at the Turkish restaurant, is where the music excited me so much that I felt like dancing.
3. All over the campus seemed to be alive with flowers.
4. Pearls are when gems are formed inside oysters.
5. In *Light in August* by William Faulkner is difficult to understand.

Exercise 21.3: Correct Sentences for Inconsistencies

1. In 60 percent of a new engine is made of plastic.
2. By using plastic makes the engine lightweight.

3. The engine can sit in a child's wagon, and the wagon can be easily pulled by them.
4. When a child does pull the wagon loaded with the powerful engine, they feel proud.
5. The new engine is called the Polimotor, and they were designed by Matthew Holtzberg.
6. When Holtzberg spoke to a recent engineers' meeting, he spoke calmly, saying most to the engine's moving parts are made of Torlon, and he also said that Torlon is a heat-resistant plastic resin.
7. In the engine block itself is made of a graphite-fabric of epoxy composite.
8. In the future is when drivers will have fewer mechanical problems because of their Polimotors.
9. In the design of the engine will probably be standard in cars in ten to twenty years.
10. According to Holtzberg, the first question everyone asks when they see a plastic engine is why the thing doesn't melt.

22 Add Omitted Words *inc*

Add missing words to complete sentences. Most incomplete sentences are sentence fragments, but some sentences that are not fragments may still be incomplete because words that complete the thought are missing.

22a Complete all comparisons.

It is easy to leave your thought incomplete, unclear, or illogical when comparing one thing with another because the comparison is obvious in your own mind. But remember, you are writing for a reader who does not know what you know.

INCOMPLETE Ace Construction Company treats its employees better.

COMPLETE	Ace Construction Company treats its employees better than other contracting firms treat their employees.
UNCLEAR	Susan is closer to me than Serena.
CLEAR	Susan is closer to me than Serena is.
CLEAR	Susan is closer to me than she is to Serena.
ILLOGICAL	The silence of the desert at night was more terrifying than a coyote.
LOGICAL	The silence of the desert at night was more terrifying than the howl of a coyote.

22b Add missing words in compound word groups.

You may leave out words in compound word groups as long as the words you leave out are common to both groups.

◆ CEOs must provide strong visible leadership for all employees and ~~provide~~ clear verbal direction for senior management.

The second *provide* is unnecessary because it is grammatically parallel with the first provide.

◆ There are only two lasting bequests we can give our children: one is roots; the other, ~~is~~ wings.

The verb *is* can be left out before *wings* with no confusion in meaning. In fact, the omission serves to emphasize wings. The added comma indicates the omission.

◆ At eighteen I knew everything; at forty, ~~I knew~~ nothing.

I knew can be omitted before *nothing.* The added comma indicates the omission.

Done properly, sentences can be strengthened by omissions. If, however, omitted words are not consistent in grammar or idiom, then the sentence is flawed.

◆ At eighteen I knew everything; now, I know nothing.

◆ Humans have a strong belief in and a desire for love.

22c Add the word *that* to prevent misreadings.

If doing so does not cause a misreading, *that* may be left out of a sentence when it begins a subordinate clause.

◆ In 1968, Criswell predicted ~~that~~ the world would end on August 18, 1999.

If there is a risk of creating confusion or a misreading by leaving out *that,* then include it.

◆ Studying his crystal ball, Criswell predicted in 1968 ^that^ the world would end on August 18, 1999.

22d Add the articles *a, an,* and *the* for grammatical clarity.

Check your sentences very carefully to see whether you have mistakenly left out articles.

◆ Negotiators cannot decide on a meeting date let alone reach ^an^ agreement.

Exercise 22.1: Add Missing Words

Rewrite the following sentences to make all comparisons complete, clear, and logical and to correct faulty omissions.

1. Many people believe that horses are more intelligent.
2. Jorge's wife Sarah always had confidence and admiration for Jorge's old horse.
3. His favorite plow horse used to plow three acres a day; now none.
4. Personally, I believe that Sarah wants a horse more than Jorge.
5. To me, smooth ride of a car is better than a horse.
6. My car is so old.
7. When my car was new, it averaged thirty miles per gallon; now, twenty.
8. I would trade in my car, except for expense.

9. No new-car dealer wants my old clunker, so my down payment will have to be cash instead.
10. I went to the Ford dealership in town and then to Chevrolet.

23 Use Appropriate Language *appr*

English can be divided into two very general categories: standard and nonstandard English. Standard English is used in most mainstream publications, business, politics, television broadcasts, and education. Nonstandard English consists of variations of standard English (especially in certain pronoun cases and verb forms) not found in the writing of formally educated people.

STANDARD	The guest *brought* homemade pie for dessert.
NONSTANDARD	The guest *brung* homemade pie for dessert.
STANDARD	Nina is the woman *who* broke the record.
NONSTANDARD	Nina is the woman *what* broke the record.
STANDARD	He sings to *himself.*
NONSTANDARD	He sings to *hisself.*

Standard American English can be divided into formal or informal (sometimes called *colloquial*) writing. Informal writing is characterized by common expressions taken from spoken English.

INFORMAL	If the mayor would *get together with* the city manager, *they'd* solve the problem.
FORMAL	If the mayor would *meet with* the city manager, *they would* solve the problem.
INFORMAL	*I don't get* why the refund took *all these* weeks to *get here.*
FORMAL	*I do not understand* why the refund took *several* weeks to *arrive.*

Informal writing is easily identified by contractions such as *they'd, don't, you're,* and *it's.* In formal writing contractions are usually written out: *they would, do not, you are, it is.* Most of the writing you do in college and in a profession—serious essays, theses, reports, and memos—will be formal.

23a Avoid slang, regional expressions, neologisms, and obsolete words.

Slang comes from a specialized, often colorful vocabulary that is related to the experience of groups with common interests, such as actors, astronauts, athletes, computer scientists, copywriters, musicians, street gangs, teenagers, truckers, and so on.

Eventually, some slang passes into standard usage. *Jazz* and *A-bomb* were once slang words but are now part of standard English. More often, slang makes its appearance, increases in use, and then shifts its meaning or becomes dated.

Generally, you should avoid using slang: It is imprecise and may be confusing or misleading to a reader.

◆ *Jean de Florette* is ~~*a downer*~~ depressing to watch. The ~~*flick*~~ film portrays ~~*a smack*~~ an intellectual from Paris who lacks the ~~*smarts*~~ intelligence to survive on a farm.

◆ The journalist was ~~*bummed*~~ stunned after the judge ~~*laid a heavy trip on him*~~ fined him for contempt of court.

Neologisms are words or terms that have come into use so recently that they may still be unacceptable in general writing. Some former neologisms, such as *astronaut, bookmobile, fallout, supersonic, and smog,* have become acceptable. But most neologisms pass quickly from use, and you should avoid using them unless they become widely accepted.

Regional expressions are common to speech in a geographical area. Do you *carry* or *drive* your friends to the mall? Do you *draw water* or *run water* from a *faucet,* a *spigot,* or a *tap?* Such regional words as these will not confuse your reader, but in writing you should avoid expressions that are not generally used outside a particular region.

◆ The committee had a ~~*right nice*~~ productive meeting. We wish ~~*you all*~~ all of you could have come.

Obsolete or *archaic* words have fallen from general use. Obsolete indicates that a word or a specific meaning is no longer used at all. *Coy* meaning "to caress" and *cote* meaning "to pass" are labeled obsolete. Archaic indicates that a word or meaning appears only in special contexts. *Anon* meaning "at once" and *methinks* meaning "it seems" are labeled archaic.

23b Use technical terms, or jargon, with care.

When writing for a group of literature specialists, you may use the terms *persona, verisimilitude,* and *motif* with confidence that your readers will understand them. These are technical terms that literature specialists freely use. Most fields and activities have technical vocabularies, and a person who studies a field or pursues an activity soon learns the specialized vocabulary that characterizes it. A person who has studied finance will use the terms *put, call,* and *margin* with ease. A skier will feel equally at ease talking about *moguls, whiteouts,* and *schussing.* But without explanation, such terms are inappropriate for a general audience. When you are writing for a general audience, therefore, avoid using technical terms. If you must use them, be sure to define them.

Exercise 23.1: Revise Using Formal English

Revise the following paragraphs by changing words or phrases that may be informal, slang, regional, obsolete, or archaic expressions, neologisms, or technical terms. Feel free to consult a dependable dictionary that includes usage labels to determine the appropriateness of expressions and to find suitable substitutes.

> In 1945 Vice President Harry S Truman unexpectedly became president when Franklin Roosevelt died in office. When Truman took the oath of office, he was so jittery that the words would not come to him and his voice petered out, so he took out a slip of paper with the oath written on it and held it on top of the Bible. Then his voice began to function, and he read the words in a real nice manner. The next day he laid his feelings on a group of reporters: "Boys, if you ever pray, pray for me now!" During his first months in office, Truman could not duck the decision to use the atomic bomb against Japan, a decision that not only brought World War II to an end but also demonstrated that human beings had created the power to waste the entire world.
>
> After the war, Truman lost the heavy-duty political support Roosevelt had previously gathered; consequently, in the 1946 midterm elections Republicans gained control of both houses of Congress for the first time since 1930. Betwixt the attacks of the opposition party and the sniping of rebellious members of his own party, Truman appeared to be on the ropes politically, yet he continued his plans to run for reelection in 1948.

23c Avoid pretentious language.

Write in simple English. Beginning writers often make their writing excessively showy, perhaps from a misconceived desire to sound impressive or even poetic. Unfortunately, the result is often pretentious.

- ◆ At sunset the beach grew quiet. ~~day's end the evening solitude descended on the sea-swept coast.~~

- ◆ This college rewards hard work. ~~is predicated on the belief that diligent and sustained effort will be rewarded.~~

COMPUTER CLINIC

Internet Jargon

The explosion of computer technology has created its own jargon. Many of the new words and phrases are seldom used in daily communication (*asynchronous transfer mode; neurobotics*). Other terms are drawn from common usage. The following ten commonly used words refer to specific computer functions.

agent. Software that learns what you want and don't want; it might retrieve information, filter incoming e-mail, or recommend music for you.

backdoor. A secret way to access a system, or an application built in by the designer.

boot. To turn on a computer or load its systems software.

bug. An error in a software program.

cookie. A unique identifier stored on your hard disk; marketers have seized on cookies to track visitors to their Web sites.

Easter egg. A cartoon, animation, or other surprise feature that programmers hide in the code of a game or application to show off their skill.

firewall. Software that keeps intruders outside a network.

gopher. A system to transfer files and to browse databases to reach sites around the Internet.

handshake. The time two modems or computers take to connect or disconnect.

virus. A digital infection hidden within a program; a virus can be harmless or destructive.

To write in simple English, always choose the common word over the fancy one. If you want to say "Drinking will destroy the liver," do not write "Imbibing alcoholic beverages in vast quantities will lead to the degeneration of one of the body's most important organs."

Exercise 23.2: Eliminate Pretentious Language

While keeping the basic meaning, revise the following sentences by using simple English.

1. The ability to orate before the multitude is accrued through repetitive effort.
2. *Vinification* is an ancient art that has been revitalized by modern technological innovations.
3. Dr. Chen's verbal meanderings amaze and mystify her students.
4. Among his peers he was the sole champion for those who wished to privatize the U.S. Postal Service.
5. We must face the dangers of an inexorable rise in population today or find an agreed-upon solution for thousands of starving infants and children in the near future.

23d Avoid sexist language.

In your writing, avoid usage that may disregard or insult your readers or that relies on stereotypes. English traditionally contains an implicit sexual bias, such as in the use of the masculine pronouns *he, him,* and *his* to refer to individual members of a given occupation or of a group composed of both men and women.

BIASED	A mystery *novelist* concentrates on *his* plot, whereas a suspense *novelist* concentrates on *his* action.
BIASED	A *doctor* must pass the state medical examination before *he* can be licensed to practice.
BIASED	*Man* must assume responsibility for the preservation of the natural world.
BIASED	*Freshmen congressmen* must serve several years before they gain enough seniority to become committee *chairmen.*

These sentences ignore the fact that women also occupy these positions or participate in these groups; thus these sentences implicitly diminish their achievements.

You can avoid sexual bias in your writing by applying several techniques.

1. Replace masculine pronouns with an article (*a, an, the*).
2. Change nouns and pronouns from singular to plural.
3. Revise a sentence to eliminate the need for a pronoun.
4. Use compounds, such as *he or she* and *him or her.*
5. Avoid the traditional masculine and feminine stereotypes by using gender-neutral language to refer to both men and women.

- ~~A m~~Mystery *novelist*s concentrate~~s~~ on ~~*his*~~ plot, whereas ~~a~~ suspense *novelist*s concentrate~~s~~ on ~~*his*~~ action.
- ~~A *d*~~D*octor*s must pass the state medical examination before ~~*he*~~ they can be licensed to practice.
- ~~*Man*~~ Humankind must assume responsibility for the preservation of the natural world.
- *Freshmen congress~~men~~* members must serve several years before they gain enough seniority to become committee *chair~~men~~*s.

Sexist	**Nonsexist**
actor, actress	actor
chairman	chairperson, chair
coed	student
councilman	councilwoman, council member
fireman	firefighter
gal Friday	assistant
man, mankind	humankind, people
policeman	police officer
poetess	poet
stewardess, steward	flight attendant
waiter, waitress	server
weatherman	meteorologist, weather forecaster
workman	worker

Exercise 23.3: Revise Sexually Biased Language

Revise the following passage to eliminate gender bias. Use any of the methods explained in this chapter.

> A writer's primary task is to fulfill the purpose of his book. He must first develop a sense of his reader and a strategy for addressing him: Whom is the essay directed to? How much does his reader know about the subject? How much time is he likely to spend reading the book? Will he want a straightforward treatment of the subject? Will he want extensive background information? These are questions every writer must ask himself. If he doesn't, he will not develop a feel for his reader, that is, for the person who sits behind his desk or in his easy chair, book in hand, under his reading lamp.

Exercise 23.4: Replace Sexually Biased Words

Find nonsexist words to replace sexist words.

1. cleaning lady
2. stewardess
3. actress
4. Father Christmas
5. Mother Nature
6. sportsmanship
7. ladylike
8. newsboy
9. anchorwoman
10. airman

24 Revise Wordy Sentences *wordy*

Make your writing concise by culling words and phrases that add nothing to your meaning. Scrutinize your sentences. Look for empty phrases, needless repetition, and euphemism. When you find such oversights, cross them out and search your vocabulary for more direct and forceful ways to say what you are thinking. Being concise does not necessarily mean that your writing will be skimpy; it means your writing will be free of useless words.

24a Avoid empty phrases.

Empty phrases do little more than add useless words to your writing. Whenever they appear in your work, cut them out or revise them.

◆ ~~In the world of today,~~ Today eighteen-year-olds can only find minimum wage jobs.

Many empty phrases develop from such all-purpose words as *angle, area, aspect, case, character, fact, factor, field, kind, nature, process, situation,* and *type.* Watch for them and cut wherever you can.

Often one word will do the work of an entire empty phrase; if so, substitute the single word for the phrase.

For	Substitute
at all times	always
at this point in time	now
at that point in time	then
at any point in time	whenever
by means of	by
come into conflict	conflict (verb)
due to the fact that	because
for the purpose of	for
for the reason that	because
give consideration to	consider
give encouragement to	encourage
in order to	to
in the event that	if
in the final analysis	finally
make contact with	call
of the opinion that	think
regardless of the fact that	although
in fact that	that
until such time as	until

Exercise 24.1: Revise Empty Phrases

Revise the following sentences by deleting empty words or phrases or by substituting single words for empty phrases.

1. At the present time, sales indicate that biographies of film stars are the type of book more readers want.
2. It is usually the case that these tales give encouragement to the public's fantasies.
3. The 1966 story of Hedy Lamarr's life was so steamy that in order to keep an aspect of her public dignity, she claimed that the book revealed too much and denounced it as obscene.

4. But at this point in time stars seem pleased to reveal shocking details of their lives due to the fact that confession sells books by the millions.
5. With big money at stake, you can easily come to the realization why Marlon Brando announced that his 1994 as-told-to publication would be candid about his love life, and why not, since it's too late for him to change his makeup.

24b Avoid careless repetition.

At times you will repeat words for parallel structure or for emphasis. But careless repetition leads to awkward, wordy sentences.

◆ The grizzly ~~bear~~ is probably North America's most ferocious bear.

◆ Economists say that the recession will continue, and I ~~continue to~~ believe them.

24c Avoid redundant phrases.

A redundant phrase says the same thing twice: *visible to the eye, large in size, cooperate together, close proximity, basic essentials, true fact.* Always revise sentences to eliminate redundancies.

◆ The central character in this novel is a mysterious figure. ~~beyond understanding.~~

The following list includes some common redundancies. Be aware of them and watch for them and others that appear in your own writing. Whenever you find a redundancy, strike it. The italicized words in the list are redundant.

advance *forward*	*important* essential
disappear *from view*	revert *back*
autobiography *of her life*	combine *together*
end result	repeat *again*
basic fundamentals	consensus *of opinion*
factual truth	round *in shape*
circle *around*	continue *to go on*

Exercise 24.2: Revise for Repetition and Redundancy

Improve these sentences by revising them for ineffective repetition and redundancy.

1. From my point of view, I believe parents do not allow their children enough time to discover their creative interests.
2. Twice a day millions of people listen to public radio while continuing on their daily schedules.
3. In the United States, American citizens often make heroes out of the country's severest critics.
4. The book puts forth an extraordinary and exceptional deception aimed at convincing readers that philosophy is superior to and better than any other intellectual pursuit.
5. Nearly square in shape and reddish brown with yellow stripes in color, the puffer fish is covered with spines that make it look more like a spiny medieval weapon than a fish.

24d Avoid excessive euphemism.

A *euphemism* is a word or phrase substituted for other words that are considered harsh or blunt. The funeral industry, for instance, substitutes *loved one* for *corpse, vault* for *coffin,* and *final resting place* for *grave.*

Common euphemisms generally refer to experiences in our daily lives: birth, bodily functions, sex, aging, death. They are often necessary for tactfulness. No doubt most of us prefer to ask a waiter for directions to the *rest room* rather than to the *toilet.*

Although common euphemisms such as *rest room* are harmless, other euphemisms, especially those created by private and public institutions, are often designed to distract us from the realities of poverty, unemployment, and war. We've become accustomed to the euphemisms *low income, inner city,* and *correctional facility* as substitutes for *poor, slum,* and *prison.* Plumbers may be referred to as *sanitation engineers,* teachers as *learning directors,* and salespeople as *account executives,* yet they still fix pipes, correct papers, and sell products. In wartime the act of burning villages and herding people into detention camps has been called *pacification,* and the lies of public officials have been euphemistically named *inoperative statements.*

Because euphemism is pervasive in our society, you must guard against its slipping into your finished work. If you identify euphemisms in your writing, rephrase them in more accurate, concrete language.

a slum
- The whole area was ~~underdeveloped and~~ crowded with ~~the~~
starving people have no more to eat than rice water.
~~disadvantaged~~, who seemed to ~~be living on a marginal diet.~~
crammed themselves into two-room hovels
Several families ~~often lived together in a small dwelling,~~
made of cardboard and sticks. The only water
they had came from tap shared by
~~sometimes with no more than~~ a single ~~water source to serve~~
fifteen or twenty such shacks.
~~them and several other homes together.~~

Use euphemism when tact calls for you to do so, but avoid using it when your work requires a direct rendering of the material. Do not use it to deceive.

Exercise 24.3: Make Sentences Concise

Make these sentences concise by eliminating jargon and euphemism and recasting them in plain, straightforward English.

1. The chairman and the director must resolve the intense feelings that arose during their recent negative encounter.
2. When I was a young girl living in a deteriorating residential section of town, I vowed to develop the capital necessary to buy a ranch.
3. Beware: preowned car dealers embellish information regarding the quality of their products to enhance their monthly revenue.
4. On the basis of information from visual surveillance, the air force chief of staff ordered the squadron to carry out a surgical bombing action over the enemy's capital.
5. My Uncle Ramsey passed away while staying overnight in a nearby motor lodge in the company of a female companion the family had never met.

25 Choose Exact Words *exact*

Find the words that best fit the meaning you wish to convey. Also develop a keen sensitivity to the differences in tone of some words. To be inexact is to risk misleading or confusing your reader.

25a Distinguish between a word's denotation and its connotation.

Denotation refers to a word's concrete meaning as found in the dictionary. **Connotation** refers to what a word implies or suggests. According to one dictionary, the word *snake* denotes "any of a wide variety of limbless reptiles with an elongated, scaly body, lidless eyes, and a tapering tail."

For some people the word *snake* may connote treachery or evil; for others, wisdom or healing. Pay close attention to both the denotation and the connotation of words. Otherwise your words might clash, as in the following sentence.

> The speaker manipulated the audience by presenting the evidence to refute their arguments.

Manipulated has the connotation of deviousness on the part of the speaker, but *refute* denotes reasonably proving something false. The two words do not fit well together. To correct the clash of meanings, the writer should use words with more compatible denotations and connotations.

- ◆ The speaker ~~manipulated~~ convinced the audience by presenting the evidence to refute their arguments.
- ◆ The speaker manipulated the audience by presenting only the evidence ~~to refute~~ that would disprove their arguments.

You must also take special care when selecting a word from among synonyms, words that have nearly the same meaning. *Depart, retreat,* and *flee; emulate, copy,* and *mimic* are two groups of synonyms. Like most synonyms, they are close in their denotations, but they differ in their connotations. Similarly, "Harold's speech was funny" conveys a different meaning than does "Harold's speech was laughable."

When the connotations of words arouse exceptionally strong feelings, we consider the words *loaded.* Loaded words appeal to emotion and bias rather than to reason. A public relations expert might claim his company is carrying on the tradition of *free enterprise* while claiming that a competitor is *price gouging.* A politician might call himself or herself a *progressive* while calling an opponent a *do-gooder.* Loaded words are the tools of propagandists; if you use loaded words, your writing will seem not only inexact but also biased.

Exercise 25.1: Select Exact Words

Replace each italicized word with a word that has a similar denotation but a connotation better fitted to the sentence.

1. To be a successful high-fashion model, a woman or a man must be *emaciated* and graceful.
2. Success also depends on an ability to improve from hearing a photographer's constant *ridicule* and to survive arduous hours in a studio.
3. Unlike actors, models are not hired because of their *quirky profiles.*
4. Instead, their facial features must be *bland,* and their bodies must seem to come from the same mold.
5. Successful high-fashion modeling has its *payoffs* but also its drawbacks—constant routine and *relentless* dieting.

Exercise 25.2: Eliminate Loaded Words

Revise the following paragraph to replace any loaded words and phrases with language that is less emotionally charged.

> Secretly, the president's agents in Congress are threatening to smother hardworking Americans with new taxes. These greedy politicians are plotting to impose a value-added tax to support social boondoggles that conservative legislators have always resisted. Patriotic taxpayers throughout the heart of the country are beginning to resist, too.

25b Do not rely exclusively on abstract and general words.

Be as concrete and specific as you can.

Abstract words refer to qualities, ideas, and actions that we cannot experience through our senses: *culture, friendship, loyalty, democracy.* **Concrete words** refer to things we can experience through our senses: *orange, blood, scream, laugh, hug, tick, swamp.*

General words refer to large groups of people or things. The word *athlete* includes everyone who seriously pursues a sport. **Specific words** refer to one particular part of a general group. *Professional athlete* limits the group of athletes to those who are paid for their athletic performances. Other specific words for *athlete* include *professional tennis player; professional female tennis player; top ten female* *tennis players;* and *Steffi Graf, one of the top ten female tennis players.* Notice that *general* and *specific* are relative terms and that language becomes more specific as it moves from the general group to a unique example of the group—from *athlete* to *Steffi Graf* in this case.

Experienced writers know the value of concrete and specific words. Inexperienced writers tend to overuse abstract and general words; consequently, their work is often inexact and lifeless.

◆ In English 170 we studied the ~~world's leading contemporary writers.~~ works of Alice Walker, Ursula K. Le Guin, Gabriel García Márquez, and Raymond Carver.

◆ After major trials, jurors are often interviewed ~~for their opinions.~~ by newspaper and television reporters who seeks to find out the jurors' versions of the deliberations.

◆ The ~~amount~~ $13,000 set by the government as the poverty level for a family of four ~~is not much to live on.~~ will not buy many $15 T-shirts or $35 jeans, let alone bread, milk, vegetables, and meat.

COMPUTER CLINIC

Computer Thesaurus

A thesaurus identifies words that have similar meanings. Word processing software will include a thesaurus that a writer can call up to find a replacement for an inexact word. A thesaurus can be very helpful when composing an essay. If you use a word that does not quite express your thought, you can highlight the word, go to Tools on the menu bar, and click on Thesaurus. A window will open that offers several replacement suggestions. You can then select the one that more accurately expresses what you want to say.

Sometimes inexperienced writers will misuse a thesaurus. Instead of using it to find the right words they need, they use it to find more abstract words, that is, words that sound more "intelligent" to their untrained ear. This practice is a mistake; writers should select words for their accuracy, not their complexity.

Exercise 25.3: Use Specific Language

Make these sentences more precise by replacing the general words and phrases with concrete and specific language.

1. The film was *thrilling.*

2. The city was *quickly destroyed.*
3. The sea was *dangerous.*
4. The senator *lost her temper.*
5. My brother *irritates me.*

25c Use idioms correctly.

An idiom is a fixed phrase with a single meaning that cannot be determined from the definitions of the individual words in the phrase. If a person said, "The waiter *flew into a rage,*" most native speakers of English would understand that the waiter became angry. If, however, a non-native speaker were to translate the phrase *flew into a rage* word by word, the meaning would seem absurd.

People learn the idiomatic expressions of their language naturally and have little difficulty understanding and using most of them. Occasionally, however, even experienced writers make errors in using an idiom that combines an adjective or a verb and a preposition. "Independent *of* outside influence" is a correct idiom, whereas "independent *from* outside influence" is not a correct phrase.

Whenever you are in doubt about which preposition to use with a word, look up the word in a dictionary. Here are common idioms and examples of their use.

abide *by*	We must abide by the rules.
according *to*	According to the evidence, he must be innocent.
agree *with* (a person)	I agree with John.
agree *to* (a proposal)	I cannot, however, agree to his proposal.
agree *on* (a course of action)	We cannot agree on a common plan.
angry *with*	The children are angry with the babysitter.
charge *for* (a purchase)	The charge for cocoa butter is excessive.
charge *with* (a crime)	The manager has been charged with fraud.
comply *with*	Everyone must comply with the regulations.
compare *to* (something in a different class)	Do not compare psychiatry to witchcraft.

compare *with* (a person)	You can compare a Freudian with a Jungian.
concur *with* (a person)	Jones concurs with Fussel.
concur *in* (an opinion)	I concur in your wish to transfer.
confide *in* or *to*	Ching had no time to confide her secret to me. She confides in her roommate.
die *of* or *from*	He may die from grief.
differ *with* (disagree)	Ruth differs with Trent over who should be a presidential candidate.
differ *from* (be unlike)	Gibson's style differs from Redford's.
differ *about* or *over* (a question)	We differ about how food should be cooked.
different *from*	Living in a dormitory is different from living in an apartment.
identical *to* or *with*	One cannot be identical to the other.
ignorant *of*	Sally is ignorant of table manners.
inferior *to*	Is a life of toil inferior to a life of ease?
occupied *by* (a person)	We found our cabin occupied by a hiker.
occupied *in* (thought)	He was occupied in thought when the pain struck.
occupied *with* (a thing)	She is occupied with a novel.
prior *to*	Prior to being married he played drums.
superior *to*	Rhonda feels superior to Linda.

25d Use figurative language carefully.

Writers use figurative language to draw a comparison between two things that are essentially different but alike in some underlying and surprising way.

By making comparisons, writers not only help their readers understand what is being said but also add vigor to their prose. The most common figures of speech are simile and metaphor.

In a **simile** a writer may express a comparison directly by using *like* or *as.*

> Her forward expression was steady and driving like the advance of a heavy truck. —Flannery O'Connor

> The bowie knife is as American as the half-ton pickup truck. —Geoffrey Norman

In a **metaphor** a writer may express a comparison indirectly, without using *like* or *as.*

> A sleeping child gives me the impression of a traveler in a very far country. —Ralph Waldo Emerson

> I refuse to accept the notion that nation after nation must spiral down a militaristic stairway into the hell of nuclear war. —Martin Luther King, Jr.

Personification and **hyperbole** are less common figures of speech. Writers use personification to give ideas, animals, and objects human qualities.

> When the wind swept through the forest, the trees moaned, and among their branches birds complained.

Through hyperbole a writer creates an exaggeration.

> Mike Finnegan's tennis game has hit bottom, unless he returns to the court another time.

To be exact, a figure of speech must always clarify a writer's thought by making it understandable in other terms. Sometimes, however, a figure of speech will miss the mark or fall flat because it is trite or overblown.

> Her smile is as warm as a crackling fire on a snowy evening.

Another figure of speech gone wrong is the *mixed metaphor,* which combines two or more incompatible comparisons.

MIXED METAPHOR	Ideas that *blaze* in his mind often *crash* in his writing.
REVISED	Ideas that *blaze* in his mind often *smolder* in his writing.
REVISED	Ideas that *race* in his mind often *crash* in his writing.

Exercise 25.4: Make Comparisons Consistent

Revise the following mixed metaphors to make the comparisons consistent.

1. The scalpel cuts through the flesh, leaving a road of blood.
2. The speaker bathed her audience in a blanket of nonsense.

3. She stirs figurative language into her writing the way a cook adds vegetables to a stew—a dash of simile, a pinch of metaphor.
4. His arms flapping, the student flew to the lectern and barked for silence.
5. Reformers once imagined that prisons could be lapidary shops where the soul would be polished after the flaws had been surgically cut away.

25e Avoid trite expressions.

A **trite expression,** sometimes called a *cliché* or *stock phrase,* is an expression that was fresh and striking at one time but by overuse has become stale.

Trite phrases include exhausted figures of speech *(hit the nail on the head),* wedded adjectives and nouns *(a well-rounded personality),* and overused phrases *(the finer things in life).*

Trite expressions may come easily to mind when you feel rushed. But when you revise your writing and come across one, strike it out and reword your thought in a fresh way. These are common trite phrases to avoid:

a must
a thinking person
all in all
all walks of life
aroused our curiosity
flat as a pancake
in a very real sense
in the final analysis
in the world of today
last but not least
method in his madness
never a dull moment
as a matter of fact
at this point in time
cold as ice
depths of despair
face the music
none the worse for wear
pure as newly fallen snow
quick as a flash
sadder but wiser
silent as the grave
smart as a whip
strong as an ox

Exercise 25.5: Eliminate Trite Expressions

Revise the following sentences, substituting fresh thoughts for trite expressions.

1. It is safe to say that Tom Pham looks like a timid tax attorney who would feel butterflies in his stomach if he ever heard a raised voice.

2. But looks are deceptive; Pham is a fierce negotiator who takes the bull by the horns and never gives an inch in collective bargaining sessions.

3. His endurance is such that he can go nose to nose with an opponent for twelve hours straight and leave the table none the worse for wear.

4. Although some see collective bargaining as child's play, Gus realizes that the incomes of two thousand union members hang in the balance.

5. He takes seriously his responsibility to get the best deal he can and never drops the ball—or a dime.

WRITER'S CLINIC

Avoid Paired Words

Sometimes referred to as "married words," paired words are combinations that seem to have been permanently joined through years of overuse.

EXAMPLES

The *grim-faced* diplomats left the negotiations without reaching an agreement.

All they could imagine was a *dark future.*

They must *face reality* and make *mature judgments.*

When you find paired words in your writing, revise by using more specific language.

REVISED

After fifteen hours of meetings, the diplomats left the negotiations without reaching an agreement.

All they could imagine was another year of civil war.

They must protect thousands of refugees or accept the responsibility for their indecision.

PART V
Sentence Errors

If you want to write, the sentence is your point of departure. Part of the art of creating a sentence is knowing the substance and elements of which it is composed. We all know, or let us assume, that sentences are made of words. But words come in various guises, whatever they are intended to hide or reveal, and so we must begin with them—seeing just what they think they are and bringing them together into the realm of sense.

—Karen Elizabeth Gordon, *novelist*

26 Rewrite Sentence Fragments *frag*

A sentence fragment is a word group that is punctuated as if it were a complete sentence. Sentence fragments are usually serious errors, suggesting that the writer does not understand the basic principles of sentence structure.

26a Revise fragmented subordinate clauses.

A group of words introduced by a subordinating conjunction (such as *when, while, although, because, if, until*) or by a relative pronoun (such as *who, which, that*) functions as a subordinate clause. Although subordinate clauses have subjects and verbs, they are not main clauses. When they are punctuated like main clauses, they are actually sentence fragments, that is, *fragmented subordinate clauses.*

You can correct such fragments by attaching the subordinate clause to a main clause, by rewriting the subordinate clause as a complete sentence, or by rewording the clause to eliminate the subordinating conjunction or relative pronoun. (See subordinating conjunctions and relative pronouns, Chapter 17.)

- Dragon stories abound in the myths and legends of people everywhere, as a study of early civilization will reveal.
- One type of dragon popular in art is a huge beast with an armorlike skin and several heads capable of breathing fire, which makes it difficult to subdue.
- Drawings from widely separated cultures show dragons that are grotesque combinations of several animals that are familiar to the people living in that area.

26b Revise fragmented phrases.

A phrase is a word group used as a noun, verb, adjective, or adverb. Since such word groups lack a subject, a predicate verb, or both, they cannot stand alone as if they were sentences. (See phrases, Chapter 20.)

Fragmented phrases can be corrected by joining them to main clauses or by rewriting them as complete sentences.

- Some scholars have spent years studying ancient texts from civilizations around the globe. Searching for a common origin of all later dragon lore.
- One candidate for the honor is Zu, a water monster of Sumerian myth. ~~who~~ was slain by Ninurta. A warrior god who took for himself the names and characteristics of all the creatures he killed.
- In Babylonian stories about battles between dragons and gods. The defeated dragons were forced to live under the sea.
- These dragons struggled constantly. To free themselves and destroy the world.

26c Revise compound predicates and word groups punctuated like sentences.

Two or more predicates joined by a coordinating conjunction form a compound predicate and share the same subject. Compound predicates should not be separated and punctuated like separate sentences.

- According to one Greek tradition, dragons paradoxically sleep with their eyes open. And see with them shut.

Word groups introduced by expressions announcing that examples or a list will follow should not be punctuated like a sentence.

- Network television ignores many sports. Such as rock climbing, skateboarding, surfing, archery, and snowboarding.

Expressions that Introduce Examples or a List

also	for example	like	or
and	for instance	mainly	such as
but	in addition	namely	that is

26d Use fragments in special situations.

Use fragments in special situations sparingly and only when your purpose is clear.

QUESTIONS AND ANSWERS	What next? Another term paper.
EXCLAMATIONS	Awesome!
IN DIALOGUE	"Of course." "Wonderful."
FOR EMPHASIS	I've been patient, understanding, attentive, and gentle. Now it's over. *No more Mr. Nice Guy!*
AS TRANSITIONS	My final point.

Exercise 26.1: Revise Sentence Fragments

Correct the following sentence fragments by (1) attaching them to main clauses, (2) rewriting them as main clauses, or (3) rewording them to eliminate subordinating conjunctions or relative pronouns.

1. Any attempt to understand the popularity of dragon stories will have to begin with their origins. Which coincide with the origins of human civilization.
2. Then, as now, people searched for explanations for the mysterious forces of nature. Because knowledge is the first step toward control.
3. As though dragons were humans' most powerful enemy. Their behavior was used to explain earthquakes, fires, storms at sea, and sudden death.
4. Chinese dragons have had a positive image, controlling rivers and bringing life-giving rain. Though they could cause considerable trouble if angered.
5. Chinese dragons have responded charitably to individual humans. Who were given wisdom and the ability to foretell the future. Because they treated the dragons with kindness.

Exercise 26.2: Revise Fragmented Phrases

Correct the following phrase fragments by joining them to the accompanying main clauses or by rewriting them as complete sentences.

1. Dragons appear in a variety of roles. Symbolizing evil cultures, wisdom to others, and power to still others.
2. Sumerians thought of dragons as embodiments of evil. A concept later attached to the devil.
3. The Gnostics, early religious cults of Europe and Asia, used a figure of a dragon biting its own tail. To symbolize the cyclic nature of time and the continuity of life.
4. To convince the people that their leaders had the dragonlike qualities of strength and goodness. Early Chinese emperors adopted the dragon as a symbol of imperial power.
5. Although you may not believe they ever existed, the image of dragons survives in art, fiction, religious stories, and dreams. In every corner of the world.

Exercise 26.3: Correcting Fragments

Correct each of the following fragments either by attaching it to a main clause or by rewriting the fragment as a complete sentence. Mark correct items with a C.

1. What explains the popularity of belief in dragons? In the absence of any scientific evidence that they ever existed.
2. Some scholars suggest that dragon stories originated from dim memories of prehistoric animals. And were passed on to later generations. Who embellished them to explain the history of their people.
3. The problem with this theory is that dinosaurs, pterodactyls, and similar animals that could have been the ancestors of dragon stories ceased to exist millions of years ago. Before human beings appeared on earth.
4. Others theorize that dragon stories represent a human psychological need. To imagine ourselves triumphant over enemies and evil forces.

5. The hero battles the many-headed monster threatening the beautiful young woman. Restores order to the world, and allows us to feel that we can control our lives, too.
6. Whatever the reason, dragons show a remarkable ability to survive. No matter how many have been killed, they are still with us.
7. Those of us who have not had the good fortune to see a live dragon can read about them. Or see them in our neighborhood theaters.
8. If books and films do not satisfy your urge to go dragon hunting. Find a damp, grassy, but rocky hillside remote from human habitation.
9. There, you may spot a particularly beautiful stone. That is really a dragon egg.
10. If you are patient, you may be witness to a dragon's hatching. Take a lunch. Sometimes it takes a thousand years.

27 Revise Run-on Sentences *run-on*

Like unintentional sentence fragments, run-on sentences are serious errors because they show that the writer is either careless or unaware of sentence structure.

In speaking, you quite naturally run clauses together, linking or separating them with breaths and pauses. In writing, you must use coordinating conjunctions or punctuation marks to link or separate clauses.

There are two types of run-on sentences: fused sentences and comma splices. When main clauses are not separated by a punctuation mark or joined by a coordinating conjunction, the result is a **fused sentence.**

FUSED SENTENCE	Spiritual insight produces one kind of knowledge (Main Clause) reading critically produces another. (Main Clause)

When main clauses are joined by a comma without a coordinating conjunction, the result is a **comma splice.**

	Main Clause / Main Clause
COMMA SPLICE	Meditation requires inactive sitting, reading critically requires active page turning.

Comma splices and fused sentences can be corrected in four ways.

1. Use a period to make two separate sentences.

◆ Some composers put notes down as rapidly as their hands can move across the paper, others write and rewrite slowly. [handwritten correction: paper. Others]

◆ In earlier centuries most composers were employed by churches or noblemen now they are usually employed by universities. [handwritten correction: noblemen. Now]

2. Use a semicolon to show a close relation between the main clauses.

◆ Some athletes work out four hours a day, others work out four days a week. [handwritten correction: day; others]

◆ For centuries, artists didn't just reimagine history sometimes they wrote its first draft. [handwritten correction: history; sometimes]

NOTE: When two main clauses are joined by a conjunctive adverb—such as *nevertheless, consequently, however,* or *therefore*—a semicolon must come before the clause containing the conjunctive adverb. (See note on conjunctive adverbs, 66g.)

◆ In earlier centuries most composers were employed by churches or noblemen however now they are usually employed by universities. [handwritten correction: noblemen; however, now]

3. Use a comma and a coordinating conjunction to show the appropriate relation between main clauses. (See coordinating conjunctions, 66g.)

◆ Painting history was drudgery, all too often it showed. [handwritten correction: drudgery, and all]

- She manages a career, a family, and the household assets, she is still the average woman.

4. Use a subordinating conjunction to introduce the less important clause. (See subordinating conjunctions, 66g.)

- Hart has an extensive collection of toy soldiers, he still spends more time searching for classic comic books.
- Mary Barkenwagen used to fear the unknown, now she faces challenges joyfully.

Exercise 27.1: Identify and Correct Run-on Sentences

Label each sentence as correct (C), fused (FS), or containing a comma splice (CS). Correct the fused sentences and comma splices in any of the four ways listed in the text.

1. Although she has studied for only two years, Laurie has already earned a black belt in aikido.
2. The meeting place for aikido practice is called a dojo the teacher is called sensei.
3. The students at Laurie's dojo work hard, many practice two or three hours every day.
4. Some of the movements are difficult to master however, everyone improves with practice.
5. Each movement is demonstrated by the sensei, he repeats the demonstration in slow motion.
6. Aikido is a fairly new martial art, it was developed in this century by Ueshiba Morihei of Japan.
7. The aikido form of self-defense involves neutralizing an attacker's power and causing him to become the victim of his own momentum.
8. Aikido students learn they do not need strength to repel an attack they use the attacker's strength against him.
9. Each training session begins with warm-up and stretching exercises then the students practice a movement until they can perform it in a smooth, seemingly effortless, motion.

10. By applying the physical and philosophical aspects of aikido to their daily lives, students learn self-defense and self-control.

Exercise 27.2: Correcting Run-on Sentences

Correct the ten comma splices or fused sentences in the following paragraph.

Jazz is an American form of music that is difficult to define there are many kinds of jazz. Almost any popular music can be played as a jazz piece such an interpretation gives it a special swing or jump. Jazz musicians take the basic idea of a piece they are playing and change it to fit a personal style personal touch is known as improvisation, consequently jazz musicians can speak directly to their audience. Jazz rhythms are syncopated they have a bounce to them stressing weak beats is at the heart of this rhythm. When jazz first started, it was always improvised. With the popularity of large dance bands that developed later, jazz arrangements were written down, at least for portions of the selection, nevertheless, individual performers improvised solos between the arranged sections. Arranging jazz is difficult it is almost impossible to write everything down on paper, individual performers must rely on their feelings at the moment to supply the rest. Each band has its own style, therefore a new performer must fit his or her personal style to the group.

28 Examine Subject-Verb Agreement *agr*

Remember: When a word refers to one person or thing it is *singular* in number. When a word refers to more than one person or thing, it is *plural* in number.

Singular	Plural
person	people
woman	women
ox	oxen
this	these
either	both
he, she, it	they

A verb must always agree with its subject in number. Singular subjects take singular verbs.

> A jet lands every four minutes.
> The winner was carried from the field.

Plural subjects take plural verbs.

> Jets land every four minutes.
> The winners were carried from the field.

When a verb immediately follows a subject, you will probably have little trouble making them agree. But sometimes you'll write a sentence that is a little more tricky. Either a subject or its number will be hard to identify.

28a Make verbs agree with their subjects even when words intervene.

Words coming between a verb and its subject often obscure an agreement error. Usually these words will modify a subject and include a noun that seems to be the subject but is not. By reading the sentence without the modifying words, you will usually be able to spot the agreement error.

- Archery [as practiced by Zen masters] require^s concentration.
- The detectives [working with the witness] ~~was~~ ^were expected to solve the theft immediately.

Expressions such as *together with, as well as, in addition to, accompanied by,* and *along with* do not make a singular noun plural.

- The major [accompanied by four scouts] ~~are~~ ^was traveling west.

28b Examine compound subjects to determine if they take a plural or a singular verb.

When two or more subjects are joined by a coordinating conjunction such as *and* and *or,* they form a compound subject. Compound subjects joined by *and* usually take a plural verb.

- Spiritual growth and psychological insight among artists ~~is~~ ^are not uncommon.

An exception to this guideline comes when the parts of a compound subject function as a single idea or refer to a single person or thing. In these cases the subject should take a singular verb.

◆ Meat and potatoes, once a staple of American cuisine, ~~are~~ is banished from low-fat diets.

◆ The Stars and Stripes wave‸s over the battlefield.

When a compound subject is preceded by *each* or *every,* the verb should be singular. Although these words refer to more than one, they imply consideration of one at a time. And when a compound subject is followed by *each,* the verb is singular, too.

◆ Every hotel, bed and breakfast, and campground ~~are~~ is filled.

◆ Diplomacy and threat each require‸s skilled execution.

When a compound subject is joined by *or* or *nor,* make the verb agree with the part of the subject nearer to verb.

◆ The James Boys or Billy the Kid ~~are~~ is the Wild West's most written about outlaw~~s~~.

Even though the preceding sentence is now correct, it does not sound right. Better to correct such a sentence by rearranging the order of the compound subject so it rings truer in a reader's mind: *Billy the Kid or the James Boys are the Wild West's most written about outlaws.*

◆ Neither the atomic bomb nor space flights ~~has~~ have influenced human events as powerfully as the Bill of Rights.

28c Generally, use singular verbs with indefinite pronouns as subjects.

Indefinite pronouns refer to unspecified subjects. Most indefinite pronouns—such as *everyone, someone, no one, everything, anybody, neither,* and *something*—are singular and take singular verbs.

◆ Most everyone in Utah support‸s keeping 22 million acres of wilderness.

◆ Neither partner, GM nor IBM, ~~are~~ is discussing the agreement.

A few indefinite pronouns—such as *all, any, none,* and *some*—may be singular or plural. Whether you use a singular or a plural verb depends on the number of the noun that the indefinite pronoun refers to.

◆ The judge announced that all of the jury ~~was~~ were present.

◆ The judge said that all of the report ~~were~~ was helpful.

28d Use singular or plural verbs with collective nouns depending on how the nouns are used and with nouns ending in *-s.*

Collective nouns—such as *army, audience, class, committee, faculty, group, herd, public,* and *team*—are singular even though they name groups of individuals. When referring to a group as a single unit, a collective noun takes a singular verb.

◆ The American public eventually sees the truth.

When you wish to draw attention to individual members of the group, a collective noun will take a plural verb.

◆ The faculty argue~~s~~ among themselves in department meetings.

Treat units of measurement like singular collective nouns when they refer to a single unit. *By mid-game one-third of the crowd was gone. Five dollars is the cost of a ticket.*

Most nouns that are plural in form but singular in meaning take singular verbs. Nouns such as *athletics, civics, economics, mathematics, measles, mumps, news, physics,* and *species* are singular and take singular verbs.

◆ Mumps in adults ~~are~~ is dangerous.

Words like *trousers* and *scissors* are regarded as plural and take plural verbs, except when used after *pair.*

◆ This pair of socks ~~have~~ has holes in the toes.

28e Examine miscellaneous subject-verb agreement problems.

A verb must agree with its subject even when the subject follows the verb. Verbs generally follow subjects. When the subject-verb word order is reversed, examine the sentence to see that the subject and verb agree.

- ◆ In the back of his mind ~~is~~ are the pain of abuse and the joy of recovery.

Do not mistake the expletives *there* and *here* for subjects. They merely signal that the subject follows the verb.

There are several strong points in his argument.

Be sure the verb following *who, which,* and *that* agrees with its subject. *Who, which,* and *that* are relative pronouns; the words they refer to are called *antecedents.* When a relative pronoun serves as a subject, the verb must agree with the pronoun's antecedent.

- ◆ Wind that blows over the peaks creates massive snow plumes.

In a sentence that uses *one of the,* examine its meaning to determine if the verb should be singular or plural.

- ◆ He is one of the critics who ~~is~~ are joining the argument.

The antecedent of *who* is *critics,* not *one.*

- ◆ He is the only one of the critics who cares.

The antecedent of *who* is *one.*

Use a singular verb when its subject is a title or words named as words.

- ◆ *Six Days and Seven Nights* seems to last at least that long.
- ◆ *Chitlins* refers to pig intestines used as food.

Exercise 28.1: Correct Subject-Verb Agreement Errors

In the following sentences, correct any errors in subject and verb agreement. If you find a correct sentence, mark it with a C.

1. A sum of over $400 million were spent to turn the Meadowlands marsh in New Jersey into a sports and entertainment complex.
2. Every domestic car and every imported car are required to pass the same safety inspection.
3. The committee are expected to announce the decision today.
4. Please bring me the pair of blue shorts that is hanging in the bathroom.
5. If you look at the map, you will see there is three different routes the mail carrier have to cover each day.
6. Our children is the only hope we have for the future.
7. The students or the teacher order the theater tickets every month.
8. All of the seventeen-page information booklet are required reading.
9. The senator commented that politics are the art of the possible.
10. Where is the pants I bought last weekend?
11. The only chance we have to win rest with the defensive linemen.
12. Managers respect the advice of employees who work hard.
13. Every one of the journalism students want to attend the conference.
14. Ham and eggs are a popular American breakfast.
15. Here are a list of all the printing shops in our area.
16. *California Classics* by Lawrence Clark Powell are interesting reading.
17. The police officer as well as the onlookers were applauding the little girl's performance.
18. All the performers are from Brazil, and all the musical selections have a Latin beat.
19. The group argue about the fund-raising activities hour after hour.
20. Jerry Hopkins and his neighbors enjoys the peaceful summer evenings at the lake.

Exercise 28.2: Correct Subject-Verb Agreement Errors

In the following paragraph, correct the errors in subject and verb agreement.

Computerized psychological testing services around the country is gaining widespread use. A report published in recent months indicate that almost everybody taking the tests are pleased by the method. The automated testing proceeds in the following fashion: Sitting before a TV-like screen, a patient answers a group of questions that demands true/false responses or offers multiple-choice answers. Either a psychiatrist or a clinician who has been trained in psychiatry sit in another room and score the data and analyze the results. Immediately following the test, doctor and patient meets to discuss the outcome and plans an initial treatment. Some critics of computerized testing claim the testing dehumanizes the doctor-patient relationship, but neither doctors using the method nor patients undergoing the process seem to agree with the critics.

29 Examine Pronoun-Antecedent Agreement *pron agr*

The antecedent of a pronoun is the word or words a pronoun refers to. An antecedent and its pronoun must agree whether they are singular or plural.

SINGULAR	The *director* took *her* cinematographer to Peru.
PLURAL	The *writers* kept working at *their* computers.

29a Examine compound antecedents with care to determine whether to use a plural or singular pronoun.

For antecedents joined by *and,* use a plural pronoun.

Hayes and King rearranged *their* priorities.

For compound plural or singular antecedents joined by *or* or *nor,* use a pronoun that agrees with the nearest antecedent.

◆ Once a year, the players or the coach host^s^ a banquet at their favorite restaurant.

When sentences that follow this convention sound awkward or puzzling, writers usually recast them.

◆ Once a year, ~~the players or~~ the coach ^or the players^ host a banquet at their favorite restaurant.

29b Generally, use a singular pronoun to refer to an indefinite pronoun that functions as an antecedent.

Indefinite pronouns refer to nonspecific persons or things.

anybody	either	everything	no one
anyone	everybody	neither	someone
each	everyone	none	something

Although they seem to be plural, they should be treated as singular antecedents in writing.

◆ Every one of the women donated time to ~~their~~ ^her^ favorite charities.

◆ Everybody passing through the office offered ~~their~~ ^his^ advice.

Traditional grammar calls for the use of the masculine pronoun *his (he)* to refer to persons of either sex when the gender of the antecedent is unknown. This practice, however, reflects a sexual bias in English. To offset the bias, you may use *his or her (he or she)* in place of a masculine pronoun. Or you may rewrite the sentence to reflect the same meaning.

◆ Everybody passing through the office offered his ^or her^ advice.

◆ Everybody passing through the office offered ~~his~~ advice.

29c Generally, use a singular pronoun to refer to collective nouns.

Collective pronouns include words such as *army, audience, class, committee, group, herd, jury, public,* and *team.* Even though they identify a class or a group with many members, collective nouns are usually singular because the members are seen as acting as a single unit.

◆ The jury of five women and seven men spoke with one voice. ~~They~~ ^It^ declared the defendant guilty as charged.

If a passage makes clear that the members of a group are acting individually, then use a plural pronoun.

- ◆ The jury members could not agree. ~~It~~ They deliberated for three days before the judge declared a mistrial.

29d Use a singular pronoun to refer to a generic noun.

Generic nouns refer to typical members of a group. They are always singular.

- ◆ A law student must study hours every night if ~~they are~~ he or she is to graduate.

Such a sentence can also be recast to reflect the same meaning.

- ◆ ~~A~~ Law students must study hours every night if they are to graduate.
- ◆ ~~A~~ Law students must study hours every night ~~if they are~~ to graduate.

29e Use accurate pronouns with *who, whom, which,* and *that.*

Who refers to persons and sometimes to animals that have been named in the passage.

> *Armando, who* lives in New Mexico, once worked as a guide to the Carlsbad Caverns.
>
> *Lassie* was the first Hollywood dog *who* had a fan club.

Which refers to things or places and unnamed animals.

> *Darby, which* has become a yuppie retreat, is located on the Bitter Root River in Montana.
>
> Tony's *cat, which* is highly curious, disappeared for two weeks.

Whose, the possessive form of *who,* can be used to refer to animals and things to avoid awkward constructions using *of which.*

◆ This is a riddle ~~the~~ whose answer ~~of which~~ no longer interests me.

◆ *Okay* is a word ~~the~~ whose origin ~~of which~~ puzzles linguists.

That also refers to things or places, unnamed animals, and sometimes to persons when they are collective or anonymous.

> The dry *hills that* border Los Angeles ignite when the Santa Ana winds sweep Southern California.
>
> The *earthquake faults that* run under Los Angeles are dangerously active.

COMPUTER CLINIC

Grammar Checkers and Sentence Errors

Grammar-checking features may, or may not, raise red flags—and that's the problem you face when using one. Too often they fail to identify errors, and too often the errors they identify are actually correct.

- Grammar checkers do not flag errors in parallel structure because computers cannot assess whether ideas are parallel in meaning.
- Grammar checkers cannot identify most missing words, although they can sometimes flag some missing verbs and articles.
- Grammar checkers cannot flag errors in modifiers (such as dangling modifiers).
- Grammar checkers cannot flag shifts in verb tense, mood, or voice.
- Grammar checkers tend to flag most sentence fragments and run-on sentences but not all of them. Sometimes they flag correct sentences as incorrect.

The best practice is to develop your own understanding of common sentence errors. Then you can serve as your own grammar checker.

Exercise 29.1: Make Antecedents and Pronouns Agree

Correct the antecedent-pronoun errors in each of the following sentences. If a sentence is correct, indicate so with a C.

1. Pearl's kitten Betsy is the one that hid under the steps.
2. Either the ranger or the campers will report the theft.

3. Sue and Beta want to change hers.
4. Anyone which cares about their grades will study every day.
5. Both groups brought its own equipment.
6. Every family in our neighborhood takes good care of their yard.
7. A skier must select his equipment carefully.
8. Neither the sales force nor the manager will receive their instructions on time.
9. Everyone passed their examinations.
10. *Humongous* is a word the origin of which is lost.

Exercise 29.2: Make Antecedents and Pronouns Agree

Rewrite the following sentences according to the directions in brackets. Be sure to make all the changes necessary to keep the agreement of pronouns and antecedents correct.

1. The catalog and the schedule of classes contain the registration information you are seeking. [Change *and* to *or*.]
2. The counselors agree that English composition should be taken in the first year of college. [Change *The counselors* to *Each counselor*.]
3. Each year the dean or the president has her portrait painted by an outstanding art student. [Change *or* to *and*.]
4. The board of trustees submitted its proposals yesterday. [Change *The board of trustees* to *Some members of the board of trustees*.]
5. Someone attending the mother-and-daughter banquet forgot her coat. [Change *mother-and-daughter* to *father-and-son*.]
6. Either the crew or the rugby team uses the weight room on Monday afternoons. [Change *Either . . . or* to *and*.]
7. The class, which usually meets on Wednesday, forgot that it had agreed to meet on Saturday. [Change *The class* to *Some class members*.]
8. By using attractive visual displays, the business manager or the budget committee chairman can communicate his plans for spending tax money wisely. [Change *budget committee chairman* to *members of the budget committee*.]

9. The bear mascot, which is paraded at all home games, was donated to the university by the game wardens' association. [Change *The bear mascot* to *Bruno, the bear mascot.*]
10. Students who study every evening will perform well on examinations. [Change *Students* to *Anyone.*]

30 Check Pronoun Reference *ref*

Pronoun reference refers to the relation between a pronoun and its antecedent. (See antecedent, 66b; agreement of pronoun and antecedent, Chapter 29.) If the pronoun reference is unclear, the sentence will confuse or misinform a reader.

30a Avoid using a pronoun to make a broad reference to an entire sentence or clause.

Sometimes inexperienced writers use *this, that,* or *it* to refer to an entire sentence or clause, which can create confusion. Rewrite such references or use a summary noun for clarification.

- ~~Mystery is what~~ [I needed the sense of mystery] I felt during my nightly walks through the streets of Paris. ~~That is what I needed.~~
- Mystery is what I felt during my nightly walks through the streets of Paris. ~~That~~ [This feeling] is what I needed.
- Good managers know when to delegate responsibility. This [knowledge] allows them to concentrate on the broader aspects of a project.
- Good managers know when to delegate responsibility, [which] ~~This~~ allows them to concentrate on the broader aspects of a project.

30b Avoid the indefinite use of *it, they,* and *you.*

In conversation *it* and *they* are often used to make vague reference to people or situations. In writing, use more precise identification.

VAGUE	*It* is said that gold prices are rising.
CLEAR	Today's newspaper predicted that gold prices will rise before next year.
VAGUE	*They* said it would rain tomorrow.
CLEAR	The KTTV weather forecaster predicts rain.

You is also commonly used in conversation to refer vaguely to people in general. In writing, however, use the more formal *one* or the less formal *a person* or *people. You* should be used as a personal pronoun.

VAGUE	When traveling in a foreign country, *you* should respect local customs.
CLEAR	When traveling in a foreign country, a person should respect local customs.

The use of *you* to refer to "you, the reader" is perfectly appropriate in all but the most formal writing.

> If *you* plan to become a history teacher, *you* should begin *your* education by reading Herodotus.

30c Make a pronoun refer clearly to one antecedent.

CONFUSING	After Yoshi studied with Kim for a week, she discovered that she still did not understand calculus.
CLEAR	After studying with Kim for a week, Yoshi discovered that Kim did not understand calculus.
CONFUSING	After Carlos bought the shingles and the boards, he discovered they were full of termites.
CLEAR	After Carlos bought the shingles and the boards, he discovered the shingles were full of termites.
CLEAR	After Carlos bought the shingles and the boards, he discovered the boards were full of termites.
CLEAR	After Carlos bought the shingles and the boards, he discovered that both were full of termites.

30d Use pronouns ending in *-self* or *-selves* only to refer to another word in the sentence.

Stacy returned the book to the library *herself.*
People who expect riches without effort are fooling *themselves.*

Avoid using pronouns ending in *-self* or *-selves* in place of a grammatically correct pronoun.

◆ Between you and ~~myself~~ me, I think our team will win.

Exercise 30.1: Correct Faulty Pronoun References

Correct the faulty pronoun references in the following sentences. You may need to change words or rewrite entire sentences. For example:

◆ Mary decided to live with Liz because ~~her~~ Liz's roommate had moved out.

1. Jason gave the notes to Raul that he had taken during the lecture.
2. After hours of lessons, he learned to water-ski, but this didn't impress his girlfriend.
3. I heard they're planning to widen the expressway to eight lanes.
4. Among Jose, you, and myself, the secret will be safe, but if we tell Alberto, we will hurt ourselves.
5. Joe Louis and Rocky Marciano were two great heavyweight boxing champions; however, after Marciano beat him in 1950, he never fought as well again.
6. I sometimes buy clothes at discount stores because they are good values.
7. As the tiny robot approached the cat it started hissing loudly.
8. The enchiladas are for ourselves and the fajitas are for them.
9. Tonya survived the three-car accident, which is evidence of her luck.
10. John changed his major and then had to drop all his classes. That's typical.

Exercise 30.2: Correcting Faulty Pronoun Reference

Rewrite the following sentences to correct faulty pronoun reference.

1. Lena saw a television movie and ate a TV dinner. She enjoyed that.
2. After she saw the movie, she turned it off.
3. Barbara combed her hair and brushed her teeth. She did it every night.
4. It was going to be cold tomorrow, they said.
5. Rita took her coat and hat from the closet and put it on the couch.
6. Although Al had neither read the novel nor seen the TV movie, he said that he might do it.
7. When you drive on a dark night in the rain, it can be dangerous.
8. They said that they will disconnect our telephone if we do not pay our bill.
9. After Carole and Joanne shared an apartment for a year, she moved.
10. I blame me for not turning it off before the generator's engine ran out.

31 Use Appropriate Pronoun Case *case*

The **case** of nouns and pronouns indicates how the words function in a sentence. Nouns and most pronouns have only two case forms (that is, the spelling of the word when it is used in a particular case): the plain form (*day, someone*) and the possessive form (*day's, someone's*).

The pronouns *I, we, he, she, they,* and *who* have three different case forms: the subjective form, the objective form, and the possessive form.

The pronouns *you* and *it* have one form for both the subjective and the objective case and a different form for the possessive case. (See possessive pronouns, 66a.)

	Subjective	Objective	Possessive
Personal Pronouns			
singular			
First person	I	me	my, mine
Second person	you	you	your, yours
Third person	he, she, it	him, her, it	his, her, hers, its
plural			
First person	we	us	our, ours
Second person	you	you	your, yours
Third person	they	them	their, theirs
Relative or Interrogative Pronouns			
singular	who	whom	whose
plural	who	whom	whose

31a Use the subjective case of pronouns for subjects and for predicate nominatives.

Alicia and *I* went shopping. [Subject]

Since Marcus and *he* returned to Detroit, *she* has been lonely. [Subjects]

The scouts who had the most badges were Salvador and *he*. [Predicate nominative]

NOTE: When the subject is a compound, as in *Alicia and I* and *Marcus and he*, beginning writers sometimes become confused about the selection of a pronoun. They would not write *Me went shopping*, but they might write *Alicia and me went shopping*. To avoid this error with compound subjects that include pronouns, try reading each subject separately with the verb.

In speech it is common practice to use the objective forms of personal pronouns as predicate nominatives in expressions beginning with *it is* or *it's: It's me, It is him, It's us, It's them*. Such use of the objective form is unacceptable in writing. Instead use the appropriate subjective pronoun, *It is I, It is he, It is we*, and *It is they*. By carefully examining pronoun use, you will avoid making this common pronoun error. (See linking verb, 66c.)

31b Use the objective case when pronouns are direct objects, indirect objects, and objects of a preposition.

Bernie met Naomi and *me* at the museum. [Direct object]

The doorman gave *us* a map of the exhibits. [Indirect object]

A man dressed in a caveman costume sat by *me* on the bench. [Object of a preposition]

Exercise 31.1: Using Subjective and Objective Pronouns

For each of the following sentences, select the correct pronoun from the pair in parentheses. Identify each selected pronoun as a subject (S), a predicate nominative (PN), a direct object (DO), an indirect object (IO), or an object of a preposition (OP).

1. The lecture on Etruscan pottery interested Nguyen and (*I, me*).
2. The ones who laughed the most were Monica and (*she, her*).
3. I know I blushed when Sonia and (*she, her*) sat near (*we, us*).
4. That group's achievement is impressive, but the faculty expected (*they, them*) to excel.
5. Jorge wanted to use the car, so I gave (*he, him*) the keys.

31c Use the appropriate case when the pronoun *we* or *us* comes before a noun.

If the pronoun functions as a subject, use *we.*

We linguists meet once a year at a major university. [We meet.]

If the pronoun functions as an object, use *us.*

A number of us mycologists regularly collect mushrooms in the foothills. [A number of us collect.]

31d When a pronoun is used as an appositive, its case depends on the function of the word it refers to.

Two chemistry majors, Margarita and *he,* won science foundation awards. [The pronoun refers to *majors,* the subject of the sentence, so it is in the subjective case.]

Science foundation awards received by two chemistry majors, Margarita and him, highlighted the program. [*Majors* is now the object of the preposition *by*, so the pronoun is in the objective case.]

Exercise 31.2: Using Proper Pronoun Case

Select the correct pronoun in each of the following sentences.

1. The artists, (*she, her*) and Shawn, will be at the festival booth all day.
2. (*We, Us*) customers are waiting for the festival to begin.
3. Many of (*we, us*) have been here since seven this morning.
4. The stormy weather ruined the day for the artists, Shawn and (*she, her*).
5. Nevertheless, (*we, us*) early birds enjoyed the chance to see the exhibits.

31e In elliptical, or incomplete, comparisons following *than* or *as,* the case of the pronoun depends on the meaning of the sentence.

In comparisons, *than* and *as* often introduce incomplete comparisons. The case of the pronoun in such constructions depends on how the incomplete clause would be completed.

Use the subjective case when the pronoun functions as the subject of the omitted clause.

I have been studying Spanish longer than *they* [have been studying Spanish].

She works as hard on projects as *he* [works on projects].

Use the objective case when the pronoun functions as the object in the omitted clause.

For information, I rely on him more than [I rely on] *her.*
I see Ngoc as much as [I see] *him.*

31f Use the objective case for pronouns that are subjects or objects of infinitives.

The attorney considered *him* to be a prime suspect. [Subject of infinitive]

He tried to trap *him* with tough questions. [Object of infinitive]

31g Usually use the possessive case of a pronoun or noun preceding a gerund.

A gerund is the present participle of a verb used as a noun. (See gerunds and gerund phrases, 68.)

What was the reason for his appearing tonight? [*His* modifies the gerund *appearing.*]

Dr. Rodriguez's running for office pleased us all. [*Dr. Rodriguez's* modifies the gerund *running.*]

The possessive is not used when the present participle serves as an adjective. (See present participles, 68d.)

The crowd watched him tottering on the tightrope. [*Tottering* is a present participle used as an adjective modifying *him.*]

I often hear Tom talking in his sleep. [*Talking* is a present participle used as an adjective modifying *Tom.*]

Avoid using the possessive with a gerund when doing so creates an awkward construction.

AWKWARD I am pleased about Nadeem's cooking dinner.

REVISED I am pleased about Nadeem cooking dinner.

BETTER I am pleased that Nadeem is cooking dinner.

Exercise 31.3: Using Proper Pronoun Case

Select the correct pronoun for each of the following sentences.

1. The president ordered (*he, him, his*) to be ready at dawn.
2. Do you know the reason for (*he, him, his*) erratic driving?
3. Bok Hee has been more generous than (*they, them, their*).
4. The whole group watched (*he, him, his*) cooking the quesadillas.
5. We wanted to prove (*he, him, his*) wrong.

31h The case of the pronoun *who* is determined by its function in its own clause.

You can usually determine which case to use in interrogative sentences by answering the question the sentence poses.

> *Who* led England to victory? [The prime minister led England to victory: subject.]
>
> *Whom* shall we hold responsible? [We shall hold her responsible: direct object.]
>
> *Whom* is the letter addressed to? [The letter is addressed to her: object of the preposition *to*.]

In dependent clauses use *who* or *whoever* for all subjects; use *whom* or *whomever* for all objects. The case of the pronoun depends only on its function within the clause, not on the function of the clause in the sentence.

> The Sisters of Mercy give help to *whoever* requests it. [*Whoever* is the subject of the clause *whoever requests it.* The entire clause is the object of the preposition *to*.]
>
> I do not remember *whom* I met at the party. [*Whom* is the direct object of *met.* The entire clause *whom I met at the party* is the direct object of the verb *do remember.*]

To determine whether to use *who, whom, whoever,* or *whomever,* substitute a personal pronoun for the relative pronoun. The case of the personal pronoun is the correct case for the relative pronoun. If necessary, change the word order of the clause.

> I do not recall (who, whom) I lent the book to.
> I lent the book to him (or her). [Objective case]

Therefore, *whom* is the correct relative pronoun:

> I do not recall *whom* I lent the book to.

Sometimes a dependent clause includes an expression such as *I think* or *he said.*

> She is the woman (who, whom) he said called last night.

To decide between *who* and *whom* in such a construction, repeat the sentence without the intervening expression.

> She is the woman *who* called last night.

Exercise 31.4: Using *Who* and *Whom*

Select the correct pronoun in each of the following sentences.

1. The one-hundred-dollar prize will be given to (*whoever, whomever*) creates the most beautiful kite.
2. (*Who, Whom*) shall I file my report with?
3. (*Who, Whom*) will clean the chalkboards?
4. The honor goes to (*whoever, whomever*) I select.
5. The master is loved most by those (*who, whom*) share his beliefs.

32 Select Accurate Verb Forms and Tense *verb*

Every verb has three principal forms: the infinitive (the plain form of the verb), the past, and the past participle.

Verb Forms

INFINITIVE	PAST	PAST PARTICIPLE
dance	danced	danced

The **infinitive** form of the verb usually appears in combination with *to,* forming a verbal that functions as a noun, an adjective, or an adverb (see 68c). A **participle** is a verbal that functions as an adjective, an adverb, or a part of a verb phrase (see 68d).

All verbs form the **present participle** by adding *-ing* to the infinitive form. Neither a present participle nor a past participle can function as the verb in a sentence unless it is combined with one or more helping verbs.

Any verb may be combined with helping (or auxiliary) verbs to express time relations and other meanings. *Shall* and *will; have, has,* and *had; do, does,* and *did;* and forms of the verb *be* (*am, are, is, was, were, been, being*) are helping verbs used to indicate time and voice. (See tense, 32a; voice, Chapter 34.) *Can, could, may, might, must, ought, shall, should, will,* and *would* are helping verbs used to indicate necessity, obligation, permission, or possibility.

You *could* learn to ski.
You *must* attend.
She *should* know better.

Verbs have either regular or irregular forms. A regular verb forms its past and past participle by adding *-d* or *-ed* to the infinitive.

INFINITIVE	PAST	PAST PARTICIPLE
live	lived	lived
jump	jumped	jumped

An **irregular verb** forms its past and past participle in a different way from regular verbs. This difference may involve a change in spelling or no change at all from the infinitive form. Spelling changes usually involve a change in vowels or the addition of an *-n* or *-en* ending.

INFINITIVE	PAST	PAST PARTICIPLE
swim	swam	swum
throw	threw	thrown
hit	hit	hit

The major difficulty you will confront in the use of irregular verbs is in selecting the correct past or past participle form. When in doubt, consult a dictionary. If a verb is regular, the dictionary does not include the past and past participle. If the verb is irregular, the dictionary includes the irregular forms.

IRREGULAR VERBS

INFINITIVE	PAST	PAST PARTICIPLE
begin	began	begun
bite	bit	bitten
blow	blew	blown
break	broke	broken
bring	brought	brought
catch	caught	caught
choose	chose	chosen
come	came	come
creep	crept	crept
dig	dug	dug
dive	dived or dove	dived
do	did	done
draw	drew	drawn
dream	dreamed or dreamt	dreamed or dreamt

drink	drank	drunk
drive	drove	driven
eat	ate	eaten
fall	fell	fallen
feel	felt	felt
find	found	found
fit	fit or fitted	fit or fitted
fling	flung	flung
fly	flew	flown
fly (baseball)	flied	flied
forbid	forbade or forbad	forbidden
forget	forgot	forgotten or forgot
get	got	got or gotten
go	went	gone
hurt	hurt	hurt
know	knew	known
lay (place or put)	laid	laid
lead	led	led
lend	lent	lent
lie (recline)	lay	lain
light	lighted or lit	lighted or lit
lose	lost	lost
pay	paid	paid
ride	rode	ridden
rise	rose	risen
run	ran	run
say	said	said
see	saw	seen
set (place or put)	set	set
shine	shone or shined	shone or shined
shoot	shot	shot
sing	sang or sung	sung
sink	sank or sunk	sunk
sit (take a seat)	sat	sat
sleep	slept	slept
steal	stole	stolen
sting	stung	stung
swim	swam	swum
tear	tore	torn
throw	threw	thrown
wear	wore	worn
win	won	won
write	wrote	written

Exercise 32.1: Practice Using Irregular Verbs

Working with another student, test yourself on the principal forms of the irregular verbs in the list above.

Exercise 32.2: Look Up Irregular Verbs

Use a dictionary to determine the correct forms of the irregular verbs necessary to complete each sentence.

1. We knew the bananas __________ a great deal, but we had __________ to love them. (*cost, grow*)
2. By the time we __________ for the airport, he had __________ less nervous. (*leave, become*)
3. The carpenters had __________ a slide and __________ it to the children. (*build, give*)
4. We had __________ our views, but they had not __________ them. (*speak, hear*)
5. I had just __________ the window when the sky __________ up. (*shut, light*)

Verb Tense

Verb forms change to show the time of the action they express. The change in time (past, present, or future) is called *tense.*

32a The present tense expresses action about something occurring now, at the present time.

I *believe* you.
The light from below *creates* huge shadows on the wall.

The present tense also serves some special functions in writing: Use the present tense to state a general truth or fact.

Automobiles *require* fuel.
A yard *equals* thirty-six inches.

Use the present tense to state what a writer does in his or her written work or to describe a character's activities in a written work.

Tonya *argues* for mandatory installation of air bags.
The hero *discovers* the truth about the Lost Canyon Mine.

Use the present tense to describe elements in artistic works.

In *Mishima,* Eiko Ishioka's designs *intrigue* the audience.

The nonsensical conversation in Philip's stories *makes* readers uncomfortable.

Use the present tense to state habitual action.

She *studies* in the library every day.
Jeff always *keeps* his car sparkling clean.

Use the infinitive form with *do* to create emphasis.

I *do get up* early!

NOTE: In all tenses you can show continuing action by using the **progressive tense,** which is the present participle of the verb together with a form of the helping verb *be.*

Li-Ching *is attending* Kettler College.

32b The past tense expresses action that occurred in the past but did not continue into the present.

I *slipped* on the icy street several times.
I *was slipping* on the ice when he grabbed my arm.

Use the infinitive form with *did* to create an emphatic form.

I *did slip* on the ice.

NOTE: Past action may be shown in other ways.

I *used to slip* on the icy streets.

32c The future tense expresses action about something that will happen in the future.

The visitors from Oxford *will debate* four of our prelaw students next week.

The visitors from Oxford *will be debating* four of our prelaw students next week.

NOTE: Future action may be shown in other ways.

The visitors from Oxford *are going* to debate four of our prelaw students next week.

The visitors from Oxford and four of our prelaw students *are* about to debate.

32d The present perfect tense expresses action occurring at no definite time in the past or action occurring in the past and continuing into the present.

Environmentalists *have enlisted* the help of sensitive businesspeople. [The action has not occurred at a specific time in the past.]

Environmentalists *have been enlisting* the help of sensitive businesspeople. [The progressive form indicates that the past action continues into the present.]

32e The past perfect tense expresses action completed in the past before another past action occurred.

I *had flown* in a glider before I flew in a single-engine Cessna. [Flying in the glider preceded flying in the Cessna.]

After I *had been flying* for three months, I gave it up. [Flying for three months preceded giving it up.]

32f The future perfect tense expresses action that will be completed in the future before another action occurs.

By the end of the year 2005, the Galaxy Probe *will have traveled* through space for fifteen years.

By the end of the year 2005, the Galaxy Probe *will have been traveling* through space for fifteen years.

32g Use an appropriate sequence of verb tenses.

Sequence of verb tenses refers to the time relation expressed by verbs in main clauses and verbs in dependent clauses, infinitives, or participles. In the sentence *The crowd cheered when he served an ace,* the past tense of the verb *cheer* (*cheered*) is in sequence with the past tense of the verb *serve* (*served*). (See subordinate clauses, 69b; verbals and verbal phrases, pp. 450–453.)

Dependent Clauses

When the verb in the main clause of a complex sentence is in any tense other than the past or past perfect, make the verb tense in the dependent clause consistent with the meaning of the sentence.

> Our political leaders hope that the federal budget will be balanced by the year 2006. [The sequence moves from the present tense, *hope,* in the main clause to the future tense, *will be balanced,* in the dependent clause.]
>
> The president of the company will visit our department after she has met with the board. [The sequence moves from the future tense, *will visit,* in the main clause to the present perfect tense, *has met,* in the dependent clause.]
>
> Kayla will change her major because she thinks that the computer field will soon be too crowded. [The sequence moves from the future tense, *will change,* in the main clause to the present tense, *thinks,* and the future tense, *will be,* in the dependent clauses.]

When the verb in the main clause is in the past or past perfect tense, use the past or past perfect tense in the dependent clause, except when the dependent clause is a general truth.

> The pianist blushed as the audience cheered. [Past tense in both the main clause and the dependent clause]
>
> The scout troop had sold a hundred coupons before the Christmas trees even arrived. [Past perfect tense in the main clause and past tense in the dependent clause]
>
> The visitors from Taiwan soon learned that Americans love Chinese food. [Although the verb in the main clause is in the past tense, the verb in the dependent clause is in the present tense because *Americans love Chinese food* is a general truth not related to a specific time.]

Infinitives

Use the **present infinitive,** which is composed of the plain form of the verb preceded by *to* (as in *to dance, to sing, to grow*), to express action that takes place at the same time as or later than that of the verb in the main clause. Use the **present perfect infinitive,** which is composed of *to have* followed by a past participle (as in *to have danced, to have sung, to have grown*), to express action that takes place before that of the verb in the main clause. (See infinitives, 68c.)

> Last July I wanted to attend summer school. [Present infinitive: Action takes place at the same time as that of the main verb, *wanted.*]
>
> They hoped to go. They hope to go. [Present infinitive: Action takes place at a time later than the main verbs, *hoped* and *hope.*]
>
> Maurice would like to have entered last week's race. [Present perfect infinitive: Action takes place before that of the main verb, *would like.* Note that *to enter,* the present infinitive, is not the correct form.]
>
> Maurice would have liked to enter last week's race. [Present infinitive: Action takes place at the same time as that of the main verb, *would have liked.*]

Participles

Use the **present participle** to express action that takes place at the same time as that of the main verb. Use the **past participle** or the **present perfect participle** to express action that takes place earlier than that of the main verb. (See present participle, 68d.)

> Running in the woods, he felt free of worries. [Present participle: The running occurs at the same time as the feeling.]
>
> Encouraged by friends, Pat decided to attend college. [Past participle: The encouragement took place before the decision.]
>
> Having danced all night, Maria slept past noon. [Present perfect participle: The dancing took place before the sleeping.]

Exercise 32.3: Use Correct Verb Forms

Select the verb form that is in sequence with the other verb or verbs in each of the following sentences.

1. The sudden ringing of the alarm clock reminded me that I (*have, had*) an appointment with the dentist in a few hours.
2. I am confident that I (*can, could*) pass the next history test.

3. I know that she will call me if she (*is, will be*) visiting the campus on her next trip.
4. Turning the corner to Rose Street, the mail carrier remembered that she (*had been, was*) bitten by a dog on this street.
5. (*Finishing, Having finished*) his shopping, Larry went to the Red Lion Inn for lunch.
6. The chief engineer will conduct further tests himself because he (*doubts, doubted*) that the first report (*is, was*) accurate.
7. Harold wrote his library report on Alice Walker because he (*knows, knew*) she (*wrote, writes*) with compassion and insight.
8. Rosa told Felipe that she (*will be, would be*) studying in the library last Friday.
9. His experiments proved that water (*boiled, boils*) at 212° F.
10. When I saw the movie, I thought that I (*will be, would be*) more frightened than I (*had been, was*).

Exercise 32.4: Practicing Past Tense

Rewrite the following paragraph as if you were living in the twenty-second century and the events had happened in the past. Change verb tenses wherever necessary. Your opening sentence will read:

> Years ago throughout Orange County, visitors seemed unable to tell where fantasy ended and real life began.
>
> Throughout Orange County, visitors seem unable to tell where fantasy ends and real life begins. One reason is theme architecture, which accounts for perhaps as much as 60 percent of the county's buildings. Within the county you can find triplex homes that look like English Tudor mansions, restaurants that look like a French chateau or a Mississippi riverboat, and a motel that resembles a Persian mosque. Theme architecture adds a dash of Disneyland to most neighborhoods. Visitors can travel from one exotic land to another within a few blocks. The variety bewilders visitors, but local residents take it in stride. The themes divide into several categories. Some homeowners prefer a Spanish mission style. Others choose the Mediterranean look. Still others want Tudor, Cape Cod, or plantation designs. One aspect of all this diversity is tragically real: As developers hack down the orange groves, they replace the trees with glittering fantasy structures.

Exercise 32.5: Practicing Future Tense

Rewrite the following passage as if the events described were going to take place at some time in the future. Change verb tenses wherever necessary. Your opening sentence will begin: Tomorrow's female writer will face . . .

> Today's female writer faces a peculiar confusion because she is susceptible to the images of women in literature. She goes to poetry or fiction looking for her role in the world, but she is disappointed. She is looking for guides, models, possibilities. But what she finds are many images of women in works by men. She discovers a terror and a dream. She encounters a Belle Dame sans Merci and a Daisy Buchanan. She does not find an image of herself, the struggling female writer.

33 Use the Appropriate Mood *mood*

The three **moods** of a verb indicate a writer's intent. The **indicative mood,** the one most frequently used, states a fact or an opinion or asks a question. The **imperative mood** gives a command or direction (usually with the subject *you* implied: *Be here at ten sharp*). The **subjunctive mood** expresses doubt or uncertainty, a condition contrary to fact, or a wish.

You will rarely have a problem with mood. In fact, the subjunctive mood, which can be problematic, is rarely used in current English. Nevertheless, you should master the remaining forms and the three uses of the subjunctive mood.

Forms of the Subjunctive

In the present tense the subjunctive mood consists of only the infinitive form of the verb no matter what the subject is. (See infinitives, 68c.)

> The choreographer urged that Boris *consider* a ballet career. [Present subjunctive]
>
> The guidelines demand that procedures *be* in effect tomorrow. [Present subjunctive]

In the past tense the only commonly used subjunctive verb form is *were.*

If I *were* retired, I would live a carefree life. [Past subjunctive]

Uses of the Subjunctive

33a Use the subjunctive form *were* to express a wish and in contrary-to-fact clauses beginning with *if.*

I wish she *were* my teacher. [But she is not my teacher: expresses a wish.]

I would be able to finish all my work if the day *were* thirty hours long. [But the day is twenty-four hours long: contrary-to-fact clause.]

33b Use the subjunctive form in *that* clauses following verbs that demand, request, or recommend.

Jano's aunt urged *that Brian save the money.*
The attorney asked *that the witness be ready to testify.*

NOTE: Often writers find substitute constructions for the subjunctive in sentences such as those above.

Jano's aunt urged Brian to save the money.

33c Use the subjunctive form in some standard phrases and idioms.

Peace *be* with you.
Heaven *forbid!*
Come rain or *come* shine.
So *be* it!

Exercise 33.1: Use the Appropriate Subjunctive Form

Revise the following sentences by using appropriate subjunctive verb forms.

1. If I was in charge, I would change our budget rules.

2. Since supply prices have soared, I wish the maximum petty cash disbursement was more than twenty-five dollars.
3. The present budget requires that a department head submits too many separate forms for a single purchase.
4. People laugh when I suggest changes, as if I was a comedian.
5. Heaven helps us.
6. Bob wishes he was captain of the team next year.
7. The officer requested that everyone calms down.
8. If Sheila was here, she would know what to do.
9. The rain is coming down hard, but if it was not, I will go for a walk.
10. The city manager decreed that all existing billboards in the city limits are take down.

34 Write in Active Rather Than Passive Voice *pass*

Voice is the quality in verbs that shows whether a subject is the actor or is acted upon.

> The Tanaka Construction Company built the Statler Bridge. [The subject *Tanaka Construction Company* is the actor.]
>
> The Statler Bridge was built by the Tanaka Construction Company. [The subject *Statler Bridge* is being acted upon.]

Effective writing is vigorous and direct. In nearly all circumstances, the active voice achieves vigor and directness better than the passive voice. Consequently, use the active voice except when you do not know the doer of an action or when you want to emphasize the receiver of an action or the action itself.

> Demonstrators from the New Earth Alliance closed the nuclear plant. [Active voice]
>
> The nuclear plant was closed by demonstrators from the New Earth Alliance. [Passive voice]

These sentences contain the same information, but each emphasizes a different point. The active construction emphasizes the demonstrators because *demonstrators* is the subject. The passive construction emphasizes the nuclear plant because *nuclear plant* is the subject.

Transitive verbs have both active and passive voice. When a verb is in the **active voice,** the subject performs the action and the object receives the action. When a verb is in the **passive voice,** the subject receives the action. (See transitive verb, 66c.)

To form a passive construction, move the direct object of the sentence ahead of the verb; it thus becomes the subject. Use a form of *be* as a helping verb; the actual subject may be contained in a prepositional phrase. (See direct object, 67e.)

> William Faulkner won a Pulitzer Prize in 1963. [Active voice]
>
> A Pultizer Prize was won by William Faulkner in 1963. [Passive voice: The direct object from the previous sentence, *Pulitzer Prize,* becomes the subject; *was* is added to the verb *won;* and the subject of the previous sentence, *William Faulkner,* becomes the object of the preposition *by.*]

Active sentences that have direct objects often have indirect objects also. When rewritten in a passive construction, either the direct object or the indirect object can become the subject, and the actual subject can be dropped. (See indirect object, 67e.)

> The committee awarded Thuy a scholarship. [Active voice]
>
> Thuy was awarded a scholarship. [Passive voice: Indirect object, *Thuy,* becomes the subject; the original subject, *committee,* is dropped.]
>
> A scholarship was awarded to Thuy. [Passive voice: Direct object, *scholarship,* becomes the subject; the original subject, *committee,* is dropped.]

Although the meaning of each of the above sentences is the same, as the subject changes so does the emphasis: from the committee to Thuy to a scholarship. The choice depends on the writer's intention.

In most situations, use the active voice for several reasons:

The active voice is more concise.

> An ancient soothsayer predicts the end of the world. [Active voice: nine words]
>
> The end of the world is predicted by an ancient soothsayer. [Passive voice: eleven words]

The active voice emphasizes the actual subject and is therefore more direct.

The detectives who investigated the case earned the admiration of their fellow officers. [Active voice]

The admiration of their fellow officers was earned by the detectives who investigated the case. [Passive voice]

The active voice is more forceful.

Starks rifled a pass to Ewing under the basket. [Active voice]

A pass was rifled to Ewing under the basket by Starks. [Passive voice]

The passive voice is appropriate in several situations:

When you do not know the doer of the action.

The clubhouse was left a shambles, and the parking lot was littered with cans and garbage.

When you want to emphasize the receiver of the action.

Tomaso was wounded by falling bricks.

When you want to emphasize the action itself.

A curved incision was made behind the hairline so the scar would be concealed when the hair grew back.

Exercise 34.1: Revise to Make Passive Sentences Active

Revise the following sentences by changing the voice from passive to active.

1. The warehouse was destroyed by fire.
2. Fortunately, or suspiciously, the paintings had been removed by the owner the day before.
3. One woman was seriously burned by falling cinders.
4. She was rushed to the emergency room by the paramedics.
5. It was reported by the fire chief that the fire was set deliberately.
6. Copies of the proposed fire guidelines were provided by the safety committee.
7. The repairs on the warehouse were done by an inexperienced contractor.
8. A detailed rendering for a new building was submitted by an architect.

9. An award is to be given to the architect by the Fine Arts Association.
10. The awards banquet will be sponsored by Arnald Forde, a well-known art collector.

Exercise 34.2: Change Passive to Active Voice

Rewrite the following passage, changing the passive constructions into active constructions.

> A poison ivy rash is considered by some to be humorous. But it is not funny at all. A rash that has the intensity of a fresh mosquito bite and lasts for several days is caused by contact with the plant. The poison ivy reaction has been studied by scientists for centuries, but no preventive pill or inoculation has been found. The poisonous substance in the plant is called urushiol. After the skin has been touched by urushiol, the exposed area will soon be covered by blisters and weeping sores.
>
> What can you do after coming into contact with poison ivy? First, the urushiol should be washed off as soon as possible. Any available hand soap and plenty of scrubbing should be used. Then take a cold shower and soap yourself all over. The course of the reaction seems to be shortened by cold water. Finally, see a doctor.

35 Select Adjectives and Adverbs with Care *adj/adv*

Adjectives and adverbs are frequently misused in writing. Errors involving adjectives and adverbs are easy to correct once you understand how the words function in a sentence.

Adjectives modify nouns and pronouns. Adverbs can modify verbs, adjectives, and other adverbs. You can form adverbs by adding *-ly* to adjectives (*rapid, rapidly; complete, completely; happy, happily; desperate, desperately*). But not all words ending in *-ly* are adverbs; some are adjectives (*womanly, lonely, saintly*). Some adverbs and adjectives have the same form (*well, late, early*), and some adverbs have two forms (*slow, slowly; quick, quickly; cheap, cheaply*).

35a Use adjectives to modify nouns and pronouns; use adverbs to modify verbs, adjectives, and other adverbs.

An adjective modifies a noun or a pronoun.

> José is a *swift* runner.
> I prefer the *checkered* one.

An adverb, not an adjective, modifies a verb.

> José ran *swiftly.*

An adverb, not an adjective, modifies an adjective.

> José is *terribly* swift.

An adverb, not an adjective, modifies an adverb.

> José ran *very* swiftly.

35b Use an adjective after a linking verb to refer to the subject; use an adverb to refer to the verb.

The most common linking verb is *be* and its forms—*am, are, is, was, were,* and *been.* Other common linking verbs include *seem, appear, become, grow, remain, prove,* and *turn,* along with verbs of the senses—*feel, look, smell, hear, taste.* When these verbs link the subject with a modifier, use an adjective as the modifier. When the modifier describes the verb, use an adverb.

> The climber felt *uneasy* about the darkening sky. [Adjective: *Uneasy* describes the climber.]

> The climber felt *uneasily* for a firm handhold. [Adverb: *Uneasily* describes how the climber used a hand to find a firm place to grip.]

35c After a direct object, use an adjective to modify the object; use an adverb to modify the verb.

> The judges ranked the wine *excellent.* [Adjective: *Excellent* describes wine.]

> She revised her papers *thoroughly.* [Adverb: *Thoroughly* describes revised.]

35d Use the words *bad* and *badly* and *good* and *well* correctly.

Bad is an adjective; *badly* is an adverb. Since verbs of the senses—*feel, look, smell, hear, taste*—require adjectives to modify the subjects, use *bad,* not *badly,* after them.

> The diners felt *bad* after the third course.
> The rendering plant smells *bad* this evening.

Good is always an adjective, never an adverb.

INCORRECT	The team played *good* last night.
CORRECT	The team played *well* last night.
CORRECT	The team played a *good* game last night.

Well may be used as either an adjective or an adverb. As an adjective, *well* has three meanings.

To be in good health:

> He seems *well* considering his ordeal.

To appear well dressed or groomed:

> They look *well* in the new uniforms.

To be satisfactory:

> All is *well.*

Exercise 35.1: Selecting Adjectives or Adverbs

Choose the correct word to complete each sentence. Explain the function of each adjective or adverb you select.

1. The band marched (*brisk, briskly*) down the field.
2. Mario felt (*bad, badly*) about the argument.
3. Choosing what car to buy is becoming (*increasing, increasingly*) difficult.
4. The driver considered the route (*safe, safely*).
5. Mai takes a (*brisk, briskly*) walk every morning.
6. The pedestrian looked (*careless, carelessly*) at the traffic.
7. Carlos shook his head (*sympathetic, sympathetically*).

8. It was an (*extreme, extremely*) clever plan.
9. The quarterback executed the play (*well, good*).
10. The pedestrian looked (*careless, carelessly*) standing there.

35e Use the correct forms of adjectives and adverbs when making comparisons.

Adjectives and adverbs have three forms or degrees: the **positive,** or plain form, which only describes; the **comparative,** which compares two things; and the **superlative,** which compares three or more things.

The comparative and superlative of most adjectives and adverbs are formed either by adding *-er* and *-est,* respectively, to the positive form or by placing *more* and *most* (or *less* and *least*), respectively, before the positive form.

Using *more* and *most* (or *less* and *least*) is the only way to form the comparative and superlative for most adverbs of two or more syllables and for adjectives of three or more syllables. Some adjectives of two syllables can add either *-er* and *-est* or *more* and *most.*

	POSITIVE	COMPARATIVE	SUPERLATIVE
ADJECTIVES	thick	thicker	thickest
	happy	happier	happiest
	beautiful	more beautiful	most beautiful
		less beautiful	least beautiful
ADVERBS	fast	faster	fastest
	often	more often	most often
	sadly	more sadly	most sadly

A few adjectives and adverbs change their spelling to form the comparative and superlative.

POSITIVE	COMPARATIVE	SUPERLATIVE
bad, badly	worse	worst
good, well	better	best
many, much	more	most
little	littler, less	littlest, least

Use the comparative form to compare two things.

In August the sea seems *bluer* than the sky.

Although the two tours cost the same, the one to Paris will be the *more* exciting.

Her client was *less* anxious today than yesterday.

Use the superlative form to compare three or more things.

Of the three agents, Bozarth has the *deadliest* charm.

Apparently the *most* skilled of all the drivers, Randolph wins nearly every race.

This novel is the *least* interesting in the series.

35f Do not use double comparatives or double superlatives.

◆ They are the ~~most~~ happiest couple I know.

35g Do not use comparative or superlative forms with words that cannot logically be compared.

Words such as *unique, perfect, dead, empty, infinite,* and *impossible* are absolute. That is, their positive form describes their only state. They cannot, therefore, be compared.

◆ Dr. Nastasi is ~~the most~~ a unique surgeon.

Exercise 35.2: Correct Errors in Adjective and Adverb Forms

Identify any errors in the use of adjective and adverb forms in the following sentences and correct the errors.

1. When the four horses turned into the stretch, My Game had the greater stamina.
2. Although he was the same height as Bridesmaid, his strides seemed the longest by a yard as Perez rose in the saddle and swung the crop to drive the thoroughbred toward the finish line.
3. My Game won in record time, proving to be the most fastest three-year-old to win the cup.
4. After the race, Perez said, "My Game is perhaps the most perfect horse I've ever ridden."
5. Whether Perez is right or wrong, today this marvelous animal was the better horse.

PART VI
Punctuation

My attitude toward punctuation is that it ought to be as conventional as possible. The game of golf would lose a good deal if croquet mallets and billiard cues were allowed on the putting green. You ought to be able to show that you can do it a good deal better than anyone else with the regular tools before you have a license to bring your own improvements.

—Ernest Hemingway, *novelist*

36 Comma ,

The comma is a critical mark of punctuation. It helps the writer show the logical relationships within a sentence by indicating groups of words that belong together and by separating words that do not. If writers fail to group and separate information logically, they risk misguiding the reader.

The comma also has several conventional uses, such as in dates and addresses. Since the comma is the most frequently used, and misused, punctuation mark, you will be well on your way to controlling punctuation errors by mastering its use.

36a Use a comma before a coordinating conjunction joining two main clauses.

When a coordinating conjunction—that is, *and, but, or, nor, yet, so,* and *for*—joins two main clauses, place a comma before the coordinating conjunction.

- The aging process is relentless, but most of us fight growing old.
- Professional athletes begin their careers out of a love for sports, and a few keep that love.
- The road was littered with household goods, for the refugees could not carry the extra weight.

NOTE: Not every coordinating conjunction in a sentence joins main clauses. Often coordinating conjunctions create compound subjects or compound predicates.

> Every Saturday the lawyer walked seven miles to the widow's cabin *and* chopped a week's supply of firewood for her.

The coordinating conjunction *and* joins two verbs, *walked* and *chopped.* It is incorrect to separate two parts of a compound predicate with a comma.

WRITER'S CLINIC

Placing Commas

To test whether you need a comma before *and, but,* or *or,* the most frequently used coordinating conjunctions, place a period before it. Then reread each part, before and after the period, without the conjunction. If each part works as a complete sentence, write your sentence using a comma before *and, but,* or *or.* If not, leave out the comma.

EXAMPLE

The printing press was invented in 1450. [but] only a small percentage of the Western world's population could read.

Because each part works as a sentence, the full sentence needs a comma before *but.*

REVISED

The printing press was invented in 1450, but only a small percentage of the Western world's population could read.

EXAMPLE

Teenagers in the 1950s had no music of their own. [and] no influence in the fashion market.

Because the second part does not work as a sentence, the full sentence does not need a comma before *and.*

REVISED

Teenagers in the 1950s had no music of their own and no influence in the fashion market.

We enjoy bagels *and* cream cheese for breakfast.

The coordinating conjunction *and* joins two nouns, *bagels* and *cream cheese;* do not use a comma.

Exercise 36.1: Using Commas with Coordinate Main Clauses

Insert a comma before each coordinating conjunction joining main clauses. If a sentence is correct, mark it with a C.

1. The British used the name *America* to refer to the British colonies and the colonists used the term *American* to refer to natives.

2. The emerging country needed to establish a name or it would always be seen as an extension of Europe.

3. In 1697 Cotton Mather popularized the word *American* to mean an English colonist in America and by 1780 our language was called *American.*

4. By 1782 a citizen of the United States was called *American* but the term *Americanism* was not used until 1797.

5. Citizens of the United States call themselves *American* but seldom remember that citizens from other Western Hemisphere countries are also American.

6. Many common names for things have interesting histories but only etomologists, word historians, study them.

7. *Hamburger,* for example, is an interesting word yet few people who eat at McDonald's know its background.

8. Russian Tartars introduced eating shredded raw meat and the practice found its way to Hamburg, Germany. Hamburg residents began cooking the meat so people began calling the result *Hamburg steak.*

9. Hamburg steak appeared in the United States around 1884 and was soon called *hamburger steak.*

10. Soon Americans were putting their hamburger steaks on a bun and *hamburger* came to mean the sandwich.

Exercise 36.2: Commas with Coordinate Main Clauses

Insert a comma before each coordinating conjunction joining main clauses. If a sentence is correct, mark it with a C.

1. Some words are unacceptable and should never be used yet the history of these words shows that they have legitimate beginnings.

2. *Ain't* is such a word and some linguists claim it is a very good and useful word.

3. The use of *ain't* began in England in 1706 and the word was soon used in America.

4. *Ain't* developed as a contraction of *am not* so it was first spelled *an't.*

5. In 1778–1779 *an't* had become *ain't* on both sides of the Atlantic but some New Englanders still pronounced it with a broad *a* like *an't.*
6. By the 1830s *ain't* was still used but many people had begun to misuse it.
7. *Ain't* was an obvious contraction of *am not* yet people began to use it as a contraction for *is not* and *are not* also.
8. Educated people began to criticize its common use for they believed it was unacceptable in all its forms.
9. Teachers say we are not supposed to use *ain't* anymore yet people still use it.
10. The educated use it with a self-conscious smirk and the uneducated use it naturally.

36b Use a comma to set off introductory phrases and clauses from main clauses.

A comma following an introductory clause or phrase shows its subordinate relationship to the information in the main clause.

INTRODUCTORY PREPOSITIONAL PHRASE

◆ By the end of next month, life in this house will change.

◆ On the north shore of Kauki, two sharks attacked surfers.

INTRODUCTORY VERBAL PHRASE

◆ To sail solo around the world, you must have courage.

◆ Beaten by relentless winds, the caravan returned to the oasis.

◆ Diving into the field, the hawk pursued its prey.

INTRODUCTORY CLAUSE

◆ If the Alaska king crab population plummets, crab fishers will be bankrupted.

◆ Whenever heavy rains hit Southern California,hillside homes begin to slide.

Be careful to distinguish verbal modifiers from verbals that function as subjects. Verbal modifiers are usually separated from the main clause by a comma; verbals functioning as subjects never take a comma. (See gerunds and gerund phrases, 68e.)

VERBAL AS MODIFIER

◆ Parachuting from an airplane,Darryl realized the joy of floating on the wind.

VERBAL AS SUBJECT

◆ Parachuting from an airplane, is Darryl's favorite pastime.

You may omit a comma after a very short introductory clause or phrase if the omission does not cause a misreading.

CONFUSING	On each weekday morning exercise class begins at six.
CLEAR	On each weekday, morning exercise class begins at six.
CLEAR	In science we need to know when to persevere and when to quit.

Usually no comma is needed to separate adverb clauses placed at the end of a sentence. (See unnecessary commas, Chapter 37.)

◆ Presidential news conferences offer more entertainment than information, because reporters do not ask pointed questions.

Exercise 36.3: Use Commas with Introductory Clauses and Phrases

Insert commas where needed after introductory phrases and clauses in the following sentences. If a sentence is correct, mark it with a C.

1. In spite of an apparently inexhaustible supply the numbers of wild creatures are being depleted because of greed.
2. If you are tempted to spend $25,000 for a leopard-skin coat remember that each coat requires the pelts of seven animals.

3. Specializing in killing and stuffing a taxidermist in California illegally offered bighorn sheep to wealthy customers.
4. After exposure he confessed and paid a fine.
5. Handicapped by low budgets authorities seem to be losing the battle against poachers.
6. With the help of naturalists, a Senate committee concluded that hunting is viewed as a traditional right in America.
7. To hunt illegally is also part of the tradition.
8. Resorting to historical records hunting enthusiasts point out that poaching on private lands was one way the poor fed themselves during tough times.
9. Hunting endangered species, stuffing them, and selling them as trophies is not the same as hunting for survival.
10. When hunting is done illegally isn't it the responsibility of authorities to arrest those involved?

36c Use a comma to set off nonrestrictive elements; do not use a comma to set off restrictive elements.

A **restrictive element** defines or identifies—that is, it restricts—the meaning of the noun it modifies and is essential to the meaning of the sentence. A **nonrestrictive element** may add important information to a sentence but is not essential to the meaning of the sentence.

RESTRICTIVE — A student who sets academic goals will graduate in four years.

The clause beginning with *who* is essential to the meaning of the sentence. Without the clause, the sentence will mean something else: A student will graduate in four years.

NONRESTRICTIVE — Robin Crisp, who studies five hours daily, will graduate in three years.

The clause beginning with *who* adds factual information but is not essential. The basic meaning of the sentence is clear without it: Robin Crisp will graduate in three years.

Restrictive clauses and phrases are not set off by commas.

◆ Citizens, who are interested in politics, should run for public office.

◆ The mechanic,/working on the Volkswagen,/lost his temper.

NOTE: Clauses beginning with the relative pronoun *that* are almost always restrictive.

◆ The belief,/that human beings,/are driven by subconscious drives is common among psychoanalysts.

◆ Medical treatments,/that are not approved by the American Medical Association,/may be dangerous.

In a restrictive adjective clause, the relative pronoun introducing the clause may be dropped when it does not function as the subject of the relative clause.

◆ A tax increase is the only way ~~that~~ our government can continue to function.

◆ Dr. Diaz could not find a politician ~~whom~~ she respected.

NOTE: Clauses and phrases modifying indefinite pronouns are almost always restrictive.

◆ Walt Disney is a genius to those,/who make animated cartoons.

◆ Anyone,/sleeping in the park,/was awakened.

Nonrestrictive clauses and phrases should be set off by commas.

◆ Venice,which is noted for its Piazza San Marco,was a favorite haunt for American writers.

◆ The right to free speech,like breathing itself,is essential to life.

NOTE: Clauses and phrases that modify proper nouns are always nonrestrictive. (See proper nouns, 66a.)

◆ Ernest Hemingway,who had an interest in art,claimed to have learned to write fine descriptions by studying impressionist paintings.

Sometimes a clause or phrase may be either restrictive or nonrestrictive. The writer must indicate how it is to be interpreted by using or omitting commas.

RESTRICTIVE	The engineers who were trained as pilots provided the technical advice.

The *who* clause restricts or defines *engineers.* The sentence means that not all engineers provided technical advice; only the ones trained as pilots did.

NON-RESTRICTIVE	The engineers, who were trained as pilots, provided the technical advice.

This sentence means that all the engineers were trained as pilots, and they gave the technical advice. The *who* clause is not essential to the meaning of the sentence.

Nonrestrictive appositives should be set off by commas; restrictive appositives should not.

A restrictive appositive defines the noun it refers to in such a way that its absence from the sentence would leave the meaning unclear.

NON-RESTRICTIVE	Ralph Williams, a frequent personality on late-night television, made millions selling used cars.
NON-RESTRICTIVE	Baby gray whales, huge creatures at birth, consume up to fifty gallons of milk daily.
NON-RESTRICTIVE	"Mending Wall," one of Robert Frost's narrative poems, deals with two differing worldviews.
RESTRICTIVE	The actor Whoopi Goldberg is known for both her comedic and her dramatic roles.
RESTRICTIVE	The Greek hero Perseus slew the dragon and freed Andromeda.
RESTRICTIVE	James Dickey's poem "Looking for the Buckhead Boys" portrays a middle-aged man's attempt to reconnect with his youth.

WRITER'S CLINIC

Set Off Nonrestrictive Elements in One of Three Ways

You will usually use commas to set off information that is not essential (nonrestrictive elements), but you may use dashes or parentheses instead, depending on the importance of the information to the meaning of a sentence.

Use commas for important information.

> No painter or sculptor, not even Michelangelo, had been as famous as Pablo Picasso was in his own lifetime.

Use dashes to emphasize nonessential information.

> Pablo Picasso—the twentieth century's dominant painter and sculptor—lived to be ninety-two.

Use parentheses for interesting but less important information.

> Picasso's *Guernica* (perhaps equaled in drama only by Goya's etchings *Disasters of War*) captures the madness of modern warfare.

Exercise 36.4: Set Off Nonrestrictive Elements

In the following sentences, insert commas to set off nonrestrictive clauses, phrases, and appositives. If a sentence is correct as written, underline the restrictive or nonrestrictive element and mark the sentence with a C.

1. Edgar Allan Poe a nineteenth-century American writer wrote the first murder mystery.
2. "The Murders in the Rue Morgue" published in 1841 presents C. Auguste Dupin the world's first modern detective.
3. In Dupin, Poe created a detective who solved murders through observation and reason often drawing a solution that appears miraculous.
4. Poe also created the "locked room" story a mystery in which a murdered victim is found in a room locked from the inside.
5. James Fenimore Cooper another American writer created the first espionage novel.

6. Cooper's *The Spy* which was based on historical notes from the American Revolution appeared even before Poe's work.
7. Cooper who is known for his romantic American Indian tales created a formula that future espionage writers would use.
8. Mark Twain who is not considered to be a mystery writer contributed to detective fiction by being the first author to use fingerprints to help solve a crime.
9. Mystery writers today must use new methods of detection since crime technology has become so sophisticated.
10. Anyone who reads or writes mysteries must wonder if science will put an end to the fine art of fictional murder.

Exercise 36.5: Combine Sentences Using Restrictive or Nonrestrictive Elements

Combine the following sentences according to the directions given in brackets. After you have combined the sentences, be sure to punctuate them correctly. For example:

> The tradition of detective stories with murder in the family is an old one. Human beings have always had murder in their hearts. [Use *since* to form an adverbial clause.]
>
> **Combined:** Since human beings have always had murder in their hearts, the tradition of detective stories with murder in the family is an old one.

1. Cain killed his brother Abel in an Old Testament story of the first murder. Cain was jealous of Abel. [Use *who* to form an adjective clause.]
2. Some serious mystery readers claim that *Oedipus Rex* is the first detective story. *Oedipus Rex* is an early Greek play. [Use an appositive phrase.]
3. Oedipus seeks his true identity. He has inadvertently killed his father and married his mother. [Use *who* to form an adjective clause.]
4. Clearly, *Oedipus Rex* is a murder mystery. The play ends ironically when the detective discovers he is the killer. [Use *that* to form an adjective clause.]
5. Shakespeare's *Hamlet* can also be viewed as a mystery. *Hamlet* is an Elizabethan tragedy. It deals with a brother murdering his

brother and ascending to the throne of Denmark. [Use an appositive phrase and an adjective phrase beginning with *that.*]

6. Hamlet must first prove that his uncle murdered his father. Hamlet was the son of the slain king. [Use an appositive phrase.]
7. Both *Oedipus Rex* and *Hamlet* concentrate on solving a family murder. They thrill many audiences today. [Use a present participial phrase.]
8. Modern detective writer Ross Macdonald also wove his mysteries around family crimes. They often use murder or a disappearance to motivate the investigation. [Use *which* to form an adjective clause.]
9. *The Galton Case* begins with a mother who wishes to be reconciled with her son. *The Galton Case* is an early Macdonald mystery. The son has disappeared without a trace. [Use an appositive phrase and an adjective clause beginning with *who.*]
10. By the novel's end, Macdonald's detective has revealed a murder and unraveled the family's snarled history. The detective's name is Lew Archer. [Use an appositive.]

36d Use commas between words, phrases, and clauses in a series consisting of three or more items of equal importance.

When three or more items, words, clauses, or phrases are arranged in a series, they should be separated from one another with commas.

- Three well-known Japanese novelists are Junichiro Tanizaki, Yasunari Kawabata, and Yukio Mishima.
- To plan successfully you must clarify the goal, define the objectives, establish a deadline, and charge ahead.
- Driving luxury sedans, eating gourmet food, and drinking fine wine are Camelita's fantasies.
- Aaron did not know who he was, where he had been, or what would happen next.

Although the final comma in a series is optional, including it can prevent misreading.

> I took the following courses: digital computers, software manufacturing, word processing, and data retrieval. [The final comma makes it clear that word processing and data retrieval are separate courses.]

NOTE: No commas are necessary between items in a series all joined by *and* or *or*.

> Whole grains and nuts and yogurt are the staples in Quintan's diet.

36e Use a comma between coordinate adjectives not joined by *and;* do not use a comma between cumulative adjectives.

Coordinate adjectives are two or more adjectives that modify the same noun or pronoun.

> Informative, imaginative, appealing advertising should be more common.

> Advertising is often no more than a deceptive, dull appeal to consumer insecurity.

NOTE: A comma is never used between the last adjective in a series and the noun it modifies.

Cumulative adjectives modify the adjectives that follow them as well as a noun or pronoun.

- ◆ His life was dedicated to achieving a single, personal goal.
- ◆ The exhibition of ancient, Tunisian mosaics will close next week.

Exercise 36.6: Using Commas in a Series

Insert commas as necessary within a series or between coordinate adjectives in the following sentences. Include the last comma in a series. If a sentence is correct, mark it with a C.

1. Early colonists brought such words as *bandit robber highwayman* and *outlaw* with them from England.

WRITER'S CLINIC

Test Coordinate and Cumulative Adjectives

Two simple tests can help you tell the difference between coordinate and cumulative adjectives. If you can change the order of the adjectives or place the word *and* between them, the series is coordinate and requires commas.

> Intelligent, sensitive, witty films are seldom produced in Hollywood.
>
> Sensitive, witty, intelligent films are seldom produced in Hollywood.
>
> Intelligent and sensitive and witty films are seldom produced in Hollywood.

The preceding adjective series meets both tests; therefore, it is a coordinate series and should be separated by commas.

> International peace organizations supported antinuclear demonstrations in the world's capitals.
>
> Peace international organizations supported antinuclear demonstrations in the world's capitals.
>
> International and peace organizations supported antinuclear demonstrations in the world's capitals.

The adjective series *international peace* does not meet either test; therefore, it is a cumulative series and should not be separated by commas.

2. Freezing weather personal dignity or increasing population demanded that the first privy be built.
3. The history of the circus goes back to the days of the Roman Empire when chariot races gladiator fights and animal shows were featured activities.
4. Hungry for adventure seeking land to farm and willing to risk life and limb, thousands of Mississippi settlers caught the Oregon fever.
5. Tall and lean brooding and gentle Abraham Lincoln was the imposing figure who led a divided confused country during the Civil War.
6. A third of the country is poorly housed, poorly fed, and poorly educated.

7. Following the Revolutionary War, farsighted courageous leaders like Benjamin Franklin, George Washington, Robert Fulton, and Albert Gallatin planned to build canals to connect towns lakes and rivers across the nation.
8. Most of the town's people were farmers or worked for small local businesses, often bartering food clothing and services.
9. At the peak of the Great Depression, bank closings bankruptcies factory shutdowns and farm and home mortgage foreclosures were at an all-time high.
10. With mustard and relish and onions, the American hot dog has been the favorite of Fourth of July picnics for one hundred years.

36f Use commas to set off parenthetical expressions that function as transitions, express afterthoughts, or offer supplemental information.

Parenthetical expressions interrupt the flow of a sentence. Transitional phrases such as *for example, on the other hand,* and *in fact* are parenthetical and usually are set off by commas.

- ◆ Driving on freeways and turnpikes, for example, is four times more dangerous than flying.

Commas are usually needed to set off conjunctive adverbs such as *accordingly, besides, consequently, furthermore, hence, however, indeed, instead, likewise, meanwhile, moreover, nevertheless, otherwise, therefore,* and *thus.* (See semicolon, 38b.)

- ◆ Several bystanders who witnessed the crime identified the thief; nevertheless, he was released from custody because of a technicality.

- ◆ Several bystanders who witnessed the crime identified the thief; he was released from custody, however, because of a technicality.

Always use commas to set off *however* when it is used as a conjunctive adverb; do not use commas to set off *however* when it is an adverb meaning "no matter how."

◆ Sixteen engineers gave similar testimony; however, the Senate committee was swayed by the attorney general's dissenting view.

◆ However, the committee votes will have no affect on the outcome.

Afterthoughts and supplemental information should be set off with commas.

◆ Mystery writers, some critics maintain, try to make sense of murder.

36g Use a comma to set off mild interjections, words of direct address, and *yes* and *no*.

◆ Oh, I didn't mean to buy so many groceries!

◆ Stop playing those video games, Don.

◆ No, I cannot be there early.

Exercise 36.7: Using Commas with Parenthetical Elements

Insert commas as necessary to set off parenthetical expressions and words of direct address in the following sentences. If a sentence is correct, mark it with a C.

1. However much Americans love their Big Macs and chocolate shakes, many are sacrificing their affair with junk food for a new commitment.
2. Bulging biceps, rippled stomachs, and yes even sinewy necks are the new shapes people yearn for.
3. Regardless of the pain and endless hours spent pumping iron men and women are dedicating themselves to furious bodybuilding.
4. Will chiseled muscles lead to healthier lives? No not if weight lifting is merely an escape from time's relentless craftsmanship.

5. Moreover many bodybuilders express their desire to become a New Age Rambo.

36h Use the comma to set off absolute phrases.

An **absolute phrase** modifies an entire sentence rather than a word or phrase, but it is not grammatically related to the rest of the sentence. Absolute phrases are always nonrestrictive—that is, they always supply important but nonessential information to a sentence. (See 67f.)

- The Doberman leaped at Rashid's throat,teeth snapping, eyes flashing anger.
- Their feet aching from the journey,the four campers climbed into their sleeping bags.
- Anuka,her fingers gripping the wheel,accelerated into the curve.

36i Use the comma to set off contrasting expressions and interrogative elements.

Love, not hate, is the essence of renewal.

Each person has the responsibility for his or her behavior, right?

36j Use the comma to set off expressions such as *she said* or *he wrote* from direct quotations.

The Tao Te Ching says, "Not collecting treasures prevents stealing."

"I cannot and will not cut my conscience to fit this year's fashions," wrote Lillian Hellman.

"One writes out of one thing only," says James Baldwin, "one's own experience."

If the expression comes between two or more sentences of quotation, use a period after the expression to indicate the end of the first sentence.

"The apartment house is nearly finished," she said. "I never thought I would see the day."

(See quotation marks, 39a.)

Omit the comma when a quotation ends with an exclamation point or question mark.

"Why all this indecision?" she asked.

NOTE: When a comma follows a quotation, always place it within the quotation marks, not after or under them.

"Of course," she replied.

Exercise 36.8: Using Commas to Set Off Certain Phrases and Quotations

Insert commas as necessary in the following sentences to set off absolute phrases, contrasting expressions, interrogative elements, and explanatory words used with a direct quotation.

1. Many food faddists like to eat natural meat not just the domesticated meat displayed in most supermarkets.
2. Natural meat is game not the kind you play on ball fields and includes a variety of wildlife found in America's forests and mountain ranges.
3. Free for the taking some game is coveted more than others. Venison for instance is the most popular game served at American tables.
4. One chef praises muskrat chili certainly not as common as Texas chili right?
5. Some food faddists see game as a preferred dish in specialty restaurants. "Seldom is the taste so aroused as when a platter of sputtering moose steaks or a brace of mallards is placed on a table" one critic writes. "It's like experiencing the American wilderness in the heart of Manhattan" he claims.

36k Use a comma according to established conventions in numbers, addresses, place names, dates, and friendly letters.

Separate long numbers into groups of three beginning from the right.

5,676 12,345 222,498 231,547,211

Separate each item in an address that is run together in a line. Do not use a comma to set off the zip code.

600 Wisconsin Avenue, South Milwaukee, Wisconsin 53172
600 Wisconsin Avenue
South Milwaukee, Wisconsin 53172

Separate each item in a place name.

I forwarded the package to Harvard University, Cambridge, Massachusetts, where she now teaches.

Separate the month and day from the year in a date.

The reception will be held at the Hilton on September 21, 1999, in the Twilight Room.

If the day precedes the month, do not use commas.

21 September 1999

Set off the salutation and close of a friendly letter.

Dear Uncle Joe Bob, Yours truly,

Exercise 36.9: Using Commas in Letters

Insert commas as necessary in the following letter, including optional commas.

March 16 1990

Dear Dat

I have just accepted a sales position with a firm in Newport Beach California about forty-five miles south of Los Angeles. The base salary is $25000 a year but with commissions I could make another $5000 to $10000.

The company will have a training position opening next month. Are you interested? Let me know. My new address is 2701 Fairview Road Costa Mesa CA 92626.

Your friend

Philip Thi

36l Use a comma to prevent misunderstanding and to show the omission of an understood word.

To prevent misunderstanding:

CONFUSING	On Monday morning schedules will be revised.
CLEAR	On Monday, morning schedules will be revised.
CLEAR	On Monday morning, schedules will be revised.

To show an omission:

- The French drink wine; the Germans,~~drink~~ beer.
- For Dr. Sanchez to give one "A" is rare; for him to give two,~~is~~ unprecedented.

COMPUTER CLINIC

Grammar Checkers and Punctuation

Just as grammar checkers are highly unreliable in flagging and correcting sentence errors, they are also unreliable in flagging punctuation errors.

- Grammar checkers generally fail to flag comma errors except before *which* and *that*.
- They tend to flag all semicolon use, but they generally fail to identify run-on sentences.
- They also tend to flag all colon and dash use, but you still need to determine whether the use is correct.
- They can be effective in identifying missing apostrophes in contractions, and they sometimes flag missing apostrophes in possessives, but not always.
- They are very effective at flagging mistakes in the use of commas and periods with quotation marks.

Obviously, until grammar-checker technology improves, you will have to proofread your work carefully for errors in punctuation, even if you use a grammar checker.

37 Unnecessary Commas *no ,*

Excessive use of the comma may confuse a reader by separating sentence elements that belong together. The following rules specify when a comma is not necessary.

37a Do not use a comma between a subject and its verb unless a sentence element that comes between them requires a comma.

- Fully grown killer whales~~,~~ are as long as thirty feet and as heavy as ten tons.
- Fully grown killer whales, which travel in pods of ten to twenty, are as long as thirty feet and as heavy as ten tons.

37b Do not use a comma between a verb and its object or its complement.

- A killer whale will eat~~,~~ anything it can catch.

37c Do not use a comma between a preposition and its object.

- Killer whales live in~~,~~ practically all the tropical oceans of the world.

37d Do not use a comma between an adverb and the word it modifies or between an adjective and the word it modifies.

- The killer whale has been described as the most socially~~,~~ intelligent~~,~~ animal in the world.

37e Do not use a comma between compound words, phrases, or dependent clauses joined by a coordinating conjunction.

◆ The engine, and the grill are the most famous features of the Rolls-Royce.

◆ A Rolls-Royce has eighty thousand parts, and takes three months to build.

◆ The Rolls-Royce is proof that fine work is still being done, and that people will pay any price for quality.

37f Do not use commas to separate restrictive elements from the rest of the sentence.

◆ The first car, created by Henry Royce and Charles Rolls, was built in 1904.

◆ Fritz Wirth's article, "An Empire on Four Wheels," appeared in January.

37g Do not use a comma after *such as* and *like.*

◆ Some writers in Spanish, such as, Gabriel García Márquez and Mario Vargas Llosa, influenced contemporary American writers.

37h Do not use a comma before the first or after the last item in a series unless a rule requires it.

◆ Reading, writing, and arithmetic, should be the spine of education.

◆ Popular college subjects today are, psychology, business, and engineering.

37i Do not use a comma to introduce indirect discourse.

◆ The Tao teaches that, muddy waters left alone will become clear.

37j Do not use a comma before *than* in a comparison.

◆ Hang gliding is more exciting, than skydiving.

37k Do not use a comma with a period, a question mark, an exclamation point, or a dash, all of which stand by themselves.

◆ "Return the money at once!", he pleaded.

Exercise 37.1: Comma Use Review

Correct the following sentences by inserting commas where they are needed and by deleting them where they are not needed. Include all optional commas. If any sentence is correct, mark it with a C.

1. The life of the Chinese heroine Meng Chiang Nu, the Pumpkin Girl, is an example of loyalty dedication and self-sacrifice.
2. The story begins with two families the Meng and the Chiang.
3. During the planting season one year each family planted pumpkins at the foot of a wall that marked the boundary of their properties.
4. Growing rapidly, pumpkin vines soon began to climb the wall and at the top they joined and produced a pumpkin larger than anyone had ever seen before.
5. According to the story the families agreed to divide the pumpkin but when they cut it they found a tiny baby girl inside.

6. To show she belonged to both the Meng family and the Chiang family they called her Meng Chiang.
7. At about the same time, the Emperor Shih Huang Ti started to build the Great Wall of China.
8. Each time the emperor's men put up a section of the wall however it collapsed before another section could be built.
9. The emperor who felt discouraged sent for the wisest men in the empire to advise him.
10. One wise man told him the only way to stop the collapse, would be to bury a living person in the wall every mile.
11. Since the wall was to extend ten thousand miles the plan would call for the sacrifice of ten thousand people!
12. Another wise man whispered to the emperor "Your Eminence living nearby is a poor man. Since his name Wan means ten thousand bury him in the wall and your great enterprise will be strong along its entire length."
13. Yes, Wan was poor, but he was not stupid.
14. When he heard of the plan he ran, and ran, and ran, until at nightfall he found himself high, in the branches of a tree in a peaceful isolated garden.
15. Beneath him he saw a beautiful girl bathing naked in a pool.
16. Of course it was Meng Chiang grown to womanhood.
17. She sang softly of love, and said aloud "If any man should see me now I would happily be his wife forever."
18. Wan forgot his own safety for a moment and climbed down from the tree and claimed his bride.
19. Unfortunately the emperor's men arrived just after the wedding seized the bridegroom and carried him off to be buried alive in the Great Wall.
20. Having heard of Wan's fate years later Meng Chiang made the hazardous journey to the wall to search for her husband's body.
21. Out of sympathy for her plight, a section of the wall collapsed, and her husband's bones fell out.
22. She was taken to the emperor who was stunned by her great beauty and vowed to marry her.

23. Seeing that the emperor was determined to marry her Meng Chiang asked only that a high altar be built in memory of her husband.

24. On their wedding day Meng Chiang climbed to the top of the altar cursed the emperor for his cruelty and threw herself to her death.

25. The emperor commanded his men to cut her body into little pieces but each piece of her flesh turned into a beautiful silver fish and her soul lives in these fish as a tribute to faithfulness.

38 Semicolon ;

Use semicolons in a limited number of situations: as a substitute for a period to indicate a close relation between main clauses and as a substitute for a comma to improve clarity.

38a Use a semicolon between main clauses.

When two main clauses are closely related in meaning and are not joined by a coordinating conjunction, you may join them with a semicolon.

◆ In Irish folklore the Sidhe (pronounced "she") spirits sometimes appear as men and women;other times they appear as birds and beasts. The Sidhe travel as clouds of dust;they rest as blades of grass.

There must be some basis for deciding whether to use two main clauses with a semicolon between them or two sentences with a period. Generally, the division into separate sentences is better. A semicolon should be used only when the ideas in the two main clauses are so closely related that a period would make too strong a break between them. (See coordinating conjunctions, 66g; comma splices and fused sentences, Chapter 27.)

Stylistically, the semicolon may be used to create a balance between closely related clauses.

◆ Mystics trust spirits; realists trust only facts.

38b Use a semicolon to separate main clauses joined by conjunctive adverbs.

◆ In folklore the Sidhe live under Ireland's rocky soil or beneath the mutinous seas; consequently, some Irish claim the Sidhe are never far from them.

NOTE: When a conjunctive adverb immediately follows a semicolon (as in the preceding example), always put a comma after the conjunctive adverb. When a conjunctive adverb does not immediately follow the semicolon, put commas before and after the conjunctive adverb.

◆ The Sidhe live on cold potatoes and milk left on hearths and at thresholds of Irish homes; when feasting, however, they resort to theft and rob Irish cellars of good wines.

38c Use a semicolon to separate main clauses joined by coordinating conjunctions.

When the main clauses are long and complex or have internal punctuation, use semicolons to separate them.

◆ The Sidhe sing in glens, dance on boulders, and play hurling in the fields; but they also curse, bicker, and fight each other.

38d Use semicolons to separate long phrases or clauses in a series if they contain commas.

◆ Partial to humans, Sidhe spirits will help them in their work; aid them in the search for hidden money, lost jewels, and buried gold; and treat their sick pets, ailing livestock, and ill children.

38e Avoid misusing the semicolon.

Do not use a semicolon to join dependent clauses or phrases and main clauses.

- According to some enthusiasts~~;~~, only ten thousand Sidhe exist.
- Some believe the Sidhe are headed toward extinction~~;~~ because fewer and fewer people believe in them.

Do not use a semicolon to introduce a list.

- Perhaps the Sidhe will join the ranks of other imaginary creatures~~;~~, such as unicorns, leprechauns, and magical dwarfs.

Exercise 38.1: Using Semicolons

Delete the unnecessary or incorrect commas and semicolons and insert the correct punctuation in the following sentences. If any sentence is correct, mark it with a C.

1. Whereas imaginary creatures may fall from memory; the real mysteries of the world will always arouse our curiosity.
2. One mystery involves strange carvings, many the size of three-story buildings, found on Easter Island, another involves cave drawings at Lascaux, France, painted fifteen to twenty thousand years ago.
3. Easter Island is tiny, volcanic, barren, and isolated; nevertheless, plenty of insects and hordes of rats live there.
4. Mysterious statues dominate the island; their threatening expressions presiding over the landscape.
5. Their faces all share similar features; such as long ears, large eyes, and jutting chins.
6. Some of the statues are toppled over, most, however, still stand, all still have topknots made from red stone.
7. The paintings in the Lascaux caves, are equally mysterious, however the mystery surrounds their purpose, not their origin.
8. Some historians claim the paintings represent hunting magic, others see in them a great symbolic idea that is beyond our un-

derstanding, still others view them as simply the result of creative impulses.

9. Whatever their motivations; the Lascaux cave painters created groups of pictures in sixty-six caves. This achievement required many skills; including the ability to extract minerals from the ground, pound them to powder, and mix them with grease.

10. As children we huddle together in the darkness and scare each other with tales of mysterious monsters, as adults we curl up under a reading lamp with a good book and wonder about the mysterious creations of humankind.

Exercise 38.2: Using Semicolons

Delete the unnecessary and incorrect commas and semicolons and insert the correct punctuation in the following sentences. If any sentence is correct, mark it with a C.

1. Many Americans are dropping coffee completely from their diets, many others are switching to decaffeinated coffee.
2. Herbal teas or health-food substitutes are reasonable alternatives to coffee drinking, they are drunk hot and offer a reason to pause during the day.
3. "I have measured out my life with coffee spoons," the poet T. S. Eliot once wrote, now, however, he might have to write, "I have measured out my life with teaspoons."
4. Coffee has been nicknamed "mud"; because the grounds look like mud once hot water has been poured through them.
5. Some people drink as much as fifteen to twenty cups of coffee a day; which makes sleeping difficult because of the caffeine.
6. Some people drink coffee to stay alert, then they cannot sleep, finally, they drink coffee the next morning because they are tired from the lack of sleep.
7. Many heavy coffee drinkers who finally quit drinking coffee experience the symptoms of withdrawal; such as headaches, depression, and listlessness.
8. Is there life after coffee consumption has ended? Coffee drinking is such a ritualized part of our experience that giving up coffee would disrupt our schedules, in fact, giving up coffee might change the very fabric of our existence.

9. Imagine having herbal tea with eggs and bacon, sipping caffeine-less cola with the morning paper, taking juice breaks, without coffee all these experiences would be equally dissatisfying.
10. Improved health is not worth the emotional price tag; coffee is the one drink for all occasions.

39 Quotation Marks “ ”

The main use of quotation marks is to assist a reader by indicating the beginning and the end of a direct quotation from speech or writing.

39a Use double quotation marks (“ ”) to enclose direct quotations from speakers or writers.

In a recent lecture on contemporary art, Professor Alvarez said, “Until the general acceptance of Georgia O’Keeffe’s work, artists were divided into two groups—artists and female painters. Now we have just one group—artists.”

Art historian Sam Hunter sees Georgia O’Keeffe’s work as emerging from and going beyond biomorphic abstraction: “O’Keeffe seemed able to invest abstract painting with fresh content and significant new forms.”

When quoting a passage that takes up more than four lines in a typewritten paper, do not use quotation marks (unless they appear in the original); instead, set off the quotation from the rest of the paper by putting it in block form. That is, indent the entire passage ten spaces (or one inch) and double-space the lines. The first line of the passage should be indented an additional three spaces (or one-fourth inch) if it marks the beginning of a paragraph.

All of us are familiar with the superstitious belief that the number 13 is unlucky. But we are not, of course, the only culture that worries about numbers. The famous linguist Charles Berlitz notes,

> In both Chinese and Japanese, the word "four," *shi*, sounds like the word "death." The Japanese often substitute another word for "four"--*yotsu*, taken

> from an alternative system of counting. License numbers using 4 in certain combinations are shunned by Chinese car owners in Hong Kong, Taiwan, and Singapore. They especially avoid the number 1414, which in speech resembles the words "definite death, definite death."

The indention of the quoted passage indicates that it is all a quotation. Note, too, that the words *four, death,* and *definite death* are placed within quotation marks because those marks appeared in the original.

When directly quoting poetry, work a quotation of one line or less into the text and enclose it within quotation marks.

> Shelley tellingly countered Ozymandias's proclamation of omnipotence with the short, ironic comment, "Nothing beside remains."

A quotation of two lines of poetry may be worked into the text of your paper or set off from it. To work the lines into the text, separate them with a slash (with one space before and after the slash) and enclose the entire quotation in quotation marks.

> In T. S. Eliot's poem "The Love Song of J. Alfred Prufrock," Prufrock's isolation is echoed in the lines "I have heard the mermaids singing, each to each. / I do not think that they will sing to me."

To set off the lines of poetry from the text, begin each line on a new line, indent it ten spaces (or one inch) unless the poet used varying indentation, and double-space the lines. Omit the quotation marks.

> In T. S. Eliot's poem "The Love Song of J. Alfred Prufrock," Prufrock's isolation is echoed in the lines
>
> I have heard the mermaids singing, each to each.
> I do not think that they will sing to me.

A poetry quotation of three or more lines should be set off from the text in block form and presented just as it is printed in the original. Do not use quotation marks or slashes.

When quoting conversation or writing fictional dialogue, put quotation marks around the exact words spoken. Do not enclose descriptive phrases or attributions in quotation marks. Begin a new paragraph for each speaker.

> "Where is he?" Mae asked, coming around the corner of the house with a mop and bucket in her hands. "Is he gone?"
>
> "I dunno, Mom," Stacy replied. "He was here a minute ago."
>
> She yawned and scratched the back of her head vigorously. "Probably gone huntin' again."

If one speaker or writer is quoted without interruption for more than one paragraph, put quotation marks at the beginning of each paragraph but at the end of only the last paragraph.

NOTE: Do not use quotation marks to enclose indirect quotations—written or spoken information that you have rewritten or summarized in your words.

> His purpose, he said, was to break with the traditions of the past and bring new life to the film industry.

39b Use quotation marks to enclose the titles of short works: articles, essays, short stories, short poems, songs, chapter titles and other subdivisions of books or periodicals, and episodes of radio and television programs.

> Shirley Jackson's “The Lottery” exposes a small community's blind obedience to tradition. [Short story]
>
> “The Microbe Hunters” is this week's episode of *Nova.* [Television episode]
>
> Chapter 2, “Entering the Aerobics Program,” tells how to take the first step toward improving the cardiovascular system. [Chapter title]

NOTE: Do not use quotation marks to enclose the titles or section titles of your own papers.

39c Occasionally, quotation marks serve to enclose a word used in a special sense.

> I had to take the job. I needed the “bread.”

Do not use quotation marks to create an ironic tone, change the meaning of a word, or justify the use of nonstandard English.

INAPPROPRIATE	Just being late to class was “traumatic” enough, but when the instructor peered over his glasses and “growled,” “Again,” I just “totally flipped.”
APPROPRIATE	Just being late to class was bad enough, but when the instructor peered over his glasses and growled, “Again,” I was really embarrassed.

39d Follow standard practice when using other marks of punctuation with quotation marks.

1. Always place commas and periods that follow a quotation inside quotation marks.

> Although Tom Bender said, “Writers who endure will always write about what they know**,**” he spent years describing the journeys of characters who became lost in exotic lands he never visited.

> Scanning the crowd for her son, she said, “It’s like looking for a needle in a haystack**.**”

2. Always place colons and semicolons outside quotation marks.

> Some of Aunt Maude’s favorite expressions are “He runs around like a chicken with its head cut off”**;** “Where there’s smoke there’s fire”**;** “Don’t count your chickens until they’ve hatched”**:** expressions from the common pot of American clichés.

3. Enclose dashes, question marks, and exclamation points in quotation marks only if they belong to the quotation.

> “That’s terrible! How can they expect—” she screamed in disbelief.

> I am sure you resent him for always asking, “But what does it all mean**?**”

> Long after she had turned the corner, she could still hear him calling, “Eva! Eva**!**”

When a dash, question mark, or exclamation point is not part of a direct quotation, do not enclose it within quotation marks.

“Something is rotten in the state of Denmark”—and I intend to find out what it is!

Have you ever wanted to tell him, “I don’t want to work here anymore”**?**

Please! Stop saying, “Something is rotten in the state of Denmark”**!**

39e Use single quotation marks (‘ ’) to enclose a direct quotation within a quotation.

“Let me remind you,” the professor said, “of the words of Edward R. Murrow, ‘We cannot defend freedom abroad by deserting it at home.’”

WRITER’S CLINIC

Paraphrasing and Quoting

Use *that* to introduce a paraphrase, but do not use *that* to introduce a direct quotation.

PARAPHRASE

Director Steven Spielberg’s mother said that she never understood her son while he was growing up.

DIRECT QUOTATION

Director Steven Spielberg’s mother said, “When he was growing up, I didn’t know he was a genius. Frankly, I didn’t know what he was.”

Exercise 39.1: Using Quotation Marks

Supply quotation marks where they are needed and place punctuation marks correctly in the following sentences. If a quotation should be set off in block form, place a B to indicate at which point the block would begin and an E to indicate where it would end. Make any other changes that would be necessary to handle a block quotation correctly. If no quotation marks are needed in a sentence, mark it with a C.

1. Of all Flannery O’Connor’s short stories, A Good Man Is Hard to Find best embodies the full range of her style.

2. O’Connor, Michael Finnegan wrote, mastered the use of caricature in character development.

3. The dictionary defines caricature as follows: The exaggeration of certain human characteristics in order to create a satiric effect.

4. The portrait of Mrs. Freeman in the short story Good Country People is an example of caricature: Besides the neutral expression that she wore when she was alone, Mrs. Freeman had two others, forward and reverse, that she used in all her human dealings. Her forward expression was steady and driving like the advance of a heavy truck. She seldom used the other expression because it was not often necessary for her to retract a statement. O’Connor even uses the name Freeman ironically because Mrs. Freeman is no more free than the speeding truck she is compared to.

5. To reveal the limited natures of her characters, O’Connor often fills their speech with stock phrases, such as Nothing is perfect; That is life; and You’re the wheel behind the wheel.

6. Sometimes her characters seem too strange to be real, but like all writers who will endure, she draws her material from life, thus following Alexander Pope’s dictate: Know then thyself, presume not God to scan; The proper study of Mankind is Man.

7. She studied people, and the absurdity of much of the world delighted her. Sally Fitzgerald writes about O’Connor’s letters, She regaled us with Hadacol advertisements; birth announcements of infants with names that had to be read to be believed; such news items as the attendance of Roy Rogers’ horse at a church service in California.

8. Could her intense interest in the absurd behavior of people continue one critic asked and still remain fresh?

9. I’ve reached the point where I can’t do again what I can do well she wrote in a letter and the larger things I need to do now, I doubt my capacity for doing.

10. Many prefer distant landscapes such as the magical kingdom in Coleridge’s short poem Kubla Khan, which begins In Xanadu did Kubla Khan / A stately pleasure-dome decree: / Where Alph, the sacred river ran Through caverns measureless to man / Down to a sunless sea.

40 Colon :

A colon has several conventional uses. It introduces sentence elements that explain, illustrate, or amplify portions of a sentence. A colon also introduces formal quotations and separates subtitles and titles, subdivisions of time, parts of biblical citations, and city and publisher in bibliographic entries.

40a Use a colon to introduce a series following a complete sentence.

Maya Angelou is best known for four volumes of autobiography**:** *I Know Why the Caged Bird Sings, Gather Together in My Name, Singin' and Swingin' and Gettin' Merry Like Christmas,* and *The Heart of a Woman.*

They stood on a hilltop and watched the crowd pour across the bridge**:** families pulling carts piled high with furniture, soldiers in torn uniforms and dragging their rifles by the strap, and children, crying, lost, helpless.

40b Use a colon after *the following* or *as follows* to introduce a statement or series.

In the upper-right-hand corner of your paper write the following**:** name, course number, assignment number, and date.

The secret to understanding history is as follows**:** whatever goes around will come around.

40c Use a colon to announce a second main clause that explains the first.

She has no doubts about her future**:** she will first attend medical school and then train as a psychiatrist.

NOTE: Capitalizing the first word of a main clause that follows a colon depends on the style you are following. (See capitals, 47a.)

40d Use a colon to introduce a final appositive.

August 6, 1945, is a day we should never forget: the day humanity ignited the earth.

40e Use a colon to introduce a long or formal quotation.

In 1962 Rachel Carson's *Silent Spring* sounded the warning:

> The most alarming of all humankind's assaults upon the environment is the contamination of air, earth, rivers, and sea with dangerous and even lethal materials. This pollution is for the most part irrecoverable; the chain of evil it initiates not only in the world that must support life but in living tissues is for the most part irreversible.

40f Use a colon to separate subtitles and titles, subdivisions of time, parts of biblical citations, and city and publisher in bibliographic entries.

The Origins of English: A Social and Linguistic History
1:13 a.m. 12:34 p.m. Matthew 4:6–10
New York: HarperCollins, 1996

NOTE: The MLA and some other styles use a period for biblical citations: Matthew 4.6–10.

40g Use a colon at the end of a formal salutation.

Dear Mr. and Mrs. Fritz: To Whom It May Concern:

40h Do not misuse the colon by placing it after a linking verb (separating the verb from its direct object) or a preposition or by placing it in a sentence that lacks a formal introduction for what follows.

- You will need~~:~~ a toothbrush, toothpaste, razor, shaving cream, and change of clothes.
- Finchamp, a well-traveled man, has lived in~~:~~ Paris, London, Rome, Dublin, and Berlin.

◆ Bluegrass music makes use of several stringed instruments, such as; banjo, guitar, mandolin, and fiddle.

Exercise 40.1: Using Colons

Correct the following sentences, inserting colons as needed.

1. After becoming rich I acquired three things I never had before, friends, relatives, and lovers.
2. The assignment for Bible as Literature is as follows, John 21, 17–30.
3. The town meeting broke up following a fiery outburst by one resident, "Either clean up the streets or declare the neighborhood a public-health hazard."
4. He drove nonstop from 530 a.m. to 530 p.m. for one reason to be present for the reading of the will.
5. The secret lesson that comes from studying poetry is simple, don't quit your day job.

Exercise 40.2: Using Colons

Use a colon to combine each group of sentences into a single sentence. You will have to revise wording and exclude some words to make the combined sentences read correctly.

1. He drove twelve hours nonstop for one reason. That reason was to arrive before the opening kickoff.
2. The philosopher Sören Kierkegaard contemplated the future with a simply stated attitude. He defined it as fear and trembling.
3. Yahoos were introduced in Jonathan Swift's *Gulliver's Travels.* They are a race of brutish, degraded creatures who have the form and all the vices of human beings.
4. Our forests, our hills, our prairies all have one thing in common. They will soon succumb to land development.
5. Propaganda devices have been given catchy names. Some of the names are "glittering generalities," "bandwagon," "testimonial," "plain folks," and "poisoning the well."

41 The Dash —

Use a dash to emphasize a sentence element and to indicate a break in tone or thought. Do not use a dash habitually in place of a comma, a semicolon, parentheses, or a period. Reserve dashes for situations calling for special emphasis or for the infrequent situation when only a dash will make your meaning clear.

In a typed paper make a dash by joining two hyphens (—) without spaces before or after them.

41a Use dashes to emphasize appositives and parenthetical expressions.

Judge Sarah Riley sentenced O'Neil—the treasurer of Local 1026 and once the friend of local politicians—to five years.

The craft of surgery—though some would call it an art—demands the steady hand of a miniaturist to work the scalpel through a web of arteries and veins.

41b Use a dash to separate a series that comes at the beginning of a sentence.

Aching feet and ankles, throbbing shins, clicking knees, and crumbling hip joints—these physical ailments result from running on asphalt or cement.

41c Use a dash for special emphasis or clarity.

Gary March decided to outrage his associates by wearing gray slacks, a brown sport coat, and a pink shirt—but no one noticed.

The meeting was attended by two consultants—a historian and a psychologist.

In the last example a dash must be used rather than a comma to make it clear that the meeting was attended by two consultants, not by four people—two consultants, a historian, and a psychologist.

41d Use dashes to show a break in tone or thought.

"I don't—well—I just can't."
"Can't what?"
"Can't seem—OK—I will if you help."

41e Use a dash to precede an author's name after a formal quotation that stands separately from the text, such as an epigraph.

Fasten your seat belts—we're going to have a bumpy night.
—Bette Davis

42 Ellipsis Mark ...

An ellipsis mark (. . .) indicates that one or more words within a quotation have been intentionally omitted, either to avoid including unnecessary or irrelevant portions of a quoted passage or to mark an unfinished statement in dialogue.

42a Use an ellipsis mark to indicate an omission in a quotation that you have edited to fit the purposes of a paper.

ORIGINAL PASSAGE

All his books in the Yoknapatawpha cycle are part of the same living pattern. It is the pattern, not the printed volumes in which part of it is recorded, that is Faulkner's real achievement. Its existence helps to explain one feature of his work: that each novel, each long or short story, seems to reveal more than it states explicitly and to have a subject bigger than itself. All the separate works are like blocks of marble from the same quarry: they show the veins and faults of the mother rock. Or else—to use a rather strained figure—they are like wooden planks that were cut, not from a log, but from a still-living tree. The planks are planed and chiseled into their final shapes, but the tree itself heals over the wound and continues to grow.

—Malcolm Cowley

EDITED WITHIN A PAPER

Malcolm Cowley praises the interconnectedness of Faulkner's work:

> All his books in the Yoknapatawpha cycle are part of the same living pattern. It is the pattern . . . that is Faulkner's real achievement. . . . Each novel, each long or short story, seems to reveal more than it states explicitly and to have a subject bigger than itself.

When a complete sentence comes before an omission, as in the sentence that ends with *achievement,* you should place a period at the end of the sentence before the ellipsis mark. Note also that a complete sentence, even if it is only part of the original sentence, is capitalized. Finally, note that although the quotation is part of a larger paragraph, an ellipsis mark is not used at the end of the quotation.

42b Use a row of evenly spaced periods to indicate that one or more paragraphs of prose or one or more lines of poetry have been omitted from a quotation.

And for all this, nature is never spent;
There lives the dearest freshness deep down things;
....
Because the Holy Ghost over the bent
World broods with warm breast and with ah! bright wings.

--Gerard Manley Hopkins, "God's Grandeur"

42c Use an ellipsis mark to indicate an unfinished statement in speech or dialogue.

Barry's nervousness got him off to a bad start: "I'm not sure how to begin. It seems as if . . . I don't know how to tell . . . I don't want to appear . . . Miss Jones . . . can I call you Mildred?"

43 Parentheses ( )

Parentheses separate incidental information from the rest of the sentence. They serve approximately the same function as commas and dashes in some situations, though each mark gives a different emphasis to the inserted information.

> Bernard Slye, the famous movie actor, was this year's grand marshal. [Commas imply that the inserted information is equal in importance to Bernard Slye.]
>
> Bernard Slye—the famous movie actor—was this year's grand marshal. [Dashes give the inserted information more emphasis.]
>
> Bernard Slye (the famous movie actor) was this year's grand marshal. [Parentheses imply that the inserted information is incidental.]

All three of the preceding sentences are punctuated correctly. Usually, however, commas, dashes, and parentheses are not used interchangeably but are used with different kinds of inserted information. (See comma, Chapter 36; dash, Chapter 41.)

> Billie Jean Stanford, one of our town's leading citizens, donated one thousand dollars to the earthquake relief fund. [Commas used for inserted information that departs from the thought of the rest of the sentence.]
>
> Billie Jean Stanford—bless her kind heart—donated one thousand dollars to the earthquake relief fund. [Dashes used for a strong break in sentence continuity.]
>
> Billie Jean Stanford (Bob's mother) donated one thousand dollars to the earthquake relief fund. [Parentheses used for inserted information of only incidental interest.]

43a Use parentheses to enclose parenthetical descriptions or explanations.

> Zablonsky Hall (its brick exterior almost entirely covered with ivy) stands at the top of the hill. [Description]

The lecture on phototaxis (the movement of an organism in response to the stimulus of light) gave Nadia the idea for her animated film. [Explanation]

If a parenthetical sentence comes between two sentences, it should begin with a capital letter and end with a period, question mark, or exclamation point.

My uncle was born in 1928. (What a year that was!) Bread was nine cents a loaf and a new Ford cost about five hundred dollars.

NOTE: Nonessential elements take no special punctuation other than the parentheses. At times punctuation marks may follow the parentheses if those marks are part of the main sentence.

When I feel my stomach churning from fear (usually on the morning of a midterm or final), I do deep-breathing exercises.

43b Use parentheses to enclose letters or figures that label items in a series.

To begin playing tennis well, you must remember these three fundamental points: (1) tennis is a sideways game, (2) the backhand stroke makes a loop, and (3) the follow-through should end high.

NOTE: When lists are set off from text, the letters and figures labeling them are usually not enclosed in parentheses.

44 Brackets [ ]

Always use brackets to enclose your own comments that explain, clarify, or correct the words of a writer you quote.

FOR EXPLANATION	Flora spoke in a soft voice to the other campers: "In all my years [she had been a ranger at Pig Pines for seven summers], I've never seen a more beautiful sunrise."

FOR CLARITY	Ibrahim, the unenthusiastic protagonist, "surveyed the wreckage [of the airplane] and smiled."
FOR COMPLETENESS	The tall, dark-haired man finally spoke: "[I] try to mind my own business. [Why don't] you do the same?"

The word *sic*, a Latin term meaning "thus it is," in brackets marks an error that you have let stand in a quotation and that you did not make when you copied the quotation.

> Roberts set the scene: "And then nite [*sic*] seemed to crush the castle under a heavy blanket of gloom."

Use *sic* only for errors, not for disagreements you may have with a writer you are quoting.

45 The Slash /

The slash, or virgule, separates lines of poetry worked into the text of a paper.

> Faustus is astounded at the beauty of Helen, whom Mephistopheles has summoned to his room: "Was this the face that launch'd a thousand ships, / And burnt the topless towers of Ilium? / Sweet Helen, make me immortal with a kiss."

The slash is also used to indicate two options.

> Students may now take eight units of credit/no-credit courses.

NOTE: Do not join pronouns with a slash when referring to non–gender-specific antecedents. Instead, use *or.*

INCORRECT	CORRECT
he/she	he or she
him/her	him or her
his/her(s)	his or her(s)

46 End Punctuation .?!

Period

46a Use a period to end sentences that are statements, mild commands, or indirect questions.

The theater department presents a Shakespearean play every year. [Statement]

Be sure to buy your tickets early. [Mild command]

My uncle asked me which play would be performed this year. [Indirect question]

46b Use periods with most abbreviations.

Ms.	Dr.	Ave.	i.e.
Mr.	Ph.D.	Blvd.	e.g.

NOTE: Although the title Ms., used before a name in place of Miss or Mrs., is not an abbreviation, it is still followed by a period: Ms. Hansen.

Generally, BCE and CE do not take periods. No periods are needed in certain common abbreviations or in abbreviations of the names of well-known companies, agencies, or organizations.

NBA	CNN	CBS	IBM
TV	USA (or U.S.A.)	NCAA	VW

Do not use periods after U.S. Postal Service (zip code) abbreviations for states.

CA	MA	VT	WY

Do not use two periods at the end of a sentence.

LaToya received her R.N.
The name on the label is William Gordon, Jr.

Question Mark

46c Use a question mark after a direct question.

What changes led to this increase in production?

46d Use a question mark within parentheses to indicate doubt about the accuracy of a date or number.

The Peloponnesian War ended in 404 BCE (?) with a victory for Sparta.

Do not use a question mark within parentheses in an attempt to indicate sarcasm. Instead shape your words to show your intention.

INCORRECT	I never saw such a hardworking (?) supermarket cashier.
REWRITTEN	John is seldom accused of being hardworking.

Exclamation Point

46e Use an exclamation point after interjections, strong commands, and emphatic statements.

INTERJECTION	Wow! Look at that little S-car go.
STRONG COMMAND	"Go away!" she shouted at the dog. "Get out of this yard!"
EMPHATIC STATEMENT	I will never give up!

Do not use an exclamation point within parentheses to indicate sarcasm or amazement. Instead shape your words to convey the meaning.

INCORRECT	Gail's winning essay (!) was printed in the *Clarion.*
REWRITTEN	I couldn't believe Gail won the contest and had her essay printed in the *Clarion.*

NOTE: Only one mark of end punctuation is used. Do not combine marks of end punctuation.

◆ How can you do this to me?!

NOTE: A period is not used as end punctuation for the title of a work. A question mark or an exclamation point is used when appropriate.

Watching God
Shopping for a New Car?
Live Now!

PART VII

Mechanics

Turning in an essay with errors is much like giving a speech without knowing you have lettuce in your teeth. No matter how brilliant your insights or how witty your anecdotes, the audience will be distracted by the green bits of lettuce stuck between your incisors.

—Chuck Dawe, *writing teacher*

47 Capitals *cap/lc*

In most writing situations, the following guidelines will help you decide when to capitalize. Whenever you are confused about whether to capitalize a particular word, you can check a good dictionary.

47a Capitalize the first word of every sentence.

The fog drifted across the field.
Who is responsible for the engine failure?
Do not touch the kettle.

NOTE: Capitalizing the first word of question fragments in a series is optional. Both of the following examples are correct.

What is the best way to become successful? *by* hard work? *through* education? *by* luck?

What is the best way to become successful? *By* hard work? *Through* education? *By* luck?

Capitalizing the first word of a sentence following a colon depends upon the style you are following. The Modern Language Association (MLA) lowercases the first word if the sentence is other than a rule or a principle. The American Psychological Association (APA) always capitalizes the first word.

MLA STYLE	The eye does more than scan the physical world: *it* reveals the soul.
APA STYLE	The eye does more than scan the physical world: *It* reveals the soul.

47b Always capitalize the interjection *O* and the personal pronoun *I* as well as contractions made with *I*, such as *I've* and *I'm.*

I beseech Thee, O Father, to help me in my troubles.

Before I write an essay, I outline the main points of my argument.

Although I've been reading French for three years, I'm still uncomfortable speaking it.

47c Capitalize key words in titles.

Capitalize the first and last words and every important word in the titles of your papers and the titles of books, plays, short stories, poems, essays, songs, films, and works of art. Do not capitalize coordinating conjunctions, articles, the *to* of infinitives, or prepositions unless they begin or end a title.

Guinness Book of World Records
"Traveling through the Dark"

NOTE: Capitalize the word immediately following a colon in a title.

The Uses of Enchantment: The Meaning and Importance of Fairy Tales

Capitalize the first word in a hyphenated compound within a title. Capitalize the other parts of the hyphenated compound if they are nouns or adjectives or are as important as the first word.

"A Clean, Well-Lighted Place"
"Mysteries of Hide-and-Seek"
The Do-It-Yourself Environmental Handbook

NOTE: The APA capitalizes prepositions of four letters or more.

One Flew Over the Cuckoo's Nest

47d Capitalize the first word in directly quoted sentences or dialogue.

In *Love and Will,* psychologist Rollo May writes, "The striking thing about love and will in our day is that, whereas in the past they were always held up to us as the *answer* to life's predicaments, they have now become the *problem.*"

"This is illegal," the detective whispered, taking the crisp twenties. "We're in it together, I guess."

NOTE: Do not capitalize the first word after an interruption between parts of a quoted sentence.

"Politicians must be courageous," the senator said, "for if they are not, they will never make unpopular decisions."

47e Capitalize the first word in every line of poetry.

To see a world in a grain of sand
And a heaven in a wild flower,
Hold infinity in the palm of your hand
And eternity in an hour.

—WILLIAM BLAKE, "Auguries of Innocence"

If the poet does not follow this convention, use the poet's style.

anyone lived in a pretty how town
(with up so floating many bells down)
spring summer autumn winter
he sang his didn't he danced his did.

—E. E. CUMMINGS, "anyone lived in a pretty how town"

47f Capitalize proper nouns, proper adjectives, and words used to form essential parts of proper names.

PROPER NOUNS	PROPER ADJECTIVES	COMMON NOUNS
Freud	Freudian	psychoanalyst
Texas	Texan	state
France	French	country

The following is a representative list of words that typically are capitalized. Do not capitalize an article that precedes a proper noun unless it is part of the noun.

SPECIFIC PERSONS, PLACES, THINGS

Pat Kubis	the Tower of London
the Atlantic Ocean	*The Old Curiosity Shop*
the Washington Monument	the Grand Canyon
Europe	the *Los Angeles Times*

HISTORIC EVENTS, PERIODS, MOVEMENTS, DOCUMENTS

Desert Storm	the Enlightenment
the Boston Tea Party	the Roaring Twenties
the Middle Ages	the Bill of Rights

NOTE: Do not capitalize centuries, as in eighteenth century, nineteenth century, and so on.

DAYS OF THE WEEK, MONTHS, HOLIDAYS

Friday	September	Fourth of July

Associations, Organizations, Government Departments, Political Parties

American Bar Association	U.S. Postal Service
League of Women Voters	House of Representatives
Boston Symphony Orchestra	Republican Party
Metropolitan Museum of Art	Democrats

Names of Educational Institutions, Departments, Courses

Westbrook College	Department of English
Chapman University	History 150

Religions, Religious Followers, Religious Terms

Christianity	Christians	God
Judaism	Jews	Judgment Day
Buddhism	Buddhists	Holy Ghost
Hinduism	Hindus	the Virgin
Islam	Muslims	Allah

NOTE: Capitalizing pronouns referring to God is optional in general writing but required in most religious writing. Do not capitalize *who, whom,* or *whose* when referring to God.

Races, Tribes, Nationalities, and Their Languages

Native American	European
Iroquois	Gaelic
African American	Asian
Irish	Yugoslav
Latino	Hispanic

NOTE: Capitalizing *black* and *white* when referring to people is optional. Both of the following examples are correct.

In American cities, Blacks and Whites are struggling to revitalize neglected neighborhoods.

In American cities, blacks and whites are struggling to revitalize neglected neighborhoods.

Names of Celestial Bodies

Mars the North Star the Big Dipper

Trade Names

Nintendo Ford Frisbee Coke Xerox

47g Capitalize titles when they come before proper names, and capitalize abbreviations for academic degrees when they come after proper names.

Chancellor Carmen Herrera	Carmen Herrera, M.D.
President Cecelia Perdomo	Cecelia Perdomo, Ph.D.

NOTE: Generally, do not capitalize titles that follow a name.

Harold Thomas, treasurer
Adelina Tapparo, professor of history

47h Capitalize abbreviations that indicate time, divisions of government, national and international organizations, businesses, and call letters of radio and television stations.

BC	A.M. (or a.m.)	NATO
BCE	P.M. (or p.m.)	IBM
FDIC	YMCA	WQXR

WRITER'S CLINIC

Capitalizing Titles

When a word that functions as a title or shows a family relationship comes before a person's name, capitalize it.

> Today Senator Boxer announced that she would seek reelection.

Also capitalize such words when they could be replaced by a name.

> The Mayor announced that she would seek reelection.

Do not capitalize such words in other circumstances.

> A mayor from California announced that she would seek reelection.

47i Avoid common mistakes in capitalization.

Do not capitalize common nouns used in place of proper nouns.

INCORRECT I plan to enroll in College next Fall.

CORRECT	I plan to enroll in college next fall.
CORRECT	I plan to enroll in Bradley College next September.

Do not capitalize the seasons or academic years or terms.

spring fall senior year winter quarter

Do not capitalize words denoting family relations unless they are part of or a substitute for proper nouns.

INCORRECT	My Mother met my Father on an ocean voyage.
CORRECT	My mother met my father on an ocean voyage.
CORRECT	Mother met Father on an ocean voyage.

Do not capitalize general directions unless they refer to specific geographical areas.

south	the South
east	the East
western	East Manhattan

Exercise 47.1: Capitalizing Words

In the following paragraph, capitalize words as necessary. Consult a dictionary if you are in doubt.

in american literature, satire has helped us examine human experience and smile. humorist kurt vonnegut jr., author of satiric novels such as *cat's cradle, slaughterhouse-five, breakfast of champions, and galapagos,* believes humankind is in trouble. "our brains," vonnegut says, "are too large." according to vonnegut, nature goofed: *homo sapiens's* highly developed cerebral lobes are responsible for the world's troubles. "our brains are terribly oversized," he says, "and must keep creating things to do." he charges that big brains are responsible for the near destruction of native american culture. humankind's big brains caused the civil war in america and world war I. big brains created the third reich in germany that led to world war II and created death camps like dachau and belsen. humankind's oversized brain made the nuclear weapons that were dropped on hiroshima and nagasaki. vonnegut believes our big brains can be used to solve all our problems, but will it happen? he does not know. after all, human beings now think they are the intellectual center of the universe, when in reality they are nothing more than a speck of dust in the milky way.

48 Apostrophe '

The apostrophe indicates possession, the omission of letters in words, and the plurals of letters and words used as words.

48a Use an apostrophe to form the possessive case for nouns and indefinite pronouns.

To form the possessive of singular nouns, plural nouns not ending in *-s*, and indefinite pronouns (such as *no one, someone,* and *everybody*), add *'s*. (See indefinite pronouns, 66b.)

> Akemi's novel is about an ex-governor's climb to the presidency.
>
> History exists because of humankind's outstanding achievement: the creation of written language.
>
> If only he could be someone's friend—anyone's—but he felt doomed to be everyone's curse.

To form the possessive of singular nouns ending in *-s*, add *'s*.

> He rushed into the boss's office.
>
> Little is known about Cheryl Moses's life in Paris during the Depression.
>
> James's reptile collection gives me an eerie feeling.

In the following examples, only the apostrophe is added because adding *'s* would make pronunciation difficult.

> James' snake collection gives me an eerie feeling.
> The court listened to Socrates' speech.

To form the possessive of plural words ending in *-s*, add only an apostrophe.

> The girls' basketball team won.

WRITER’S CLINIC

Checking Apostrophes to Show Possession

You can check to see if you need to use an apostrophe to indicate possession by rewriting a sentence, using *of.*

A *persons right* to speak freely is protected by law.

REWRITTEN

The *right of a person* to speak freely is protected by law.

CORRECTED

A *person’s right* to speak freely is protected by law.

The victory was the Mustangs’ first.

To form the possessive of compound words, add *’s* or an apostrophe (following the rules for forming possessives) to the last word only.

My son-in-law’s job is threatened by military cutbacks.

When two or more nouns show joint possession, add *’s* to the last noun in the group.

Raoul, Gus, and Meera’s business is facing stiff competition.

When two or more nouns show individual possession, add *’s* to each noun in the group.

Raoul’s, Gus’s, and Meera’s businesses are facing stiff competition.

Exercise 48.1: Using Apostrophes

Insert apostrophes as needed in the following sentences.

1. *Sophies Choice* advanced William Styrons reputation as Americas leading novelist.
2. A kangaroos hop can span forty-two yards.
3. Grooves and Flags fates are intertwined.
4. The Childrens Book Shoppe on 15th Street holds Kids Time, an hour of storytelling, three times each week.

5. Fathers Day and Mothers Day are celebrated yearly, but no special day has been designated for fathers- and mothers-in-law.

48b Do not use an apostrophe with possessive pronouns, such as *his, hers, its, ours, yours, theirs,* and *whose.*

The manuscript is *theirs;* the income is *ours.*
If you want the truth, it is *yours.*

NOTE: Be careful not to confuse the possessive pronouns *its, whose, your,* and *their* with the contractions *it's* (it is), *who's* (who is), *you're* (you are), and *they're* (they are).

48c Use the apostrophe to mark omissions in contractions.

it's (it is)	don't (do not)	o'clock (of the clock)
we're (we are)	you're (you are)	class of '57 (class of 1957)

48d Use *'s* to form the plurals of letters and words used as words.

When speaking publicly do not use *well*'s, *huh*'s, and *you know*'s.

I got two *A*'s and three *B*'s.

NOTE: Letters and words used as words are italicized, but the *'s* is not italicized as part of the word. (In handwritten and typed papers, italics are indicated by underlining. See italics, Chapter 50.)

Exercise 48.2: Using Apostrophes

Delete or insert apostrophes in the following sentences. Correct any mistakes in possessive pronouns. If any sentence is correct, mark it with a C.

1. Mississippi is spelled with four *s*s and four *i*s.
2. Whos 57 Ford is this? Hers or his?
3. Its the house on the corner.
4. She became rich in the state's lottery.
5. His *what ifs* make the world sound gloomy.
6. It was our mistake, not hers.

7. Who's responsibility is it?
8. The summer of 1992 was as hot as an angry dragon's breath.
9. *Whys* and *how comes* seem to breed on the tongue of every four-year-old.
10. Many writers confuse *their* or *there* with *theyre* and *your* with *youre.*

49 Abbreviations *ab*

In most writing, avoid using abbreviations unless they are commonly accepted.

49a Abbreviate titles before a proper name, if you wish.

Mr. Douglas Miner
Mrs. Catherine Rojas
Prof. Wilma Steward
Gen. Doyle Fujimoto
Ms. Florence Nesbitt
Dr. Hanh Tran
Rev. Marion Sylvester
Msgr. Ramon Alvarez

NOTE: Do not abbreviate a title when it is not used with a proper name.

INCORRECT	The Maj. deployed the volunteers in an awkward formation.
CORRECT	The major deployed the volunteers in an awkward formation.
CORRECT	Maj. Olson deployed the volunteers in an awkward formation.

49b Abbreviate titles immediately following proper names.

Yung Kee, M.D.
Sumi Inoue, LL.D.
Donald Sporakowski, Ph.D.
Maude Cook, Ed.D.

NOTE: You may use abbreviations for academic degrees without proper names.

She has one goal—to earn an LL.D. by 2004.

49c Use familiar abbreviations for names of corporations, organizations, and countries.

NBC FBI IRS USA (or U.S.A.) AFL-CIO

NOTE: If a name that you plan to use repeatedly is not well known and can be abbreviated, you may write the full name followed by the abbreviation in parentheses the first time you use it; you may then use the abbreviation throughout the paper.

> Parents, teachers, and students formed the Committee for Educational Excellence of Orange County (CEEOC) to improve classroom teaching. CEEOC raises money to support experimental programs that might go unfunded because of limited state resources.

49d Use the commonly accepted abbreviations *a.m., p.m., BCE, CE, no.,* and the symbol *$* with specific dates and numbers only.

12:01 a.m. (or A.M.)	1:00 p.m. (or P.M.)
21 BCE	CE 1061
no. 12	$5,501

NOTE: BCE always follows a date; CE always precedes a date.

49e Use common English and Latin abbreviations in tables, footnotes, reference lists, and comments placed inside parentheses.

Hobson, Sydney, et al. *A Hiker's Guide to South America.* 4th ed. 3 vols. New York: Wainwright, 1989.

The four defendants (i.e., Humphreys, Kettler, Rodda, and Gandy) had to be restrained.

49f Do not abbreviate personal names, calendar terms, courses of study, divisions of written works, units of measurement, or geographical names.

PERSONAL NAMES

◆ Edw. Walden wrote three unpublished books. [correction: Edw~~.~~ → Edward]

NAMES OF DAYS, MONTHS, AND HOLIDAYS

◆ The ~~Mon.~~ Monday before ~~Xmas~~ Christmas is the earliest I begin to shop.

◆ Virgos are born during the second half of ~~Aug.~~ August and the first half of ~~Sept.~~ September

NOTE: MLA style abbreviates the name of the month in the list of works cited; APA style, however, spells out the name of the month in the reference list. (See 57c.)

EDUCATIONAL COURSES

◆ You must take ~~lit.~~ literature and ~~bio.~~ biology to finish the general education requirements.

DIVISIONS OF WRITTEN WORKS

◆ ~~Sec.~~ Section 4, ~~ch.~~ chapter 3 is due next week.

UNITS OF MEASUREMENT

◆ The car skidded 106 ~~ft.~~ feet and 7 ~~in.~~ inches

NOTE: Long, familiar phrases, such as *miles per hour,* are usually abbreviated (mph).

> The Porsche nosed into the turn at 120 mph, fishtailed, and then screeched down the highway.

GEOGRAPHICAL NAMES

◆ The outstanding characteristic of ~~L.A., Calif.~~ Los Angeles, California, is that it seems to be able to stretch itself from the ~~Mex.~~ Mexican border to San Francisco.

◆ He grew up in Huntington ~~Pk.~~ Park on Randolph ~~St.~~ Street near Miles ~~Ave.~~ Avenue

NOTE: Certain familiar abbreviations for countries are acceptable: USA (or U.S.A.).

50 Italics (Underlining) *ital*

Use underlining to represent italic (or *slanted*) type when distinguishing certain titles, words, and phrases in typed and handwritten papers.

50a Underline the titles of books, periodicals, newspapers, pamphlets, plays, films, long poems, long musical compositions, television and radio shows, and works of visual art.

(See quotation marks, 39b.)

When underlining a title, be precise. Do not underline an initial article (*a, an, the*) unless it is part of the title.

BOOKS	The Color Purple
MAGAZINES	Time
NEWSPAPERS	The New York Times, the Los Angeles Times
PAMPHLETS	Life in the Fast Lane
LONG POEMS	The Waste Land
PLAYS	Death of a Salesman
FILMS	A Beautiful Mind
TV PROGRAMS	X Files
RADIO PROGRAMS	The Shadow
MUSICAL WORKS	The Nutcracker Suite
VISUAL ART WORKS	Mona Lisa
COMIC STRIPS	Doonesbury
SOFTWARE	Norton's Utilities

NOTE: Names of legal documents, the Bible, and parts of the Bible are not underlined.

INCORRECT	The Bill of Rights contains the first ten amendments to the Constitution.
CORRECT	The Bill of Rights contains the first ten amendments to the Constitution.

INCORRECT	The Bible is composed of the Old Testament and the New Testament.
CORRECT	The Bible is composed of the Old Testament and the New Testament.

50b Underline the names of spacecraft, aircraft, ships, and trains.

Discovery   Titanic   Orient Express   Spirit of St. Louis

50c Underline non-English words and phrases that have not become common expressions.

Harrods, Europe's largest department store, tries to live up to its motto--Omnia, omnibus, ubique--everyone, everything, everywhere.

Foreign words that have been absorbed into English do not need to be underlined. For example, the words *cliché* and *genre,* both French, are commonly used in English and therefore are not underlined. When in doubt, consult a dictionary to see if a foreign word or phrase should be underlined.

NOTE: Most commonly used foreign abbreviations—i.e., etc., ibid. op. cit., sic—are not italicized.

50d Underline words, letters, numbers, phrases, and symbols when they are referred to as such.

When writing a paper, you should not use & for and.

Someone had painted an X on the oak.

The voters are tired of maybe and perhaps.

"Mind your p's and q's" was my grandmother's favorite expression.

NOTE: You can use quotation marks instead of underlining to set off a word you are defining. Both of the following styles are correct, but use one style consistently throughout a paper.

Bumbershoot, which is slang for umbrella, is the result of merging umbr from umbrella and shoot from parachute.

"Bumbershoot," which is slang for "umbrella," is the result of merging "umbr" from "umbrella" and "shoot" from "parachute."

50e Underlining may be used to show emphasis.

I wrote that I wanted the entire amount.

Excessive underlining, however, will only distract the reader and diminish the emphasis.

I wrote that I wanted the entire amount.

50f Do not underline the titles of your own papers.

Propaganda: Five Ways to Trick a Consumer

Do underline the title of another work included in your title.

The Message of The Autobiography of Malcolm X

51 Hyphen *hyph*

Use the hyphen to divide words, form compounds, and add some prefixes, suffixes, and letters to words.

51a Use a hyphen to indicate that a word is broken at the end of a typed or handwritten line.

Emergency volunteers, medical workers, and federal avia-
tion experts began sifting through the wreckage.

NOTE: Be sure to divide words between syllables. Whenever you are unsure of the syllabication of a word, check a dictionary. Do not break a one-syllable word.

51b Use a hyphen to form certain compound words.

cross-reference	clear-cut
mother-in-law	half-moon
deep-fry	bull's-eye
jack-o-lantern	great-grandfather

NOTE: Since most compound words are not hyphenated, check a dictionary whenever you are uncertain about whether to hyphenate a compound word.

51c Use a hyphen to join two or more words that serve as a single descriptive word before a noun.

The one-eyed, one-armed cowboy could hold his own in any two-bit joint he stumbled into.

In Pentagon jargon, two-syllable names indicate jets, and one-syllable names indicate piston-driven aircraft.

Since taking a course in crafts, Beth has produced some well-designed furniture.

The twenty-year-old adventurer will lecture tomorrow.

NOTE: When the descriptive phrase comes after the noun, the words usually are not hyphenated.

Beth's furniture is well designed.

The adventurer, who is twenty years old, will lecture tomorrow.

But when such a phrase is used as a noun, it is hyphenated.

The adventurer, a daring twenty-year-old, will lecture tomorrow.

51d Use a hyphen to spell out the compound numbers twenty-one to ninety-nine and fractions.

seventy-five ninety-nine one-half three-fourths

51e Use a hyphen to join certain prefixes, suffixes, and letters to words.

Use a hyphen to join a prefix to a word beginning with a capital letter.

Those who criticize foreign policy are sometimes accused of being anti-American.

Use a hyphen between words and the prefixes *self-*, *all-*, and *ex-* (meaning formerly) as well as the suffix *-elect.*

self-control ex-student president-elect all-encompassing

Use a hyphen to join single letters to words.

Z-transfer U-turn T-shirt F-sharp

51f Use suspended hyphens for hyphenated words in a series.

My *mother-*, *father-*, and *brother-in-law* graduated from high school.

51g Use a hyphen to avoid confusion.

In creating compound words, use a hyphen rather than doubling vowels and tripling consonants.

- The current college administration has an antiintellectual attitude.
- When the wind blows, the chimes make belllike music.
- The concept of a college without walls is like a wallless room—full of wind.

Use a hyphen to avoid ambiguity.

re-creation (something created anew)
recreation (a diverting activity)
re-sign (to sign again)
resign (to give up a position)

52 Numbers *num*

Follow established conventions when writing numbers.

52a Spell out any number consisting only of one or two words.

Eighty-five cyclists started, but only *twenty-one* finished.

The race covered *four hundred* miles of tough Mexican desert over a period of *three* days.

52b Use figures for any number that requires more than two words to spell out.

In Kobe, Japan, 5,300 people lost their lives in an earthquake that left over 200,000 homeless.

NOTE: Be consistent. If there are several numbers, some composed of one or two words and others of more than two words, use numerals for all of them. Also, if numbers are used frequently in a discussion, use numerals for all of them.

52c Use a combination of figures and words for numbers when such a combination will keep your writing clear.

The president invited fifty 10-year-olds to the Easter celebration.

52d Use figures for dates; time; addresses; scores and other numerical results; percentages, decimals, and fractions; pages and divisions of written works; and exact amounts of money.

DAYS AND YEARS

November 11, 2002 423 BCE CE 1492 the 1990s

The forms *1st, 2nd,* and so on, as well as *fourth, fifth,* and so on, are sometimes used in dates but only when the year is omitted: *December 5th, December fifth.*

TIME OF DAY

12:15 p.m. 1300 hours 5:43 a.m.

If you are not using a.m. or p.m., write the time in words.

We will meet at twelve-thirty, and we will leave at one o'clock.

ADDRESSES

4345 Sandburg Way   4 Upper Newport Plaza

SCORES, STATISTICS, RESULTS OF SURVEYS

The Hawks beat the Hornets 133 to 102.

You must score over 600 to qualify.

Out of the 500 surveyed, 498 recognized the name *Tyrone Power,* but only 56 knew he had been an actor, and 16 said they had never seen "one" but had heard they were great to drive.

PERCENTAGES, DECIMALS, FRACTIONS

23 percent (or 23%)   98.6   12⅓

PAGES AND DIVISIONS OF WRITTEN WORKS

page 3, pages 110–124	chapter 2	volume 5
act 4	scene 1	lines 5–22

EXACT AMOUNTS OF MONEY

$100,871 $19.76 $123 million

52e Spell out any number that begins a sentence.

Two hundred thirteen [not 213] voted for the amendment.

Revising the sentence may be more effective than spelling out the number.

The amendment passed 213 to 0.

Exercise 52.1: Writing Numbers

Correct the faulty use of numbers in the following sentences. If any sentence is correct, mark it with a C.

1. In Super Bowl V at Miami's Orange Bowl, Dallas and Baltimore were tied thirteen to thirteen with 5 seconds left when the Colts' Jim O'Brien kicked a field goal.
2. 42.5 million people live in Congo, which has a growth rate of three point three percent.
3. Massive mud slides have been known to reach speeds of sixty mph.

4. On October 18th, 1864, 15 Confederate raiders robbed 3 banks in St. Albans, Vermont, and buried $114,522 in gold and currency, $82\frac{1}{2}$ percent of the town's total capital.
5. Nearly 1,000 fans were turned away from the auditorium gates even though they had paid as much as $34.50 for seats.

53 Spelling *sp*

Nobody improves poor spelling without working at it. To get started, use a dictionary to check the spelling of words you are uncertain about. If you write on a word processor, use the Spellcheck program to check the spelling in each paper you write, but be careful—a Spellcheck program won't distinguish among words that sound the same but are spelled differently, such as *accept, except; their, there, they're; who's, whose; its, it's;* and *won, one.* Also compile a personal list of spelling demons, the words you frequently misspell, such as *occasion, separate, rhythm, negotiator, strategy.* When you use a word on your demon list, double-check its spelling. Finally, remember that basic spelling guidelines and lists of commonly misspelled words will help you eliminate spelling errors.

53a Place *i* before *e* except after *c* or when pronounced like *a* as in *neighbor* or *weigh.*

I BEFORE *E*	chief, grief, belief, brief, fierce, frieze, sieve
E BEFORE *I*	ceiling, conceit, receive, freight
EXCEPTIONS	either, neither, foreign, forfeit, height, leisure, weird, seize, sheik.

53b Usually drop a silent final *e* before a suffix that begins with a vowel. Usually keep the silent final *e* before a suffix beginning with a consonant.

DROP THE *E*	come + ing = coming	force + ible = forcible
	fame + ous = famous	love + able = lovable
EXCEPTIONS	dying, singeing, mileage, noticeable, courageous	

KEEP THE *E*	care + ful = careful arrange + ment = arrangement
EXCEPTIONS	awful, ninth, truly, argument, judgment

53c When a final *y* follows a consonant, change *y* to *i* before a suffix except when the suffix begins with *i.*

With *y* before a consonant:

try + ed = tried   messy + er = messier

With *y* before a vowel:

obey + ed = obeyed   sway + s = sways

With a suffix beginning with *i:*

apply + ing = applying   try + ing = trying

53d Double the final consonant before a suffix beginning with a vowel if the word has only one syllable or is stressed on the last syllable.

drop + ing = dropping   stop + ed = stopped
forget + ing = forgetting   submit + ed = submitted

53e Form plurals correctly.

Add *s* to form the plurals of most words. Add *es* to form the plurals of words ending in *-s, -sh, -ch,* or *-x.* For most words ending in *y,* change the *y* to *i* and add *es.*

book, books	dress, dresses	bush, bushes
fox, foxes	fly, flies	church, churches

Form the plural of hyphenated words by adding *s* to the main word.

son-in-law, sons-in-law

Form the plural of family names ending in *-y* by adding *s,* such as *McCurry, McCurrys.*

Form the plural of most nouns ending in *-f* or *-fe* by adding *s.* But the plural of some of these nouns is formed by changing the *f* to *v* and adding *s* or *es.*

chief, chiefs	dwarf, dwarfs	roof, roofs
calf, calves	knife, knives	leaf, leaves

COMPUTER CLINIC

Spell Checkers

A spell checker is a valuable software asset, but it won't solve all your spelling problems. For example, a spell checker will not flag commonly confused words such as *illusion* and *allusion* or *accept* and *except*. It will not flag words that sound alike but have different meanings and spellings, such as *all together* and *altogether* or *there* and *their*. It will not show you how to spell words not in its dictionary, but it will flag them so you can check the spelling in your dictionary. Nevertheless, a spell checker is useful because it will flag most typos and most misspellings, allow you to correct the errors on the screen, and integrate the changes throughout the text with one click of the mouse.

Form the plural of words ending in *-o* following a vowel by adding *s*, but form the plural of most words ending in *-o* following a consonant by adding *es*.

radio, radios	mosquito, mosquitoes

Exception: Form the plural of musical terms ending in *-o* by adding *s*.

piano, pianos	solo, solos

The plural of a few nouns is formed by irregular methods.

child, children	goose, geese	mouse, mice
ox, oxen	tooth, teeth	woman, women

Some nouns borrowed from French, Greek, and Latin retain the plural form of the original language.

alumnus, alumni	analysis, analyses
basis, bases	datum, data
medium, media	criterion, criteria

Some nouns are the same in plural and singular forms.

deer	Chinese	species	trout

Exercise 53.1: Using Spelling Guidelines

Complete the following words by filling in the blanks with *ie* or *ei*, whichever is correct.

1. w__rd
2. p__ce
3. perc__ve
4. n__ce
5. th__f
6. l__sure
7. c__ling
8. ach__ve
9. for__gn
10. rec__pt

Add the final suffix to the words below. Be able to explain the rule that applies to each word. Use the dictionary to check your work.

11. unwrap + ed
12. stubborn + ness
13. plant + ing
14. ski + ing
15. commit + ed
16. casual + ly
17. move + ing
18. merry + ly
19. argue + ment
20. write + ing

Write the plural forms of each of the following words. Be able to explain your spelling according to the rules for forming plurals. Refer to a dictionary when in doubt.

21. father-in-law
22. cameo
23. wife
24. loss
25. box
26. crisis
27. loaf
28. alumnus
29. Kelly
30. approach

Commonly Confused Words

Many spelling errors come from confusion over the meaning and correct spelling of commonly used words. Learn the spelling and the meaning of the following commonly confused words.

accept	to receive
except	to exclude
advice	counsel (noun)
advise	to give advice (verb)
affect	to influence (verb)
effect	a result (noun); to accomplish (verb)
all ready	prepared
already	previously
brake	to stop
break	to smash
buy	to purchase
by	near

capital	accumulated wealth; city serving as government seat
capitol	building in which legislative body meets (lowercase for state, uppercase for federal)
choose	to select
chose	past tense of *choose*
cite	to quote
sight	ability to see
site	a place
complement	something that completes
compliment	flattering remark
conscience	moral sense (noun)
conscious	aware (adjective)
coarse	rough (adjective)
course	path, procedure, process (noun)
decent	moral (adjective)
descent	a way down (noun)
dissent	to disagree (verb); difference of opinion (noun)
desert	to abandon (verb); barren land (noun)
dessert	last course of a meal
formally	in a formal manner
formerly	previously
forth	forward
fourth	after third
hear	to perceive by ear (verb)
here	in this place
heard	past tense of *hear*
herd	group of animals
instance	an example
instants	moments
its	possessive of *it*
it's	contraction of *it is*
lead	to show the way (verb); a metal (noun)
led	past tense of *lead*
lessen	to make less
lesson	something learned
loose	to free from restraint (verb); not fastened (adjective)
lose	to misplace; to be deprived of (verb)
passed	past tense of *pass*
past	no longer current (adjective); an earlier time (noun); beyond in time or place (preposition)

peace	absence of strife
piece	a part of something
plain	clear (adjective); level land (noun)
plane	airplane; carpenter's tool
principal	most important (adjective); leader (noun)
principle	basic truth or law (noun)
right	correct (adjective)
rite	ceremony (noun)
write	to record (verb)
road	a driving surface
rode	past tense of *ride*
stationary	unmoving
stationery	writing paper
their	possessive of *they*
there	in that place
they're	contraction of *they are*
to	toward
too	also; excess amount
two	the number following one
weak	not strong
week	Sunday through Saturday
weather	condition of climate
whether	if, either
who's	contraction of *who is*
whose	possessive of *who*
your	possessive of *you*
you're	contraction of *you are*

Exercise 53.2: Using Commonly Confused Words

For each of the following sentences, identify the correct word in parentheses.

1. The ancient temple was the (*cite, sight, site*) of mysterious rituals.
2. The coat does not (*complement, compliment*) the dress.
3. Her job is to (*advice, advise*) the board, not make (*its, it's*) decisions.
4. You must contribute (*weather, whether*) you want to or not.
5. The boys were not (*conscience, conscious*) of the damage they did.

6. I think I know (*who's, whose*) thumbprint that is.
7. He stands as (*stationary, stationery*) as a statue.
8. There is a (*principal, principle*) cause for his joy—money!
9. Can you identify the (*affect, effect*) of the chemical?
10. (*Accept, Except*) for Roberta, no one was in the house last night.

Frequently Misspelled Words

Learn to spell frequently misspelled words. The following is a list of one hundred commonly misspelled "demons."

absence	February	privilege
academic	foreign	probably
accidentally	forty	procedure
accommodate	friend	proceed
achieve	fulfill	quantity
across	government	quiet
all right	grammar	quite
already	harass	quizzes
apparent	height	receive
appearance	independent	reference
athletic	intelligence	referred
attendance	license	referring
believe	luxury	reminisce
benefited	maneuver	repetition
Britain	marriage	rhythm
business	mathematics	ridiculous
calendar	misspelled	sacrifice
candidate	neither	safety
cemetery	ninth	salary
definite	occasion	satellite
desperate	occur	secretary
develop	occurrence	seize
dilemma	optimistic	separate
dining	parallel	sergeant
embarrass	pastime	similar
emphasize	personnel	sincerely
existence	precede	sophomore
familiar	prejudice	specimen
fascinate	prevalent	strategy

subtly	tendency	vengeance
succeed	thorough	weird
succession	tragedy	writing
surprise	usually	
temperament	vacuum	

Exercise 53.3: Frequently Misspelled Words

Test yourself on the list of frequently misspelled words by asking someone to read the words aloud so that you can spell them.

PART VIII

Special College Essays

Writing is about getting something down, not about thinking something up. Whenever I strive to "think something up," writing becomes something I must stretch to achieve. It becomes loftier than I am, perhaps even something so lofty, it is beyond my grasp. When I am trying to think something up, I am straining. When I am focused on just getting something down, I have a sense of attention but not a sense of strain.

—Julia Cameron, *poet and journalist*

54 The Argument Essay *arg*

An argument essay is distinguished from other essays because it has an *argumentative edge*—that is, the writer takes a stand on a controversial issue.

In writing, critical thinking finds its most direct expression in argumentation. By using argumentation, writers attempt to change or reinforce a reader's opinion or to move that reader to take action. Often an argument essay may be emotionally charged, appealing to a reader's feelings with emotional detail or biased language. This is called *persuasive argument.* Or an argument essay may be highly rational, appealing to a reader's intellect with logical discussion. This is called *logical argument.* Political writing relies heavily on persuasive argument, whereas academic writing relies heavily on logical argument. With the exception of highly scientific argument, however, an argument essay seldom appeals only to emotion or only to reason.

The ancient Greeks, who formulated the underlying concepts of logic, identified three factors crucial to the construction of an effective argument:

1. *Logos*, or the quality of arguing soundly, refers to the quality of the evidence—that is, examples, facts, statistics, authority statements, reasonable interpretations.
2. *Pathos,* or the feeling dimension of language, refers to the ability to connect with a reader's emotion—that is, values, attitudes, and psychological needs.
3. *Ethos,* or credibility and honesty, refers to how writers present themselves—that is, knowledgeable, trustworthy, logical or ignorant, shiftless, erratic.

An effective argument usually blends *logos, pathos,* and *ethos.* The exact mixture varies with the audience and your purpose.

54a Write a purpose statement for an argument essay.

Identifying the purpose of an argument essay is similar to identifying the purpose of any college essay (review 4a and 6a), that is, a purpose statement should identify the subject and how you wish to develop it. Consider the following examples.

> I want to argue that the use of animals in scientific research is necessary to protect humankind.

The writer will discuss animals used in scientific research. The method of development is also clear. The writer will argue that research using animals is necessary.

> I want to convince my readers that campus police should be armed.

The subject is arming campus police, and the writer will argue to do so.

> I will argue that films featuring characters who smoke cigarettes should carry the surgeon general's warning that smoking is hazardous to a smoker's health.

Here, too, the subject—films featuring characters who smoke—and the method of development—to argue that the public should be warned about the hazards of smoking—are clear.

54b Develop and evaluate evidence to support your argument.

When writing an argument, you are interpreting evidence, not merely presenting facts and opinions. It will usually be the power of your interpretation that wins the day, not the innate truth or falsity of the evidence you marshal in support of your position. Always remember, evidence presented without careful, thoughtful interpretation will not influence most readers (review 2a, 2b, 2c).

If any of your evidence is based on research, you must acknowledge your sources. There are several types of evidence you can use in an argument essay, but some types are more convincing than others.

Facts and Statistics

Often the most convincing argument you can develop is based on facts and statistics. Facts and statistics, when used appropriately, are irrefutable but will not carry an argument in themselves. Instead, they serve as the basis for an inference. For example, research from the Industry Safety Council in Washington, DC, points out the following facts about automobile tires.

- Americans wear nearly 50 million pounds of rubber off their tires every two weeks, enough to make 3.25 million new tires from scratch.
- Some 240 to 260 million tires are discarded each year in the United States.

- Billions of tires currently fill up landfill space.
- It takes half a barrel of crude oil to produce the rubber in one truck tire.

In themselves these facts are merely surprising in their magnitude, but if used to argue a case for recycling tires, they could be compelling.

When using facts and statistics, you must be sure the inferences you draw are reasonable. No one, for example, can dispute the fact that four powerful advocates of African American rights—John F. Kennedy, Malcolm X, Martin Luther King Jr., and Robert Kennedy—were assassinated in the 1960s. But the interpretation of this fact as proof of a powerful anti–civil rights conspiracy is highly debatable.

Informed Authorities

In daily life we rely on a variety of authorities. Dentists evaluate the condition of our teeth. Critics recommend films and books. Weather forecasters tell us to prepare for rain or sunshine. In an argument essay you can rely on authority to support your opinion, but you must be sure your authority is an expert in the field. To argue for special psychological treatment for children who are victims of natural catastrophes, you would rely on developmental psychologists, not law enforcement officers. To argue for government-supported child care, you should rely on educational experts, not political activists.

Avoid using recognized experts in one field as authorities in an unrelated field. For example, a Nobel Prize–winning biologist might have opinions about the economy but is probably not an authority on the economy.

Also avoid using biased authorities. For example, a film executive's opinion about the social effects of violence in popular movies probably will not be an objective opinion.

Avoid using *nameless* authorities. Although "doctors maintain," "three hundred scientists surveyed," and "nationally recognized educators" are often cited by advertisers, to do so in an argument essay would detract from its credibility.

Personal Observations

You can rely on your own observations and the observations of others as evidence to support your opinion. In fact, often the most vivid and dramatic evidence results from personal observations. A traveler's report from a foreign country; a friend's exchange with law enforcement officers; your own encounter with the college bureaucracy; a visit to a polluted river, beach, or industrial site—all can add color and significant information to an argument essay.

When using personal observations as evidence, do all you can to present accurate information. You know how accurate a description of your own experience is because you lived it, but when you present the experience of others, you are in effect vouching for its veracity. It is often wise, therefore, to include more than one account of the same event.

Personal observations become even more compelling when used in conjunction with other forms of evidence. For example, to develop an argument to convince officials to protect an ecologically sensitive salt marsh, you might visit the site and report your observations. If your observations can also be supported by authorities, facts, and statistics, then your observation and the argument's validity will be difficult to challenge.

54c Confront the opposition.

During the evidence-gathering process, keep in mind that you must confront the opposing arguments you identified when planning a strategy. If you neglect to confront the opposition, your essay will be ineffective because you will not have dissuaded the reader from those opposing arguments. By confronting objections to your position, you are actively convincing readers that your arguments are sound and that you are a reasonable person, thus making your case even stronger. You can confront opposing arguments by showing that they are unreasonable, unfair, or even weak and emotional. If, however, the opposing position is so compelling that it is not easily dismissed, then concede its strength and go on to make an even stronger case for your position.

One effective strategy to use when planning your essay is to develop a list of arguments that support your position and a list of arguments that oppose your position.

List Supporting Arguments

Begin by developing a list of arguments you might use to support your position. Suppose you want to argue that films featuring characters who smoke cigarettes should carry the surgeon general's warning. You might develop a list of supporting arguments similar to the following:

- Scientific evidence shows that smoking is hazardous to health.
    Smoking causes lung cancer.
    Smoking affects the fetuses of pregnant women.
    Smoking causes emphysema.
- Because of the health hazards of smoking, advertisements for cigarettes have been banned from television and radio. Moreover, cigarette advertisements in magazines carry a warning of the health hazards of smoking.
- Many classic films feature romantic characters who smoke. A famous actor, Humphrey Bogart, died of lung cancer.
- Many current films perpetuate smoking by featuring romantic characters who smoke.
- Several cigarette companies realize the advertising value of having film characters smoke their brands and have paid film companies to feature their brands.

List Opposing Arguments

Once you have listed supporting arguments, list opposing arguments. An effective tactic for developing a list of opposing arguments is to discuss the issue with someone who disagrees with your position. The discussion can provide you with valuable information you might have overlooked. Here is a list of arguments opposing the labeling of movies that feature characters who smoke.

- There is no practical way to evaluate the impact on viewer behavior of characters who smoke in films.
- Much information already exists about the hazards of smoking, so film viewers must already be aware of the dangers.
- Films reflect reality. Many people smoke, so why should films be held accountable for reflecting that reality?
- Forcing film companies to label films would be just one more government attempt to interfere with free expression in the arts.

Reconsider Your Position

After developing lists of supporting and opposing arguments, you might reconsider your position. Perhaps the supporting arguments are weak and the opposing arguments are strong. In this situation you would probably be unable to convince readers that you are right, even though you still believe in your original position. Perhaps your position is oversimplified, too extreme, or merely rooted in a preference. In these situations you might rethink your position, attempting to search beyond the obvious in order to modify your extreme thinking or to rephrase your preference so you can support it.

54d Write an argumentative thesis statement and sketch a plan.

An argument is predicated on an "assertion," that is, an opinion you want a reader to accept or an action you want a reader to take. When stated in a sentence, the assertion is referred to as a **proposition** or **thesis** (review Chapter 6). Take a stand in your thesis; that is, clearly state your position so readers will have no doubt about your sympathies.

> Television stations should not be allowed to broadcast children's programs that feature violent encounters.
>
> Class attendance should not be a factor in grading.
>
> The high-fashion fur industry should be stopped.

Sometimes you might identify the opposing position in your thesis statement.

> Although censoring magazines that feature nudity would violate freedom of expression, these magazines should not be sold in community vending machines.
>
> Even though some ranchers will lose livestock to wolf packs, for ecological reasons wolves should be reintroduced into the western national parks.
>
> Police maintain that they do not target college-age drivers, but the evidence shows that police consistently abuse their authority near the university.

Notice that in each of these statements the writer takes a clear stand on a debatable point, one with which reasonable people could disagree.

Once you have written a clear thesis statement, you are ready to plan the development of your essay in sentence form. The points you state in your development plan can serve as topic sentences for the finished essay. Your thesis statement and development plan, therefore, will give you a sketch or rough outline for your final paper. Consider the following example. The writer wanted to argue that movie violence should not be censored. Furthermore, he wanted to convince his readers that the skillful use of violence heightens audience interest.

THESIS	Despite charges that movie violence triggers social violence, the evidence shows that no causal relationship exists between imaginary violence and human behavior, and, moreover, violence used skillfully in movies heightens audience interest.
DEVELOPMENT	• Some movies use violence in irresponsible ways. • No study has shown a causal connection between movie violence and actual violent behavior. • Since violence pervades real life, viewers demand that movies depict violence to reflect reality. • Although many movies feature gratuitous violence, others use skillfully crafted violence to engage viewers in positive ways. • Even such mild fare as *Bambi* and *The Wizard of Oz* use carefully crafted violence to heighten viewer awareness. • The careful crafting of violence to achieve dramatic purposes has its roots in classical literature.

The development pattern of this essay is clear. The author would first write an introduction that presents the thesis statement. She would then concede that many movies feature gratuitous violence, but she would also point out that even if gratuitous violence is a characteristic of many films, it still has no proven effect on audience behavior. Next, the writer would develop the supporting arguments: violence is part of real life; skillfully crafted violence engages viewers in positive ways; even classic children's films use violence; and finally, violence plays a significant role in literature in general.

54e Arranging an argument inductively or deductively.

To be convincing, evidence must be arranged so that it all makes sense to a reader. Presenting evidence logically is the most important part of argument writing.

There are two logical approaches to arranging evidence: inductive and deductive. Remember, an *inductive* argument moves from the particular details to generalization. Whenever you begin by first presenting evidence and end by making a logical conclusion from the evidence, you are using inductive reasoning (review 3b). A *deductive* argument is the opposite, and it is similar to college essay arrangement. Whenever you begin with a generalization you assume to be true, consider a specific case of that generalization, and then arrive at a conclusion, you are probably using deductive, or *syllogistic,* reasoning (see 3c). Should you ever include an actual syllogism in an argument? No, but sometimes an argument can be reduced to syllogistic form.

NOTE: Review Chapter 16, Argument Paragraphs, before writing an argument essay.

54f Write an argument essay with a reader in mind.

While writing and revising an argument, always keep an eye on your readers. Since you can't be all things to all readers, you might find it helpful to lump them into one of three general categories and then address them appropriately.

Supportive readers already agree with you. There's no need to overload your argument with dry facts and statistics for them. You can emphasize *pathos* over *logos*—that is, rely more on emotion and less on information. Touch the right emotional nerve, and this crowd will carry you away on its shoulders.

Wavering readers are uncommitted or uninformed readers. They are the ones you want to move by using both *logos* and *ethos,* that is, by presenting solid evidence and by establishing your trustworthiness and honesty. Establish the right image, and they will hop on your bandwagon.

Hostile readers are apathetic, skeptical, downright mean. Convincing them of anything is like trying to pull an angry bull's tooth with pliers. Just the facts, please—simple facts, dramatic facts, any facts that will penetrate their intransigence. *Ethos* won't help much, they already see you as a low-down schemer trying to sell them snake oil, and *pathos* will come back at you like a nail-filled mud pie. Just keep writing calmly and rely on *logos.* It's hard to spit in the face of truth.

54g Use the Toulmin model to examine an argument.

Philosopher Stephen Toulmin has developed a way to examine the strength of an argument, one that can help you check if you are covering everything you should. It is a simple system to use in ordinary thinking situations, and it reflects how most people use their minds. It is now called the *Toulmin model,* and it consists of three main elements:

The *claim* is the conclusion you draw from your examination of the information: the thesis.
The *grounds* are the pieces of information related to the issue: the evidence.
The *warrant* is the principle that links the evidence to the thesis: the assumption.

How does the Toulmin model work? Here's a simplified example: Someone makes the suggestion that you and your roommates would have fun camping during the upcoming weekend. You respond by saying, "We can't. We have an examination in freshman composition on Monday."

CLAIM	We can't go camping.
GROUNDS	We have a midterm examination.
WARRANT	Students should stay home and study before a test.

Often a warrant is left unstated because it is usually so obvious that the listener will fill it in. *Students should study the weekend before a test* is a warrant—an assumption behind the claim and the grounds—that most college students would agree with. Sometimes, however, a listener might fill in a different warrant. Suppose that one of your roommates has a warrant that says *Students should relax before a test.* He or she could insist that everyone go camping. You might think this view strange or even unreasonable until you clarified the conflicting assumptions behind each other's thinking.

Notice that a warrant is similar to the generalization used in a syllogism (review 3c) or the conclusion of an inductive chain (review 3b). You could easily argue:

Students who have a test on Monday shouldn't camp the weekend before.

All of us have a test on Monday.

Therefore, we shouldn't go camping Friday, Saturday, and Sunday.

By using Toulmin's model to identify warrant, claim, and grounds, you can see that the warrant links the claim and the grounds and whether it should be stated explicitly or left implicit. The model will also help you clarify, or even qualify, your claim and help you determine if you have enough information to convince a reader that your claim is justified.

A Student Argument Essay

Examine the following essay by student-writer Allison Ko in response to this freshman composition assignment:

> Select a controversial subject that is frequently in the newspapers. Write a 500- to 750-word logical argument that takes a position on the subject. Be sure to account for the opposing position within your essay. If the subject you select has undergone extensive public discussion, assume that your reader is familiar with the general elements of the debate and develop specific evidence based on your own observations, reading, and experience.

After your first reading of the essay, return for further study by examining the comments in the margin. (Key sentences are italicized.)

Title announces Ko's position.

War on Drugs: A Losing Battle

Introduction sets up the thesis statement.

Are we winning the war against drug use? Last week our local police arrested a narcotics dealer and confiscated over $2 million in cocaine. The Register even published a front-page story under the headline, "Cops Make Record Drug Bust." The "bust" was heralded as a victory in our community's effort to win the war on drugs. But such front-page stories are misleading. Local, state, and federal law enforcement agencies will never win the war on drugs. In fact, we are wasting valuable resources, restricting constitutional freedoms, and overcrowding our prisons in our effort to combat drug use. By making drug use illegal, we have created a "Prohibition" atmosphere with an increase in crime. *The only way to win the war on drugs is to legalize drug use.*

Thesis has an argumentative edge.

First discussion paragraph opens with an opposing view.

Politicians who support the war on drugs tell us that if we legalize what are now illegal drugs, we are sending our children the wrong message. To do so would be saying, "Yes, drugs can ruin your and your family's lives. They can kill sooner or later. We don't advise you to use them, but if you want to, we'll make them available to you at the neighborhood drugstore." *Nothing could be further from the truth.* Ask any of our school principals. Drugs are already available at neighborhood "drugstores." Police officers will tell you the same story. Furthermore, they will tell you if any mildly enterprising teenagers want to score drugs, they can do so within ten minutes of home. Moreover, there is no sound research that indicates legalizing drugs would create more users. Common sense may say so, but common sense, as has been proven time and time again, is commonly wrong.

Transition sentence shifts to Ko's position.

Paragraph closes with a clincher.

Second discussion paragraph opens with opposing view.

Those who actively campaign against drugs say drug use is our country's biggest social problem. One anti-drug champion recently claimed that over half of all murders were committed by people under the influence of drugs. He said that most street crime and home burglaries were committed by people who needed money for drugs. The high crime rate caused by drug use is a problem, but if drugs were legalized and sold at a reasonable price, then addicts would not have to steal to pay for their addiction. But as long as drugs are illegal and costly, the drug-related crime rate will not drop.

Ko agrees with opposing view but says her position will solve the problem.

Third discussion paragraph opens by pointing out a major

When anti-drug champions trumpet the high crime rate caused by drug use, they ignore the

flaw in opposition thinking.

country's biggest drug problem. It is not marijuana, heroin, amphetamines, or barbiturates. It is alcohol abuse. The alcohol manufacturers and marketers want us to believe that alcohol is not a drug, but it is a drug. Like all illegal drugs, it affects the senses, alters the drinker's psychology, and becomes addictive with prolonged use. According to Mothers Against Drunk Driving, drunken drivers kill someone in America every 32 minutes. Should we therefore prohibit alcohol consumption again? Of course not. We shouldn't because there are many more responsible drinkers than there are abusers.

Analogy links illegal drug use with legal alcohol use.

Transitional paragraph clearly reminds readers of Ko's position.

Instead we now treat alcohol abuse as a medical or psychological problem, and we pass laws that restrict when and where people may drink. I believe all drugs should fall in the same classification as alcohol, and we should end the war on drugs.

Ko extends the legal-drug-use analogy in more detail. She is relying on logos, that is, the development of a reasonable argument, to sway her reader.

Instead of incarcerating drug abusers, we should treat them the same as we do alcohol abusers and help them to lead normal lives in society. There are many responsible people who can and do use drugs recreationally without any harmful effect to themselves or to society. There are religious sects who use peyote, marijuana, and mushrooms without becoming helpless addicts. And the Netherlands has proved that decriminalization of drug use does not cause a collapse of society or an increase in crime.

Conclusion offers an appeal to ethos. Ko claims to be forthright and honest and calls for action.

I am not an advocate of drug use. In fact, I believe there are many harmful drugs that nobody should become involved with. But I am against laws that make drug use a crime instead of a health problem. Let us start a drug education campaign that uses facts rather than propaganda and grant amnesty to all nonviolent prisoners of the drug war.

Exercise 54.1: Analyze an Argument

Review Allison Ko's essay. Does she effectively use *logos, pathos,* and *ethos?* Find specific examples in her essay.

Exercise 54.2: Applying the Toulmin Model

Apply the Toulmin model to Allison Ko's essay. Identify the claim, the grounds, and the warrant.

WRITER'S CLINIC

Conversations and Arguments

A written argument has the same give-and-take as a lively conversation. The main difference is that in a lively conversation you probably feel more confident of what you know, and someone is right there in front of you, asking questions that make you think.

An effective tactic for beginning the writing process is to hold an imaginary conversation. Begin with your fingers on the keyboard or wrapped around a pen. Relax for a moment and imagine someone you know who is informed on the issue you've selected to write about. Then, after a few moments of reflection, begin the conversation.

The Other Person	You
What's your point?	I claim that . . .
I doubt it, what's your evidence?	One point is . . . Another point is . . .
How about this counter argument . . .	That's true, but it doesn't explain . . .
Why are you so sure?	For these reasons, first . . .
What other arguments work against your claim?	I must admit that . . .
How strong is your claim?	I have to limit it to . . .

Once you've fully developed an imaginary conversation, you are ready to fill in the weaknesses of your argument and begin the formal phase of the writing process.

Exercise 54.3: Writing an Argument Essay

Write an argument essay in which you express one of your own deeply felt opinions. If the subject you select has undergone extensive public discussion, assume that your reader is familiar with the general elements of the debate and develop specific evidence based on your own observations, reading, and experience. Use the following list to spark your thinking, but do not feel bound by the subjects. Remember, the suggestions are merely broad subjects; any one of them must be narrowed and focused.

1. Euthanasia
2. Censorship
3. Television violence
4. Film ratings
5. Legalized drugs
6. Animal rights
7. Student codes of conduct
8. Disruptive behavior in public places
9. Subliminal messages in music
10. People on public assistance should work
11. Sex education in public schools
12. Hiring quotas
13. Smoking in public places
14. Alternative ways to combat drug use
15. The power of the beauty myth

55 The Essay about Literature *lit*

Much of your writing in college will be in response to written texts. For example, in American literature you might read a novel, a poem, or a play and write an interpretive essay to explain the work's theme. In history you might read a significant government document and write an analytical essay to explore the assumptions that underlie its intent. In psychology you might read two conflicting views of the mind's structure and write a comparison essay to show how they are similar and different.

Even though the content of written works might be very different, the general strategies for writing about them always apply, no matter what the content. For any such assignment, you can use the basic structure of a college essay. The thesis should embody the purpose; the discussion paragraphs should be organized around topic sentences, each of which develops one subpoint of the thesis; and the conclusion should end the paper in a satisfying way. But within this general structure you should also adhere to several practices common to essays about written works.

To prepare to write about a written work, you must read the assigned work with care. Take notes, reread, identify a subject for your essay, and highlight passages to support your position. Once your preparation is complete, you can begin the writing process.

55a Formulate a thesis statement and develop a plan.

No one can examine every aspect of a written work in a brief essay; consequently, you must decide on a topic by selecting a single aspect of your subject. Then develop a limited thesis statement that announces the topic and expresses your attitude toward it. (See thesis statement, 6c.) A thesis developed in response to a written work can take many forms.

AN INTERPRETATION OF CHARACTER IN A SHORT STORY

In "The Chrysanthemums," John Steinbeck portrays a character who senses but cannot understand the need to communicate her deepest feelings.

AN ANALYSIS OF A CENTRAL IMAGE IN A POEM

"Buffalo Bill's defunct" by e. e. cummings offers an ambiguous image of an American folk hero.

AN EVALUATION OF WRITING TECHNIQUES IN AN ESSAY

Simpson creates this realistic portrait of a hospital emergency room through the effective use of descriptive techniques.

Once you have developed a working thesis statement, you can sift through the evidence you have identified and develop a plan as you would for any essay. (See informal plan, 6b; formal plan, 6d.)

55b Write an introduction that represents the work and highlights the thesis.

Unless you are absolutely certain that your readers are familiar with the work, use the introduction to acquaint them with it. The most efficient way to represent the work is to summarize it.

Your summary should be brief, perhaps no longer than eight to ten sentences. When summarizing do not get bogged down in tedious detail that will only distract your readers. Instead, create an overview with just enough detail to make your readers feel comfortable as they enter the discussion part of your essay.

While writing the summary, follow several common practices.

- In the first sentence state the author, the title, and the author's main purpose as you interpret it.
- Follow the opening sentence with a quotation that supports your interpretation.
- Throughout the summary section, and whenever appropriate in the discussion and conclusion, attribute quotations and ideas to the author.
- Use the historical present—the present tense of your main verbs—in the summary section and throughout the essay.
- After stating the author's full name in the opening, use only the last name in the summary section and throughout the essay.
- End the introduction with the thesis you plan to develop.

In an evaluation of writing techniques, one student wrote the following detailed summary of George Simpson's "The War Room at Bellevue."

Opening sentence names author, title, and the writer's purpose.

George Simpson in "The War Room at Bellevue" describes a typical Friday night in the Bellevue Hospital to show why its emergency team is so highly respected. Simpson writes, "Why do injured cops drive by a half-dozen other hospitals to be treated at Bellevue? They've seen the Bellevue emergency team in action." In vivid detail, Simpson describes the nightly events that

Quote effectively introduced. Note the use of historical present tense.

Writer uses vivid detail and continues to attribute to Simpson: "Simpson writes," "Simpson describes," "Simpson creates."

Closes with thesis statement.

unfold in the ER and the victims of accidental injuries, poisonings, suicide attempts, overdoses, stabbings, and shootings. From the moment "An ambulance backs into the receiving bay, its red and yellow lights flashing . . ." to the end when "blood spatters on the floor" from a knife wound, Simpson captures the grinding pace and traumatic conditions doctors and nurses face. Although few of his readers will ever actually see the inside of the Bellevue Emergency Room, all of them will leave the essay with a powerful sense that they have experienced an ER's nightly reality. *Simpson creates this realistic portrait of an emergency room through the effective use of descriptive techniques.*

If your reader is familiar with the work, an introduction may be composed of snippets of detail. In an introduction to an analysis of setting as it relates to character in Guy de Maupassant's "Moonlight," one student wrote the following.

Opening sentence names author, title, and the writer's central purpose.

Historical present tense is used throughout introduction.

Effective use of attribution.

Closes with thesis statement.

Guy de Maupassant's "Moonlight" deals with a psychological awakening. The principal character, Father Marigan, is a self-satisfied woman-hater who believes he understands "God . . . His plans, His wishes, His intentions." Marigan's awakening comes when he is symbolically seduced by moonlight into realizing, to his dismay, that God's plan includes love between a man and a woman. *Throughout the story de Maupassant uses setting to reinforce the characterization of Father Marigan and to convey the idea that love is natural and good.*

55c Write a discussion that develops the thesis.

The discussion section of an essay about a written work is like the discussion section of any well-constructed college essay: it should be developed around subpoints expressed in topic sentences. Arrange the discussion according to significant ideas, not necessarily by the structure of the written work you are examining.

Support Observations with an Extended Quotation

One way to develop the topic sentence is by combining your observations with an extended quotation that supports them, as in the following discussion paragraph from an analysis of Flannery O'Connor's "Revelation." (See direct quotations, 39a.)

Topic sentence sets up discussion.

O'Connor creates a conflicting portrait of Mrs. Turpin. We see her from the inside and the outside. Throughout the story she professes Christian love and charity, but in her mind she judges others by superficial standards. For example, at night before sleeping she categorizes and judges people by their economic condition:

Comments set up extended quotation that follows.

> On the bottom of the heap were most colored people . . . next to them--not above, just away from--were the white trash; then above them were the homeowners, and above them the home-and-land owners, to which she and Claud belonged. Above she and Claud were people with a lot of money and much bigger homes and much more land.

Extended quotation in block format (see 39a).

This judgmental vision of Mrs. Turpin ends in confusion when rich blacks who own land and "white trash" who've grown rich don't fit into her scheme, but she solves the problem by mentally consigning everyone--white, black, rich,

Closing comments tie the quotation to the opening assertion.

and poor--to boxcars headed for a gas oven, a grim reference to Nazi Germany and the result of categorical thinking when carried to its limits.

Support Observations with Specific Summary

Other paragraphs in the discussion might be developed by accurately summarizing specific aspects of the content of a work as they relate to your point. Consider the following discussion paragraph from an analysis of *Oedipus Rex*.

Topic sentence opens paragraph.

Summarized points support the assertion in the topic sentence.

Sophocles uses the imagery of sight and blindness for ironic effect throughout the play. It is blind Tiresias, the prophet of Apollo, who is the god of foresight and insight, who sees more clearly than those who have eyes. Early in the play, Oedipus promises to bring the dark secret of Laius' death to light for all to see, yet he does so while still blind to his own moral faults. After blinding himself near the play's end, Oedipus sees who he really is and what he has done. Ironically, throughout the play, Oedipus prides himself on his clear-sightedness, but by the end he recognizes that this pride has blinded him.

Support Comments with Brief Quotations

You might also use very brief quotations from a work to support your observations, as does this discussion paragraph from a critical evaluation of *Serpentine*.

Topic sentence sets up the discussion.

Series of brief quotes that support assertion in the topic sentence.

A minor flaw in the book comes from Thompson's flagrant use of clichés in place of more thoughtful prose. He writes, "It was the dead of winter, 1967, and the prison walls were cold as ice." He refers to Sobhraj's courtroom chicanery as a "bag of tricks." His girlfriend clung to him "like moss on an oak." He tries to

Closes by linking back to topic sentence.

pass off their tawdry affair as an "epic romance more poignant than Romeo and Juliet." Trite expressions such as these mar every page and blemish an otherwise captivating work.

55d Write a brief conclusion.

The conclusion should briefly summarize your thesis and the major subpoints, and it should end with your general view of the work. Here is an effective conclusion from an analysis of Flannery O'Connor's "Revelation."

> Clearly, O'Connor's "Revelation" takes a careful reader into the shadowy mind of a bigot who gains awareness through a personal catastrophe. O'Connor seems to be offering a positive message--that is, there is even hope that a bigot such as Mrs. Turpin can learn not to judge others by the weight of their wallets or the color of their skin.

55e Write a precise title.

A title should be brief and should express the idea your essay examines. If the title of the work is included in your essay title, only it should be italicized or put within quotation marks, as appropriate. (See quotation marks, 39b; italics, 50a.)

> e. e. cummings's "Buffalo Bill's defunct": The Backside of a Folk Hero
>
> Imagery in Oedipus Rex
>
> Mrs. Turpin's Revelation

55f Identify your quotations and specific references.

In a brief essay about literature, you might be allowed to omit complete citations for primary sources. If so, you should still identify the location of each quotation and specific reference you make. After the quotation or reference, place the page number or numbers from the original work in parentheses and close the sentence with the end punctuation mark after the last parenthesis. (See parenthetical citations, 58c.)

> Hemingway ends the story on an ironic note: "After all, he said to himself, it is probably only insomnia" (72).

> Near the end of his life we find that Gimpel has achieved peace. He now understands that soon all illusion will be swept away. He believes he will truly see without the confusion of ridicule and deception. He will see what is real (85-86).

55g Use the present tense of verbs.

The dominant verb tense in an essay about a written work—whether fiction, nonfiction, drama, or poetry—should be the present tense. (See present tense, 32a.)

> In The Executioner's Song Mailer *re-creates* life as it *is lived* in the rural West. He *evokes* people struggling to make a living in gas stations, roadside cafés, movie theaters, small factories, country stores, and on farms. It *is* a world filled with pickup trucks, six-packs, country music, Monday Night Football, deer hunting, motorcycles, and honky-tonk violence. The city slicker *is* suspect, and the easy buck *is* hard to find. The four-wheel-drive Ford truck, not the sleek Mercedes, *is* the status symbol.

55h Avoid common mistakes in essay writing.

Do not summarize excessively. Summarize enough of a work only to clarify your thought or a point. A summary should always serve a clear purpose.

Do not refer to authors by their first names. Furthermore, do not refer to them by title (Dr., Prof., Mr., Mrs., Miss, Ms.). After giving an author's full name in the introduction, refer to him or her by last name throughout the rest of the essay.

Do not miscopy a direct quotation. Always recheck any quotation you use to be sure you have copied it accurately.

Do not set off the title of a work with commas when it follows the word *story, tale, novel, story, book, poem,* or *play.*

INCORRECT	In his poem, "Traveling through the Dark," William Stafford reflects on humankind's relation to nature.
CORRECT	In his poem "Traveling through the Dark," William Stafford reflects on humankind's relation to nature.

A Student Essay about Literature

Examine the following essay by student-writer Kirk Rensfield in response to this reading assignment:

> Select one of the seven literary works read for the unit "On Living and Dying" and write a 500- to 750-word analysis. Explore how effectively the short story, literary essay, or poem you select captures the experience of living or dying. Emphasize "writing techniques" in your essay by linking them to the work's larger implications.

After your first reading, reread Rensfield's essay along with the comments in the margin. To further prepare yourself for this assignment, you should also read George Orwell's "A Hanging," which you will find in most anthologies of essays or in the library in a copy of his collected essays.

The cryptic title is drawn from Orwell's tale.

One World Less

George Orwell in "A Hanging" describes a condemned man's march from a prison cell to his execution by hanging. Orwell begins the march simply: "We set out for the gallows. Two warders marched on either side of the prisoner . . . two others marched close against him, gripping him by the arm and shoulder." Eight minutes later, the prisoner is declared dead by the officer in charge. He "reached out with his stick and poked the brown body; it oscillated slightly. 'He's all right,' said the superintendent." The words of the officer's pronouncement may skirt the reality

Introduction sets up thesis statement, follows writing about literature conventions:
1. Names author, title, and purpose.
2. Attributes, using author's last name.
3. Uses quotes.
4. Keeps to the historical present.
5. Closes with thesis.

that a man has just died; Orwell, however, does not blink from that reality. *Although few readers of "A Hanging" will actually see someone hanged, all will leave the essay with a strong sense of what the experience must be like.*

First discussion paragraph opens with topic sentence.

Supports topic sentence with specific detail and quotations from the story.

Orwell creates a vivid reality by generally maintaining an objective perspective, much like a camera photographing the event. For example, like a movie camera moving from a long shot, to a medium shot, to a close-up, Orwell establishes the atmosphere and location of his tale. He begins with an overview, "It was Burma, a sodden morning of the rains." He then moves to the jail yard, "A sickly light, like yellow tinfoil, was slanting over the high walls into the jail yard." He then moves even closer by describing the condemned cells, "a row of sheds fronted with double bars, like small animal cages." Each cell was ten-by-ten feet and held only a plank bed and a pot for drinking water. There, "Brown, silent men were squatting at the inner bars." Finally, his camera concentrates on the prisoner to be hanged, a "Hindu, a puny wisp of a man, with a shaven head and vague liquid eyes."

Second discussion paragraph opens with a transitional phrase and a topic sentence.

Even though the opening perspective seems emotionally detached, Orwell is actually using first person point of view. Throughout the story, the unnamed narrator reports the event much like an objective newspaper reporter, but in one brief passage he does reflect on the experience. Orwell uses the narrator's reflection to create the story's dramatic tension. Orwell writes,

> I saw the mystery, the unspeakable wrongness, of cutting a life short when

Block quotation used as support for topic sentence.

> it is in full tide. This man was not dying, he was alive just as we are alive. All the organs of his body were working--his bowels digesting food, skin renewing itself, nails growing, tissues forming--all toiling away in solemn foolery. His nails would still be growing when he stood on the drop, when he was falling through the air with a tenth-of-a-second to live.

Follows up quotation by relating it to topic sentence.

Indeed, the narrator thinks about the significance of taking a life; he, nevertheless, continues the relentless march toward the noose. But it is his reflection on life that elevates the story to a higher dimension.

Third discussion paragraph gives background, then states the topic sentence.

Experience is composed of two facets: the outer and inner realities. Orwell captures outer reality in great detail that is expressed in a detached, even solemn, tone. *But he also captures inner reality through the narrator's thoughts.* They are far from detached. In fact, they roil with boiling language, and they move from the particular reality of this hanging to the universal reality of every person's death.

Uses block quotation to support opening assertion.

> He and we were a party of men walking together . . . understanding the same world and in two minutes, with a sudden snap, one of us would be gone--one mind less, one world less.

Closes paragraph with interpretation of quote.

The narrator is beginning to see that all humans will "be gone." And that with each passing, there will be "one mind less, one world less."

The narrator's thoughts round out the experience of an encounter with death. The

Conclusion opens with rephrasing of thesis and restatement of major point.

external descriptive detail creates the dramatic experience of this particular hanging, but the narrator's internal reflections on death universalize the experience all humans will ultimately face.

Exercise 55.1: Writing about a Written Work

Select an anthology of literature that includes fiction, poetry, and drama, such as X. J. Kennedy's *Literature* or Sylvan Barnet, Morton Berman, and William Burto's *An Introduction to Literature.* Browse through the book to find a work that interests you. After reading the work several times, compose a five- to seven-paragraph explication of a brief poem or passage or an analytical examination with character, plot, point of view, setting, symbol, or theme as the subject.

56 The Essay Exam *exam*

In taking an essay exam, you face two important tasks: knowing and understanding the course content, and writing clearly and effectively about it in the time allowed.

The first task means that you will need to study your class notes and review the course textbook in many of the same ways you would for any other kind of exam.

The second task requires that you plan your writing before the exam and then briefly plan again when you read the exam question and prepare to answer it.

Guidelines to Prepare Yourself for the Exam

Begin planning for a timed essay exam as early as possible. Pay attention at the start of the course to the kinds of tests mentioned in the class syllabus or by the instructor. If you know a course will require an essay exam, take notes that focus on relating key concepts and events discussed in lectures and readings.

Also keep any handouts or quizzes given during the course, and pay particular attention to information related to special films, field trips, or presentations by guest speakers.

Since you will need to study the course content as well as prepare for writing about it effectively, give yourself enough time before the exam to prepare adequately for both tasks.

Review Major Course Concepts

Refer to the course syllabus and the table of contents in your textbook to prepare a list of major topics to study.

Be especially sure to include any topics to which a large portion of class time was devoted—such as a series of lectures, special demonstrations, guest speakers, or a class project.

Beneath each topic, list any significant events, examples, persons, dates, or definitions associated with it. As you study for the exam, relate the listed topics and supporting information to your class notes, assigned readings, and any handouts or other course material.

Use Direction Words to Write Practice Questions

An essay exam question usually includes important *direction words* describing how you are to answer. Words like *compare, define, list, show, summarize,* and *evaluate* specify the way your instructor wants you to respond and indicate the scope of the answer he or she expects. As you review major topics covered in the course, you can use such direction words to create and study for potential exam questions.

For example, suppose that in addition to assigned readings about youth gangs, your sociology course also included several lectures on that topic. You would want to use a variety of direction words (shown in bold) to devise potential essay questions about youth gangs:

> ***Define*** gang membership as viewed by Peters and Walton and ***show*** how gang activity in central Los Angeles fits that definition.
>
> ***Compare*** and ***contrast*** the values of two different types of youth gangs we have studied in this course.
>
> ***Explain*** the appeal of gang membership beyond the teenage years.

Generating six to ten questions like these will familiarize you with direction words that may appear on the exam, as well as provide you with a means of focusing your preparation.

Prepare a List or Outline

Once you have created a number of potential exam questions, choose one of them and write a brief informal outline of the relevant main points to be discussed. An informal outline for the last question above, for example, might look like this:

I. The appeal of gang membership beyond the teenage years
   A. Lack of maturity
   B. Desire to maintain youth
   C. Social and financial dependency
   D. Community prestige

Make an outline such as this for each of the potential questions you devise. You can then use your outlines as a study guide as well as a preliminary plan for writing a practice essay.

Write a Practice Response

Rehearsing a response to likely exam topics will build your confidence and prepare you to handle other questions as well.

Select two or three topics that the instructor emphasized or that you feel important for other reasons. Devise a potential exam question for each topic, and allow yourself thirty or forty minutes (the usual time allowed for most exam essays) to write a response.

When you have finished, review what you have written for clarity, organization, a clear thesis, and the inclusion of relevant information and examples.

Make corrections to the essay as needed by adding omitted material or deleting anything that did not address the question directly. This practice will reinforce good essay-writing habits and help you to remember the material better.

Make a Spelling List

Your instructor will expect you to be familiar enough with key terms and concepts from the course to be able to spell them correctly.

If you are a weak speller, practice writing words you expect to use in your exam responses, especially those terms that are central to the course. For an exam in a psychology class, for example, you might need to practice writing terms such as *neurosis, Jungian,* and *paranoid;* for an exam in biology, you may want to rehearse words like *synapse, protozoa,* and *cellular.*

Make a list of any such terms that you find difficult, and practice writing them correctly before an exam. Preparing in this way will not only improve your spelling; it will also increase your familiarity with the words and the concepts behind them.

Prepare Yourself for the Exam

After studying and mentally preparing all you can for an essay exam, also make sure you are physically ready to do your best. Get a good night's sleep before the exam, and be sure to eat a healthy breakfast or lunch beforehand. You want to be ready to devote all your energy and attention to the exam, not to staying awake or listening to your stomach growl.

56a Writing an essay exam.

Be on time for the exam, and bring any necessary items such as a test booklet, pen or pencil, notes (if allowed), a computer disk, or other permitted items. Once you have the exam in hand, take time to read it carefully and to plan your response.

56b Reading and understanding the question.

Writing an acceptable response on an essay exam requires that you read and understand the essay question accurately. Do not make the mistake of rushing through the question to formulate a hasty, inaccurate response. Instead, take the time to read the entire exam carefully.

Next, underline the essay question and highlight the direction words in it:

> In a paragraph or two, *discuss* the ways in which evolution may be correctly described as both a theory and fact.
>
> Briefly *summarize* Jesperson's case against same-sex marriages and *evaluate* his three major arguments.

If you are unsure about what the exam directions say or what is being asked in the exam question, ask your instructor or the exam proctor for clarification.

56c Planning your time.

As you read the exam instructions, make a point of circling the time allowed for the test. Consider the steps involved in completing the exam, and decide how long you can take for each. The majority of your time will go for writing the essay response, but you will also need to read and understand the essay question, plan your response, and revise and proofread your finished essay. Allocate enough time for each of these steps, and avoid giving any one of them more time than you can afford.

56d Planning your answer.

Briefly plan your essay response by using the exam question's key words (e.g., *define* or *trace*) to direct the form of your answer. Jot down in rough outline form the main points you intend to discuss, and use clustering or other techniques to generate supportive details or examples. Use the outline of your main points as a working plan for writing the essay.

56e Writing your response.

An essay exam does not allow you the time to write an introduction and accompanying thesis statement, as you normally would do with other essays. For this reason, you should begin discussing the main points of your response immediately after an opening statement. Begin the essay with a clearly stated sentence that rephrases the exam question itself and serves as the main idea for the rest of the response.

EXAM QUESTION

Explain why Spanish rule in the early nineteenth century did not expand into what later became the northwestern United States.

QUESTION REPHRASED

Spanish rule in the early nineteenth century did not expand into the future northwestern United States because of opposition from the French and economic conditions within Spain itself.

EXAM QUESTION

Compare the wedding rites of the Tair people of West India with one or more traditional American wedding ceremonies.

QUESTION REPHRASED

The wedding rites of the Tair people are far simpler than traditional American ceremonies, but they are also more legally and morally binding.

Use statements such as these to announce your answer and focus your response. Develop the rest of the essay by discussing the main points and supportive information you listed in the working outline you made earlier.

As you complete the essay, write steadily and neatly. Do not expect to recopy your work, as that would sacrifice valuable writing time. Instead, plan to proofread your answer and write in necessary corrections.

Answer the Question

Be sure that you answer the question that is asked and not a different one. Direction words in a question will call for specific kinds of responses—for instance, asking you to *define* a set of terms, *trace* a development, or *identify* and *evaluate* a cause. If you do something other than what is asked—like offering examples instead of defining terms or identifying but not evaluating—your instructor will most likely consider your answer incomplete and give you a low score.

In addition, take care not to wander off the question asked and into one you think you know more about. No matter how well you write on a different topic, your instructor is unlikely to give you credit if you did not answer the exam question. Keep your working outline in front of you, and refer at times to your thesis statement in order to stay on track.

Finally, keep in mind that not all written exams require essay-length answers. Some may ask you to respond to each question in a few sentences, while others may ask for a paragraph or two. When a

WRITER'S CLINIC

The 15-Minute Response

Some instructors require unannounced, written responses to reading assignments. One kind of response might ask you to apply information. Another might ask you to summarize key points. No matter what the assignment calls for, it is essential to employ three important tactics:

1. Get organized: Quickly list key points in any order and then make a scratch outline to rearrange them logically.
2. Begin quickly: State your purpose in the first sentence and create a blueprint of what will follow.

    President Lincoln had three criteria when he selected Ulysses S. Grant and William T. Sherman as his generals.

3. Use clear transitions: Begin each point with a brief sentence that starts with a clear transition.

    First, Lincoln expected his generals to have courage.
    Second, Lincoln expected his generals to be loyal.
    Third, Lincoln expected his generals to fight.

Remember that your reader wants you to answer two implicit questions: Have you read the assignment? Did you understand it?

question explicitly asks you to respond *in a certain length,* make sure your answer stays near the specified range. This is the approximate quantity of writing your instructor has determined is necessary to compose a satisfactory answer.

56f Revising and proofreading.

When you have finished your essay, take a few minutes to reread it for completeness and to make minor corrections. If you have left out words or even a sentence or two, add them neatly, using a caret (^) to show where each fits into your writing. Also neatly cross out any irrelevant material and replace it with more pertinent content. Be sure your sentences are complete and that they make sense. Check for punctuation and spelling errors, paying special attention to the spellings of key terms and names of places and individuals. Before you hand in the essay, make sure your name and other necessary information appears on the test booklet cover or at the top of each page.

PART IX

The Research Paper

Despite the telephone, computers, and other information-transmitting technology, the volume of paper work in organizations increases annually. Somebody writes that stuff. It may well be you. Can you predict whether one day you will be publicity chairman of a group? Make public speeches? Design and write brochures, sales materials, procedure manuals? Once you have developed it, writing facility is transferable; you don't need a special course in a specific kind of writing.

—Roger Garrison, *Writer*

57 Researching a Paper *res*

A research paper is a formal composition based on an investigation of detailed information and other writers' ideas about a topic rather than solely on your own attitudes and experiences. No doubt you have opinions about a number of topics, but unless you have taken many courses or read extensively, you probably do not have an *informed* opinion about a given topic. Writing a research paper offers you the opportunity to develop an informed opinion and to apply your thinking and writing skills to an objective discussion of a topic. Unlike the personal essay, which grows from personal experiences and viewpoints, the research paper grows from an in-depth study and a careful examination of the ideas of other writers.

A research paper is more than a summarized version of what others have said or written, however. Ideally, your research paper represents a synthesis of your own perceptions, attitudes, ideas, and experiences supported by information gained from other sources. In most cases, those sources are materials in your college or community library. You can use these materials to enlarge, to strengthen, to define, or otherwise to complement your own basic views about a subject. No one expects you to solve a major world problem as a result of your research, but if you have done your work seriously and thoroughly, you will gain a broader and more informed view than any one source alone has yet provided.

57a Find and limit a topic suitable for research.

If your instructor has not already given you a specific research assignment, allow yourself time to select an appropriate topic for research. The best way to start your search is by examining your own interests and experiences.

1. Begin with Topics That Interest You

Your favorite section of the newspaper; the kinds of books, magazines, or films you enjoy; and a particular textbook chapter that excited your curiosity are all strong clues to your real interests. Try brainstorming to develop a list of hot topics. Discuss them with class members. Narrow the possible topics to one or two. The best ingredients for a successful paper are your own understanding of, and enthusiasm for, a subject.

2. A Suitable Topic Allows Room for Discussion

To choose an appropriate research topic, you also must be aware of what your paper can achieve. Since most research papers attempt to add new dimensions or perspectives to a body of ideas already expressed by others, process or how-to papers or those that merely summarize already known information ("the major decisions during John F. Kennedy's presidency") are not good choices. Strictly philosophical subjects or topics based on personal beliefs—"the nature of reality," "Loyalty to one's government comes before loyalty to one's family," "Public nudity should be left to personal choice"—should be avoided. Such topics are based on opinion and often do not require research for objective evidence and do not lend themselves to objective discussion. Look for a topic that allows you to explore areas that still need discussion or review, such as an unsettled and continuing problem or a little-known situation. Whether the sale of handguns should be controlled in this country, for example, might prove a suitable problem to investigate for a research paper. An examination of student binge drinking (as in the sample research paper by Cynthia Delgado beginning on p. 386) could also produce an informative, researched discussion.

3. Narrow the Topic to Manageable Size

The topic of your research paper should allow you to generate enough discussion to fulfill your instructor's requirements about length and about the kinds of sources you should use for your research. A subject that is too narrow, such as whether the shopping mall provides enough security for Christmas shoppers, or too recent, such as the credibility of the United States government if weapons of mass destruction are not uncovered in Iraq, will not work because there will not be enough written material for you to build on.

Likewise, some topics may be so large or already have so much written about them—the events leading up to President Nixon's resignation, for example—that you cannot expect to learn enough in a few weeks' time to write about them convincingly. In such instances, you will need to narrow the focus of your paper, just as you did when developing a thesis or writing the personal essay.

Sometimes reviewing the general sources for a broad subject can help you see particular ways to narrow the approach or to shift the emphasis of a topic. Often the topic itself becomes more refined only after you have begun researching it, and it may not evolve into its final form until the completion of the paper. For instance, if you were to begin with a broad topic, such as "art" or "psychology," you might find yourself moving gradually toward a narrower topic in the manner illustrated on the following page.

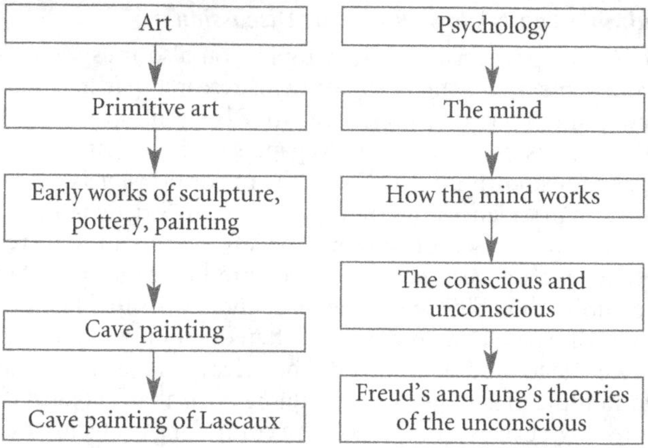

Narrowing a topic from the general to the specific is seldom as smooth or orderly as the illustrations above might make the process seem. Usually you will have several false starts, but reading in a general subject area will help you find your way.

Education major Cynthia Delgado, the author of the sample paper, moved quickly from the general subject of alcohol abuse in society to a more focused one on college drinking. Yet even as she began reading about this narrower topic, Delgado discovered that there were still many aspects to be discussed, too many for a single paper. Finally, she decided that her keenest interest was in one major issue: the problem of student binge drinking and what colleges were doing to reduce it. She liked this subject because it was current and relevant to her own campus and her fellow students. At first Delgado had trouble finding adequate sources, but once she became more familiar with the library and the vast resources of the Internet, she found plenty of material dealing with the problem of student binge drinking, as well as information about how colleges and universities were responding to it.

Do not rush the essential step of narrowing the topic to something that interests you and that can be easily researched. Careful selection and limitation of the right topic can save you time and work later and can provide an early foundation for a successful finished product.

57b Use the library and other resources.

Use reference books to get an overview of your topic and to evaluate its appropriateness for your assignment. In addition to encyclopedias, dictionaries, almanacs, indexes, guides, atlases, and book reviews, your library's reference section probably contains a large selection of special reference sources, ranging from *The Encyclopedia of Evolution* to the *Guinness Book of Records.*

A complete listing of the hundreds of reference books would be impractical here. The following is a sampling of the variety of sources available. Survey your own library for the reference books most applicable to your topic. You will also find that many of these resources are available on CD-ROM or online at your campus library, as well as through the Internet.

GENERAL ENCYCLOPEDIAS

Encyclopedia Americana
The New Encyclopaedia Britannica

THE ARTS

Art Books: A Basic Bibliography on the Fine Arts
Encyclopedia of World Art

BUSINESS AND ECONOMICS

Business Index
Business Periodicals Index
Encyclopedia of Computers and Data Processing
The Encyclopedia of Management
Marketing Terms: Definitions, Explanations, and/or Aspects

HISTORY

Dictionary of American History
An Encyclopedia of World History

LITERATURE, THEATER, FILM, AND TELEVISION

Bibliography of American Literature
The Complete Encyclopedia of Television Programs
Contemporary Authors
International Index of Film Periodicals
Macmillan Dictionary of Films and Filmmakers
Play Index
The New York Times Encyclopedia of Television
Short Story Index

MUSIC

Bibliographic Guide to Music
The New Harvard Dictionary of Music
The New Grove Dictionary of Music and Musicians

Philosophy and Religion

The Philosopher's Index: An International Index to Philosophical Periodicals and Books
Religion Index One: Periodicals

Social Science

Bibliographical Guide to Psychology
Handbook of Social Science Research
Social Science Citation Index

Sciences

Applied Science and Technology Index
Biological Abstracts
Environmental Periodicals Bibliography
General Science Index
Index Medicus

Unabridged Dictionaries

The Oxford English Dictionary
Webster's Third New International Dictionary of the English Language

Special Dictionaries

Dictionary of Contemporary Usage
Dictionary of Modern English Usage
Modern American Usage
The New Roget's Thesaurus of the English Language in Dictionary Form

Biographical Reference

Dictionary of American Biography
Webster's New Biographical Dictionary
Who's Who in America

Atlases and Gazetteers

Columbia Lippincott Gazetteer of the World
Rand McNally New Cosmopolitan World Atlas

Almanacs and Yearbooks

Britannica Book of the Year
Facts on File Yearbook
Information Please Almanac
Reader's Digest Almanac and Yearbook
World Almanac and Book of Facts

1. Use the Card Catalog to Find Books on Your Topic

The best guide to the books available is your library's card catalog. Whether on microfilm or microfiche, on a computer screen, or in the traditional card tray, the library's catalog alphabetically lists and cross-references its holdings by subject, author, and title. Special information given with each entry can supply useful data about a book's publication date, whether or not it includes illustrations, and its length. You can locate books on your topic by looking under the author, title, or subject heading. (See the computer catalog sample below.) There are two widely used classification systems—the Dewey decimal system and the Library of Congress system. The system a library uses has no effect on your library work; it merely determines the call number of any book.

123 RECORD MATCHES AFTER TERM BINGE
6 RECORDS MATCHED THE SEARCH
Type DI to Display the records

Screen 001 of 001

NMBR	DATE	TITLE	AUTHOR
0001	2002	Binge drinking blowout the extreme dangers of	
0002	2001	Bulimia: the binge-purge compulsion	Stubbs, Janice M
0003	2000	Men's health concerns sourcebook	
0004	2002	Overcoming binge drinking	Kellogg, Katherine
0005	1999	Colleges and alcohol	Tyner, Robert
0006	2000	Controlling uncontrollable urges	

Type DI NMBRs for specific titles

A catalog computer screen

2. Use Periodicals for More Focused Information About Your Topic

Periodicals are valuable sources of more specific or current information. Many different indexes catalog the various kinds of journals, magazines, newspapers, and other periodicals, and certain guides are more useful to the general researcher than are others. One such source is the *Reader's Guide to Periodical Literature,* which provides a monthly, quarterly, and annual index to the most widely circulated magazines in the United States.

General subject heading

Explanatory information

ALCOHOL AND COLLEGE STUDENTS

Article title — Another pass from Dartmouth {elimination of single-sex fraternities over problem of alcohol abuse} W. F. Buckley, *National Review* v51 no6 p63 Ap 5 1999 — Author

•Campus crackdown [in loco parentis] N. Schaefer, il *National Review* v51 no6 p31+ Ap 5 1999

Journal Title

Volume, issue number, page, and date — Contains illustrations

Index from Reader's Guide to Periodical Literature (1999)

Articles listed in the *Reader's Guide* are cross-referenced under author, title, and subject. Information about each entry is listed in a condensed form explained in the front of every volume of the *Reader's Guide.* Above, for example, are entries on "alcohol and college students" that Cynthia Delgado used for her research paper.

In addition to magazines, newspaper articles are important contemporary sources for research. While most libraries can store no more than a few nationally circulated or local newspapers, most university and college libraries have copies of several major newspapers on microfilm. Articles are usually listed in a separate index, such as *The New York Times Index,* which lists news articles, first by general subject, then in chronological sequence according to the dates they appeared in the newspaper. Like entries in the *Reader's Guide,* subject headings in *The New York Times Index* are cross-referenced by "see" and "see also" directions. An additional feature is that each entry in *The New York Times Index* describes the length of the article as either short (S), medium (M), or long (L). This feature can help you decide whether the article is likely to yield enough information to make researching it further worthwhile.

Cynthia Delgado consulted her college library's Infotrac system and discovered a wide range of potential research sources, such as *The New York Times, Time* magazine, *The Journal of the American Medical Association,* and *The Chronicle of Higher Education.* Such sources provided Cynthia with a variety of points of view on the topic of campus binge drinking.

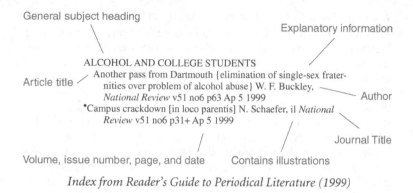

In addition to consulting the *Reader's Guide* and *The New York Times Index* for sources, Delgado wanted to find discussions written for audiences with more scholarly interest in the subject of alcohol and college drinking than the general public may have had. She knew

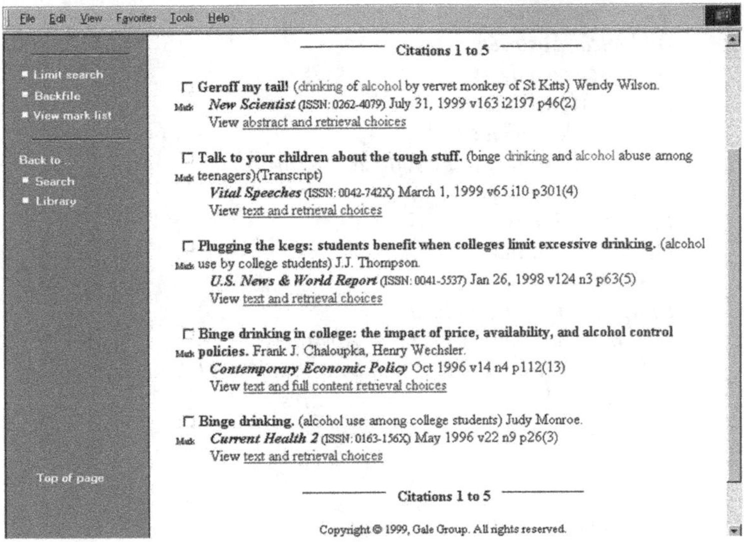

An Infotrac screen showing search results

that her library contained several reference sources intended for readers interested in researching topics within certain academic disciplines. Such discipline indexes, for example, as *Social Sciences Index*, *Arts and Humanities Index*, and *Applied Science and Technology Index* report results of research studies or other scholarly information not generally addressed in popular magazines and newspapers. Thus, because her topic fell within the discipline of sociology, Delgado consulted the *Social Sciences Index*. Although she looked first under "binge drinking," a "See" note directed Delgado to other subject headings, where she eventually found the magazine and journal sources shown in the sample *Social Sciences Index* entry on the following page.

Besides the *Reader's Guide* and the discipline indexes already discussed, most libraries contain a number of other guides to periodical literature on general and specialized subjects. The list that follows is representative of the most common indexes to periodical literature. Investigate your own library's holdings and use such sources to compile your bibliography.

Abstracts of Popular Culture
Alternative Press Index
The American Humanities Index
Bibliography and Index of Geology

Biography Index
Biological Abstracts
Book Review Digest
Book Review Index
Business Periodicals Index
Cumulative Index to Periodical Literature
Economics' Abstracts
Education Index
Humanities Index
Index Medicus
Index to Jewish Periodicals
International Political Science Abstracts
MLA International Bibliography of Books and Articles on the Modern Languages and Literatures
The Music Index

Main subject heading

College students

See also

Alternate subject headings — Graduate students
Women college students

Major subject heading — Alcohol use

Alcohol and sexual assault in a national sample of college women. S. Ullman and others. bibl *J Interpers Violence* v14 no6 p603-25 Je 1999 — Journal title

Alcohol risk reduction for fraternity and sorority members. N. G. Harrington and others. bibl *J Stud Alcohol* v60 no4 p521-7 Jl 1999 — Includes a bibliography

Drinking, binge drinking, and other drug use among southwestern undergraduates: three-year trends. M. E. Bennett and others. *Am J Drug Alcohol Abuse* v25 no2 p331-50 My 1999

Article title — An examination of the utility of server intervention to reduce alcohol-related problems in college students. R. Turrisi and others. bibl *J Appl Soc Psychol* v29 no3 p622-38 Mr 1999

Gender congruence in confirmatory and compensatory drinking. R. J. Williams and L. A. Ricciardelli. bibl *J Psychol* v133 no3 p323-31 My 1999

Male and female recipients of unwanted sexual contact in a college student sample: prevalence rates, alcohol use, and depression symptoms. M. E. Larimer and others. bibl *Sex Roles* v40 no3-4 p295-308 F 1999 — Multiple authors

Volume, issue number, pages, and date

Entry from Social Sciences Index (September 1999)

Poole's Index to Periodical Literature (1802–1906)
Popular Periodical Index
United States Government Publications

3. Use Computer Databases to Supplement your Library's Resources

Perhaps your library subscribes to one or more of the numerous computer database services that give users immediate access to a vast library of information on a multitude of subjects. Using such databases, you can peruse a comprehensive bibliography of your subject,

COMPUTER CLINIC

Finding Online Government Sources

You can find current information relevant to nearly any research topic by investigating federal and state government databases on the Internet. Sites such as Town Hall <http://www.town.hall.org/> and Thomas <http://www.thomas.loc.gov/>, for example, provide links to useful databases for both state and federal government agencies. By going to Fedworld <http://www.fedworld.gov/>, you can access thousands of United States government reports on topics ranging from the environment to skateboarding safety. The following list includes some of the most generally useful government resources online and the Internet address, or URL, for each.

Congressional Quarterly	<ftp://ftp.ncu.ed>
Council of State Governments	<http://www.csg.org/>
Federal Register	<http://ww1.access.gpo.gov/GPOAccess/sitesearch/su_docs_aces/desc004.html>
Fedworld	<http://www.fedworld.gov/>
Government Printing Office	<http://www.access.gpo.gov/>
Guide to U.S. Congress	<http://www.policy.net/capweb/congress.htm>
National Library of Medicine	<http://www.nlm.nih.gov/>
State and Local Government Information	<http://www.piperinfo.com/piper/states.html>
Thomas (local governments)	<http://www.thomas.loc.gov/>
Town Hall	<http://www.town.hall.org/>
U.S. Bureau of the Census	<http://www.census.gov/>
U.S. Congress person	<http:www.stardot.com/zipper>
U.S. Senate	<http://www.senate.gov/>
U.S. Supreme Court Decisions	<ftp:marvel.loc.gov>

read related encyclopedia articles, and find answers to specific factual questions. You can also have all the on-screen information printed so that you can keep a copy and use it when you wish. We suggest, though, that you begin the search for information in your library and turn to computer databases only to fill a gap in the library's resources.

4. Use Primary and Secondary Sources in your Research

Primary sources are the original materials about which secondary sources are written. They include novels, short stories, plays, poems, letters, journals, government documents, surveys, reports of experiments, interviews, and oral histories. Using primary sources puts you in direct contact with the raw material from which your paper will develop. Through this contact, your own analysis can become an integral part of your research paper.

Secondary sources are written materials about your topic, including books, magazines, newspaper articles, encyclopedia entries, pamphlets, and other works that examine, analyze, or report facts. Delgado used several books, reference works, and articles as secondary sources of information to complete her paper.

57c Gather information and prepare a working bibliography.

When you have decided on a topic, you will be ready to start gathering information about it. Most of your research data will probably come from the reference books, general books, and periodicals available in your college or community library. Systematically investigate each of these three major sources to establish a preliminary bibliography for your paper.

A working bibliography helps you determine whether your chosen topic is researchable in your library. It also helps you keep track of the available sources you need to seek. Finally, the working bibliography provides a handy source of information you will need for evaluating your sources during the writing stage, for citing sources in your text, and for completing your list of works cited.

Keep your Working Bibliography on Index Cards

Keep your working bibliography on 3-by-5-inch index cards, with a separate card for each source you consult. To find the source easily, or for reference if you need the work later, record the library call number.

Record the information you would need to list the source in your paper's Works Cited section. For a book, this information includes the author's name (or the editor's name followed by "ed."), the title

HV
5135.39
W397
2002
Wechsler, Henry, and Bernice Wuethrich. Dying to Drink: Confronting Binge Drinking on College Campuses. Emmaus, PA: Rodale, 2002.

Bibliography card

of the book (underlined), the place of publication, the publisher's name, and the year of publication.

For a magazine or journal article, list the author's name, the title of the article (in quotation marks), the title of the magazine or journal (underlined), the volume or issue number if the source is a journal, the date of publication, and the page numbers on which the article appears.

A sample bibliography card for a book with a single author is shown above. Other kinds of sources will require slightly different information. Follow the guide to documentation forms (59a and 59b) to learn what information to record for any source you may need to locate again or to include in your paper's Works Cited list.

Bibliographic formats vary among disciplines. They all, however, have the same intent—to make sure the writer includes the information that a reader needs to find those same sources. Section 59c contains a list of guides for disciplines using documentation styles other than those of MLA or APA.

The forms presented in this text follow the guidelines of the Modern Language Association (MLA) and the *MLA Handbook for Writers of Research Papers* (2003). But before beginning to record bibliographic information, check with your instructor about the format you should follow for your research paper. (American Psychological Association [APA] guidelines are discussed in 59b.) Then carefully follow the handbook, taking care during the final typing of your paper to use the spacing and punctuation shown in the illustrations. Also be sure to notice how bibliographic form—the form you will use in your Works Cited list—differs from in-text citation form. (See parenthetical citations, 58c.)

57d Reading and writing for a tentative thesis and working outline.

When you have set up a working bibliography (usually about fifteen sources for a college paper), you will be ready to examine your research materials more closely. Your first efforts should be directed toward preliminary reading and establishing a tentative thesis and working outline.

Preliminary reading consists of skimming the most promising materials in your bibliography to give yourself an expanded overview of the topic. You should gain a more detailed sense of the scope and complexity of the topic and a familiarity with the kinds of information you will compare and analyze during the research process. Work quickly by using tables of contents and indexes to locate information. At this point, take notes only for general information about the topic. Once you have explored enough material, you will start to form an idea (or sharpen an already existing one) of the central point you want to develop in your paper.

1. Develop a Tentative Thesis Statement

Begin by developing a tentative thesis statement, no more than one or two sentences, that presents and limits your topic (see Chapter 6). The tentative thesis may actually change during further research or in the writing stage of the paper, but at this point it will add focus and organization to your research. Cynthia Delgado's preliminary reading revealed two major issues related to campus binge drinking: the dangerous amounts of alcohol many students were consuming and the efforts colleges and universities were making to reduce that amount. She decided to include these ideas in her research paper, so she formulated the following as a *tentative* thesis statement:

> Binge drinking among today's college and university students has become so rampant that schools are responding with a variety of new policies and programs.

2. Develop a Working Outline

Your preliminary reading and your tentative thesis statement should aid you in establishing a working outline for the paper (see Chapter 6). As with everything you have done so far, the working outline need not be in permanent form; it is an early guide, a flexible blueprint to aid you in organizing your research, arranging your ideas logically, and making sure you have not left out any important aspects of your topic. The working outline may simply state the tentative thesis and then list supporting ideas. Delgado's working outline was roughly organized around the major ideas in her evolving thesis statement and the research materials she found to support it.

> Despite nationwide efforts by everyone from college presidents and national organizations to the U.S. Congress over the last ten years, studies continue to show that little progress has been made in changing a persistent, destructive, and too often lethal "drink till you puke" culture on American college campuses.
>
> BACKGROUND TO THE PROBLEM
> — 2001 study shows 70.3% of students drink; 44.4% binge drink.
> — College drinking has been a long-standing problem, but today is excessive and harmful.
>
> DANGERS OF BINGE DRINKING
> — Students are suffering personally as well as academically.
> — Students are dying as a result of binge drinking.
> — Binge drinkers do harm to others as well as themselves.
>
> WHO'S DRINKING
> — Student drinking in general is pervasive and extensive.
> — Fraternity and sorority members drink the most, also athletes.
> — There are increases in the number of women who drink heavily.
>
> WHY STUDENTS ARE DRINKING SO MUCH
> — Students expect to drink in college as part of the campus culture.
> — Some drink to fit in socially.
> — Some are attracted by the "forbidden" aspect of alcohol.
> — The alcohol industry promotes drinking on campuses.
>
> WHAT COLLEGES ARE DOING ABOUT THE PROBLEM
> — Many are becoming stricter about enforcing rules and alcohol laws.
> — Most have instituted alcohol education programs.
> — Some are contacting parents.

Notice that the working outline need not be complete. At this stage, it is useful in roughly charting the direction the paper may finally take and in pointing out the research that still needs to be done.

57e Take effective notes.

Using Note Cards

Begin the next step in the research process by using note cards to record information from and about your sources. Although there are many ways to keep research notes, storing them on cards is the most practical: cards are more durable than loose slips of paper; they are more easily organized than entries on notebook pages; and unlike computer-stored notes, the cards can go with you and are available for reference anywhere you do research. You will find large 4-by-6-inch index cards the most practical since they provide plenty of space for content and are easily distinguished from the smaller 3-by-5-inch bibliography cards you have been keeping.

Make a habit of using note cards to create consistent and useful records throughout your research. Start by skimming your sources, then reading closely those that appear promising. Analyze information and take notes as you proceed. What you select to read and decide to take notes about should correspond to the major categories of ideas listed earlier on your working outline (57d). Use these categories to direct your research and as topic headings, written at the top of the note cards, by which you can easily identify and organize the information you record. Expect to create additional headings for the note cards as your later reading suggests. Use a separate card for each note, even if two notes come under the same heading or from the same source.

Since you will undoubtedly need to document the sources for any note material included in your paper, be sure to record the name of the author and the page numbers for each piece of information you record. The sample summary card on p. 363 demonstrates a basic format for note card information.

Maintaining Academic Integrity by Avoiding Plagiarism

To maintain academic integrity, you must avoid plagiarism, the worst form of intellectual dishonesty a student can commit. Plagiarism occurs when a student writer presents another writer's language or ideas as if they were his or her own.

The consequences for students who plagiarize material by incorporating it in their work—whether deliberate or unintentional—can be severe. Colleges and universities treat plagiarism as an act of theft that can result in punishment ranging from receiving a failing grade in a course to expulsion from school.

In its most pernicious form, plagiarism occurs when a writer submits an essay written by another student or an essay purchased through a mail-order or online service. Plagiarism may also occur when a writer borrows heavily throughout an entire essay from a single source without properly acknowledging the source or without acknowledging the extent to which the writer relied on the source. For example, a common form of plagiarism occurs when a writer acknowledges direct quotations from a source but does not acknowledge his or her paraphrasing or summarizing the source material in other parts of the essay, thus creating the appearance that the material is the writer's original work.

Other times, plagiarism can be accidental. Accidental plagiarism occurs when a writer relies on a source and either forgets or neglects to acknowledge its author in the text of his or her essay and Works Cited. Such lapses frequently occur in several forms:

- Failure to identify a direct quotation with quotation marks
- Failure to adequately paraphrase a passage in the writer's own language
- Failure to clarify the source of a paraphrased passage following a direct quotation
- Failure to credit sources for ideas integrated into the essay

To maintain academic integrity in your writing, adhere to the following as guidelines during the research and writing process.

1. *Employ correct note-taking methods.* Learn the differences among summary, paraphrased, and quotation. Know when and how to use each and employ them correctly.
2. *Make a bibliographic card for every note source.* Consistently include on each note card the name of the source's author, title of the work, and the page number(s) for any language you copy or adapt and for each piece of information you record.
3. *Use quotation marks.* On your note cards and in your essay, put quotation marks around any language you reproduce directly from the source.
4. *Be scrupulous about identifying material downloaded from the Internet.* The Internet is a vast resource for information. it is easy to download material and then cut and paste it into an essay. Just as you must be scrupulous about acknowledging your traditional

sources, you must also be scrupulous about acknowledging your Internet sources.

5. *Check and recheck your note cards.* During the writing process be sure to integrate your sources into your text accurately. Check and recheck your information and acknowledgments for accuracy.
6. *Cite information accurately.* Cite the source in the text and the Works Cited section whenever you include material from the notes in your final paper.

For experienced instructors, plagiarism is easy to spot. At the most obvious level, a plagiarized essay might not address the assignment or might not read like student work or perhaps read unevenly, revealing that a writer has not acknowledged a significant source used throughout the essay. Moreover, since there are tens of thousand of plagiarized essays available on the Internet, instructors have become determined to fight the problem. As a result, Web sites such as plagiarism.org and turnitin.com now give instructors the ability to determine if suspect essays have indeed been plagiarized.

Rather than close on this cautionary note, you should be encouraged to approach the process of researching and writing a research essay as your opportunity to learn what authorities have said about a subject and to develop your own opinion while acknowledging the work of those who have come before you.

Note-Taking Techniques

Information you store on note cards must be not only accurate but also useful, worth the time you spend writing it down. Using the right recording methods will allow you to tailor notes to your expected needs for the paper and keep you from over recording information or writing too little because of inefficient note-taking methods. You can ensure the value of your notes and the time you spend on them by practicing four standard techniques for recording information: summarizing, paraphrasing, using quotation, or combining quotation and paraphrase.

Summarizing

Summarizing is a technique for quickly recording information in a condensed form and in your own words and style. Summarize whenever you need only a few facts or statistics from a source and are not concerned about having a larger, more detailed record of its content or an author's perspective. Summarizing is also useful for broadly characterizing the general contents of a source or for registering your own reactions (e.g., "Describes state laws on home schooling. Not as complete as Baker article.").

Convenience and brevity are the keys to effective summarizing. Focus on recording only main points or useful facts, possibly adding a brief note to yourself when doing so seems helpful. Write the notes quickly, without too much concern for your own wording and style. Use synonyms and other wording or symbols to express the information in your own way, but also take care not to distort the meaning of the original. Avoid simply copying words and sentences from the original, since this defeats the purpose of summarizing by taking more time, and it leads easily to plagiarism. If you must retain certain exceptional wording from the source, enclose it in quotation marks. Include the author's name and the page number for the summarized material on your note card in case you want more information later or need to list the source in your paper's Works Cited section.

The following paragraph comes from one of the sources Cynthia Delgado used for her paper on college binge drinking. The sample note card below the original paragraph shows how Delgado summarized information from it. Notice that the card includes a topic heading to help her locate and organize the note material later.

ORIGINAL

> Congress passed a measure this year that says colleges may notify parents if their son or daughter is caught violating an alcohol policy. But colleges are not required to do so, and many are still weighing the pros and cons. Some legal experts argue that the law violates a student's rights, and some campus officials believe it undermines their efforts to encourage independence and personal responsibility.
>
> —Mary Beth Marklein,
> "College Alcohol Policies Balance Rights, Privileges."

SUMMARIZED NOTE

Notification of parents

Marklein, "College"

Congress passed law making it OK for schools to notify parents when students violate alcohol rules. Might violate student rights, so some colleges are not sure they want to use it; others feel it would take away from student's responsibility.

Paraphrasing

You **paraphrase** information by clearly restating it in your own words. Paraphrasing is useful when you need to make a source's language or style more understandable and when it needs revision to match the style and flow of your own writing if you later include the material in your paper. Unlike a summary, which condenses original material into its essential meaning, a good paraphrase captures the sense of each part of the source, whether the source is a single sentence or several pages. For this reason, a paraphrase has no typical length, although it is seldom much shorter or longer than its source.

Your goal in paraphrasing is to recreate the entire original in different, clearer language, accurately conveying the source's meaning as well as the attitude of its author. As you interpret the original, remember that the way ideas are stated can change or add to their meaning. Be sure your paraphrase reflects the less evident as well as the obvious aspects of the source's language and style by paying attention to the author's word choice, emphases, qualifications, and overall tone. To serve as a later reminder for yourself and to indicate an author's attitude to your own readers, it is often helpful to include brief phrases that describe the manner in which the source's author relates the original (e.g., "Jenkins argues . . ." or "Henderson concedes that . . .").

Do not make the mistake of simply rewriting the original by rearranging its parts or integrating its words and sentence structures with your own. (Whether or not you cite the source, this practice amounts to plagiarism because the reader will assume the paraphrase is composed of your own wording.) Instead, always rewrite the source in your own style and language, taking care to use synonyms and other words that accurately capture the sense of the original. If you feel you must retain certain exceptional wording from the source, enclose it in quotation marks.

The following examples demonstrate the difference between unsuitable paraphrasing and paraphrasing that achieves its purpose. Notice how the first, poor paraphrase incorrectly repeats words and phrases from the source (shown here in italic type).

ORIGINAL

Public schools have, apparently willingly, assumed the role of "holding tanks." Social contact limited strictly to "peers" (defined as everyone of the same chronological age) is a fraud. The world for which we have the responsibility of preparing young people is *not* full of their peers. It is full of people both

older and younger, from social strata both higher and lower. What are we teaching about this very real world? Not much.
—Bob Pike, "Why I Teach My Children at Home"

POOR PARAPHRASE NOTE

Pike says that *public schools* seem too willing to serve *the role of "holding tanks,"* places where the *social contacts* children have are *limited strictly* to their *chronological peers.* This is simply *fraud. We have the responsibility of preparing* children for a world populated by people *younger* as well as *older,* and from different levels of society. What lessons are they learning about the *real world?* Very few (564).

BETTER PARAPHRASE NOTE

Pike complains that schools seem deliberately to serve as isolated, fraudulent environments in which children socialize only with others their own age. However, the world for which education readies these children is, he insists, populated by people of all ages and from all levels of society. The education we give children about the world beyond the classroom amounts to very little (564).

In contrast to the first paraphrase, the second version effectively rewords the source to avoid unintended plagiarism. In addition, the second paraphrase more accurately conveys the disgruntled attitude of the original author by using such terms as *complains* and *insists* to characterize the way he presents his argument. The first version, in contrast, uses only the much less descriptive word *says,* which communicates nothing of the irritation implied in the source.

Once you have written your paraphrase, compare it with the original to make sure you have not omitted key details or distorted the meaning. Remember also to record the author's name and the page number of the source on your note card so you can properly document the paraphrase when you use it in your paper.

Using Quotation

Take down the precise words of a source when you sense that what is said can be used to strengthen your research paper's discussion. Quote selectively and accurately, with the expectation of giving your reader only enough quoted material to convey and support your ideas. Blend single words, phrases, and sentences directly into your own writing as much as possible to keep your discussion flowing and to maintain your style.

> By arguing that people "don't want more taxes, just fewer criminals ruining their neighborhoods," Philips ignores the question of how we pay for more law enforcement.

Keep in mind that a quotation introduces the voice of another writer. Used excessively, it may suggest that you are depending too heavily on others for ideas. When used sparingly and accurately, however, quotation can bring variety and a sense of immediacy to a discussion.

The following are some of the most effective uses for quotation.

1. Quote from a source to lend authority to what you say. Use the quotation to reinforce your point, not to make it for you.

   > To do their job right, schools first need more money for teachers, which is why the prestigious 1991 *President's Report on Education* called low teacher salaries "the single greatest roadblock to this nation's quest for educational excellence."

2. Use quotation when summary or paraphrase would sacrifice the accuracy, precision, or eloquence of the original.

   > The world's largest single radio telescope has "27 receivers moving on Y-shaped railway tracks, with each arm of the Y stretching 20 km."

   > Americans have historically agreed in principle with Henry David Thoreau, who said, "That government is best which governs least."

3. Use quotation to provide brief examples of language, as when you discuss a literary work or analyze a political speech.

   > Melville describes the whale as "primal," "preadamic," and "as elemental as the substance it swims in."

4. Use quotation when the original may appear extreme or of questionable veracity.

   > Linguist Mary Hiller states that "half of the world's 6,000 known languages will disappear in the next fifty years because no children living today speak them."

Remember always to put quotation marks around any quotation and to include documentation of the source, in both your notes and your paper. Failure to provide either of these each time you quote is plagiarism. Be careful also not to distort the original or to quote out of context. Although you must always use the exact language of the original whenever you quote, there are acceptable methods for

WRITER'S CLINIC

Using Ellipses in a Direct Quotation

Whenever you quote directly from a source, you must reproduce all words, phrases, and sentences exactly as they appear in the original. You may, however, make changes to eliminate irrelevant language from a quotation. In doing so, you must indicate the omitted material by using an *ellipsis,* three spaced periods (. . .), wherever the missing language appeared in the original.

Original material to be quoted:

> These laws, written in response to a national concern for our resources, are necessary to preserve America's last remaining wilderness areas and to provide a valuable heritage for future generations. Our children will be grateful. The world will be a better place for us all.

Quotation with omitted material indicated by ellipses:

> According to Senator Carter (87), "These laws . . . are necessary to preserve America's last remaining wilderness areas . . . for future generations."

When omitting material that appeared at the beginning of a sentence in the original, you can avoid an unnecessary ellipsis by including relevant parts of the original in your own sentence:

> According to Senator Carter (87), these new laws have become "necessary to preserve America's last remaining wilderness areas . . . for future generations."

If you include an ellipsis at the end of a quotation, add a concluding period after the ellipsis.

Ellipsis appearing at the end of a sentence:

> According to Senator Carter (87), these new laws have become "necessary to preserve America's last remaining wilderness areas . . . ."

Similarly, include a period after an ellipsis to indicate the omission of a whole sentence from a quotation.

Ellipsis used to omit an entire sentence in a quotation:

> According to Senator Carter (87), these new laws have become "necessary to preserve America's last remaining wilderness areas . . . . The world will be a better place for us all."

If your instructor prefers that you indicate that an ellipsis has been added to the original, you may also place square brackets around the ellipses: "These laws [. . .] are necessary to preserve America's last remaining wilderness areas [. . .] for future generations."

altering a quotation to blend with the grammar of your own writing or to suit other needs. For example, use ellipses to show that you have omitted material from a quotation (see ellipses, 42a) and place brackets around your own comments when they interrupt the quotation (see brackets, Chapter 44).

Combining Quotation and Paraphrase

You can sometimes reduce the amount of information you need to quote by combining quotation with paraphrase. The technique is simple: use quotation when the exact wording of the original is important, and paraphrase any part whose meaning, but not whose precise language, is worth recording. You must be careful when using quotation and paraphrase together to distinguish quoted material from paraphrasing by means of clearly written quotation marks. Use ellipses and brackets to alter quotations as necessary to maintain sense or to omit unnecessary material. The following example demonstrates how to use quotation and paraphrase to record information on a note card.

> Pike argues that when schools serve more like "holding tanks" and limit student contact only to peers, they are "a fraud." The real world "for which we . . . [prepare children] is *not* full of their peers." It includes "older and younger" people from various social levels. "What are we teaching [children] about this very real world? Not much."

57f Twenty student questions, twenty answers.

Research is a complicated activity that raises innumerable questions. The following are common questions asked of instructors, with answers that may help your own research.

1. **I want to write a paper arguing against child abuse. I know a lot has been written on the subject. Is that a good choice for a topic?**
   First, who would argue against you in favor of child abuse? That is, are there two sides to the question? A topic like this might lead you into a discussion of morality, which would be too philosophical for a research paper. You would need to concentrate on arguing a thesis about some unsettled issue or problem related to child abuse, such as prevention, laws, or some aspect that needs further investigation.

2. **I have scoured all the reference indexes and the card catalog, but I have found only three sources on my topic. Where do I go next?**
There are other places to look—pamphlets, other libraries, or some community sources of information. At this point, though, you may need to reconsider your topic. It might be too recent an idea, and perhaps not much has been written about it. Or it might be so narrow or so broad that it is not identified in any index or catalog. Try to redefine the topic along the lines of other ideas you have seen in sources, or develop another topic entirely.

3. **A book I need for my research is not available in any convenient libraries. Is there any way for me to get the book or find out about it?**
Yes. You can ask the librarian to get the book through interlibrary loan from another college or university. Or use the *Book Review Digest* or a similar guide to find a comprehensive review of the book. You may find the information you need in the review, which itself will serve as a research source for your paper.

4. **For my paper I want to interview a friend. Is that a good primary source?**
Use interviews with careful judgment. In most cases the people you choose to interview should be in a position to speak objectively and knowledgeably about the subject. They should also be able to give you insights or information not available in regular, published sources—that is why you have to interview them instead of using the library. If your friend or anyone else fits these broad criteria, use that person as a source to reaffirm or illustrate the information you obtain from more broadly available and recognized authorities.

5. **I couldn't find a date of publication, but I found a copyright date. How do I cite that date?**
In most cases, the copyright date and date of publication are treated as the same. If both are supplied, give the publication date. If only the copyright date is included, give that date.

6. **My book source was published in three different cities. Which do I cite?**
Cite the first city or place listed.

7. **I've gone on the Internet and found almost a hundred sources for my topic. How do I decide which ones to use for my paper?**
   Use sources that appear the most reliable in terms of their being current, provided by an authority, unbiased in the viewpoints they present, and relevant to your topic. In many instances, you should consult Internet sources with the same discrimination you use for regular library sources or other materials for research.

8. **Out of a total of twelve sources so far, six of my preliminary works cited are from one major magazine. Is that all right?**
   Your list of works cited should be balanced in terms of both the categories of sources you use (books, magazines, and so on) and the specific publications within each category. Any one source or category of source presents a limited point of view. Try to include as many viewpoints as possible, although you do not have to ignore any source.

9. **My paper topic has a long and fascinating history. How much of that history should I include?**
   Include only as much history as is relevant to your thesis or to a current situation. For the most part, keep histories to a minimum, focusing your paper's content on the development and support of your thesis statement.

10. **I need to use a number of technical terms in my paper. What is the best way to make sure my reader understands them?**
    For general college papers, keep technical vocabulary to a minimum. Recast technical terms in familiar wordings whenever possible. Refer, for example, to poikiloterms as "cold-blooded animals." Or use descriptive phrases to define unfamiliar terms: "Such pinnate, featherlike leaves are common to these plants." Finally, ask yourself if the terms are really necessary to convey your point. If not, leave them out.

11. **My paper seems like a paragraph-by-paragraph summary of my sources. Where do my own ideas come in the paper, and how do I express them?**
    Your thesis statement is *your* most important opinion in the paper and should control the organization and presentation of material. Be sure your thesis is truly an argumentative one, and then argue it as you would any idea you believe in and can support with ample evidence. Take time to review both

your sources and your own attitude toward what you have learned in your research. Compare, evaluate, define, make concessions, analyze, and comment just as you would in any thorough discussion.

12. **I find little information that needs to be cited in my ten-page paper. Are three or four citations enough for a paper this long?**
Probably not. A lack of citations results from inadequate use of your research data or weak support of your own arguments. Very likely, too, you have not always given credit to your sources as you should. Review the paper's content to be sure that you have offered supportive evidence from your research and that you have properly cited the sources of that evidence.

13. **I remember hearing something about using abbreviations like *ibid., loc. cit.,* and *op. cit.* for subsequent references. What are they for?**
These abbreviations formerly were used for specific kinds of subsequent references. Scholarly groups and universities, however, have generally abandoned them in favor of the simplified method described in this text.

14. **One major work I read disagrees with several others on an issue important to my paper. How do I handle this situation?**
Give careful consideration to the authority and evidence of all sources, and base your discussion on what you feel is a fair representation of the case. Provide an explanatory note to inform your readers of the differing opinion and to explain briefly the rationale for your presentation in the paper.

15. **I have a magazine title with no capital letters. Do I write the title that way in my paper?**
Capitalize according to standard practices. Commercial, popular writing often emphasizes visual impact over traditional uses of punctuation. Unless you know that such variations are part of the author's purpose, capitalize and punctuate all titles in accordance with standard rules.

16. **Where can I find sources other than those in my library?**
Go to public agencies, departments within your school, businesses, local museums, and special-interest groups or societies. Such groups usually have pamphlets or other material available for the public as well as special libraries devoted to their particular activities.

17. **I heard a lecture in one of my classes and took notes on it. Is that a good primary source?**
Yes. Be sure your notes are accurate. For your paper, cite the lecturer, place, and date, and identify it as a lecture.

18. **After writing the first draft, I can tell that my paper is shorter than the length required by my instructor. What should I do?**
Check to see that you have supplied ample support for your thesis and that you have discussed all relevant aspects of the topic. Is the issue you are writing about really as simple as you have made it sound? Is your thesis too narrow or obvious to allow much discussion and presentation of evidence? Perhaps you need to broaden your subject. If time allows, ask your instructor to look over the draft with you to see what parts might need fuller treatment.

19. **I have cited six works in my paper, but I want to include in my list of works cited all twelve sources I listed in my working bibliography. Is that right?**
No. Only the works cited in the text of your paper should appear in your Works Cited. Distinctions are sometimes made between works *cited* and *consulted,* but if you have not used a source for other than common background information, it should not be cited.

20. **How should I refer to an author? Should I use the full name or Dr., Mr., Mrs., Miss, or Ms.?**
Simply use the full name without titles the first time you refer to an author. Then use only the last name throughout the rest of the paper. If, however, you have more than one author with the same last name in your Works Cited, use their full names throughout the paper.

58 Writing a Research Paper *res*

58a Revise the thesis and outline.

After completing the reading and note taking for your paper, you probably will have changed your concept of the paper's content and organization. At this point you will start to revise your thesis and then your outline. Begin by sorting the note cards by topic and then arrange them in a way that parallels your tentative outline. This process will show whether you have adequate material to support the points in your outline. Once the sorting is completed, evaluate your tentative thesis and working outline with an eye for revision. Then begin to rearrange the note cards and rework the tentative thesis to fit the concept you see emerging from the material you have collected.

After rereading and taking notes, Cynthia Delgado decided that her paper needed to emphasize the extent to which her research showed that binge drinking was not only widespread but terribly destructive of student lives. She also knew that she wanted to talk about the steps colleges and universities were taking to reduce the amount of drinking on their campuses. She revised her tentative thesis statement to reflect these ideas.

TENTATIVE THESIS STATEMENT

> Because binge drinking continues to be a problem on America's college and university campuses, schools are beginning to treat student alcohol use as a serious problem.

REVISED THESIS STATEMENT

> Despite nationwide efforts by everyone from college presidents and national organizations to the U.S. Congress over the last ten years, studies continue to show that little progress has been made in changing a persistent, destructive, and too often lethal "drink till you puke" culture on American college campuses.

Having sorted her cards and revised her thesis, Delgado found that the tentative outline needed revision. She had come across a satiric national advertisement directed at student binge drinking during her research, and she now decided to use it in the first part of her paper. In addition, she now understood that many of the new programs and policies schools were putting into effect were having positive results. She wanted to talk about these results in her paper, but not in such a way that her reader would think the problem of binge drinking was getting solved. (Refer to Delgado's working outline on p. 359.) The following are the beginning sections of her revised outline.

Revised Outline

EXTENT OF THE PROBLEM

— 2001 study shows that 70.3% of all college students drink; 44.4% of them binge drink.

— College drinking has been a long-standing problem, but today is excessive and harmful.
— College students consume large and excessive amounts of alcohol.

DANGERS OF BINGE DRINKING

— Students' devotion to alcohol is excessive and out of control at most campuses.
— Students are suffering personally as well as academically.
— The annual death toll of students dying from alcohol abuse keeps increasing.
— Binge drinkers harm themselves as well as others.

WHO IS DRINKING THE MOST

— Fraternity and sorority members, as well as athletes, drink the most.
— College students spend more money on alcohol than on most other things they buy.

Once Delgado completed this stage of the revision process and arranged her notes according to the headings of the revised outline, she was ready to develop the final outline by following the formal outline form. (See final plan for an essay, 6d.) Delgado's formal sentence outline is on p. 385, preceding her research paper. If you compare the formal outline to the working and revised outlines, you will see how much more information she included and how she rephrased the sentences for accuracy in the formal outline.

58b Write the first draft.

You can begin writing the paper at any point in the outline, perhaps writing the middle paragraphs before the introductory and concluding paragraphs. Delgado began her research paper with an example that she considered both highly interesting and significant. The national ad ironically reassuring students that they sometimes needed those "five or six drinks the night before that big test" seemed to her an effective way to emphasize the real seriousness of her subject and grab her reader's attention at the same time. She read a draft of her introduction to a classmate, and she also discussed the other sections she had planned for the paper. Delgado's classmate urged her to keep the introduction she had planned. It was, he assured her, something student readers would relate to and want to know more about. From that conversation Delgado learned an important lesson about writing:

Sometimes just talking about your ideas helps to improve them and gives you confidence that you are thinking effectively about your topic.

58c Acknowledge your sources.

Acknowledging sources for your paper lends it authority and credibility and provides readers with information to locate the sources for themselves. To a large extent, in fact, the value of your paper's content and your own integrity as a writer depend on how accurately and fairly you make use of and credit the ideas you borrow from other writers. (See avoiding plagiarism, pp. 360–362.) As you write the paper and integrate information from your sources into it, follow standard documentation practices to ensure accurate acknowledgment of your sources.

Parenthetical Citations: MLA Documentation Style

Acknowledge sources in your paper by naming them in brief parenthetical citations as explained below and in the examples provided in "A Documentation Guide" in Chapter 59. The Modern Language Association (MLA) recommends that sources be acknowledged within parentheses placed directly in the text. In this system of parenthetical citation, numbered notes, although rarely necessary, serve only to identify supplementary or explanatory comments (see p. 381).

Use parenthetical citations to acknowledge quotations (except for common sayings or well-known quotations), summaries, paraphrases, the opinions of others, lines of thinking you adopt, and statistics. In short, use parenthetical citations whenever you borrow information that is not commonly known or believed, especially by people generally acquainted with your subject. Do not provide parenthetical citations for facts or common knowledge, such as that hydrocyanic acid is a colorless, poisonous liquid or that Abraham Lincoln was the sixteenth president of the United States.

Because a parenthetical citation must always designate a specific entry alphabetically listed in Works Cited, the information in the citation must clearly direct a reader to that entry. Usually, but not always (see examples below), the author's last name and a page reference are enough to identify the source and the specific location from which you have borrowed material.

> The wings of jetliners built in Europe or the USSR are more difficult to inspect and maintain than those built in the U.S. because of the way they are manufactured (Seo 28).

Page references never include *p.* or *pp.* If you are referring to several consecutive pages, join the page numbers with a hyphen—for example: (Seo 78-81). When referring to two or more individual pages in one citation, use commas to separate them—for example: (Seo 16, 41, 63). If the work consists of only one page, list the page number in the Works Cited entry and do not include it in the parenthetical citation: (Birnbaum).

Keep parenthetical citations as concise as possible so that the interruption in your text is minimal. You are required to give only enough information to guide a reader to the specific source you have fully identified in Works Cited. If you have integrated into your text any information that should be included in the parenthetical citation, such as the author's name, you need not include that in the citation.

> Wilson Bryan Key has taken the mystery from subliminal-advertising discussions. He claims to have found subliminal messages in vodka ads (99).

Keep your paper as readable as possible. Insert parenthetical citations before a period or comma as close to the borrowed material as possible and outside quotation marks, when directly quoting a source.

> In her 1979 essay collection <u>The White Album</u>, Joan Didion sounds confused by random violence and personal terror (15-20), but by 1982 its meaning has become clear to her: "I came to understand, in a way I had not understood before, the exact mechanism of terror" (<u>Salvador</u> 21).

If the borrowed material is set off from the text, the parenthetical citation follows the final punctuation. (See quotation marks, 39a.)

> In contrast to great art works, Oates sees literary criticism as a refined form of communication between writer and reader. She writes,
>
> > If the greatest works of art sometimes strike us as austere and timeless, with their private music, as befits sacred things, criticism is always an entirely human dialogue, a conversation directed toward an audience. (2)

To acquire skill in accurately acknowledging your sources in parenthetical citations, study their use in Cynthia Delgado's paper and review the following examples, paying close attention to the details of form and punctuation.

Entire Work

At times you may wish to acknowledge an entire work rather than a specific part of the work. In this case, include the author's name in the text rather than in a parenthetical citation. Since the reference is to a work in general, you are not required to cite a page number.

> Peter Brooks's analysis of plot and plotting is established on basic psychoanalytic principles.

Part of an Article or of a Single-Volume Work

When you refer to specific passages or when you quote directly from a work, you must give the relevant page reference in the parenthetical citation.

> Campbell's point is stunningly clear: "Communication is not confined to radios, telephones, and television channels. It occurs in nature, wherever life exists" (67).

> Most people spend more time picking a car than they do a doctor and hospital (Mathisen 63-64), but obviously you can't kick tires in a doctor's office, and if you attempted the equivalent in a hospital--laying your foot into a $600,000 CAT scanner--you would get some very nasty looks indeed.

If another author listed in Works Cited has the same last name as the one you are acknowledging, give the first initial as well as the last name: (L. Sanders 34).

For a work with two or three authors, give all the last names. If, however, there are more than three authors, give one last name followed by *et al.*: (Scholes et al. 28-29).

If you list more than one work by a single author in Works Cited, give the title or a shortened version after the author's name: (Barthes, Images 12-13).

Multivolume Work

In the parenthetical citation for a multivolume work, include the volume number followed by a colon, a space, and then the page reference: (Kroos 1: 210-15). If you refer to an entire volume in general rather than to specific pages, place a comma after the author's name and include *vol.:* (Kroos, vol. 1). If you place the information in your text, write out *volume* and the numeral: Kroos's volume 1 covers the first . . . . Use arabic numerals rather than roman numerals to indicate volume numbers.

> "Feeling-toned complexes" were defined by the early psychiatric community as "failures to react" (Jung 8: 93).

> At first the prose is groping, unsure of its footing, but midway through the work, sharp portraits of avant-garde artists emerge (Nin, vol. 1).

Work Listed by Title

For a work alphabetized by title in your Works Cited, use the title or a shortened version of the title in the parenthetical reference. To make tracing the reference easier for your reader, begin the citation with the word by which the work is alphabetized. If you are acknowledging a one-page article, omit the page reference.

> A debit card, according to MasterCard's president Hogg, "looks like a credit card but works like a check" ("Now It's the No-Credit Card").

> The Planning Commission Handbook clearly states that land development is not the landowner's god-given right, but is a privilege granted by a public agency (31-32).

Work by a Corporate Author

Because the names of corporate authors are often long, identify them in your text and cite the specific page reference in the parenthetical citation. When necessary, you may offer a shortened version of the name in the parenthetical citation.

> The Commission on Post-Secondary Education in California states that remedial education in the University of California and State University systems has dramatically increased (5-10).

Fiction, Poetry, Drama, and the Bible

When citing the Bible and other literary works available in more than one edition, include the appropriate unit—that is, chapter, book, scene, line. In general, use arabic numerals rather than roman numerals in citing volumes or divisions of a work. Roman numerals may be used in citing acts and scenes of a play.

For a novel, give the page number first, a semicolon and space, and then the divisions, using appropriate abbreviations with periods.

> Politics, the undercurrent of the novel, sweeps Julien from one extreme to another. Nowhere is this more evident than in the description of the king's visit to Verrières (Stendhal 115-26; pt. 1, ch. 18).

For extended works of poetry, give the division reference first, followed by the line reference. Use a period with no space to separate the two. Do not give a page reference.

> Antenor described Odysseus's power as a powerful orator: "But when he let the great voice go from his chest, and the words came / drifting down like the winter snows, then no other mortal / man beside could stand up against Odysseus" (Homer 3.221-23).

If the poem is short or not divided into books or cantos, give only the line reference. When acknowledging only line numbers, use *line* or *lines* in the citation, but after you have established that the numbers designate lines, use only numbers.

> "For the Anniversary of My Death" begins with the suggestion that after death the soul starts a journey through time "Like the beam of a lightless star" (Merwin, line 5). The poem ends with Merwin's affirmation of concrete experience, behind which lies the mystery of existence.
>
> > As today writing after three days of rain
> > Hearing the wren sing and the falling cease
> > And bowing not knowing to what. (11-13)

For a play give the act, scene, and line references, using periods without spaces to separate the divisions. You may use roman numerals in citing acts and scenes.

> The imagery of futile battle is also found in the "To be, or not to be" soliloquy (Shakespeare 3.1.56-89).

For the Bible give the book title, chapter, and verse, using periods to separate the divisions. Within the parenthetical citation (but not in the text itself) you may abbreviate a book title, using a period to end the abbreviation–for example, "Gen." for *Genesis,* "Rev." for *Revelation.*

> In the opening verses of the Book of Job (1.1-5), Job appears to have fulfilled the blessing that God had bestowed on humankind when Adam and Eve were created, "Be fruitful, multiply, fill the earth and conquer it" (Gen. 1.28).

Indirect Sources

Whenever possible, draw your material from an original source, but at times you will need to rely on an indirect source for information. For instance, you may need to use someone's published account of what another person has said. When you do quote or paraphrase from an indirect source, you must indicate in the parenthetical citation that you have done so by putting *qtd. in* ("quoted in") before the acknowledgment of the source, unless, of course, you have clearly indicated in your text that you are relying on an indirect source.

> Poet Michael McClure claims Mailer had a strong belief that he would only be listened to if he were irreverent. When people asked Mailer to moderate his irreverence, he would say, "Hey, I feel irreverence, and there's truth in the irreverence" (qtd. in Manso 281).

Two or More Sources in a Single Parenthetical Citation

To acknowledge more than one source in a single citation, cite each work as you normally would but separate the citations with a semicolon and a space.

> Whenever we open another novel, we embark on an adventure in which we have a chance to become a new person in the sense both that we can assume the imaginary

role the writer thrusts at us and that we can reformulate ourselves by discovering what had previously seemed to elude our consciousness (Gibson 265; Iser 294).

When multiple references in a single citation would be too long, acknowledge them in a note instead. (See explanatory notes section that follows.)

Explanatory Notes: MLA Style

Explanatory notes have a limited use in the MLA system of documentation. Notes are used to offer definitions, provide translations, make comparisons between sources, or generally furnish information not strictly pertinent to the immediate discussion in the text.

Identify notes in your text by numbering them consecutively throughout with superscript (raised) arabic numerals. The numerals correspond to notes appearing either in footnotes at the bottom of the page or on a page titled "Notes" placed at the end of the paper before Works Cited.

TEXT REFERENCE

Although colleges in the United States had historically assumed close supervisory roles over students since the late eighteenth century,[1] the 1960s introduced changes in social attitudes that resulted in fewer restrictions on campuses and new regard for the rights of students to be treated as adults (Kleiner 74).

NOTE

[1]Until the 1960s, colleges and universities continued to act in loco parentis, that is, legally responsible for minors in the absence of their parents. Changes in social attitudes and the fear of being sued for any involvement in student affairs then pushed schools toward a more "hands-off" approach to supervising students. Today, fear of being sued for not taking more responsibility has pressured colleges and universities to address campus drinking problems more aggressively. See Kleiner, 74.

58d Complete the final draft.

After you have completed the first draft, put your paper aside for a day or two if possible. This will give you a chance to return to it with a fresh approach. Reread the entire draft carefully several times and at least once aloud to listen for missing transitions or awkward constructions. Watch for careless grammar, spelling, or punctuation mistakes. More important, examine the content to see that you have kept to your thesis, provided ample evidence to support the assertions in your topic sentences, and integrated your own views with those of your sources to create a balanced whole. As a last step, check your citations and list of works cited to be sure they are correct in form, content, and punctuation.

Guidelines for Typing the Research Paper

Although formats for research papers vary, the following guidelines are the most common practices for typing the title page, outline (if required), quotations, citations, and Works Cited. Unless otherwise noted, all typing should be double spaced. Additional information is covered in Chapter 9.

Title page. Center the title about a third of the way down the page. Do not underline it or put quotation marks around it unless the words would also be underlined or quoted in the paper's text. Ten lines down from the title, center your name. Beneath your name, type the course title, the instructor's name, and the date, each on a separate line.

Your instructor may prefer that you follow the MLA guidelines, which recommend not using a separate title page. If you are to follow the MLA style, present the identifying information on the first page of the text. Place your name, your instructor's name, the course number and section, and the date on separate double-spaced lines in the upper-left-hand corner of the page, observing the same left-hand margin as the text. Double-space below the date and center your title; then double-space between your title and the first line of the text.

Outline. On a separate page, center the word *Outline* one inch from the top. Two lines below, type the thesis statement, followed by the outline itself. Use standard outline form, with the various topic levels successively indented and numbered with roman or arabic numerals and lowercase or uppercase letters as required. The outline included in Cynthia Delgado's paper begins on page 385.

Quotations. Indent quotations requiring more than four typed lines ten spaces from the left margin (or one inch), double-spacing throughout (see 39a). Do not put quotation marks around an indented quotation. When quoting two or more paragraphs, indent the first line of each paragraph three additional spaces (or one-fourth inch). The parenthetical citation appears at the end of the indented quotation, following the period or other end mark. Shorter quotations, not indented, should be enclosed in double quotation marks.

Other punctuation marks. Most computer keyboards have bracket keys. For a dash, use either two unspaced hyphens (—) without space on either side or an em dash, if available.

Notes. Starting on a new page, center the word *Notes* one inch from the top, with the first entry two lines below the title. Indent the note number, raised, five spaces from the left margin, leaving no space between the number and the first word of the note. All subsequent lines of the note begin at the left margin. Double-space within each note and between notes.

Works Cited. Type the words *Works Cited* on a new page, centered, one inch from the top. Begin the first alphabetized entry at the left margin two lines below the title. Remember to cite the first author with the last name first; subsequent authors' or editors' names in the same entry are typed in regular order; subsequent lines of an entry are indented five spaces. When you have more than one work by the same author, the name is not repeated; instead, type three hyphens followed by a period. Double-space throughout. Follow periods with only one space.

After you have typed the final version of the paper, carefully read it again for errors in typing. Include, in order, an outline, the text of the paper, the notes, and the list of works cited. Other sections, such as an appendix or glossary, if they are included, precede the notes. When you are satisfied that you have written and typed the paper in a manner that fulfills your own goals and the requirements of your instructor, make a photocopy to keep for yourself and present the original copy to your instructor.

58e Examining a sample research paper.

Cynthia Delgado's research paper, which follows, illustrates the advice given in this chapter. She followed the style for citations and list of works cited given in the *MLA Handbook.* The comments accompanying the paper identify specific points about the research paper format as well as some of the decisions Delgado made while writing.

Delgado i

Include title page if paper has outline and instructor requires it.

Center title one-third down the page.

College Binge Drinking: Can Students Dry Out?

Cynthia Delgado

English 101

Professor Janet Kramer

May 5, 2003

Center and double-space name, course information, and date.

Number all pages after title page in upper-right-hand corner, ½" down and 1" from the right. Delgado ii

Center outline 1" from top.

Outline

Thesis: Despite nationwide efforts by everyone from college presidents and national organizations to the U.S. Congress over the last ten years, studies continue to show that little progress has been made in changing a persistent, destructive, and too often lethal "drink till you puke" culture on American college campuses.

Outline organized by topics.

I. Introduction: The large number of college students engaging in excessive alcohol consumption and binge drinking
II. Harmful effects
    A. Personal and academic problems
    B. Deaths
III. Campus drinkers
    A. General patterns
    B. Fraternity and sorority members and athletes
IV. Causes of excessive student drinking
    A. Campus culture
    B. Alcohol industry influence
V. Campuses responses
    A. Stronger policies and enforcement
    B. Restrictions on alcohol
    C. Other practices
VI. Persistence of the problem

Double-space throughout outline; 1" margins on both sides.

Delgado 1

Center title on first page; double-space after title throughout.

College Binge Drinking:

Can Students Dry Out?

Opening sentences introduce the general topic "college drinking" and references the quotation that follows.

In 1993 the following statements were made by students responding to a national survey on college drinking in 1993 (Wechsler "Binge"). The unfortunate fact is that identical responses could as easily have come from students answering the same survey today, a full decade later.

This example supports the assertion in the opening sentences and relates to the thesis stated in the introduction's last sentence.

> Several people were drunk at this fraternity party. Some of the guys were kicked out because they were so drunk they were urinating on the walls. The entire place reeked of beer, and people were covered in it.
>
> I was having a great night. I drank at least 15 beers, and then I completely blacked out. This is not uncommon for me.

Use single quotation marks for material quoted in source.

As anyone familiar with contemporary college life knows, campus traditions like "Nude Olympics," pub crawls, keg parties, chug-a-lug challenges, "fourth-year fifths" (drinking a fifth of hard liquor after the final football game of one's senior year), and spring break bashes are as popular and widely ingrained in campus culture today as ever--if not more so. In fact, the all-too-common belief among many students is that in order to have fun at college, 'you're going to have to get drunk,' and not to do so will only make you 'feel weird' (Okie.) Thus despite nationwide efforts by everyone from college presidents and national organizations to the U.S. Congress over the last ten years, studies continue

First paragraph concludes with thesis statement.

to show that little progress has been made in changing a persistent, destructive, and too often lethal "drink till you puke" (Nuwer 16) culture on American college campuses.

The problem of college drinking is hardly new. Overconsumption of alcohol has been a recognized and serious problem on America's campuses for at least the last four decades (Nuwer 20). The large numbers of students who drink excessively on campuses has long been documented by a variety of research efforts, most notably the 1993, 1997, and 1999 national College Alcohol Survey (CAS) sponsored by the Harvard School of Public Health. The CAS findings and other studies have revealed that disturbingly high numbers of students not only binge drink but also consider any occasion a reason to consume alcohol. The reasons student binge drink are multiple, but studies also show that most students who binge drink do so with the clear intention of getting solidly drunk (Dickinson; Smith and Smith; Wechsler and Wuethrich 55). All together, frequent binge drinkers make up less than a quarter (23%) of all college students but consume nearly three-quarters (72%) of all the alcohol college students drink (Wechsler and Wuethrich 6).

Use abbreviation after first naming item fully.

Cite joint authors with and *between names; semicolon separates multiple sources.*

Numerals and percent symbols used when paper contains frequent numbers.

Cite multipage source by author and page number.

While current studies show that the majority of today's students drink moderately or even abstain from alcohol (Wechsler et al., "Trends" 210), what has college officials and others worried is the number of students who continue to drink both excessively and often, despite

Use "et al." when source has more than three authors; list source title for multiple works by same author.

major increased efforts on the part of colleges and universities to educate students about the harmful effects of alcohol abuse, especially binge drinking. Results of the 2001 CAS,[1] for example, showed that two out of every five respondents had indulged in a recent bout of binge drinking, defined as consuming five or more drinks in a row by a male and four or more for a female. What surprised--and disappointed--researchers is that percentage of binge drinkers overall--44.4% of those responding to the survey--did not change between 1993 and 2001[2] (Wechsler et al., "Trends" 207).

Additionally, although the 2001 CAS showed a slight decrease in binge drinking among Hispanic (34%), Native American (34%), African American (22%), and Asian (26%) students, there was also an increase (32% in 2001 versus 25% in 1993) in the percentage of women who frequently engaged in binge drinking. Given the efforts by colleges throughout the country in the last ten years, researchers had hoped for significant declines in the number of students who binge drink. "You would expect a drop," said Henry Weschsler, director of the survey. "It hasn't happened yet" (Okie).

Capitalize names of races or ethnic groups.

Quotation integrated into the paper's text.

This is not to say that binge drinkers are indulging alone. So entrenched is the culture of drinking among college students in general that when both Michigan State and Washington State University tried to cut back on student drinking and partying privileges in 1999, mobs of drunken students rioted in protest (Farrish). In

2000, at James Madison University in Virginia, over seven hundred students confronted riot police and state troopers trying to control a "progressive" (i.e., consuming alcohol in several successive places) drinking party. That same year the administration at the University of Dayton, Ohio, indefinitely suspended Homecoming because of 'extensive and excessive drinking and trashing of the student neighborhoods' (Wechsler and Wuethrich 5-6).

The unrestrained popularity of alcohol results in students consuming far more than is safe, especially by those who binge drink. In survey after survey, college binge drinkers report in higher numbers than other students that alcohol has led them to do things they later regretted: missing classes, forgetting where they have been or what they did, falling behind in school work, arguing with friends, forgetting where they were, getting hurt, driving after drinking, having unplanned sexual activity, not using protection during sex, damaging property, and getting in trouble with the police (Wechsler and Wuethrich 177).

The most tragic fact, however, is that in too many instances students are literally drinking themselves to death:

Bullets list examples by year.

- In 1999, a Penn State student celebrating her twenty-first birthday died after being hospitalized with a blood alcohol content of 0.682%--twice the level that normally sends a person into a coma. The young woman had taken part in a tradition of consuming at least

Delgado 5

twenty-one birthday drinks at a series of local bars ("Binge").

- In October 2000, a student choked to death on his own vomit after passing out from consuming near-lethal amounts of alcohol during a "big brother/little brother" fraternity night at Old Dominion University in Norfolk, Virginia (Argetsinger).
- In November 2001, an Ohio State University student and fraternity member died after consuming a lethal amount of alcohol while celebrating his twenty-first birthday. The Franklin County Coroner said when the young man died, he had a blood-alcohol content of 0.36--three times the legal limit defining someone as intoxicated (Solvig).
- In September 2002, a nineteen-year-old University of Maryland student with blood alcohol levels far in excess of the legal limit for driving died in a car crash following a raucus "bid night" party of the campus Phi Kappa Sigma house. His death was the second fraternity-related death at the campus that year (Okie).

Sadly, these few examples represent only a small fraction of the tragic damage caused by student abuse of alcohol. Not only do the binge drinkers harm themselves, but others endure the consequences of their indulgences as well. According to Harvard's director of the School of Public Health and head of the national CAS studies, nonbinging students experience "widespread harm as a result of others' misuse

Delgado 6

of alcohol," ranging from "interrupted study and sleep to destruction of property, assault, and unwanted sexual advances" (Wechsler, Austin, and DeJong 2). Data from a recent study for the National Institute on Alcohol Abuse and Alcoholism show that drinking by college students contributes to 1,400 deaths, half a million injuries, and 70,000 sexual assaults or date rapes a year. The study also reports that more than 600,000 students between the ages of 18 and 24 are assaulted by another student who has been drinking, and that 25% of all college students have academic problems caused by their own excessive drinking (Task Force 15).

Dangerous drinking and its too-often fatal results are not limited to any particular kind of college or groups of students, although patterns do emerge. In general, college students who drink the most include males, whites, members of fraternities or sororities, athletes, and some first-year students (Task Force 19). If any groups stand out as leaders in campus drinking, fraternities, sororities, and athletes are in the forefront. Although binge drinking has declined among fraternity and sorority house residents from 83.4% in 1993 to 75.4% in 2001, fraternities and sororities are still major arenas for student binge drinking (Wechsler et al., "Trends" 207). Research shows that 73% of college fraternity members are binge drinkers, as are 57% of sorority members (Wechsler and Wuethrich 6).

Cite committee author by shortened name.

It is hardly surprising, then, that the national 2001 College Alcohol Survey conducted by Wechsler and others shows that fraternity members are more likely (75.1% versus 48.6%) than their nonfraternity peers to be binge drinkers, with similar results (62.4% versus 40.9%) reported for sorority and nonsorority members (Wechsler et al., "Trends" 204). As one study of college drinking points out, "For students who do not already drink heavily when they begin college, joining a Greek organization is a sure way to start" (Wechsler and Wuethrich 37).

Other studies have shown that athletes who are also members of a fraternity or sorority drink three times as much alcohol as independent, nonathletic students; a majority of those Greek male and Greek female athletes also describe themselves as binge drinkers (Cashin, Presley, and Meilman 66). College athletes, in fact, are "more likely than other students to binge when they drink and more likely to say that getting drunk is an 'important reason' for drinking" (Wechsler and Wuethrich 55).

Although researchers can essentially agree about who binge drinks and how often, the increased role of alcohol in student lives derives from a number of factors. Some experts on excessive campus drinking argue that society enhances alcohol's attraction as something "forbidden" by keeping the legal age for buying it at 21 (Smith and Smith). For many students, especially freshmen, excessive drinking may be a part of a mistaken effort to fit in socially or to find companionship at college (Bruffee). Some studies suggest that students bring their previous

Delgado 8

bad habits with them when they come to college (Task Force 20), while others blame the too-easy accessibility of alcohol on campus, at open parties, or throughout surrounding neighborhoods. As some students see the situation, they have been taught to think of heavy drinking and partying as part of the "real" college experience (Kleiner 75). For such students, the alcohol-oriented culture of a campus makes drinking unavoidable as well as easy. As one campus interviewer discovered, "Anyone can get a keg, they say, or find someone of legal age who will. The local bars card them, 'but that's a joke'" (Dickinson).

Double quotation marks around single indicate quoted material appeared between double marks in source.

A number of authorities agree that the biggest contributors to excessive student drinking are the alcohol producers themselves. There is no denying that student drinking represent a huge, lucrative market. A 1994 study, for example, showed that college drinking accounted for about 10% of the U.S. alcohol market, or $10 billion annually (Task Force 44). Current data shows that today's college students nationally spend $5.5 billion on alcohol each year, more than they spend on soft drinks, tea, milk, juice, coffee, and schoolbooks combined (Wechsler and Wuethrich 4). Such spending has not been ignored by the alcohol industry. As one study explains,

Indent long quotations ten spaces from left.

> The fact that so many U.S. college students binge drink today indicates a failure not only of our best and brightest but also of higher education, local law enforcement, and to some extent our own attitudes. At the same

Delgado 9

> time it represents booming economic success for the alcohol industry which, like Big Tobacco, has been targeting young adults as part of its marketing master plan for years. And big alcohol is still on the offensive. (Wechsler and Wuethrich 24)

Cite source after final period in long quotation.

The presence of "Big Alcohol" on college campuses is undeniably extensive, ranging from sponsoring and advertising at athletic events to actually funding campus alcohol research and education programs. As a 2002 study by the National Advisory Council on Alcohol Abuse and Alcoholism points out, alcohol advertisements not only cover the walls of college sports arenas but permeate campus extracurricular life to an extent far greater than allowed to other noncampus business entities (Task Force 15).

What to do about excessive campus drinking and its causes has colleges and universities scrambling for answers. Some experts argue that schools need to begin by simply getting tougher about campus drinking. In the opinion of Harvard's Henry Wechsler,

> Students who become drunk and disorderly should be made to take responsibility for messes they have created: They should have to clean up vomit in the bathrooms made unusable on weekends, help care for drunken students at the college health center, repair damage from vandalism, and

> pick up litter. The punishment should fit the crime.
>
> But with repeat offenders, colleges need to consider enforcing a "three strikes and you're out" policy for alcohol-related violations of the student conduct code. ("Getting")

When author is named in text, cite title only if multiple works.

Stronger approaches may indeed have merit. Campus crime reports show that nationwide arrests for alcohol violations at colleges and universities have risen steadily for the last six years. Police and safety experts attribute the increase not to more alcohol use by students but to more aggressive enforcement efforts and toughened policies by college and university campuses. Michigan State University's tough stance on campus liquor infractions, for example, has twice resulted in a record number of arrests for the school. Students appear to have gotten the message. According to a university spokesperson, students are "definitely being more careful about where they drink." Rather than risk arrest, would-be drinkers make the decision to "stay inside and not cause trouble," he says (Nicklin).

Cite only author's name for single work, one page.

Other campuses have opted for milder but no less effective kinds of policing. Student paramedics at Duke University in Durham, North Carolina, patrol large parties to provide medical attention or emergency room service to overintoxicated students in need of assistance, for example (Okie). In addition, several schools have begun requiring freshmen to live on

Delgado 11

campus, and many now require live-in adult supervisors or resident advisers in dorms as well as fraternity and sorority housing (Task Force 24). And although the practice is controversial, such schools as the University of Delaware, Vanderbilt, and Virginia Tech are using the authority of a recent amendment to the Higher Education Act to inform parents whenever a student under 21 violates drug or alcohol laws.

Colleges and universities recognize that easy accessibility to booze on campus needs to change also. Several campuses--including the University of Connecticut, Lehigh University, and Villanova--are promoting more nonalcoholic events on campus, and several have changed their academic calendars to eliminate days when presemester celebrations or long weekends encourage drinking parties (Farrish). To keep alcohol off the campus, Washington University in St. Louis has instituted substance-free dormitories, and the University of Kentucky now prohibits alcohol being sold on campus property and bans drinking in undergraduate housing. In similar efforts, both the University of Wisconsin-Madison and the University of Colorado recently stopped selling beer in sports arenas, and the University of Iowa has closed down an on-campus bar and banned alcohol in the Greek system (Kleiner 74).

Schools have also turned to pressuring local bars, as well as fraternities and sororities, to help reduce binge drinking where it most often occurs. Several campuses are working with local bars to enforce ID checks and convince owners that it is in their best interest to eliminate traditional "birthday crawls": ritual celebrations in which honorees drink their way from pub to pub and consume the number of free drinks--and more--that matches their age (Kleiner 75). Perhaps recognizing the difficulty of controlling alcohol among its member groups, at least two national fraternities have announced in the past year that they will go dry, and the chapter in which a Massachusetts Institute of Technology student died from binge drinking has been suspended by the national organization (Bruffee).

In addition, some schools are adopting what has been dubbed a "social-norms" approach to combat excessive drinking. The strategy is based on the assumption that many students try to conform to social expectations by drinking to a level they perceive as the norm. Through marketing social-norm information, schools attempt to correct misconceptions about campus alcohol use by advertising the majority numbers of students who abstain from alcohol or refrain from excessive drinking. Campuses such as the University of Arizona, Northern Illinois University, and Western Washington University have reported declines in binge drinking as a result of using such strategies (Marklein).

Rhetorical question provides a transition and introduces the topic sentence.

Can all these efforts make a dent in the numbers of students who continue to binge drink? There is some indication that continuing campus efforts may have an effect on student drinking. The 2001 CAS study noted slight but important increases, for example, in the percentage of college students who reported they had had some type of education about abuse at their colleges. The survey also showed an increase in students who abstain from alcohol--though the percentage increase was the same as the additional growth in the number of students who binge drink, evidence of a polarization among students who avoid alcohol and those who overindulge in it (Wechsler et al., "Trends" 210).

Concluding example reinforces thesis statement.

While there are some positive developments in the fight against college binge drinking, however, some college officials fear students are already too inundated with information about the effects of alcohol and antidrinking campaigns, while others criticize such efforts as misdirected and coming too late in students' lives (Farrish). And although more students may be abstaining from alcohol and many are changing their habits, the deadly tradition of binge drinking continues. Last spring, a student at Case Western Reserve University died from head injuries suffered after an evening of excessive drinking at a fraternity house party. Following his death, all 17 fraternities at the university agreed to review university alcohol regulations and to ban alcohol at parties ("College"). The ban was for only six weeks, however, further evidence that, as colleges and universities continue to learn, some traditions are as hard to change as students.

Delgado 14

Center the title "Notes" at the top of the page.

Notes

[1]The most recent CAS was administered between February and April 2001, and yielded replies from 10,000 full-time undergraduate students at 119 U.S. colleges and universities.

"See" note refers reader to source cited in the paper and listed in Works Cited.

[2]The percentage was even higher among certain subgroups of respondents. For example, among "traditional" college students between 18 and 23 years of age who drank any alcohol at all in the past year, a whopping 70.3% were binge drinkers. See Wechsler et al., "Trends," 207.

Delgado 15

Center the title Works Cited at top of the page.

Works Cited

Argetsinger, Amy. "Students Find Alcohol Learning Curve a Deadly One." Washington Post 16 Apr. 2002: B1.

List entries with no author alphabetically by title.

"Binge Drinking on the Rise, Penn State President." Buffalo News 28 Aug. 1999. 6 Dec. 2002. ⟨http://library.northernlight .com?PN199908...d=YTVTSgMeHk95 DHQdB mEPVABT&cbx=0%253B1004⟩.

Bruffee, Kenneth A. "Binge Drinking as a Substitute for a 'Community of Learning.'" Chronicle of Higher Education 5 Feb. 1999: B8.

An article from a journal.

Cashin, Jeffrey R., Charles A. Presley, and Philip W. Meilman. "Alcohol Use in the Greek System: Follow the Leader?" Journal for the Study of Alcohol 59.1 (1998): 63-70.

An online newspaper article without page numbers.

"College Binge Drinking Worries." AP Online. 27 Aug. 1999. 4 Dec. 2002. ⟨http://library .northernlight.com?EA199908...d=YTVTS gMeHk95DHQdBmEPVABT&cbx= 0%253 B1004⟩.

An article in a weekly magazine.

Dickinson, Amy. "No School for Sots: The Family Dinner Table Is the Place to Train Your College-Bound Kids to Think--Not Drink." Time 13 Sept. 1999: 85.

Farrish, Katherine. "Ad Campaign Warns Students of Dangers of Binge Drinking." Hartford Courant 11 Sept. 1999: C-4.

Separate continuous page numbers with a hyphen.

Kleiner, Carolyn. "Schools Turn Off the Tap." U.S. News & World Report 30 Aug. 1999: 74-75.

Delgado 16

Marklein, Mary Beth. "Schools Seeing Some Indication of Success after Crackdown on Booze." USA Today 15 Nov. 1998. 26 Nov. 2002. ⟨http://researcher.sirs.com/cgi-bin/res-a...le-display? 092220+binge+drinking+college⟩.

Alphabetize entries by author's last name.

Nicklin, Julie L. "Colleges Report Increases in Arrests for Drug and Alcohol Violations." Chronicle of Higher Education 28 May 1999: A39.

Book title includes subtitle after colon.

Nuwer, Hank. Wrong of Passage: Fraternities, Sororities, Hazing, and Binge Drinking. Bloomington: Indiana UP, 1999.

An article from a newspaper. Cite newspaper page numbers as they appear in the source.

Okie, Susan. "Drinking Lessons as Alcohol Problems Grow: Colleges Seek New Remedies." Washington Post 16 April 2002: F1.

Smith, Michael Clay, and Margaret D. Smith. "Treat Students as Adults: Set the Age at 18, Not 21." Chronicle of Higher Education 12 Mar. 1999: B8.

Solvig, Erica. "Student Drank Lethal Amount, Report Shows." Columbus Dispatch 30 Nov. 2001: 03C.

A work authored by a committee.

Task Force of the National Advisory Council on Alcohol Abuse and Alcoholism, National Institute on Alcohol Abuse and Alcoholism. A Call to Action: Changing the Culture of Drinking at U.S. Colleges. Washington, DC: National Institutes of Health, 2002.

Wechsler, Henry. "Getting Serious about Eradicating Binge Drinking." Chronicle of Higher Education 20 Nov. 1998: B4.

List individual works by the same author before listing those in which author is part of a group of authors. List works alphabetically by title.

Wechsler, Henry, et al. "Binge Drinking on Campus: Results of a National Study." Higher Education Center. October 2001. 24 Nov. 2002. <http:www.edc.org/hec/pubs/binge.html>.

Wechsler, Henry, et al. "College Binge Drinking in the 1990s: A Continuing Problem. Results of the Harvard School of Public Health 1999 College Alcohol Survey." Journal of American College Health 48.5 (2000): 199-210.

A book with two authors.

Wechsler, Henry, and Bernice Wuethrich. Dying to Drink: Confronting Binge Drinking on College Campuses. Emmaus, PA: Rodale, 2002.

A work with three authors. For online sources, include the date of publication followed by the date you accessed the material. Give online address or URL, not underlined, between angle brackets, with final period following last bracket.

Wechsler, Henry, Bryan Austin, and William DeJong. "Secondary Effects of Binge Drinking on College Campuses." Higher Education Center. 1 Nov. 2000. 16 Dec. 2002. <http://www.edc.org/hec/pubs/effects.htm>.

A work with more than three authors.

Wechsler, Henry, et al. "Trends in College Binge Drinking during a Period of Increased Prevention Efforts: Finding from 4 Harvard School of Public Health College Alcohol Surveys: 1993–2001." Journal of American College Health 50 (Apr. 2002): 203–217.

59 A Documentation Guide *doc*

59a Guide to MLA *Works Cited* and parenthetical note forms.

Examples of the MLA *Works Cited* and parenthetical note forms (if different from the standard style detailed in 58c) follow this list of sample resources.

General Books

1. A Book with One Author
2. Two Books with the Same Author
3. A Book with Two or Three Authors
4. A Book with More Than Three Authors
5. A Book with a Corporate Author
6. A Book with a Later Edition
7. A Book in More Than One Volume
8. A Book Reprinted or Republished by a Different Publisher
9. A Book in a Series
10. A Book with an Editor
11. A Book with Two Editors
12. A Book with an Author and an Editor
13. A Book with an Introduction, Foreword, or Afterword
14. A Book That Has Been Translated
15. A Book That Includes a Quotation from Another Work
16. A Selection from an Anthology, Collection, or Critical Edition
17. A Book with a Title in Its Title
18. A Book with a Publisher's Imprint
19. An Anonymous Book

Periodicals

20. An Unsigned Article in a Magazine
21. A Signed Article in a Magazine
22. An Article in a Journal with Continuous Pagination in Each Volume
23. An Article in a Journal with Separate Pagination in Each Issue
24. An Unsigned Newspaper Article
25. A Signed Newspaper Article
26. A Letter to the Editor

27. An Unsigned Editorial
28. A Signed Editorial

Encyclopedias

29. An Unsigned Article from an Encyclopedia
30. A Signed Article from an Encyclopedia

Electronic, Computer-Based, and Online Sources

31. Regularly Published Material on CD-ROM
32. Online Newspaper, Magazine, Journal, or Other Database Material
33. A Work from a Library or Personal Subscription Service
34. A Home page for a Course from an Academic Department
35. Personal Homepage
36. Electronic Books and Other Complete Texts
37. E-mail, Discussion Lists, and Online Postings

Other Sources

38. An Unsigned Pamphlet
39. A Signed Pamphlet
40. A Government Publication
41. A Published Conference Proceeding
42. An Unpublished Dissertation
43. A Dissertation Listed in *Dissertation Abstracts* or *Dissertation Abstracts International* or a Published Dissertation
44. A Film or Videocassette
45. A Television or Radio Program
46. A Biblical Citation
47. A Poem
48. A Play
49. A Performance of a Play
50. A Musical or Audio Recording
51. A Work of Art
52. An Interview
53. A Personal Letter
54. A Lecture or an Address
55. A Cartoon or Comic Strip

General Books

1. A Book with One Author

Alder, Ken. The Measure of All Things: The Seven-Year Odyssey and Hidden Error That Transformed the World. New York: Free press, 2002.

2. Two Books with the Same Author

Morris, Edmund. Dutch: A Memoir of Ronald Reagan. New York: Random, 2000.

---. Theodore Rex. New York: Modern Library, 2002.

3. A Book with Two or Three Authors

Wechsler, Henry, and Bernice Wuethrich. Dying to Drink: Confronting Binge Drinking on College Campuses. Emmaus, PA: Rodale, 2002.

Manning, Marable, Leith Mullings, and Sophie Spencer-Wood. Freedom: A Photographic History of the African American Struggle. New York: Phaidon, 2002.

4. A Book with More Than Three Authors

Andrews, Sam S., et al. Sugar Busters for Kids. New York: Ballantine, 2001.

[Avoid lengthy citations in the text and elsewhere by listing only the first author's name (in reverse order), followed by a comma and the abbreviation *et al.*, meaning "and others," as shown here. Cite all the authors in the order they are listed on the source's title page (as shown below) only when necessary.]

Andrews, Sam S., Morrison C. Bethea, Luis A. Balart, and H. Leighton Steward. Sugar Busters for Kids. New York: Ballantine, 2001.

5. A Book with a Corporate Author

Upstream: Salmon and Society in the Pacific Northwest. Committee on Protection and Management of Pacific Northwest Anadromous Salmonids. Washington, DC: National Academy, 2001.

6. A Book with a Later Edition

Cialdini, Robert B. Influence: Science and Practice. 4th ed. Boston: Allyn & Bacon, 2000.

7. A Book in More Than One Volume

Yehoshua, H. L., and T. R. Barry. A History of British Philosophy: 1890–1995. 2 vols. London: Barrow, 1999.

8. A Book Reprinted or Republished by a Different Publisher

Davis, Carl. When We Were at War: A Recollection of the Vietnam Era. New York: Chaney, 2002.

9. A Book in a Series

Rentor, Michael. Our Forests: A Brief History. Ecology Ser. 2. New York: Hadden, 2003.

10. A Book with an Editor

Bryant, John, ed. Tales, Poems, and Other Writings. By Herman Melville. New York: Modern Library, 2001.

11. A Book with Two Editors

Sontag, Kate, and David Graham, eds. After Confession: Poetry as Autobiography. St. Paul: Graywolf, 2001.

12. A Book with an Author and an Editor

Fitzgerald, F. Scott, and Zelda Fitzgerald. Dear Scott, Dearest Zelda: The Love Letters of F. Scott and Zelda Fitzgerald. Ed. Jackson R. Bryer. New York: St. Martin's 2002.

[Use this form when the work of the book's author(s) is your subject. An entry focusing on the work of the editor would appear as below.]

Bryer, Jackson R. Dear Scott, Dearest Zelda: The Love Letters of F. Scott and Zelda Fitzgerald. By F. Scott Fitzgerald and Zelda Fitzgerald. New York: St. Martin's 2002.

13. A Book with an Introduction, Foreword, or Afterword

Hancock, Herbie. Preface. Sonic Boom: Napster, MP3, and the New Pioneers of Music. By John Alderman. Cambridge, MA: Perseus, 2001. xvii-xviii.

[Use this form when your focus is on the writer of the introduction, foreword, or afterword. Otherwise, cite only the author of the source.]

14. A Book That Has Been Translated

Dostoyevsky, Fyodor. The Best Short Stories of Fyodor Dostoyevsky. Trans. David Magarshack. New York: Princeton Review, 2001.

15. A Book That Includes a Quotation from Another Work

Matts, Richard. Another Look at Democracy. Boston: Pitts, 2002. Parenthetical note: (qtd. in Matts, 121)

16. A Selection from an Anthology, Collection, or Critical Edition

Allende, Isabelle. "The Argonauts." Herencia: The Anthology of Hispanic Literature of the United States. Ed. Nicolos Kanellos. New York: Oxford UP, 2002. 1982–87.

17. A Book with a Title in Its Title

Kent, Larry K. A Student Guide to James Joyce's Ulysses. Boston: Casing, 2003.

[As shown above, do not underline the title of a book (or other form of art) when it is included within the title of another work. Make sure, however, that you underline the rest of the main work's title.]

18. A Book with a Publisher's Imprint

Fraser, Antonia. Marie Antoinette: The Journey. New York: Nan A Talese-Doubleday, 2001.

19. An Anonymous Book

America's Multi-Cultural Future: Where Are We Headed? San Francisco: Orion, 2002.

20. An Unsigned Article in a Magazine

"Coffee Jitters." Science News 4 Jan. 2003: 5.

21. A Signed Article in a Magazine

Grossman, Lev "Can Freud Get His Job Back." Time 20 Jan. 2003: 76-80.

22. An Article in a Journal with Continuous Pagination in Each Volume

Teller, Sharon R. "What Huck Finn Did to the River: Ecology and Art at Odds." New Literary History 33 (1999): 529-38.

23. An Article in a Journal with Separate Pagination in Each Issue

Nochimson, Martha, P. "Ally McBeal: Brightness Falls from the Air." Film Quarterly 53.3 (2000): 25-32.

24. An Unsigned Newspaper Article

"Weed Killer Found to Sexually Deform Frogs" New York Times 17 Apr. 2002, natl. ed.: A17.

25. A Signed Newspaper Article

Trounson, Rebecca. "Shake-Up at Nuclear Facility." Los Angeles Times 3 Jan. 2003: A1.

26. A Letter to the Editor

Bristol, David. Letter. Chronicle of Higher Education 29 June 2001: B17.

27. An Unsigned Editorial

"War Is Never the Right Option" Opinion 23 (2002): 4.

28. A Signed Editorial

Seideman, David. "Editor's Note." Audubon Dec. 2002: 10.

29. An Unsigned Article from an Encyclopedia

"Artificial Intelligence." The Encyclopedia Americana. 2001 ed.

30. A Signed Article from an Encyclopedia

Ward, John J. "Mark Twain." Encyclopedia of American Authors. Ed. Susan N. Scott-Dale. New York: Ross, 1999.

31. Regularly Published Material on CD-ROM

Mandell, Rachel, ed. The Sonnets of William Shakespeare. CD-ROM. New York: Anthem, 1999.

32. Online Newspaper, Magazine, Journal, or Other Database Material

Often a URL is long and complicated. For example:

Wade, Nicholas. "Scientists Say Human Genome Is Complete." New York Times on the Web 15 April 2002: N. pag. 10

July 2003 <http://www.nytimes.com/2003/04/15/science/15GENO.html?ei=5070&en=ee8f85bcaad7f8bd&ex=1052020800&pagewanted=all&position>

Whenever a reference is long and complicated, you may give the URL of the site's search page or home page. In such cases, follow the URL with *Path*: and give the sequence of links that lead to the source page. For example:

Wade, Nicholas. "Scientists Say Human Genome Is Complete." New York Times on the Web 15 April 2002: n. pag. 10 July 2003 <http://www.nytimes.com>. Path: Health; Genetics.

Posner, Richard A. "Strong Fiber After All." Atlantic Online. Jan. 2002. N. pag. 22 Jan. 2002. <http:theatalantic.com/2002/01/posnerhtml>.

[For an online entry, give the date you accessed the source before the URL. Use *N. pag.* when a bibliography source has no page numbers.]

Torp, Daniel. "In Cochise's Footsteps." Journal of Western History. 4.2 (2002): 45-48. 23 June 2003. <http://jwhon.org/jwh03/vol4/borter7.html>.

33. A Work from a Library or Personal Subscription Service

"Why Children Don't Read." Educator 15 Mar. 2002 Newspaper and Magazine Index Group. Infotrac. Pasadena Public Library, Pasadena, CA. 3 June 2003 <http://www.ci.pasadena.ca.us/services.asp>.

Koller, Harold. "Web Sties You Can't Afford to Visit." Business America 2 Mar. 2003: 34-36. Electric Lib. 8 May 2003 <http://www.elibrary.com>.

34. A Home Page for a Course or Academic Department

Hoffman, Lynne. American Literature. Course home page. January-May 2003. Department of English, Orange Coast College. 19 Mar. 2003 <http://www.hofflit.occ.cccd.edu/departments/instruction/litlang/index.html>.

[List a course home page by the instructor's name, followed by a description and other relevant information as shown here.]

American Studies Program. Dept. home page. California State College, Long Beach. 3 June 2003 <http://www.csulb.edu/colleges/cla/ais/main.html>.

35. A Personal Home page

Abbott, Cheryl. Favorites home page. 22 June 2002 <http://www.fallsapart.com.lists.html>.

36. Electronic Books and Other Complete Texts

James, Henry. The Portrait of a Lady. New York: Collier, 1917. 10 Dec. 2002. <http://www.bartleby.com/311/1-55.html>.

37. E-mail, Discussion Lists and Online Postings

Hatter, Julie. "Membership Requirements." E-mail to the author. 14 May 2002.

Pollet, Jack. "Weapons on Campus." Online posting. 7 Feb. 2003. Webtalk. 12 Feb. 2003 <http:web.campus.uclb.edu/comp/ldtag.htm>.

[For a posting from an e-mail discussion list or online posting of any kind, include the description *Online posting* after the document title in quotation marks.]

38. An Unsigned Pamphlet

Preventing Mold and Fungus Growth Inside and Outside Your Home. San Diego: Bayside, 2003.

39. A Signed Pamphlet

Florida Committee on Education. Every Child Needs a Computer: Education for Today and Tomorrow. Miami, 2002.

40. A Government Publication

Cong. Rec. 18 June 2002. S4584. Florida State. Joint Committee on Language Education. Standards for Elementary Grade Language Instruction. Tampa: Greydon, 2002.

41. A Published Conference Proceeding

Hanes, Joycelyn S. Preparing for Tomorrow: Communications in the Twenty-First Century. 37th International Communications Conference. Detroit, MI: Society for International Communications, 20 Oct. 2002.

42. An Unpublished Dissertation

Bohanon, Margaret Ann "'Wild Women Don't Have the Blues': African-American Women Blues Singers and Working Class Resistance." Diss. Case Western Reserve U. 2001.

43. A Dissertation Listed in Dissertation Abstracts, Dissertation Abstracts International, or a Published Dissertation

Arsena, Paula C. "Politics of the Street: Culture and Practices of Ghetto Life in New York City." Diss. Johns Hopkins U. 2002. DA 57 (2002): 8302A.

Rancourt, Norman Vincent. The Legal Aspects of the Rights of the Public Secondary Student Relative to School Testing for Drugs. Diss. U of Bridgeport, 2002. UMI, 2002. 3056679.

[Add the pertinent abbreviation *DA* or *DAI* and the item's entry number in *Dissertation Abstracts* or *Dissertation Abstracts International* after the basic information about the dissertation. For a published dissertation or one published by University Microfilms International (UMI), underline the title. Include the UMI order number for the latter type of entry if you wish.]

44. A Film or Videocassette

Polanski, Roman, dir. and prod. The Pianist. Perf. Adrian Brody. Focus, 2002.

Grant, Kelly P. "Team Building Tips." Videocassette. Rockland, 2002.

45. A Television or Radio Program

"I Live Alone." Dateline NBC. Rpt. Jack Talent. NBC. KNBC, Los Angeles. 4 Mar. 2002.

Springer, Jerry, host. "Spring break." Jerry Springer. WMOR, Tampa. 19 Apr. 2002.

46. A Biblical Citation

The New Oxford Annotated Bible with the Apocrypha: New Revised Standard Version. 3rd ed. Oxford UP, 2001.

[Cite versions of the Bible as you would a book in the example given here.]

47. A Poem

Escobedo, Alonso de. "La Florida." Herencia: The Anthology of Hispanic Literature of the United States. Ed. Nicolos Kanellos. New York: Oxford UP, 2002. 1211-19.

48. A Play

Goldsmith, Oliver. She Stoops to Conquer. The Longman Anthology of Drama and Theater: A Global Perspective. Eds. Michael L. Greenwald, Roger Schultz, and Robert Dario Pomo. New York: Longman, 2000. 1018-1034

49. A Performance of a Play

Dir. Jason Colter. Perf. Linda Maer. Golden Gate Theater, San Francisco. 9 Sept. 2002.

[Along with the author's name and title of the work, cite principal performers and their roles as pertinent to your paper's content. Also include the place and date of the performance.]

50. A Musical or Audio Recording

London, Jack. The Call of the Wild and Other Stories. Audiocassette. Read by Treat Williams and Jason Miller. Listening Library, CXL 634, 1999.

[After the name of the distributor or manufacturer—Listening Library in this example—list recording numbers, if given, and the publication date.]

51. A Work of Art

Rodin, Auguste. The Thinker. Metropolitan Museum of Art, New York.

Van Gogh, Vincent. Self-Portrait. The Louvre, Paris. Illus. in Masters of the Brush: Great Painters and Their Art. Ed. Mary K. Pollard. New York: Candleprint, 2002. 46.

52. An Interview

Ngyuen, Steve. Personal interview. 10 Mar. 2003.

53. A Personal Letter

Siddons, Janet. Letter to the author. 4 June 2002.

54. A Lecture or an Address

Margon, Bruce. "Cosmic Recycling: We Are made of Stars." Twenty-Fourth Annual Faculty Lecture. U of Washington, 25 Jan. 2000.

55. A Cartoon or Comic Strip

Gregory, Alex. Cartoon. New Yorker. 13 Jan. 2003: 76.

Trudeau, Gary. "Doonesbury." Los Angeles Times. 16 Mar. 2003: C6.

59b APA documentation style.

The American Psychological Association (APA) style of documentation is frequently used in courses in psychology and other social sciences. Although all documentation styles require essentially the same information, each has its own conventions of arrangement, punctuation, and abbreviation.

Parenthetical Citations: APA Style

The APA parenthetical style cites the last name of the author and the date of publication, separated by a comma. For some citations, these two items of information are the only ones necessary, but page references should be added when you present a direct quotation or refer to specific information rather than general concepts. Notice the following examples.

AUTHOR AND DATE ONLY

Surveys show a majority of college and university students who say they binge drink are white males, although significant numbers of self-identified Hispanic, Native

American, Asian Pacific Islander, and African American students also report that they binge drink (Kalb, 1997).

DATE ONLY

Kalb (1997) points out that surveys show a majority of college and university students who say they binge drink are white males, although significant numbers of self-identified Hispanic, Native American, Asian Pacific Islander, and African American students also report that they binge drink.

AUTHOR, DATE, AND PAGE

Most studies indicate that students are "drinking more, drinking to get drunk, and suffering more severe consequences from excessive drinking" (Keeler, 1998, p. 76)

[For direct quotations, include the page number. Use "p." for *page* and "pp." for *pages.*]

By their third or fourth year of college, most students seem either to have "brought their drinking under control or dropped out because of personal and academic problems brought on by excessive indulgence" (Myer & Torson, 1998, p. 34).

[Join the names of multiple authors with an ampersand: &.]

Most experts agree that the problem of campus drinking cannot be solved by any single approach, regardless of its apparent success with some students (Myer & Torson, 1998; Hanchett, Krueger, & Davis, 1997).

[For more than one source, list them in alphabetical order by the first authors' names, and separate the citations by a semicolon.]

References: APA Style

In APA style, the works cited are listed at the end of the paper in a section titled "References." As you study the following examples of APA reference listings, notice carefully the order in which information is given, the use of punctuation and capitalization, and spacing between items.

Only the most frequently encountered situations are illustrated here. For a comprehensive guide, consult the *Publication Manual of the American Psychological Association*. 5th ed. Washington: APA, 2001.

Guide to APA Reference and Parenthetical Note Forms

Examples of APA reference and parenthetical note forms follow this list of sample resources.

1. A Book with One Author
2. A Book with More Than One Author
3. A Book in More Than One Volume
4. A Book with an Editor
5. A Printed Newspaper Article
6. A Daily Newspaper Article Available Online
7. A Printed Article in a Weekly or Monthly Magazine
8. An Article in an Online Monthly Magazine
9. An Article in a Journal Listing Volume Numbers Only
10. An Article in a Journal Listing Volume and Issue Number
11. An Online Article Based on a Print Source
12. An Article in an Encyclopedia or Other Reference Source
13. A Message Posted to a Newsgroup or Other Online Forum

APA Style for Books

1. A Book with One Author

Horgan, J. (2003). *Rational mysticism: Dispatches from the border between science and spirituality*. Boston: Houghton.

2. A Book with More Than One Author

Livingstone, M., & Hubel, D. H. (2002). *Vision and art: The biology of seeing*. New York: Abrams.

3. A Book in More Than One Volume

Holton. J. R., Pyle, J., & Curry, J. A. (Eds.). (2002). Encyclopedia of atmospheric science (Vol. 1). London: Academic.

4. A Book with an Editor

Hawking, S. (Ed.). (2002). *On the shoulders of giants: The great works of physics and astronomy*. Philadelphia: Running.

APA Style for Periodicals

5. A Printed Newspaper Article

Wilson, J. (2003, January 3). Appeal to save trees is issued. *Los Angeles Times*, p. B3.

6. A Daily Newspaper Article Available Online

Knowlton, B. (2003), January 16). Inspectors find empty warheads able to carry chemical agents. *New York Times.* Retrieved January 17, 2003, from http://www.nytimes.com/

7. A Printed Article in a Weekly or Monthly Magazine

Mason, B. (2003), February). Season of fire. *Discover*, 24. 32-39.

8. An Article in an Online Monthly Magazine

Ezzell, C. (2003, February). Why? The neuroscience of suicide. *Scientific American, 228.* Retrieved March 6, 2003, from http://www.sciam.com/article.cfm?chanID=sa006&articleID =0006AF90-5BC7-1E1B-8B3B809EC588EEDF

9. An Article in a Journal Listing Volume Number Only

Wurz, P., Bochsler, P., Paquette, J. A., & Ipavich, F. M. (2003, January 20). Calcium abundance in the solar wind. *The Astrophysical Journal, 583*, 489-495.

[List all authors' names, but after a sixth name use *et al.* (the Latin abbreviation for "and others") to indicate the remaining authors of the article.]

10. An Article in a Journal Listing Volume and Issue Number

Kunzig, L. L., Hadder, B., & Blaser, P. G. (2003). Risks and benefits of cloning. *Journal of Medical Research, 53*(2), 45-51.

[Give the issue number in parentheses after the volume number.]

11. An Online Article Based on a Print Source

Gross, H. T., & Samuelson, P. (2002). New color variations among cowry species from south coast of Sri Lanka [Electronic version]. *International Conchologist, 3*(2), 22-24.

[Include the bracketed statement *Electronic version* if the online and published versions are the same. Omit the statement and add the date you retrieved the article if they differ.]

Gross, H. T., & Samuelson, P. (2002). New color variations among cowry species from south coast of Sri Lanka. *International Conchologist, 3*(2), 22-24. Retrieved June 4, 2002, from http:www.iconch/articles/june/html

APA Style for Encyclopedias

12. An Article in an Encyclopedia or Other Reference Source

Trapp, H. R. (2002). Capital punishment. In *The Encyclopedia Britannica.* Chicago: Encyclopedia Britannica.

[When no author's name is given for an entry in the source, place the article title in the author position, as in the example following.]

Artificial intelligence (1993). In *The Columbia Encyclopedia.* Boston: Houghton.

[If subjects are not ordered alphabetically in the reference source, include the page numbers of the article after the reference source's title, as shown below.]

Pollution of rivers and lakes. In *The Random House Encyclopedia* (pp. 296-97). New York: Random.

13. A Message Posted to a Newsgroup or Other Online Forum

Rollart, G. (2002, December 10). Dangerous speed bumps [Msg 6]. Message posted to http:groups.yahoo.com/group/trafiicsafety/message6.

59c CSE and other documentation styles.

Documentation styles different from MLA and APA styles are used in the natural and applied sciences. In these styles, each in-text (or parenthetical) citation is a number, which is the reason these documentation styles are frequently called the "number-system style." The number in the in-text citation always corresponds to a full citation in the list of sources located at the end of the research project. The citations in the reference include the name of the author(s), title, and other publication information.

The requirements for arranging and punctuating citations vary among these documentation styles. You must, therefore, be sure which style your science instructor wants you to follow. Sources for common style manuals you might need to use are:

American Chemical Society: *Handbook for Authors of Papers in the American Chemical Society Publications.*
American Institute of Physics: *Style Manual for Guidance in the Preparation of Papers.*
American Mathematical Society: *A Manual for Authors of Mathematical Papers.*
Council of Science Editors: *Scientific Style and Format.*

Of the number-system documentation styles, the one most commonly used in undergraduate research is one advocated by the Council of Science Editors (CSE). Besides a system similar to APA's author year system, CSE documentation style offers writers two number-system choices:

1. Sources are alphabetized and numbered in the reference section.
2. Sources are numbered in the reference section as they appear in the text.

Parenthetical Citations

Whether the alphabetized or sequential numbering system is used, the numbers placed in an in-text citation correspond to the number of the source listed in the reference section. The numbers themselves, placed within the text, can be enclosed in parentheses or brackets or can be raised above the line (you must, of course, follow one prescribed style consistently throughout your paper—in other words, do not use brackets for some citations and parentheses for others). For example, the source of the following excerpt would be the third item listed in the numbered reference section.

> The unique scent of a spring meadow, for example, may appear to come from a single source when in reality it comes from a multitude of fragrances mingling in the air and stirred together by breezes (3).

If you need to document a specific reference, the page number or numbers (using *p.* to indicate one page and *pp.* to indicate more than one page) follow the number assigned to the source.

> In some animals the sense of smell functions as an early warning system. "Even in slumbering felines, the nose can catch a whiff of danger and rouse the beast to action" (5, p. 23). In other animals, however, especially those that have been long domesticated, the sense of smell is not so acute and may have diminished to the point at which they can barely use it to find their dinner bowls (5, pp. 25-27).

You can refer to more than one source in a single in-text citation, and if you need to cite a source already cited in your paper, refer to it by its original number.

> The human nose fails miserably from disuse (3, 5). Early human hunters could smell an animal downwind before the eye ever picked it out of the brush, and Native American warriors could smell a nearby enemy before they heard a war cry (3, 6).

References

Title the reference section Literature Cited, References Cited, or References. Center the title at the top of the page. When listing your sources, follow these general guidelines.

1. Arrange the sources either alphabetically or sequentially as they appear in the text.
2. Number each source.
3. Neither underline nor place quotation marks around titles.
4. As a general guideline, capitalize only the first word in the title except proper nouns. For example: The urban coyotes of Los Angeles.
5. Begin with the author's last name. In place of an author's first name, use initials. If the source has multiple authors, separate their names with a semicolon.
6. The title of the source follows the author's name and ends with a period.
7. For books, the city of publication follows the title and ends with a colon. The publisher follows and ends with a semicolon, which

is followed by the year of publication, and the entire entry is closed with a period.

8. For journal articles, the name of the journal follows the title of the source. The volume number follows the name of the periodical and ends with a colon, which is followed by the page numbers, a semicolon, and the year of publication; the entire entry is closed with a period. A journal title may be abbreviated, unless it is composed of a single word.
9. For popular magazine articles, the name of the magazine followed by a period comes after the title of the article. The date of publication (year, month, and day) follows the magazine title and ends with a colon, which is immediately followed by the page number. The entire entry is closed with a period.

Use the following sequentially arranged References Cited page as a guide to help you create your own reference section.

Sample Reference List

References Cited

POPULAR MAGAZINE	1. Stein, RS. Earthquake conversations. Sci Am 2003 Jan: 72-79.
JOURNAL ARTICLE	2. Madsen, KM. A population-based study of measles, mumps, and rubella vaccination and autism. N Eng J Med 2002;347:1477-82.
BOOK	3. Canup, R. and Righter, K. editors. Origin of the earth and moon. University of Arizona Press, 2000. 670p.
CORPORATE AUTHOR	4. World Health Organization. Legal status of traditional medicine and complementary/alternative medicine: A world-wide review. 2001. New York; 189p.
MULTIPLE BOOK AUTHORS	5. Morris, HL, James, MT, Pollis, J, and others. Molecular biology and human progress. Berkeley: Bridge, 2002. 288p.

BOOK WITH AN EDITOR

6. Ridley, M, editor. The best American science writing. New York: Ecco, 2002. 211p.

STANDARD WORKS WITH EDITORS BEGIN WITH TITLE

7. Encyclopedia of social and cultural anthropology. Barnard, A, and Spencer, J, editors. London: Routledge; 2002. 688p.
8. McGraw-Hill dictionary of scientific and technical terms. 6th ed. Parker, SP. editor. New York: McGraw-Hill; 2002. 2380p.

When typing your References Cited page, double-space throughout and begin the second and subsequent lines of that entry directly under the first letter of the first line, not under the numeral. If your project requires citations more complicated than these basic examples, check the *CSE Scientific Style and Format* for more detailed information.

PART X

Communicating in the Workplace

Often you will find yourself embarking on an article so apparently lifeless—the history of some institution, or some local issue such as storm sewers—that you quail at the prospect of keeping your readers, or even yourself, awake. Take heart. You will find the solution if you look for the human element. Somewhere in every drab institution are men and women who have a fierce attachment to what they are doing and are rich repositories of lore.

—William K. Zinsser, *journalist*

60 Business Letters *bus*

A business letter should be brief, to the point, and representative of your best writing skills. The tone, even if you are writing a letter of complaint, should be courteous. As in all writing, observe the conventions of grammar, usage, and punctuation. Take extra care in proofreading the letter before sending it.

Business Letter Formats

A business letter usually follows one of three basic formats: block style, modified block style, or simplified style.

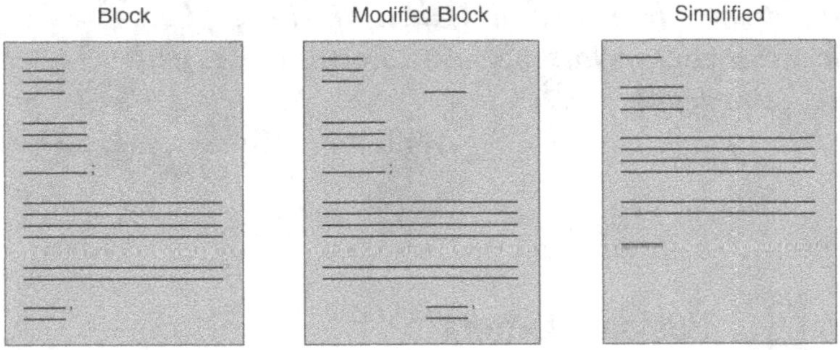

Block Style. Block style is the most formal layout for business letters and is usually written on letterhead stationery. To type a letter in block style, begin all the elements—including date, inside address, salutation, body, and close—flush with the left margin. If there is a second page to a block-style letter, begin the content just below the top margin; don't center it on the depth of the page.

Modified Block Style. Modified block style appears less formal. Type a modified block letter the same as one in block style, beginning every line at the left margin, with one major exception: The date and the signature lines must begin at the center of the page.

Simplified Style. The simplified style is usually used for form letters, correspondence with unknown parties, and mass mailings. It is not often used for personal business correspondence. Type a letter in simplified style by lining up all the elements flush with the left margin, as in block style. A major difference, however, is that you include no salutation or complimentary close. The body of the letter begins immediately after the inside address (or after the subject line), with no salutation such as *Dear Ms. Dunlap.* Similarly, include your name and signature right after the last line in the body, with no intervening close such as *Sincerely* or *Yours truly.*

Elements of Business Letters

Return Address Heading. The heading of a business letter includes the sender's return address and the date the letter was written. If you use letterhead stationery, include only the date, typed two line spaces (that is, double spaced) below the letterhead. Don't abbreviate the names of streets, avenues, boulevards, and the like, but do use postal abbreviations for names of states.

> 2701 Fairview Road
> Costa Mesa, CA 92626
> September 21, 2000

The return address should always be flush left on the page, regardless of which letter format you follow. The date should also be flush left if you are using block or simplified style; the date should begin at the center of the page, however, if you are using modified block style.

Inside Address. The inside address includes the recipient's name, title, and mailing address. If the person's title is short, include it following the name and a comma. If the title is long, place it on the line below the name. Write the company name as it usually appears. Again, do not abbreviate the names of streets, avenues, or boulevards. Do use postal abbreviations for states.

> Dr. Robert Sanchez, Chair
> Department of Linguistics
> University of California, Irvine
> 2000 Campus Drive
> Irvine, CA 92612

Begin the inside address two lines below the return address heading and *always* on the left-hand side of the page.

Salutation. Greet the reader with a salutation. You have several options:

1. If you know the person you are writing to, use the name that appears in the inside address: *Dear Dr. Sanchez.*

2. If you are not writing to a particular person and do not know whether the person is male or female, you may use a general salutation: *Dear Sir* or *Dear Madam* (but not *Dear Sir or Madam*).
3. If you are writing to an organization in general, you may greet someone by position: *Dear Dean of Students.* Or you may greet the organization: *Dear Southwest Services.*

When greeting women use *Ms.* unless you know that the recipient prefers *Mrs.* or *Miss.* Always type the salutation two lines below the inside address and end the salutation with a colon.

Subject Line. If you wish to highlight the subject of your letter, type a subject line. A subject line briefly names the subject of the letter. Use the word *subject* or the abbreviation *re* (Latin for "thing"), followed by a colon, to identify your letter's content. Several styles are acceptable.

Subject: Student Aid
SUBJECT: Study Abroad
Re: Part-Time Employment
RE: Drop Policy

Type the subject line two lines below the letter's salutation.

Body. If possible, keep a business letter to one page in length but never more than two pages. Structure a business letter in three main parts:

1. An *introduction* paragraph that states the purpose of the letter and establishes a courteous tone.
2. One or more *body* paragraphs that develop major points and provide details.
3. A brief *conclusion* paragraph that thanks the reader and suggests possibilities for further action.

Begin each line of the text of a letter at the left margin. Double-space between paragraphs to set them off from each other.

Close. Choose a close that reflects the tone—formal or informal—of the salutation and the rest of the letter: *Sincerely yours, Sincerely, Yours truly, Best regards, Cordially.* Capitalize only the first letter.

Begin the close two lines below the last line of the body. Except for modified block form, align the close with the return address heading, flush left. Follow the close with a comma.

Name and Signature. Type your name four lines below the close. Add any title you hold that may be relevant to the letter's content

(*Student Body Vice President*). If you have addressed a letter's recipient by his or her last name, sign your letter with your full name.

Enclosures. If you include other material with a letter, add an enclosure notation at the left margin, two lines below your name. You may write out or abbreviate the notation for *enclosure* (*encl.*) or *enclosures* (*encls.*). List important enclosures by name or type. Multiple items should be listed and indented below the notation, or use parenthetic numerals to indicate their quantity.

Enclosure: Transcripts
Encl: Class Schedule
Enclosures: (2)
Encls:
  Photograph
  Copy of Birth Certificate

Copies. If copies of your letter are being sent to other persons, add a *carbon copy* notation (*cc*) two lines below your typed name or the enclosure notation (if there is one).

cc: Dean William Walsh
CC: Ms. Margaret Johns
Copies to Rodger Faubel
  2715 Orange
  Tustin, CA 92619

When your letter contains sensitive information and you do not want the recipient to know that copies are being sent to others, use a *blind carbon copy* notation on the copy sheets only.

bcc: Internal Revenue Service
BCC: Donald Rayneman, Attorney at Law

Postscripts. Since a postscript may suggest a last-minute, casual addition, it should rarely be part of a business letter. If you want to include one to emphasize a point not covered in the body of the letter, use the abbreviated form *P.S.*, *PS*, or *PS:* to identify it. Type the abbreviation two lines below the last notation.

P.S. I truly look forward to the four weeks of intense training IBM offers.

Paper and Typing or Printing. Use a good quality paper—20-pound weight, white bond. Write on one side of the paper, single-spacing between lines and double-spacing between paragraphs. Allow 1″ margins on the left- and right-hand sides of the paper. Right-hand margins may be left "ragged," that is, "unjustified," if printed. Type or print letters in black or dark blue ink.

Envelope. Use a business-size (no. 10) envelope. It should be the same width as your letter and about one-third its height. Type your name and address in the upper-left-hand corner. Include any instructions, such as *Attention Accounts Payable,* below that address. Beginning just to the left of the center of the envelope, type the recipient's name, title, and mailing address, as you did for the inside address.

Robin Hanna
12 Antares Avenue
Irvine, CA 92612

Dr. Rene Thursten
University of California
2000 Campus Drive
Irvine, CA 92612

61 Memorandum Form *memo*

Unless you are using preprinted company or commercial stationery, begin a memorandum (memo) by typing *MEMORANDUM* at the top of the page. Centering, capitalizing, and underlining are optional.

Two line spaces beneath the heading, type a block of standard information elements: *TO, FROM, DATE, RE* (or *SUBJECT*). Double-space these elements and type them in capitals or with the first letter capitalized. Follow each element with a colon, advance several spaces, and type in the relevant information, keeping each item aligned with the one above it.

Begin the body of the memo two lines below the last element. Single-space the body and begin flush with the left margin (or indent the first line five spaces).

Do not include a closing signature element, but you may add your handwritten initials next to your name or end the memo with your signature, centered at the bottom.

When the memo includes copies or enclosures, note them the way you would in a business letter.

MEMORANDUM

TO: Fine Arts Staff

FROM: Donna Jennings, Chair, Fine Arts

DATE: September 29, 2001

RE: Budget Allotment Meeting

I have several requests to purchase supplies and equipment from department members. Although our supply and equipment budget has been increased by 20% above last year's, we still do not have enough discretionary moneys to accommodate all the requests. As a result, the budget committee will meet to rank the requests by how each one most directly addresses the needs of the entire department. You are invited to attend the meeting and address the committee regarding any proposal before it. The meeting will be held in the Fine Arts Conference Room on October 15, at noon.

Encl: Proposal List

62 Résumé and Cover Letter *résumé*

A *résumé* should be an easy-to-read summary of your qualifications for a job. A job résumé usually includes a cover letter that states your interest in a specific position and describes your general abilities.

Creating a Résumé

A résumé follows no standard form, but there are general principles you should follow.

1. Be brief. Keep the length to one or two pages, no more.
2. Stick to the point. Give only the information someone needs to determine whether you are an applicant worth interviewing.
3. Organize résumé information. Arrange the information in categories relevant to the position.
4. Write in brief, active phrases. Summarize information in each category in language that suggests you will be an assertive, proactive employee.
5. Concentrate on the particular position. Tailor a résumé so that the information reflects the experience required for the position.

Personal Data. List your name, address, and telephone number where you can be reached during business hours. Include a fax number or an e-mail address, if you have either. Do not include your age, marital status, race or ethnicity, religion, height, or weight, all of which the law forbids employers from considering.

Career Objective. You may include a brief statement of a long-range goal or specific job interests. Keep such a statement brief, no more than a line or two: *Hope to secure a management position in banking. Strong interests in sales and marketing.* Do not use such statements to misrepresent yourself.

Education. List all schools you have attended from high school on, the most recent first. Include the years you attended, the diplomas and honors you have received, and your area of study. If you did not receive a diploma, list the number of units you completed. Do not mention particular courses you took, but if any of those courses relate to the position, present them in the cover letter.

Employment History. List your most recent job first. Include each employer's name and address, and identify the position you held. Use short phrases and action verbs to describe your responsibilities: *Taught painting to third graders. Previewed video-game proposals.*

Activities. You may include a section indicating other activities, memberships, hobbies, skills, or awards that might interest an employer. Do you speak a foreign language? Did you serve as an officer on your campus? Keep in mind that the activities you mention should relate to the position.

References. Before you provide an employer with a list of references, be sure everyone listed will support your application. Once that is accomplished, you may provide employers with references in one of three ways.

Tom Jenkins
2415 Mann Street
Laguna Beach, CA 92676
(949) 494-0499
tjenkins@aol.com

Career Objective

To be employed with a law firm specializing in international contracts and business negotiations.

Education

1999-present	California State University, Long Beach	
	Major: History	Minor: English
	Degree: B.A., History	
1995-99	University High School	
	Diploma: Graduated with honors	

Employment History

1999-present Forde and Mulrich
12 MacArthur Avenue
Newport Beach, CA 92644
Duties: Political Research. Responsible for researching statewide and local election initiatives. 15 hours weekly.

1998-99 University Park Library
221 Sandburg Way
Irvine, CA 92912
Duties: Assistant to the Senior Research Librarian. Maintain research materials. Conduct research on special request. 10 hours weekly.

Activities and Interests

- President of University High chapter of the Green Party, 1998
- Member of the Sierra Club
- Active participant in tennis, camping, and cross-country bicycling

References

Placement Office
California State University, Long Beach
Long Beach, CA 92888
(310) 772-0559

1. Indicate near the bottom of a résumé that *References are available upon request.* If the employer asks for them, you will provide the list.
2. Create a section titled *References.* Type the names, titles, addresses, and phone numbers of several individuals—teachers, former employers, community leaders—who will vouch for your skills and character.
3. File your complete résumé and cover letter with your school's placement center. On your job application, indicate that your résumé, including references, is available through the placement office, and include the phone number. Keep your on-file résumé current; review it each time you apply for a job.

Although there are several acceptable résumé formats, the sample here is the most commonly used.

Writing a Cover Letter

Keep a cover letter brief. Avoid repeating what is in the résumé. Express your interest in the position, request an interview, and refer the recipient to the enclosed résumé.

Because a company may have several job openings, it is good practice to begin the cover letter by identifying the position you want and by telling specifically when and how you heard about it. Next, briefly refer to an aspect of your résumé that would be particularly relevant to the position. End the cover letter by stating your desire for an interview. Throughout the letter, follow standard business letter guidelines.

63 Fax and E-mail *fax/e-mail*

Treat electronic communications such as faxes and e-mail with the same care as traditional business correspondence.

Sending a Fax

Use the following guidelines when communicating by fax.

1. Since a fax may be received in a mail room or other common area, keep in mind that it may be read by others before being given to the intended recipient. You may prefer to send personal, confidential, or sensitive material by traditional correspondence.

2. Select a letterhead, font sizes, images, and colors that will fax clearly. To ensure readability, use 12-point type for all contents, and remember that colors other than black may not transmit clearly. Avoid sending or retransmitting copies of a fax with fuzzy print or hazy images.
3. Include a cover sheet with your name and your company name, address, and telephone number as well as a fax or e-mail address where you can be reached in case of transmittal problems. Also indicate the total number of pages you are sending (including the cover sheet).
4. Check your fax machine's readout to ensure proper transmission and receipt of your fax, or follow up the transmittal with a telephone call to verify that it was received.

Keep in mind that a fax may not be an acceptable form of communication for all business correspondence. When it is, however, following the above guidelines will help to ensure the effectiveness of your fax and the receipt of a timely response.

Sending E-mail

Although e-mail messages are frequently informal, those written for business purposes need to be easily understood and professional in form and content. Use the following guidelines when transmitting e-mail in a professional environment.

1. If possible, compose offline. This will allow you to compose, revise, and edit any drafts, and it will provide you with a file copy and backup. Once you have finished writing your e-mail, use your computer's Copy function to insert it into the e-mail program.
2. Structure your e-mail so it is easily read. Check for spelling errors and follow standard punctuation and grammar practices. Use indentation, paragraph divisions, capitalization, bullets, and headings as needed to separate content and organize it for a reader.
3. Guide the recipient to the point of your e-mail by including a clear subject line identifying your message's content or purpose.
4. Try to limit an e-mail correspondence to no more than one full screen in length because a lengthy e-mail message is difficult to read on-screen. Use your e-mail program's Attachment function to send additional content as an attached file.
5. Send copies only to those directly concerned with matters treated in your e-mail. Sending unwanted communications takes up other people's time and appears unprofessional.

Like a fax, an e-mail may not be appropriate for all types of business correspondence. For instance, because e-mail programs do not always accurately transmit or reproduce formatting, the original spacing and organization of, say, a résumé that you sent may well be altered. In most instances, you should use e-mail for routine business matters or to communicate with those you have already corresponded with by traditional means.

Finally, keep in mind that e-mail is not necessarily a confidential form of communication. Even after you have deleted an e-mail from your message center, it still exists somewhere on your computer system and perhaps on your company's and server's systems as well. Many companies issue guidelines to employees about the appropriate uses of e-mail, warning against using it to discuss personal or potentially litigious topics.

64 Creating an Effective Web Site *web*

Over the last few years, the World Wide Web (WWW) has experienced tremendous growth. Federal and state governments, large and small businesses, and most academic institutions have their own Web sites. Yet the use of Web sites is not limited to government, business, and academic institutions. You, as an individual, may create a Web site for your own personal use or as part of a school or work assignment.

To build an effective Web site you must familiarize yourself with the technical aspects involved in the project. Begin by going to *www.builder.com/Authoring/Basics.* This Web site will give you an overview of the basic computer language, Hypertext Markup Language (HTML), that Web masters use to create documents for the WWW. You can also get helpful information on how to go about building your site at *www.builder.com.*

Once you grasp the fundamentals of Web site construction, you must organize and design, that is, you must plan the "vision," or "look," of your Web site.

64a Organize your site.

Keep your personal Web site organization and design simple and basic. Construct it for your Web audience. More than likely it will be made up of people who are surfing for information, which is much different from browsing for information in a library. Web surfers tend to be impatient; they want information—now! If your Web site is haphazardly organized and designed, it will not hold their interest. Remember, with one click of the mouse they can surf away into cyberspace.

64b Start with a well-organized home page.

Begin by setting up a visually appealing and user-friendly home page. The home page should be clutter-free yet have enough information to entice visitors to the site and clearly explain the site's contents. Use the home page to announce your site's main areas. Visitors can then click on to the main areas to reach the subsections.

To organize your home page effectively, take a few minutes to brainstorm some ideas for the page. Consider what your overall vision should be for the site. What is your main message? Is there something you want to showcase? What attention-getting language will work? How can you entice visitors deeper into the site? As you brainstorm, use arrows that move from main sections to subsections to be sure that the material follows a logical sequence.

64c Use a visually appealing design.

Some Web sites are eye-catching and some are duds. To make your site exciting, use interesting graphics. Just as you imagined your site's content, imagine its colors and graphics. Should there be a recurring visual element or a flashing banner? photographs? dramatic color? For a crash course in Web site design, visit *www.builder.com/Graphics/Graphics101/?st.bl.fd.tsl.feat.1284.*

64d Add appropriate links to other sites.

Effective Web sites offer many layers of information by linking to other sites. Links give Web surfers other resources besides yours. When you link up with other sites, be sure to evaluate them first. Visit them yourself to be sure they are appropriate for your audience.

Also, since Web sites come and go without notification, check your links frequently to make sure that they are still in effect. If any have closed down, remove them from your site.

64e Carefully proofread your site.

There is nothing more embarrassing than having a Web site that is riddled with spelling and grammatical errors. Just as you would proofread a college paper before submitting it, you should proofread your site before launching it.

As you proofread, do not let the graphics distract you. Concentrate on the language, or you risk missing an obvious error. Also have a group of friends or colleagues review the site for spelling, grammatical, and content errors. A final reminder: Always identify the sources of the material you have integrated into your site.

65 Oral Presentations *oral pres*

Most people are struck by stage fright when asked to speak in front of others. In fact, many professional stage actors confess that they frequently experience stage fright before the curtain goes up.

But refusing at the last moment to step onto the stage is not an option for an actor, just as refusing to complete an oral assignment is usually not an option for you, no matter how much you might dread risking embarrassment.

Although the prospect of public speaking is no doubt daunting, there are some simple guidelines you can follow in preparing and delivering an oral presentation. By following these guidelines you can tame your initial fear to a manageable edginess, which in itself can make your presentation a success.

The Speaker-Audience Relationship

Just as you must establish a writer-reader relationship when you write an essay (see section 4a), so too you must establish a speaker-audience relationship when you speak in front of a group. In both instances, you are obligated to know a good deal about your subject. Also in both instances, you are obligated to organize your material carefully so that you clearly communicate it to a reader or to a listening audience, whichever the case may be.

Also, just as it is necessary in writing to carefully rewrite the early drafts of an essay to make it as clear and graceful as possible for your reader, it is necessary in speaking to rehearse your presentation over and over again so that it, too, becomes as clear and graceful as you can make it for your listener.

Finally, when you actually make the oral presentation to an audience, just as you do in writing, you can employ several simple speaking principles to make your speech informative, clear, interesting, and, possibly, even entertaining.

There is no standard oral presentation. The nature of your assignment will dictate the kind of presentation you will make. But virtually all oral presentations succeed or fail well before the speaker ever stands in front of an audience. So although the kind of presentation you might be required to make will vary, the principles you must employ to make a success of any oral presentation are constant:

- You must carefully organize your material;
- You must repeatedly rehearse your presentation;
- You must use sound speaking techniques when delivering your presentation.

65a Organize your presentation

A solid oral presentation normally has three elements:

Announce your subject and purpose. After a brief, casual, and polite lead-in, such as "Thank you, Professor Bibbit, for the opportunity . . ." or "I appreciate Ms. Chiselwit's invitation to address you today . . . ," straight-forwardly announce your subject and purpose:

> I chose to read Ken Kesey's *One Flew over the Cuckoo's Nest* for this presentation. I would like to outline for you why I think the novel should be required reading for all college freshmen.

Or,

> Ms. Chiselwit asked me to discuss some effective ways to market and sell our standard copper-plated widgets. I will discuss some of the methods I have used lately that have proved particularly successful, at least to me.

Choose an effective method of presentation. There are several ways to organize an oral presentation, some more effective than others. Select the one that makes you feel comfortable.

Memorizing your presentation. Inexperienced speakers often try to memorize their presentations. Although many believe memorization is the path to perfection, it is often the least effective method of oral presentation, it is all too easy for an inexperienced speaker to forget a word or two because of nervousness, then panic and draw a complete blank. Furthermore, a speaker other than a professional actor who attempts a memorized speech often loses effective voice inflection, thus losing verve and spontaneity of spoken language. Finally, the speaker of a memorized speech seldom makes eye contact with the audience, being so caught up on concentrating on the selected words stored away inside his or her head.

Reading Your Presentation

Reading a presentation has most of the drawbacks of a memorized speech, but it is not all bad. A good actor, for instance, can make an extremely effective reading. And sometimes it can be effective to read short passages from other people's texts to reinforce your ideas.

Using Notes

Generally, using notes as an aid in giving your oral presentation is considerably more effective than reciting or reading a written speech. It's easier to have normal voice inflection when you're using notes to jog your memory. It is also easier to make eye contact with your audience, to move away, at least briefly, from your lectern, and to use gestures to emphasize your points and give some visual variety to your audience. All these things make your presentation more dynamic. There is, however, one minor drawback to using notes. It's possible to drop your note cards out of nervousness and, thus, get them accidentally shuffled out of order. Unless you've numbered the cards, putting them back in order could prove difficult and embarrassing.

If you do employ notes, use note cards—and number them. They're easy to handle. Make sure the notes on each card are brief. You don't want your attention riveted on the cards; that would be almost as ineffective as reading. The only extended writing on a card should be a direct quote from another writer that you use to back up one of your points.

Using an Outline

Your oral presentation, whether you memorize it, read it, or use notes, needs to be tightly organized. The most effective method of tightly organizing your presentation is by outlining it. And then using that outline as a memory jog has a few advantages over using note cards. If you accidentally drop a page of an outline, it is much easier and quicker to get it back in proper order. Using an outline can also be a bit less physically constraining than using notes, particularly if you have your outline or the main points of your presentation on display for your audience on a visual aid such as a chalkboard or overhead transparency. Doing so allows you to move away from your lectern more freely and make eye contact with your audience more easily. We discuss these and other visual aids later in this chapter.

Check section 6d in this text for the characteristics of a formal outline. There we point out that formal outlines include a thesis statement, or in oral presentation more often a statement of subject and purpose that serves as a thesis, and the various levels of detail that explain the subject and purpose. The outline of this chapter looks like this:

Oral Presentations

I. Introduction
II. Speaker-Audience Relationship
III. Organizing Your Presentation
  A. Introduction
  B. Announcing your subject and purpose
    1. Casual and polite lead-in
    2. Explicit, simple statement
      a. Example 1
      b. Example 2
  C. Choosing your method of presentation
    1. Memorizing
    2. Reading
      a. advantages
      b. disadvantages
    3. Using notes
      a. advantages
      b. disadvantages
    4. Using an outline
      a. advantages
      b. example of chapter outline
IV. Rehearsing Your Presentation
  A. Introduction
  B. Rehearsing alone
    1. Reading aloud
    2. Reading into an audiocassette
    3. Speaking with only notes or an outline
    4. Speaking in front of a mirror
  C. Rehearsing in front of others
V. Delivering Your Presentation
  A. Introduction
  B. Using appropriate pace

C. Using visuals
D. Moving around the room
E. Making eye contact
F. Answering questions
G. Ending your presentation

VI. Conclusion

65b Rehearse your presentation

Professional stage actors begin their rehearsals months before they will ever perform in front of a live audience. They rehearse over and over and over again, and their rehearsals progress from the simple to the more complex.

They begin by reading their scripts silently to themselves. They then read aloud, testing different pacing, voice modulations, and verbal emphasis—but still by themselves. Next they read with a director and other actors reading their own parts. Eventually, they add gestures and movement to their reading. Finally, their lines memorized by this time, they recite their lines with gestures and movement, but without a script. They will finally perform in front of test audiences in order to make further adjustments to their performances before the play officially opens.

Making a relatively brief oral presentation might be a bit simpler but, nevertheless, requires substantial rehearsal time if the presentation is to succeed. Normally, the more you can rehearse the better your presentation will be. Like a professional actor, you will have more success if you organize your rehearsals by moving from the simple to the more complex.

Rehearsing Alone

Begin by writing out your entire presentation or by making a very detailed outline. Then read your work or speak from your outline aloud. Reading or speaking aloud is important. Believe it or not, you have to get used to hearing your own voice. You also must determine how long your presentation will take to make sure it will fit into your allotted time.

Then read or speak into an audiocassette. Listening to your voice come out of a machine will give you an entirely different perspective on what you sound like. You will now hear yourself as others hear you. At this point you can more easily make adjustments to your pace, tone, and verbal emphasis.

The final stage of rehearsing alone is speaking in front of a mirror, preferably a full-length mirror. Now you will see yourself as your audience will see you. If you haven't as yet added gestures and movement to your presentation, now is the time to do so. If you have already added these elements, now is the time to revamp them to make them more effective.

Rehearsing in Front of Others

Ideally, you should rehearse in front of an audience that is similar to your perspective audience. But practically, you will probably rehearse in front of a roommate or two, or a brother or sister, or a parent, or a husband or wife, or any friend willing to listen and, possibly, give advice. This is an important stage in your preparation because speaking in front of a breathing human being is substantially different from speaking to your image in a mirror. The more you are able to rehearse in front of others, the more your fear of speaking in front of an audience will subside and transform itself into an edgy nervousness when you actually make your presentation. Being just slightly nervous before you give your speech can actually make you a more effective speaker. An edginess can often enliven your presentation and emotionally connect you to your audience. Extreme nervousness, however, can render you oblivious to almost everything except your own state of mind. Being too relaxed can make you oblivious to your audience by catching you up in your own performance so you don't clearly recognize how your audience is responding to you.

65c Deliver your presentation

If you have prepared for your oral presentation by carefully organizing it and repeatedly rehearsing it, your presentation is headed for a success. As we said earlier, virtually all oral presentations succeed or fail well before a speaker ever gets in front of an audience. Once in front of an audience, though, you will still have to employ the following sound speaking techniques. But, of course, you will have practiced all of them during your rehearsals.

Using Appropriate Pace

There are two important factors in striking the appropriate pace for your speech. The first is to time your presentation so you start and finish within the time frame you've been given without either rushing or dawdling. A nervous and unpracticed speaker tends to rush, whereas a speaker without much to say stretches thin material even thinner by speaking too slowly.

Writers must use clear visual conventions to make their message clear for their readers. Indented paragraphs indicate the basic units of thought that combine to form an essay's total meaning. Individual sentences are the building blocks for the paragraphs. Sentence punctuation clarifies the meaning of each sentence. Speakers should also give their audience visual clarifications (see "Using visuals" later), but must rely primarily on voice to make verbal clarifications. That means raising and lowering the voice at appropriate places, speeding and slowing the pace, and pausing to give emphasis.

Using Visuals

When you organize your material, plan to use visuals. Visuals help you to pace yourself, as well as help clarify and emphasize your points. For a short talk, keep your visuals as simple as possible. Handouts, chalkboards, poster boards, flipcharts, and transparencies and slides, for instance, are readily available and can be easily used in classroom and small business presentations. But whatever kind of visual aid you choose to employ, use common sense in implementing it. All visuals must be big enough to be easily seen by your entire audience. All visual aids must be simple and uncluttered. When you use a visual, never turn your back to your audience when you use it or waste time writing on a chalkboard or overhead transparency while your audience waits. Anything you use must, therefore, be prepared before your presentation.

Moving Around the Room

Because just listening to a speaker is pretty much a static activity for a listener, you can make your speech more interesting by simply moving around a little bit. Even minimal movement helps. On occasion, take a step away from your lectern and stand next to it to make a point or two before you move back to your notes. Or walk to the chalkboard you're using to underline or check one of your points. Or move away from your lectern with a copy of the handout you distributed before your presentation to direct your audience to one of the points listed there. Any kind of movement that appropriately fits into your presentation gives visual variety to your audience and makes your presentation more interesting.

Making Eye Contact

You cannot engage your audience unless you look at them. This means looking them in the eyes, not at the top of their heads. Look around the room as you speak, pausing for moments with individuals. If you don't look your audience in the eyes, you give them the impression that it's really not necessary for them to be there.

Answering Questions

Most of the time when you give an oral presentation you will answer questions at the end. If you do answer questions, there are two important guidelines for you to follow: (1) Listen to the entire question so you fully understand it, and (2) Never try to answer the question if you don't know the answer.

When you take a question, look the questioner in the eye, nod at appropriate times, never speak until the questioner is through, and then repeat the question, asking the questioner if you have it right, so that you, the questioner, and the rest of the audience all have the same understanding. Then answer the question as simply as you can.

Never try to bluff if you don't know the answer to a question. Your audience will always recognize and resent a bluff. There is absolutely nothing wrong with saying, "I don't know," or "That's an aspect of the problem I've never considered," or if it is a question of fact that you don't know but could easily find out, "I don't have that information with me today, but I could bring it to our next meeting, if you'd like."

Ending Your Presentation

Whether or not you answer questions, end your presentation as simply and straightforwardly as you began it: "I've found these sale techniques particularly effective; maybe you will to." "Maybe some of you now agree with me that Ken Kesey's *One Flew over the Cuckoo's Nest* should be required reading for college freshmen. Or maybe some of you are now interested in reading the novel yourselves to come to your own conclusions." "If there are no more questions, I'd like to thank you for your attention."

If you diligently organize your material, repeatedly rehearse your presentation, and then use sound speaking techniques when you deliver your talk, there is every reason to expect your speech will be a success.

PART XI

Background in the Basics

When you study grammar in school, you are actually studying what you already "know." Note that the verb know *needs those quotation marks because we're not using it in the usual sense. Your grammar knowledge is largely subconscious: You don't consciously know what you "know." When you study grammar you are learning* about *those grammar rules that you use subconsciously every time you speak—as well as every time you listen and make sense of what you hear.*

—Martha Kolin, *writer*

66 Parts of Speech *gr*

There are eight parts of speech in English: nouns, pronouns, verbs, adjectives, adverbs, prepositions, conjunctions, and interjections. The same word can function at different times as more than one part of speech. To identify a word's part of speech, determine how the word is used in a sentence. The word *coach,* for instance, may function as a noun in one sentence and as a verb in another.

NOUN	The *coach* has a gentle way with players.
VERB	I *coach* my daughter's softball team.

66a Nouns.

Nouns name persons, places, things, or ideas. They may be classified as proper, common, abstract, concrete, and collective.

Proper nouns name particular persons, places, things, or events. They should be capitalized: Charles Dickens, London, Christmas.

Common nouns do not name particular persons, places, things, or events. They are not capitalized: writer, city, holiday.

Abstract nouns name intangible qualities, ideas, or characteristics: love, democracy, courage.

Concrete nouns name tangible things that can be perceived through the senses: wind, rain, pencil, nose, knife, needle.

Collective nouns name groups of individuals: audience, family, army, herd, jury, squad. (See agreement of collective nouns and verbs, 28d; of collective nouns and pronouns, 29c.)

NOTE: **Compound nouns** are composed of more than one word: *high school, crosswalk, sister-in-law, Labor Day.* (See hyphen, 51b; forming the possessive case, 48a; forming plurals, 53c.) A dictionary will list a compound noun as a single entry. Referring to a dictionary is especially important for determining capitalization of compound nouns. (See capitals, 47f.)

66b Pronouns.

Pronouns take the place of nouns. In the following sentences, the pronoun *him* substitutes for *John Franklin,* and the pronoun *them* substitutes for *fans.*

John Franklin ran eighty yards for a touchdown. Six fans ran onto the field to greet him before officials chased them back to the stands.

The word that a pronoun replaces is called the **antecedent** of the pronoun. *John Franklin* is the antecedent of *him,* and *fans* is the antecedent of *them.*

Pronouns are classified as personal, possessive, reflexive, relative, interrogative, demonstrative, and indefinite.

Personal pronouns refer to a person or a thing. They have plural and singular forms.

	SINGULAR	PLURAL
FIRST PERSON	I, me	we, us
SECOND PERSON	you	you
THIRD PERSON	he, she, him, her, it	they, them

Possessive pronouns are forms of personal pronouns that show ownership or relation. (See case, Chapter 31.)

my, mine	his	its	their, theirs
your, yours	her, hers		our, ours

Reflexive pronouns are formed by combining personal pronouns with *self* and *-selves.*

myself	ourselves
yourself	yourselves
himself, herself, itself	themselves

A reflexive pronoun indicates that someone or something named in a sentence acts (or reflects) upon itself.

Margo looked at herself in the mirror.

Reflexive pronouns that are used to emphasize a noun or pronoun are sometimes called **intensive pronouns.**

Margo herself will perform the ceremony.

Relative pronouns introduce adjective clauses. (See subordinate clauses, 69b.)

who whom whose that which

The couple who performed the tango won first prize.

Interrogative pronouns are used in questions.

who	whom	whose	which	what

Whom did you call?

Demonstrative pronouns point to or identify a noun. (See pronoun reference, Chapter 30.)

this	that	these	those

That is your problem.
This is the question: How will we raise the money?

Indefinite pronouns function as nouns in a sentence but do not take the place of a specific person or thing. Following are some common indefinite pronouns.

all	any	anyone	each
another	anybody	anything	either
everybody	most	nobody	some
everyone	one	none	somebody
many	neither	several	something

Somebody will reap the benefits.

66c Verbs.

A verb may express physical action (*dance, walk, jump*), mental action (*dream, guess, trust*), or state of being (*is, are, were*). A sentence must have a main verb to be complete. (See sentence, 67b; sentence fragments, Chapter 26.)

The year 2000 *ended* much like any other year.

Action verbs are classified by whether or not they must be followed by an object, that is, a noun or pronoun that names what is acted upon.

A *transitive verb* takes an object. (See direct object and indirect object, 67c.)

The pitcher tossed the ball.
The voters believed the politician.

An *intransitive verb* expresses action that has no object.

The pitcher smiled.
The stream runs through the canyon.

Although some verbs are transitive only (*destroy, send, forbid*) and others are intransitive only (*tremble, chuckle, happen*), most verbs can function as either transitive or intransitive.

TRANSITIVE	The guide explained the danger.
INTRANSITIVE	The guide never explained.

Linking verbs express a state of being or a condition rather than an action. The most common linking verbs are forms of *be,* such as *am, is, are, was, were.* Words such as *appear, become, feel, grow, look, smell,* and *taste* function as both linking verbs and action verbs. These verbs link the subject of a sentence with a predicate nominative or predicate adjective—a noun, pronoun, or adjective that identifies or modifies the subject. (See subject, 67a; predicate nominatives and predicate adjectives, 67f.)

The butler is the killer.

The predicate nominative *killer* identifies the subject *butler.*

The silence became frightening.

The predicate adjective *frightening* modifies the subject *silence.*

Many linking verbs also function as transitive as well as intransitive verbs.

LINKING	The butler *looked* gloomy.
INTRANSITIVE	The butler *looked* for an escape.
LINKING	Carmen's hair *grew* gray from shock.
TRANSITIVE	Mr. Higgins *grew* plums.

Helping Verbs and Verb Phrases

A verb often includes one or more **helping verbs,** sometimes called **auxiliary verbs.**

Common Helping Verbs

am	has	can (may) have
are	had	could (would, should) be
is	can	could (would, should) have
was	may	will (shall) have been
were	will (shall) be	might have
do	will (shall) have	might have been
did	has (had) been	must
have	can (may) be	must have
		must have been

The verb and its helping verb(s) form a verb phrase.

The comet *has been approaching* earth for two years.

In some sentences the verb and its helping verb are separated.

> The day *has* finally *arrived.*
> *Did* they *reach* Georgia?

(See tense, Chapter 32; passive voice, Chapter 34.)

66d Adjectives.

Adjectives modify nouns and pronouns. To modify a word means to limit it—that is, to make its meaning more definite. Adjectives limit in three ways.

1. **By describing.**

   A *tall* woman stepped from the *curious* crowd.
   The *white* and *black* car won the race.

2. **By pointing out which one.**

   That man is my brother.

3. **By telling how many.**

   Twelve children and *several* parents attended.

Adjectives normally are placed directly before the words they modify, but sometimes a writer places descriptive adjectives after the words they modify.

> The stallion, *long* and *lean,* galloped past us.

Predicate adjectives generally follow linking verbs and modify the subject of a sentence. (See predicate adjective, 67f.)

> The runners were *tired* and *thirsty.*

Adjectives or Pronouns?

A word may be used as more than one part of speech. This is especially true of the words listed below, which may serve as adjectives or pronouns depending on the way they function in a sentence.

all	either	one	these
another	few	other	this
any	many	several	those
both	more	some	what
each	neither	that	which

ADJECTIVE	*This* book is overdue. *Those* books are on reserve.
PRONOUN	*This* is the overdue book. *Those* are the books on reserve.

The definite article *the* and the indefinite articles *a* (used before words beginning with a consonant sound) and *an* (used before words beginning with a vowel sound) may also be classified as adjectives.

66e Adverbs.

Adverbs modify verbs, adjectives, other adverbs, and groups of words. Adverbs most commonly modify verbs by telling how, when, where, or to what extent.

HOW	He reads carefully.
WHEN	He reads late.
WHERE	He reads everywhere.
EXTENT	He reads widely.

Adverbs sometimes modify adjectives and other adverbs.

> She is *truly* dedicated. [Modifies the adjective *dedicated*]
> She studies *terribly* hard. [Modifies the adverb *hard*]

Adverbs sometimes modify groups of words.

> *Unfortunately,* I cannot attend the wedding. [Modifies the whole sentence]

Many adverbs end in *-ly,* but not all words that end in *-ly* are adverbs.

> The day was chilly, but the group jogged briskly through the park. [*Chilly* is an adjective; *briskly* is an adverb.]

66f Prepositions.

A preposition shows the relation of a noun or pronoun to some other word in a sentence. Prepositions usually introduce a word group called a **prepositional phrase,** which always consists of the preposition and an object of the preposition—a noun or pronoun that relates to another word in the sentence.

> The effect of pesticides threatens wildlife in marshes.

Pesticides is related to *effect* because it specifies which effect. *Marshes* is related to *wildlife* because it indicates where wildlife is threatened. The prepositions *of* and *in* indicate the relations between these words. (See prepositional phrases, 68a.)

Prepositions usually show direction or position. The following words are among the most common prepositions.

above	at	beyond	into	under
across	before	by	of	up
after	behind	down	on	upon
against	below	during	out	with
along	beneath	for	over	within
among	beside	from	through	without
around	between	in	to	

Around the corner and *beyond* the tracks the road turns.

Groups of words, such as *along with, according to,* and *in spite of,* sometimes serve as prepositions. (See idioms, 25c.)

According to the latest report, the company is nearly bankrupt.

66g Conjunctions.

Conjunctions join words, phrases, or clauses. They are usually classified into three categories: coordinating conjunctions, correlative conjunctions, and subordinating conjunctions.

There are seven **coordinating conjunctions:** *and, but, or, yet, for, nor,* and *so.* (See subject and predicate, 67a, 67b; main clauses, 69a; compound sentences, 70.)

Oranges, lemons, *and* limes are citrus fruits.
The fish bite in the morning *or* after sundown.
The comet hit, *but* no one saw it.

Correlative conjunctions are always used in pairs: *both . . . and; not only . . . but also; either . . . or;* and *neither . . . nor.*

Both the California condor *and* the Maryland darter are struggling to survive.

Neither animal *nor* plant species are safe from human encroachment.

Subordinating conjunctions begin subordinate clauses. Some common subordinating conjunctions, several of which also function as prepositions, are *after, although, because, before, if, since, so that, though, unless, until, when, where,* and *while.* (See subordinate clauses, 69b.)

Humans must uncover their fears *before* they can uncover their courage.

When psychology develops a model of human nature, it will not be based solely on neuroses and character disorders.

NOTE: Conjunctive adverbs join main, or independent, clauses. Words such as *consequently, furthermore, hence, however, indeed, moreover, nevertheless, subsequently, therefore,* and *thus* are conjunctive adverbs. (See main clauses, 69a; semicolon, 38b.)

Paralysis was President Franklin Delano Roosevelt's only experience with defeat; *consequently,* he never revealed the extent of his handicap.

Statistics show that advertising generates sales; manufacturers, *therefore,* will continue to support Madison Avenue copywriters.

66h Interjections.

Interjections express surprise or strong emotion and have no grammatical relation to sentences. Examples of interjections are *Oh! Wow! Ah! Ouch! Hey! My goodness!*

Ouch! I bit my tongue.

Exercise 66.1: Review

Name the part of speech of each italicized word in the following paragraph, using the abbreviations N for noun, PRO for pronoun, V for verb, ADJ for adjective, ADV for adverb, PREP for preposition, C for conjunction, and I for interjection.

Medical school instructors *believe* that good care *begins* with a record of a patient's medical history; *therefore,* the *skill* of *diagnosis* rests on the simple act of talking with a patient. The doctor must listen, *ask* important questions, and *not only* hear what the patient says *but also* hear what the patient does not say. *This* discussion will enable the doctor to create a diagnosis and a *treatment* plan. *Although* medical interviewing has been part of the *diagnostic* process since medicine began, authorities are *officially* recognizing that *it* is the foundation of any successful treatment. The next time your doctor begins *with* a discussion of your medical history, do not protest with "*Oh no,*" not again," but instead appreciate the importance of this process.

67 Parts of Sentences *gr*

Effective writing starts with clear, grammatical sentences. A sentence is a group of words that contains a subject and a predicate and is not dependent on another group of words to complete its meaning. (See subordinating conjunctions, 69b; main clauses and dependent clauses, Chapter 69.)

NONSENTENCE	Although the celebration ended with a fireworks display.
SENTENCE	The celebration ended with a fireworks display.
SENTENCE	How did the celebration end?

Subject and Predicate

67a Simple subject and complete subject.

The **simple subject** is the word or words that act, are acted upon, or are described.

> *Quail Hill* rises at the end of University Drive.
> *Birds* have been nesting among the rocks and shrubs.
> Bundled in coats, *students* stroll to the peak each evening.

Sometimes the subject *you* is implied.

> Speak to us! [Meaning *You* speak to us.]

The **complete subject** includes the simple subject and the group of words that modify the simple subject.

> *The student rally* began at noon.
> *The candidate from Benson Hall* will speak at two o'clock.

67b Simple predicate and complete predicate.

The **simple predicate,** sometimes referred to as the **main verb,** is the word or words that tell what the subject did or how it was acted upon.

> Quail Hill *rises* at the end of University Drive.
> Birds *have been nesting* among the rocks and shrubs.

Bundled in coats, students *stroll* to the peak each evening.

The **complete predicate** is the group of words that includes the simple predicate and its modifiers.

The student rally *began at noon.*
The candidate from Benson Hall *will speak at two o'clock.*

67c Compound subject.

A compound subject consists of two or more subjects that are joined by a conjunction and that have the same predicate.

Samuel King and *William Black* took the first aerial photographs.

Either *he* or *she* will fly the balloon.

67d Compound predicate.

A compound predicate consists of two or more main verbs that are joined by a conjunction and that have the same subject.

The rumble of the train *echoes* through the valley and *rolls* over the hills.

Space shuttles will *fly* to the moon and *return* with payloads of minerals.

Complements

Some sentences express the writer's thought by means of a subject and a predicate only: *He worked. She arrived.* Most sentences, however, have within the complete predicate one or more words that add to the meaning of the subject and simple predicate.

They appointed *a new president.*
He is *an engineer.*

These elements are called **complements,** and they function as direct and indirect objects and as predicate adjectives and predicate nominatives. (See verbs, 66c.)

67e Direct objects and indirect objects.

A **direct object** is a word or word group that receives the action of a main transitive verb. A direct object answers the question What? or Whom?

The Civic League invited *Julio to speak.*
She teaches *fifth grade.*

The **indirect object** of a verb precedes the direct object and usually indicates to whom or for whom the action is done.

The caretaker gave *Kim* the key.

To identify an indirect object, reconstruct the sentence by using the preposition *to* or *for.*

The caretaker gave the key *to Kim.*

Now *Kim* no longer functions as the indirect object but as the object of the preposition *to.*

67f Predicate adjectives and predicate nominatives.

A **predicate adjective** is an adjective that follows a linking verb and modifies the subject of the verb.

The animals seem *restless.*

A **predicate nominative** is a noun or pronoun that follows a linking verb and renames or identifies the subject of the verb.

The man with gray hair is *Mr. Sumato.*

Exercise 67.1: Complements

Underline and identify the direct objects (DO), indirect objects (IO), predicate adjectives (PA), and predicate nominatives (PN) in the following sentences.

1. Metaphors create vivid images in people's minds and in their hearts.
2. Highly charged images can become trademarks or handicaps for politicians.
3. Lincoln's "a house divided" won him success, but Hoover's "a chicken in every pot" brought him scorn.
4. In fear of using vivid language, many politicians give us empty phrases.
5. This vague use of language often sounds dull.

68 Phrases *gr*

Words in sentences function not only individually but also in groups. The most common word group is the phrase, a group of words that may function as a noun, a verb, an adjective, or an adverb.

68a Prepositional phrases.

Prepositional phrases begin with a preposition and end with a noun or pronoun. They function as adjectives or adverbs. (See prepositions, 66f.)

> The fibula *of the left leg* is broken.
> As she turned, her mask fell *to the floor.*

68b Appositive phrases.

An appositive phrase is a noun or pronoun with modifiers that is placed near another noun or pronoun to explain, describe, or identify it.

> The Wolves' Den, a hangout for college intellectuals, caught fire.
>
> My brother *David not James* works nights.

Usually an appositive follows the word it refers to, but it may also precede the word. (See comma, 36c.)

> A thrilling love story, John and Marsha's romance would make a wonderful film.

Exercise 68.1: Prepositional and Appositive Phrases

Combine each group of sentences into one sentence by using prepositional phrases and appositives. You may need to revise wording and exclude some words to make the new sentences read correctly. For example:

> The purpose is to enrich a person's life. This is the purpose of a college education. A college education is the best investment anyone can make.
>
> The purpose of a college education, the best investment anyone can make, is to enrich a person's life.

1. History is the foundation of any liberal arts education. It is a basic subject. History is in most curricula.
2. Sigmund Freud visited the United States. Freud is the father of psychoanalysis. He came to the United States in August and September. The year was 1909.
3. Bodybuilders seem dedicated. They are both male and female. The dedication is self-torture.
4. Personal forgiveness can be granted only by victims, not by observers. Forgiveness is a kind of moral embrace. The embrace is between two people.
5. Upton Sinclair wrote radical novels. Most of his novels are about corruption of the capitalistic system. He was a California candidate for governor in 1934.

Verbals and Verbal Phrases

A **verbal** is a verb that does not function as the simple predicate of a clause. Instead, verbals (which include infinitives, present participles, and past participles) function as nouns, adjectives, and adverbs.

68c Infinitives and infinitive phrases.

Infinitives and infinitive phrases function as nouns, adjectives, and adverbs. An infinitive phrase includes the infinitive—the plain form of a verb preceded by *to*—as well as its complements or modifiers. (See verb forms, Chapter 32.)

> Her favorite pastime is *to dance.* [Noun: names pastime]
> I have three choices *to offer* you. [Adjective: modifies choices]
> He seems eager *to gain* knowledge. [Adverb: modifies eager]

68d Participles and participial phrases.

Participles and participial phrases are verb forms that function as adjectives. Present participles end in *-ing* (*running, laughing, flying*). Past participles usually end in *-ed* (*flopped, jumped, dangled*), but a few end in *-en* (*beaten*), and some change entirely (*begun, swum, brought*). (See note on gerunds, 68e; verb forms, Chapter 32.)

> *Tired,* the runner slumped to the ground. [Past participle: modifies runner]

The *developing* crisis dominated the news. [Present participle: modifies crisis]

Participial phrases consist of a participle and its complements or modifiers.

The cat *howling through the night* belongs to Caesar.

Glutted with inexpensive imports, the automobile market has declined.

Beaten by Lady Luck, the gambler quit the game.

Exercise 68.2: Verbals and Verbal Phrases

Combine each group of sentences by using infinitive and participial phrases. Follow the directions in brackets after each group. You may need to add words, delete words, and/or change tenses. Example:

Time ticks away in relentless beats. It is a major preoccupation of most Americans. [Use a present participial phrase.]

Ticking away in relentless beats, time is a major occupation of most Americans.

1. The Navy keeps accurate world time. This is the Navy's tremendous responsibility. [Use an infinitive phrase as the subject.]
2. Atomic clocks outstrip the performance of the solar system. Every two years atomic clocks must be reset. [Use a present participial phrase.]
3. The Naval Observatory operates about fifty atomic clocks. They are stored in climate-controlled vaults. [Use a past participial phrase.]
4. Navigation satellites are accurate. They are accurate enough to locate an oil well. They are even accurate enough to guide a battleship through fog. [Use two infinitive phrases joined by *or.*]
5. Our lives are conditioned by a steady television diet. Our lives are measured in increments as regular as television commercials. [Use a past participial phrase.]

68e Gerunds and gerund phrases.

Gerunds and gerund phrases function as nouns. A gerund is the present participle of a verb, formed by adding *-ing* to the infinitive. It is used as a noun.

Dreaming leads to creation.

A gerund phrase consists of a gerund and its complements or modifiers. Like the gerund, the gerund phrase is used as a noun.

I love *dancing until dawn.*
Flying to Rome is costly.

NOTE: Since both gerunds and present participles end in *-ing*, they are sometimes confused. You can avoid confusing them by determining their function in a sentence. Gerunds function as nouns. Present participles, when not serving as part of the predicate, function as adjectives.

SUBJECT	*Running* keeps me fit for tennis.
PARTICIPLE	The water *running* in the kitchen is a nuisance.

Exercise 68.3: Gerund and Present Participial Phrases

Write two sentences for each of the following words, using the word in a gerund phrase and in a present participial phrase. For example, using the word *diving:*

GERUND	Diving from the ten-meter board is thrilling.
PARTICIPLE	Diving beneath the surface, he saw a world of splendid color.

1. hoping
2. drifting
3. flinging
4. washing
5. speaking

68f Absolute phrases.

An absolute phrase consists of a noun and (usually) a participle, plus modifiers, that add to the meaning of a sentence but have no grammatical relation to it.

An absolute phrase differs from other phrases because it does not modify a particular word but instead modifies an entire sentence. An absolute phrase may appear almost anywhere in a sentence.

The palm tree swayed, *its slick leaves shimmering with light.*

A magnifying glass raised to his eye, Sherlock Holmes examined the weapon.

The two of us worked the entire night—*Barbara at the computer and I at the tape recorder*—transcribing our field notes.

Exercise 68.4: Absolute Phrases

Combine each group of sentences using absolute phrases. You may need to add or omit words and change tenses. For example:

> The players were leaning over their cards. They were chatting softly. The poker game continued for hours.
>
> The players leaning over their cards and chatting softly, the poker game continued for hours.

1. Her novel was finished. Renee decided to vacation in Paris.
2. The Mercedes skidded to a stop in the rain. Its brakes were squealing. Its taillights were glowing.
3. The horses rounded the turn. Their nostrils were flaring. Their necks were stretching toward the finish line.
4. The mysteries of the earth have been explored. The 1990s adventurer will turn to the secrets of the mind.
5. The lifeguard sat on the sand. Suntan lotion was glistening on her back, and the wind was gently lifting her hair.

69 Clauses *gr*

A **clause** is a group of words that has a subject and a predicate. There are two kinds of clauses: main clauses (sometimes called independent clauses) and subordinate clauses (sometimes called dependent clauses).

69a Main clauses.

Main clauses form grammatically complete sentences. They may stand alone or be joined by coordinating conjunctions (see 66g), by conjunctive adverbs (see note, 66g), or by semicolons (see 38a, 38b). (Also see comma, 36a.)

The cobra is a poisonous snake. Its bite is often fatal.
The cobra is a poisonous snake, and its bite is often fatal.
The cobra is a poisonous snake; indeed, its bite is often fatal.
The cobra is a poisonous snake; its bite is often fatal.

69b Subordinate clauses.

Subordinate clauses do not form grammatically complete sentences. They are usually introduced by a subordinating conjunction (see 66g) or a relative pronoun (see 66b).

Subordinate clauses function as nouns, adjectives, or adverbs within a sentence. The exact relation in a sentence between the thoughts expressed in a dependent clause and the main clause is indicated by the subordinating conjunction or relative pronoun that joins them.

An **adjective clause** modifies a noun or pronoun. It often begins with a relative pronoun (*who, whom, whose, that, which*) that refers to or is related to a noun or pronoun that precedes it. (See comma, 36c.)

The trumpet player *who left the stage* fell asleep in the lounge.

Anything *that stands on the seafront* will be leveled by the storm.

Karla is the spy *Smiley seeks.* [The relative pronoun *that* or *whom* is understood.]

An **adverb clause** modifies a verb, an adjective, or an adverb. It begins with a subordinating conjunction such as *when, although, whenever, since, after, while, because, where, if, that,* or *than.*

Whenever he is asked, he plays the banjo.
I am happy *because it is Saturday.*
She studies more effectively *than I do.*

A **noun clause** is a subordinate clause that functions as a noun. It may serve as subject, predicate nominative, direct object, indirect object, or object of a preposition. The noun clause is likely to begin with a relative pronoun. (See complements, 67e, 67f.)

SUBJECT	*That life is difficult for some* means little to insensitive bureaucrats.
OBJECT	He described *what he wanted.*

Exercise 69.1: Subordinate Clauses

Combine each group of sentences by using subordinate clauses as indicated in the instructions in brackets. You may need to change some words to avoid repetition. For example:

> Few people have heard of hydrocephalus. Hydrocephalus affects at least a million families. [Use *although* to form an adverb clause.]
>
> Although few people have heard of the disease, hydrocephalus affects at least a million families.

1. Hydrocephalus is caused by a buildup of fluid in the brain cavity. Hydrocephalus is often called "water on the brain." [Use *which* to form an adjective clause.]
2. As many as eight thousand babies are born with the defect every year. This number does not relieve the mark of shame attached to the disease. [Use *that* to form a noun clause.]
3. Some doctors have attempted to educate the public about the defect. These doctors are prominent in the medical profession. Many people still believe that any child suffering from it will develop a head perhaps twice the normal size. [Use *although* to form an adverb clause and use *who* to form an adjective clause.]
4. Enlarged heads can be avoided. Doctors have developed an operation for hydrocephalics. The operation drains the fluid to avoid retardation in the patient. [Use *because* to form an adverb clause and use *that* to form an adjective clause.]
5. The surgical procedure has brought new hope to the parents of children suffering from the disease. They still worry about the future of their children. [Use *although* to form an adverb clause.]

70 Sentence Patterns *gr*

Sentences can be classified according to their structure (simple, compound, complex, or compound-complex) and their purpose (declarative, imperative, interrogative, or exclamatory).

Sentence Structures

Simple sentences have only one main clause and no dependent clauses, although they may have several phrases.

> Years ago the family of a bride would supply the groom with a dowry. [One main clause]
>
> The bride and the groom were not consulted about the choice of a mate and sometimes met each other for the first time on the day of their wedding. [One main clause with a compound subject and a compound predicate]

Compound sentences have two or more main clauses but no dependent clauses.

> Chauvinism has fueled many political skirmishes, but jingoism has ignited wars. [Two main clauses joined by a comma and the coordinating conjunction *but*]
>
> Some people are flattered into virtue; other people are bullied out of vice. [Two main clauses joined by a semicolon]

Complex sentences have one main clause and at least one subordinate clause.

> Although he was a cunning investor, Bennett went bankrupt. [One main clause and one dependent clause beginning with the subordinating conjunction *although*]

Compound-complex sentences have at least two main clauses and at least one dependent clause.

> If they wish to live fully, most people need amusement to relax, and many people need intellectual challenges to develop their minds. [Two main clauses joined by a comma and the coordinating conjunction *and* and one dependent clause beginning with the subordinating conjunction *if*]

Sentence Purposes

A **declarative sentence** makes a statement.

> Spelunking requires the skill of a mountain climber and the courage of a coal miner.

An **imperative sentence** gives a command or makes a request.

> Don't walk on the grass.

Please stay off the grass.

(See implied subject, 67a.)

An **interrogative sentence** asks a question.

Which point of view is most valid?

An **exclamatory sentence** expresses strong feeling.

The mountains are glorious!

Exercise 70.1: Sentence Structure and Purpose

Write sentences according to the following directions.

1. Write a simple, declarative sentence that states a fact about your campus.
2. Using the coordinating conjunction *or,* write a compound sentence about a friend.
3. Write an interrogative sentence directed to a politician.
4. Write a declarative compound-complex sentence directed to a parent.
5. Write an imperative sentence that gently directs a child.
6. Write a complex sentence that deals with a foreign country.
7. Using a semicolon, write a compound sentence that deals with a sports event.
8. Using *who,* write a compound-complex sentence describing a friend.
9. Write a series of three simple sentences followed by a complex sentence that deals with a subject you read about in a newspaper.
10. Using a variety of sentence structures, describe a place that is important to you. Identify each sentence as simple, compound, complex, or compound-complex.

PART XII

Background for Multilingual Writers

I am a writer. And by that definition, I am someone who has always loved language. I am fascinated by language in daily life. I spend a great deal of my time thinking about the power of language—the way it can evoke an emotion, a visual image, a complex idea, or a simple truth. Language is the tool of my trade. And I use them all—all the Englishes I grew up with.

—Amy Tan, *novelist*

71 Omitted Words *esl*

Do Not Omit Expletives, Subjects, or Verbs

Are three chapters to read this week has a common second language error. The writer left out a word, the expletive *there.* Corrected, the sentence should read, *There are three chapters to read this week.*

English does not allow you to omit expletives, subjects, or verbs. English does allow you to omit *you* in commands—that is, when *you* is understood: *Read the directions with care.* If your first language allows for these omissions, stay alert! Acceptable omissions in your first language may not be acceptable in English.

- ◆ [I w] ~~W~~orry about my life span because I smoke.
- ◆ Cultural knowledge [is] important.
- ◆ Jorge Lopez, [who] studied karate, broke a brick with a hand.

An expletive, *there* or *it,* may be required in sentences where the subject follows the verb.

- ◆ [It is] ~~Is~~ easy to make mistakes.
- ◆ Children believe [there] are scary creatures in the night.

Remember, *is, are, was,* or *were* cannot begin a clause unless the clause is a question, such as *Are you awake?,* or an exclamation, such as *Was I sick!*

Exercise 71.1: Omitted Words

Read the following paragraph. Find the missing subjects and verbs and add them to the text.

> Government loans to college students the lowest in ten years. The president very concerned. Appointed a committee to investigate falling income. Will not meet until next September. The president unhappy about the slow start. Is one

of the problems the president promised to solve during his campaign. Are thousands of needy students in the United States cannot afford a college education. Are unhappy about this problem. Is little hope. Seems to be an unfair policy.

72 Noun Markers *esl*

Use Noun Markers

English nouns frequently have markers. Noun markers are words indicating a noun is coming (though the noun might not be the next word). The command *Read stories* is wrong, unless the writer means all stories, which would not make much sense. Corrected, it would read, *Read the stories.*

	COMMON NOUN MARKERS
ARTICLES	a car; the car; an automobile
NUMBERS	12 cats; seven dogs
POSSESSIVE NOUNS	Van's stories; China's goal
POSSESSIVE PRONOUNS	my, our, your, his, her, its, their
OTHER PRONOUNS	all, every, any, each, either, neither, few, many, more, most, this, that, these, those, much, several, some, whose

Other words may be placed between the marker and the noun.

> *The* shiny new *motorcycle* belongs to her.
> *Twelve* white *ducks* swim in the lake.
> *Jon*'s hopeless *whining* gets nothing done.
> *Her* demanding *schedule* is exhausting.

Of all the noun markers, articles (*a, an, the*) can be troublesome.

Definite Article: *the*

Use *the* before nouns that are specifically identified.

> Wear *the* boots you bought in Santa Fe.

> Raul had *the* most interesting performance.
> *The* sun rose at six.

A careful reading of the examples above shows that each noun in question is specifically identified by the context.

> I couldn't find the reason for the computer error no matter how hard I tried. After I read the manual the reason became clear.

At first the *reason* is unidentified, so you could use the indefinite article *a.* But *reason* is identified when the writer mentions it the second time; it is the specific *reason* that the writer found that caused the computer error.

Because it is used only with nouns specifically identified, *the* should not be used with plural or noncount nouns when the meaning conveyed is *generally* or *all.*

- ◆ The cost of printing ~~the~~ magazines is usually paid for by advertising revenue.
- ◆ Health magazines report studies about drinking ~~the~~ coffee.

Generally, do not use *the* with proper nouns. Proper nouns name people, places, and things: *Leslie Woo, Mexico, Shea Stadium.*

There are exceptions. Some plural proper nouns naming places, such as *the Pyrenees, the Sierra Nevadas, the Alps, the Great Lakes,* take the definite article. Furthermore, some countries have an official name that may take *the* and a shorter, more commonly used name that does not take *the.*

Formal Name	Common Name
the Italian Republic	Italy
the Commonwealth of Australia	Australia
the Hashemite Kingdom of Jordan	Jordan
the Principality of Liechtenstein	Liechtenstein
the United States of America	America

In all these cases the article *the* is used with the descriptive portion of the name, *republic, commonwealth, kingdom, principality, states,* but not with the actual name.

Indefinite Articles: *a, an*

Use the indefinite article *a* or *an* for singular count nouns not specifically identified.

Most nouns refer to things that can be counted, such as *one horse, three cars, five dollars.* Some nouns refer to things that can't be counted, such as *news, fog, sand.*

If a singular count noun is not specifically identified, use *a* or *an.*

Apple started a revolution in personal computers.
Deacon has an interesting insect collection.

Which should you use, *a* or *an?* That depends on the sound of the word following the article. Use *a* before consonant sounds and *an* before vowel sounds.

a rabbit	an awkward rabbit
an umbrella	a blue umbrella

A word beginning with the letter *h* may have either an initial consonant sound if it is aspirated (*hole*) or an initial vowel sound if it is not aspirated (*heiress*).

a hand	an hour

Don't use *a* and *an* with plural nouns.

◆ Mariko borrowed money to cover ~~an~~ expenses.

◆ The exhibit consisted of ~~a~~ hastily arranged groupings of native costumes.

Generally, don't use *a* and *an* with noncount nouns.

Teresa wrote on pollution.

While you are shopping, please get coffee and soap.

Generally use an article when you show a particular amount of a noncount noun by placing a count noun first and using *of.*

a bag of rice	a pile of sand

Exercise 72.1: Noun Markers

In the following paragraph, determine if an article should be used in a space, and if so, which article—*a, an,* or *the.*

______ hundred years ago, human beings lived ______ average of forty-five years. Then came ______ flush toilet. Invented by Thomas Crapper in 1860, ______ toilet has been "______ biggest variable in ______ extending life span," according to Professor Gary Ruvkun, ______ geneticist at Harvard University.

In the remainder of the paragraph, determine where articles should be added or deleted.

Human wastes in water can transmit the cholera, diarrhea, and salmonellosis. In developing world, where only 34 percent of population has access to the toilets, life spans can be up to 30 years less than average in the industrialized countries.

73 Verb Combinations *esl*

Use Correct Verb Combinations

Van had three tests, but only two difficult has a common second language error: The writer has not used a correct verb combination. Corrected, the sentence would read, *Van had three tests, but only two were difficult.*

English sentences often require combinations of helping verbs and main verbs.

Helping Verbs. Helping verbs appear before main verbs. Some main verbs will not be complete without helping verbs.

- The mail ^will^ *arrive* soon.

There are twenty-three helping verbs. Nine are called *models;* they work only as helping verbs. The others, which are forms of *do, have,* and *be,* can also work as main verbs.

HELPING VERBS

Three forms of *do:* do, does, did
Three forms of *have:* have, has, had
All forms of *be:* be, is, was, were, are, am, been, being
Modals: can, could, may, might, must, shall, should, will, would

After modals and *do, does, did,* use a plain verb.

may dance	might fly	should bring
do swim	does feel	did hurt

◆ My web page may expand~~s~~ my clientele.

◆ Your answer does not convince~~s~~ me.

◆ Did you finish~~ed~~ your projects?

After *have, has, had,* use the past participle to form the perfect tense.

have driven   has contributed   had slept

◆ Those hungry guys must have ~~eat~~ eaten the leftovers.

◆ Julia has accomplish^ed nothing this weekend.

◆ Luis had finish^ed his sculpture just in time.

After the helping verbs *is, was, were, are, am,* use a present participle to form one of the progressive tenses.

is going   was swimming   were eating
are studying   am thinking

◆ Jason was work~~ed~~ing on his car.

Be and *been* must be preceded by other helping verbs and followed by a present participle to form one of the progressive tenses.

can or *could* be
may, might, or *must* be
shall or *should* be
will or *would* be
has, have, or *had* been
can or *could have* been
may, might, or *must have* been
shall or *should have* been
will or *would have* been

◆ Rod ^will be leaving soon.

◆ Minh ^has been studying late.

After the helping verbs *is, was, were, are, am,* use a past participle to form the passive voice.

is repeated   was thrown   were submitted

are appreciated am assisted

◆ The truth is reveal[ed] in strange ways.

Be, been, and *being* must be preceded by other helping verbs and followed by a past participle to form the passive voice.

is, was, were, are, or *am* being
can or *could* be
may, might, or *must* be
shall or *should* be
will or *would* be
can have or *could have* been
may have, might have, or *must have* been
shall have or *should have* been
will have or *would have* been

◆ My dog may have been save[d] by its veterinarian.

◆ The photos were being mount[ed] in the albums.

Intransitive verbs, those expressing action with no direct object, cannot be used in the passive voice.

◆ The actor was grinn~~ed~~[ing] broadly.

Exercise 73.1: Correct Verb Forms

Identify the correct verb form for each set of verbs in the following sentences.

1. Scientists (have studied, have study) the effects of exercise on people for years.
2. Information, which (was release, was released) in August, indicates that exercise (is contributing, is contributes) to a longer life expectancy.
3. Further research on exercise suggests that some older people (be coping, may be coping) with mental disorders better because of daily exercise.
4. Unfortunately, many residential communities for the elderly (do not offer, do not offering) enough exercise classes.

5. Now the National Institutes of Health (is encourage, is encouraging) more organized exercise programs across the nation.

Phrasal Verbs. Phrasal verbs combine a verb with a preposition or an adverb. Often phrasal verbs have both idiomatic and literal meaning. For example, *look up* may be used literally to mean *focus on something above you* or idiomatically to mean *search for information.*

Phrasal verbs are either separable or nonseparable depending upon whether an object can be inserted between the verb and the particle. *Clean up,* for example, is a separable phrasal verb, as in *This weekend I will clean the house up.* Generally, phrasal verbs have been common in informal writing, but now they are appearing more frequently in formal writing.

Phrasal verbs must be learned in context. Nevertheless, the following list will help you understand phrasal verbs. Nonseparable phrasal verbs are marked [N].

COMMON PHRASAL VERBS

ask out (ask for a date)
bring up (mention casually; raise a child)
call off (cancel)
call up (call on a telephone)
come across [N] (meet or find unexpectedly)
drop in or drop by [N] (visit unannounced)
drop off (leave someone or something at a place)
fill out (complete a form)
get along with [N] (have a comfortable relationship)
get over [N] (recover from something)
give up (stop trying)
go over [N] (review)
hand in (submit)
help out (assist)
keep on (continue)
leave out (omit)
make up (become friendly again; do past work; invent)
pass away [N] (die)
point out (call attention to)
put away (store; lock up; drink heavily)
put off (postpone, avoid)
run out of [N] (have no more)
take off (leave; remove something)
take over (control; take charge)
turn down (reject)
wrap up (complete)

When the direct object is a pronoun, a phrasal verb must be separated.

◆ I will help out him with biology.

Exercise 73.2: Correct Phrasal Verbs

Decide which phrasal verb, similar in meaning to the verb in brackets, should be used in the following paragraph.

> Artists must [submit] their entries for the exhibit by Friday, but they are always late. Most artists [postpone] creating their work until the last minute. By starting so late, they cannot [complete] a painting or sculpture on time. Too often judges [reject] late entries. Artists often [invent] dramatic excuses for being late. Last year, one artist actually said, "The dog ate it."

Verbs Followed by Gerunds and Infinitives. Some verbs may be followed by gerunds but not infinitives. Some may be followed by infinitives but not gerunds. Some may be followed by either gerunds or infinitives.

A gerund ends in *-ing* and functions as a noun, such as *cooking, studying, painting.*

An infinitive consists of a verb's plain form usually preceded by *to: to attend, to believe, to convince.*

VERB WITH GERUND	Did he *mention running* in Mason Park?
VERB WITH INFINITIVE	This light *is guaranteed to work* fifteen hours on two batteries.

Verbs Followed by Gerunds But Not Infinitives.

admit	discuss	mind	recall
appreciate	enjoy	miss	resent
avoid	escape	postpone	resist
consider	finish	practice	risk
delay	imagine	put off	suggest
deny	mention	quit	tolerate

Authorities *will not tolerate writing* on buildings.

Verbs Followed by Infinitives But Not Gerunds.

afford	demand	hope	pretend
agree	deserve	learn	promise

appear	endeavor	manage	refuse
ask	expect	mean (intend)	seem
are	fail	need	threaten
claim	guarantee	offer	wait
choose	happen	plan	want
decide	hesitate	prepare	wish

Some verbs followed by an infinitive must have a noun or pronoun between the verb and the infinitive, such as *advise, allow, cause, caution, challenge, condemn, convince, dare, direct, encourage, forbid, invite, permit, persuade, require, teach, tell, warn.*

> I *urge* you *to enter* the race.
> William *advised* Nona *to avoid* the park after dark.

Some verbs may be followed directly by an infinitive or may have a noun or pronoun between them and an infinitive, such as *ask, expect, need, want.*

> I *want to dance* until midnight.
> I *want* you *to dance* with me until midnight.

Verbs Followed by Gerunds or Infinitives.

bear	deserve	love	remember
begin	read	neglect	start
hate	prefer	stop	can't bear
intend	regret	try	can't stand
continue	like		

> The institute *will start researching* the effects of laughter.
> The institute *has started to research* the effects of laughter.

Exercise 73.3: Correct Gerunds and Infinitives

Complete the following sentences with a gerund or an infinitive.

1. Counselors want students [understand] course requirements.
2. They want students [study] the course catalog.
3. They also suggest [examine] and [memorize] college department requirements.
4. Moreover, counselors caution students not [ignore] [read] the detailed requirements for graduation.
5. The Advisory Office would appreciate [know] each student's graduation plans.

74 Faulty Repetitions *esl*

Delete Faulty Repetitions

Childhood it is the leading cause of stress among children has a common second language error. The writer has unnecessarily referred to *childhood* with the pronoun *it.* Corrected, the sentence would read, *Childhood is the leading cause of stress among children.*

Reread your sentences carefully. Delete any words that unnecessarily refer to or repeat other words in a sentence.

- Driving ~~this~~ is my favorite method of travel.
- The slim woman with short hair ~~she~~ is my doctor.
- Professor Park, who lectured on Korea, ~~she~~ used humor to make her points.
- That was the year when we graduated ~~then~~.
- The party will be held in the restaurant where we held the graduation dinner ~~there~~.
- Carl's business trip was made miserable by the clients whom he was visiting with ~~them~~.

Exercise 74.1: Faulty Repetitions

Draw a line through the unnecessary words in the following sentences.

1. The Statue of Liberty, which is located in New York harbor, it was given to the United States by France.
2. A love letter was on the front seat of Tom's Honda where it would be easily found there.
3. The sun it was so hot the sand sizzled.

4. The game occurred on Saturday when thousands of people were at home then.
5. Six people they were honored, and more than fifty they were mentioned.

75 Present and Past Participles *esl*

Use Present and Past Participles Correctly

The interesting events interested TV viewers shows how forms of a plain verb can be used as an adjective and main verb. But when you use the present or past participles of a plain verb as an adjective, be sure to do so correctly.

Present participles, such as *moving, running, dancing, flying,* and past participles, such as *moved, ran, danced, flew,* when used as adjectives may precede the noun they modify, or they may follow a linking verb, such as forms of *to be* (*am, are, is, was, were*).

Present Participle Used as an Adjective

We saw an *interesting* movie.
The movie we saw was *interesting.*

Past Participle Used as an Adjective

All *interested* people should attend the debate.
Many people were *interested* in the debate.

As you can see from the examples above, the present participle describes the agent causing the feeling or reaction (*movie was interesting*), and the past participle describes the person or thing having the feeling or reaction (*interested people*). In your writing, use the proper participle form for verbs such as these:

amazing, amazed
amusing, amused
annoying, annoyed
boring, bored
confusing, confused
depressing, depressed
disturbing, disturbed
embarrassing, embarrassed
exciting, excited
exhausting, exhausted
fascinating, fascinated
frightening, frightened
interesting, interested
shocking, shocked
surprising, surprised
thrilling, thrilled

Sometimes writers make the mistake of unnecessarily repeating a verb form. They mistakenly use the present participle as an adjective and a past participle of the same verb as the main verb.

- The ~~exciting~~ movie excited us.

Exercise 75.1: Using Participles Correctly

Identify the correct participle for each sentence.

1. People across the country were (shocking, shocked) by the news of the explosion in Oklahoma City.
2. The news on television showed how (frightening, frightened) and (confusing, confused) everyone was.
3. The death and destruction left the residents of the Oklahoma City area very (depressing, depressed).
4. However, the rescue of victims who had been trapped for hours was (amazing, amazed), and people were (thrilling, thrilled) to learn that some people survived.
5. Even though the emotional response of people around the nation was strong, nothing could relieve the families of victims, who were (grieving, grieved) over their losses.

Glossaries

Glossary of Usage

Glossary of Grammatical Terms

Glossary of Usage

The entries in this glossary are words and phrases that frequently cause problems for inexperienced writers. Based on recent editions of dictionaries and usage guides, the suggestions for standard written English included in this glossary represent current practice among experienced writers. You should avoid using words and phrases labeled *nonstandard,* and use entries labeled *colloquial* sparingly and with care. They are used primarily in informal speech and writing and, therefore, are usually inappropriate in college and business writing.

a, an Use *a* before a consonant sound, *an* before a vowel sound.

a history	a university	a one o'clock meeting	a *C*
an hour	an undertow	an orphan	an *F*

aggravate *Aggravate* means "make worse." In writing it should not be used in its colloquial meaning of "irritate" or "annoy."

agree to, agree with *Agree to* means "consent to" a plan or proposal. *Agree with* means "be in accord with" a person or group.

ain't Nonstandard for *am not* or *aren't.*

all right *All right* is always two words. *Alright* is a misspelling.

all together, altogether *All together* means "in a group," "gathered in one place," or "in unison." *Altogether* means "wholly" or "completely." *They made the jungle trek all together rather than in small groups. I did not altogether approve of the plan.*

allusion, illusion An *allusion* is a reference to something. An *illusion* is a deceptive appearance. *Dr. Conn fills his lectures with classical allusions. Despite the hard facts, she clings to her illusion of true love.*

a lot *A lot* is always written as two words. *Alot* is a common misspelling.

among, between *Among* is used to refer to three or more people or things. *Between* is used with two people or things. *Half the treasure was divided between the captain and the ship's owner, the other half among the crew.* Sometimes *between* is used with more than two if the relationship concerns individual members of the group with each other. *The treaty between the five countries guarantees access to deep water ports.*

amount, number *Amount* refers to a quantity of something that cannot be counted. *Number* refers to things that can be counted. *A large number of salt-water fish requires an aquarium that holds a tremendous amount of water.*

an See *a, an.*

and etc. *Et cetera* (etc.) means "and so forth"; *and etc.,* therefore, is redundant.

and/or A legalism that many people consider awkward in college and business writing.

anxious, eager *Anxious* means "nervous" or "worried." *Eager* means "enthusiastically anticipating something." *I am eager to start the trip across the desert but anxious about the weather.*

anyone, any one *Anyone* means "any person at all." *Any one* refers to a particular person or thing in a group. Similar definitions apply to *everyone, every one, someone, some one. Anyone with the price of membership can join. Any one of the seniors might have started the brawl.*

anyplace Colloquial for *anywhere.*

anyways, anywheres Nonstandard for *anyway* and *anywhere.*

as Avoid using *as* for *because, since, while, whether,* and *who. Because* [not *as*] *the firm is almost bankrupt, buying a computer is out of the question. We doubt whether* [not *as*] *they can continue.*

as, like See *like, as, as if, as though.*

awful An overused word for *bad, shocking, ugly.* Colloquially, *awful* substitutes for intensifiers meaning "very" or "extremely."

awhile, a while *Awhile* is an adverb. *A while* is an article and a noun. *Awhile,* therefore, can modify a verb but cannot serve as an object of a preposition. *After six hours on the road, they rested awhile. After six hours on the road, they rested for a while.*

bad, badly *Bad* is an adjective and should be used in formal writing to modify nouns and as a predicate adjective after linking verbs. *Badly* should be used only as an adverb. *The doctor felt bad. The tenor sang badly.*

being as, being that Colloquial for *because. Because* [not *Being that*] *the sun has risen each morning of your life, you may expect it to rise tomorrow.*

beside, besides *Beside* means "next to." *Besides* means "except" and "in addition." *The older sister stood beside her father. Besides one stranger, only relatives were on the bus.*

between See *among, between.*

bring, take Use *bring* to carry something from a farther place to a nearer one. Use *take* to carry something from a nearer place to a farther one. *Take these pages to the printer and bring me yesterday's batch.*

bunch *Bunch* should not be used to refer to a crowd or group of people or things. Reserve it to refer to things that grow fastened together, such as grapes and bananas.

burst, bursted, bust, busted The verb *burst* means "fly apart," and its principal parts are *burst, burst, burst.* The past tense *bursted* is nonstandard. *Bust* and *busted* are considered slang and so are inappropriate in college or business writing.

can, may *Can* indicates ability, and *may* indicates permission. Colloquially, *can* is used in both senses. *If I may use the car, I believe I can reach the store before it closes.*

center around *Center on* is more accurate than *center around.*

climactic, climatic *Climactic* refers to a climax. *Climatic* refers to climate.

compare to, compare with *Compare to* means "regard as similar." *Compare with* means "examine for similarities or differences." *The boy compared his father's bald head to an egg. The investigator compared the facts of the Rineman case with the facts of the Billings incident.*

continual, continuous *Continual* means "often repeated." *Continuous* means "unceasing" or "without a break." *My afternoons are continually interrupted by telephone calls. The waves lap continuously at the shore.*

convince, persuade Careful writers use *convince* when someone changes his or her opinion. They use *persuade* when someone is moved to take action. *The attorney convinced several students that capital punishment is immoral. The attorney persuaded several students to demonstrate against capital punishment.*

could of Nonstandard for *could have.*

credible, creditable, credulous *Credible* means "believable." *Creditable* means "praiseworthy." *Credulous* means "inclined to believe just about anything." *Hitchcock's fantastic stories are hardly credible; nevertheless, as a director he got creditable performances from his actors regardless of whether or not the audience was craedulous.*

criteria, data, phenomena *Criteria* is the plural form of *criterion.* Careful writers use *criteria* only in the plural sense. *The criteria were so ill phrased that they were hard to apply. Data* and *phenomena* are plurals of *datum* and *phenomenon,* respectively. They should be treated as plural forms. *New data suggest the drug is harmful. Today's unexplainable phenomena are tomorrow's scientific explanations.*

data See *criteria, data, phenomena.*

deal Colloquial and overused for *bargain, transaction,* or *business transaction.*

differ from, differ with *Differ from* means "be unlike." *Differ with* means "disagree."

different from, different than *Different from* is idiomatic and widely accepted. *Different than* is acceptable when it precedes a clause. *An elephant is different from a mastodon. Paris was different than I had expected.*

disinterested, uninterested *Disinterested* means "impartial." *Uninterested* means "bored" or "indifferent."

don't *Don't* is a contraction of *do not* and should not be used for *does not,* whose contraction is *doesn't. Although the performance doesn't begin for an hour, I still don't think Bernice will be ready.*

due to Many people object to the use of *due to* as a preposition that means "because of" or "owing to." *The class was canceled because of* [not *due to*] *low enrollment. Due to* is acceptable when used as a subject complement. In this position it usually follows a form of *be. His unpredictable behavior is due to alcohol.*

eager See *anxious, eager.*

enthused Colloquial for "showing enthusiasm." The preferred adjective is *enthusiastic.*

etc. See *and etc.*

everyday, every day *Everyday* is an adjective meaning "used daily" or "common" and is always written as a single word. *These are my everyday shoes. Every day* is composed of the noun *day* and the adjective *every* and is always written as two words. *I leave campus every day at 3 p.m.*

everyone, every one See *anyone, any one.*

everywheres Nonstandard for *everywhere.*

every which way Colloquial for *in every direction* or *in disorder.*

expect Colloquial when used to mean "suppose" or "believe." *I suppose* [not *expect*] *the Reynolds clan is still squabbling about the settlement of the will.*

explicit, implicit *Explicit* means "expressed directly or precisely." *Implicit* means "expressed indirectly or suggested." *The threat was explicit—"I'll break your nose!" Although his voice was gentle, his body carried an implicit threat.*

farther, further *Farther* refers to actual distance. *Further* refers to additional time, amount, or other abstract matters. *I cannot walk any farther. Further encouragement is useless.*

fewer, less *Fewer* refers to items that can be counted. *Less* refers to a collective quantity that cannot be counted. *The marsh has fewer ducks living in it, but it also has less water to support them.*

finalize Avoid using *finalize* for the verb *complete.*

former, latter *Former* refers to the first named of two things or people. *Latter* refers to the second of two named. *First* and *last* are used to refer to items in a series of three or more. *Gina and Jose are very successful; the former is a dentist, the latter a poet. Jogging, biking, and swimming require tremendous endurance; the last requires the most.*

further See *farther, further.*

get A common verb used in many colloquial and slang expressions. *Get wise, her prattling gets me,* and the like. Using *get* in such ways is inappropriate in college and business writing.

goes Nonstandard when used instead of *says* or *said* to introduce a quotation. It should not be used to indicate speech. *He said* [not *goes*], *"Leave me alone."*

good, well *Good* is an adjective; *well* is an adverb. *Dr. Hunato is a good golfer. She strokes the ball well. Well* should be used to refer to health. *You look well* [not *good*]. *Are you feeling well* [not *good*]*?*

had ought, hadn't ought Nonstandard for *ought* and *ought not.*

half *Half a* or *a half* is appropriate, but *a half a* is redundant. *We drank half a* [not *a half a*] *gallon of soda.*

herself, himself See *myself, herself, himself, itself, yourself.*

hisself Nonstandard for *himself.*

hopefully *Hopefully* means "with hope." *They prayed hopefully for the blizzard to stop. Hopefully* is used colloquially to mean "it is hoped" in place of *I hope;* however, *I hope* is preferred in college and business writing. *I hope* [rather than *Hopefully*] *the blizzard will stop.*

illusion See *allusion, illusion.*

implicit See *explicit, implicit.*

imply, infer *Imply* means "suggest." *Infer* means "conclude." *Irving implied that he had studied for the quiz, but I inferred that he was unprepared.*

in, into *In* indicates a location or position. *Into* indicates movement or change. *Beata is in the study with a clairvoyant, who is in a trance. I must go into Murkwood, but I don't want to fall into danger. Into* has also come colloquially to mean "interested in" or "involved in" something, which is an inappropriate use in college and business writing. *My brother is interested in* [not *into*] *restoring Victorian houses.*

individual, party, person *Individual* should be used to refer to a single human being when expressing that person's unique qualities. *Each individual has a right to pursue his or her interests within the law.* When not emphasizing unique qualities, use *person. A romantic person will love the Austrian countryside.* Except in legal documents, use *party* to refer to a group. *Who is the missing person* [not *party*]?

infer See *imply, infer.*

in regards to Nonstandard for *in regard to* or *regarding.*

into See *in, into.*

irregardless Nonstandard for *regardless.*

is because See *reason is because.*

is when, is where A common predication error in sentences that define. *"Bandwagon" is a propaganda device by which* [not *is when* or *is where*] *advertisers urge consumers to become one of the millions buying their products.*

kind, sort, type These are singular words and take singular modifiers and verbs. *This kind of butterfly is rare in North America.* When referring to more than one thing, *kind, sort,* and *type* must be made plural and then take plural modifiers and verbs. *These kinds of butterflies are rare in North America.*

kind of, sort of Colloquial when used to mean *somewhat* or *rather. The picnic was rather* [not *sort of*] *dull.*

lay See *lie, lay.*

learn, teach *Learn* means "acquire knowledge." *Teach* means "dispense knowledge." *I must teach* [not *learn*] *the children better manners.*

leave, let *Leave* means "go away." *Let* means "allow" or "permit." *Let* [not *leave*] *me finish the job. The firm should have let* [not *left*] *her resign.*

less See *fewer, less.*

let See *leave, let.*

liable See *likely, liable.*

lie, lay These verbs are often confused. *Lie* means "recline," and *lay* means "place." In part, they seem to be confusing because the past tense of *lie* is the same as the present tense of *lay.*

lie ("recline")	*lay* ("place")
lie	lay
lay	laid
lain	laid
lying	laying

Lay (meaning "place") is also a transitive verb and as such takes an object. *Don't forget to lay the book on my desk. Today I laid the tile, and tomorrow I'll be laying the carpet. Lie* (meaning "recline") is intransitive and as such never takes an object. *The book lay on my desk for weeks. I can't waste time lying in bed; I've lain there long enough.*

like, as, as if, as though *Like* is a preposition and introduces a prepositional phrase. *As, as if,* and *as though* usually function as subordinating conjunctions and introduce dependent clauses. In college and business writing, do not use *like* as a subordinating conjunction. *The sky looks as if* [not *like*] *the end of the world is near.*

like, such as When introducing a representative series, use *such as.* To make a direct comparison with an example, use *like. The 1980s produced some powerful hitters in tennis, such as Borg, Connors, and McEnroe, but I want to play a game of strategy like Vilas.*

likely, liable *Likely* is used to express probability. *Liable* is used to express responsibility or obligation. *She is likely to finish the project before the weekend. Mr. Wert is liable for his son's destructive behavior.*

lots, lots of Colloquial for *a great deal, much,* or *plenty.*

may See *can, may.*

may be, maybe *May be* is a verb phrase, and *maybe* is an adverb meaning "perhaps."

may of Nonstandard for *may have.*

media, medium *Media* is the plural form of *medium.* Use plural modifiers and plural verbs with *media. These kinds of mass media—television, radio, newspaper—influence our emotional attitudes.*

might of Nonstandard for *might have.*

most Colloquial when used for *almost.*

must of Nonstandard for *must have.*

myself, herself, himself, itself, yourself These and other *-self* pronouns are reflexive or intensive—that is, they refer to or intensify a noun or another pronoun in a sentence. *The family members disagree among themselves, but I myself know how the inheritance should be divided.* Colloquially these pronouns often are used in place of personal pronouns in prepositional phrases. This use is inappropriate in college and business writing. *None of the team except you* [not *yourself*] *has learned to rappel.*

no way Nonstandard for *no.*

nowhere near Colloquial for *not nearly. Brytan's game is not nearly* [not *nowhere near*] *as good as Schrup's.*

nowheres Nonstandard for *nowhere.*

number See *amount, number.*

OK, O.K., okay All are acceptable spellings, but avoid using them in college and business writing.

party See *individual, party, person.*

people, persons *People* refers to a collective mass and emphasizes faceless anonymity. *Persons* refers to individuals who make up the group and emphasizes separate identity. *People surged into the convention hall. Several persons angrily denounced the membership's reluctance to act.*

percent, percentage Both *percent* and *percentage* refer to numbers and should be used only in actual references to statistics. Avoid using them to replace the word *part. The major part* [not *percent*] *of my trouble is caused by mismanagement. Percent* is always preceded by a number (*60 percent; 45 percent*), and *percentage* follows an adjective (*a major percentage*). In formal writing *percent* should always be written out (not %).

person See *individual, party, person.*

persons See *people, persons.*

persuade See *convince, persuade.*

phenomena, phenomenon See *criteria, data, phenomena.*

plus Nonstandard for *moreover. Nguyen Enterprises has a fine economic future; moreover* [not *plus*], *it offers young executives many tax-free perquisites.*

raise, rise Two commonly confused verbs. *Raise (raising, raised, raised),* meaning "force something to move upward," is a transitive verb and takes a direct object. *Rise (rising, rose, risen),* meaning "go up," is an intransitive verb. When the subject of a verb is being forced to move upward, use a form of *raise. Increasing the interest rate will raise monthly mortgage payments.* When the subject of a verb is itself moving upward, use a form of *rise. Unsteadily the ailing man rose from the chair.*

real, really *Real* is an adjective; *really* is an adverb. *The linebacker was really* [not *real*] *tough to block.*

reason is because Use *that* instead of *because* in the phrase *reason is because,* or rewrite the sentence. *The reason the MG stalled is that* [not *is because*] *the oil had leaked from the crankcase.*

respectfully, respectively *Respectfully* means "with respect" or "showing respect." *Respectively* means "each in the order given." *He respectfully expressed his opposition to the plan.* The Collector, The Optimist's Daughter, *and* The Human Comedy *were written by John Fowles, Eudora Welty, and William Saroyan, respectively.*

rise See *raise, rise.*

says, said See *goes.*

sensual, sensuous *Sensual* refers to pleasures of the body, especially sexual pleasures. *Sensuous* refers to pleasures perceived by the senses. *The poet's sensual desires led him to create the sensuous images readers find in his work.*

set, sit Two commonly confused verbs. *Set (setting, set, set),* meaning "put or place," is a transitive verb and takes a direct object. *Sit (sitting, sat, sat),* meaning "be seated," is an intransitive verb. When you mean "put something down," use a form of *set. Ralph set the paint beyond the child's reach.* When you refer to being seated, use a form of *sit. Don't sit in the wet paint.*

shall, will *Shall,* which was once used to form the simple future tense in the first person, has been replaced by *will. I will deal with him later.* In first-person questions that request an opinion, *shall* is the correct form to use. *Shall I march? Shall we strike?*

should, would Use *should* when expressing a condition or obligation. Use *would* when expressing a wish or customary action. *If they should appear, you must be prepared to battle. He would nap each afternoon when he was on vacation.*

should of Nonstandard for *should have.*

sit See *set, sit.*

someone See *anyone, any one.*

sort See *kind, sort, type.*

sort of See *kind of, sort of.*

such as See *like, such as.*

sure Colloquial when used as an adverb for *surely* or *certainly. Barnett surely* [not *sure*] *was correct in his cost estimate.*

sure and, sure to, try and, try to *Sure to* and *try to* are the preferred forms. *Try to* [not *try and*] *attend.*

than, then *Than* functions as a conjunctive used in comparisons, *then* as an adverb indicating time. *I would rather be in class than* [not *then*] *at work.*

that, which *That* always introduces a restrictive clause. *Which* may introduce a restrictive clause or a nonrestrictive clause. Many writers prefer to use *which* to introduce only nonrestrictive clauses. *This is the class that requires six outside reports. This class, which requires six outside reports, meets once a week.*

theirselves Nonstandard for *themselves.*

then See *than, then.*

try and, try to See *sure and, sure to, try and, try to.*

uninterested See *disinterested, uninterested.*

use to, suppose to Sometimes carelessly written for *used to* and *supposed to.*

wait for, wait on *Wait for* means "await." *Wait on* means "serve."

ways Use *way* when referring to distance. *The trout stream is only a little way* [not *ways*] *from here.*

well See *good, well.*

which See *that, which.*

which, who Never use *which* to refer to people. Use *who* or *that* to refer to people and *which* or *that* to refer to things.

who, whom Use the relative pronoun *who* to refer to subjects and subject complements; use the relative pronoun *whom* to refer to the object of the verb or preposition. *The award was given to the person who deserved it. The award was given to whom?*

will See *shall, will.*

would See *should, would.*

yourself See *myself, herself, himself, itself, yourself.*

Glossary of Grammatical Terms

absolute phrase A phrase that modifies a whole clause or sentence rather than a single word and is not joined to the rest of the sentence by a connector. It consists of a noun and a participle: *Hands trembling, she opened the envelope. Our original plan looks best, all things considered.* See *phrases;* also 68f, 36h.

abstract noun See *noun.*

active voice See *voice.*

adjective A word used to modify a noun or pronoun. It tells what kind, how many, or which one: *Careless drivers must attend seven hours of that class.* A **predicate adjective** follows a linking verb and describes the subject of the sentence: *The speaker was nervous.* See also 67f.

adjective clause A dependent clause that modifies a noun or a pronoun. See *clause.*

adjective phrase Any phrase that modifies a noun or pronoun. See *phrase.*

adverb A word used to modify a verb, an adjective, another adverb, or a whole phrase, clause, or sentence. Adverbs tell how, when, where, or to what extent. *He speaks hurriedly.* [*Hurriedly* modifies *speaks* by telling how.] *She was never ambitious.* [*Never* modifies *ambitious* by telling when.] *Our dog wanders everywhere.* [*Everywhere* modifies *wanders* by telling where.] *He is quite easily confused.* [*Quite* modifies *easily* by telling to what extent.] See also 66e.

adverb clause A dependent clause that modifies a verb, an adjective, another adverb, or a whole clause. See *clause.*

adverbial conjunction See *conjunctive adverb.*

adverb phrase Any phrase used as an adverb. See *phrase.*

agreement The correspondence in person, number, and gender between two words. A verb must agree with its subject in person and number. A pronoun must agree with its antecedent in person, number, and gender. A demonstrative adjective (*this, that, these, those*) must agree with its noun in number. See also *gender, person, number;* also Chapters 28, 29.

antecedent The word or group of words that a pronoun refers to. *When Stacy graduated, she immediately took a job in New York.* [*Stacy* is the antecedent of the pronoun *she.*] See also Chapter 29.

appositive A noun or group of words used as a noun, placed next to a noun or pronoun to explain, describe, or identify it: *The lawyer, a Harvard graduate, easily won her first case.* Most appositives are nonrestrictive and are set off with commas. See also 68b, 37c.

article *The* is a definite article. *A* and *an* are indefinite articles. Articles are classed as adjectives. See also 66d.

auxiliary verb See *helping verb.*

case The form of nouns and pronouns classified according to how they function in a sentence. English has three cases: the **subjective** to indicate the subject of a verb or a subject complement; the **objective** to indicate the object of a verb, verbal, or preposition; and the **possessive** to indicate ownership. Nouns and most pronouns change form only in the possessive case (*cathedral's, everyone's*). All other uses require only the plain form (*cathedral, everyone*). The personal pronouns *I, we, he, she,* and *they* and the relative or interrogative pronoun *who* have three case forms. The personal pronouns *you* and *it* have a separate possessive form. See also Chapter 10.

clause A group of words that has a subject and a predicate. A **main (independent) clause** forms a grammatically complete sentence: *He ran all the way to the station.* Main clauses can be joined to other main clauses with coordinating conjunctions, conjunctive adverbs, or semicolons. (See 66g, Chapter 38.) **Subordinate (dependent) clauses** are not sentences and must be joined to a main clause to form a grammatically complete sentence: *Although he was tired, he ran all the way to the station.* Dependent clauses function as adjectives, adverbs, and nouns. See also Chapter 69.

collective noun See *noun.*

comma splice An error occurring when main clauses are joined only by a comma: *Last summer we went camping, everyone laughed at my inability to pitch a tent.* See also Chapter 27, 69a.

common noun See *noun.*

comparative degree See *comparison.*

comparison Adjectives and adverbs have three forms: the **positive degree,** which only describes [*large*]; the **comparative degree,** which compares two things [*larger*]; and the **superlative degree,** which compares three or more things [*largest*]. See also 22a.

complement A word or group of words that completes the meaning of a subject, an object, or a verb. Complements function as **direct objects, indirect objects, predicate adjectives,** and **predicate nominatives:** *The manager opened the door* [direct object]. *Please send me a letter* [indirect object]. *The sea was calm* [predicate adjective]. *Her father is an accountant* [predicate nominative]. See also Chapter 67.

complete predicate See *predicate.*

complete sentence See *sentence.*

complete subject See *subject.*

compound Words or groups of words of two or more parts functioning as a unit. **Compound words:** *brother-in-law, lifeguard.* **Compound constructions:** *Betty and Joe* [compound subject] *flew to Chicago. The children giggled and blushed* [compound predicate]. See also 67c, 67d.

compound-complex sentence See *sentence.*

compound predicate See *compound.*

compound sentence See *sentence.*

compound subject See *compound.*

concrete noun See *noun.*

conjunction A word that connects and shows the relation between words, phrases, and clauses. **Coordinating conjunctions** (*and, but, or, nor, yet, for,* and *so*) connect items of equal grammatical rank: *The beauty of the scenery and the friendliness of the people make British Columbia an attractive tourist area.* **Correlative conjunctions** (*either . . . or, not only . . . but also,* and so on) are used in pairs: *You may choose either the vase or the picture.* **Subordinating conjunctions** (*when, while, if, although, because,* and so on) introduce dependent clauses and connect them to main clauses: *The carnival activity began when the sun went down.* See also 66g.

conjunctive adverb An adverb used to connect two main clauses: *Susan practiced faithfully; therefore, she improved rapidly.* See also 66g.

coordinating conjunction See *conjunction.*

correlative conjunction See *conjunction.*

count/noncount noun Count nouns are nouns that may be used in singular or plural form (e.g., *textbook, textbooks; assignment, assignments*). Noncount nouns may be used in singular form only (e.g., *advice, homework*). See Chapter 72.

dangling modifier A modifying phrase or clause that does not sensibly connect to any word in a sentence. See also 20f.

degree See *comparison.*

demonstrative pronoun See *pronoun.*

dependent clause See *clause.*

direct address A noun or pronoun used parenthetically to indicate the person or group spoken to: *I believe, friends, that we will win this election.*

direct discourse The presentation of the exact words, spoken or written, of another: *Steven asked, "Where have you been?"* **Indirect discourse** reports the words of another in paraphrase or summary form: *Steven wanted to know where we had been.* See also 21e.

direct object See *object.*

double negative Two negative words used in the same construction: *I didn't have no reason to stay home.* Double negatives are nonstandard English. The sentence must be revised: *I didn't have any reason to stay home* or *I had no reason to stay home.*

elliptical construction A construction in which one or more words are omitted but understood. *Bob types faster than Margaret* [*types*]. See also 32e.

expletive The word *there, here,* or *it* followed by a form of the verb *be* and used to begin a construction in which the subject follows the verb: *It is easy to spend money foolishly.* [To *spend money foolishly* is the subject of *is.*] See also 28e.

finite verb A verb that makes an assertion about a subject. A finite verb can function as the main (or only) verb in a sentence: *On weekends I work in the garden.* Gerunds, infinitives, and participles are nonfinite verbs and cannot function as main verbs in a sentence. See *verbal.*

fragment See *sentence fragment.*

fused sentence An error occurring when main clauses are joined without a coordinating conjunction or semicolon: *We traveled to Georgia it was a good trip.* See also Chapter 27.

future perfect tense See *tense.*

future tense See *tense.*

gender The classification of nouns and pronouns as masculine (*man, he*), feminine (*woman, she*), or neuter (*house, it*). See also *agreement;* Chapter 28.

genitive case Same as possessive case. See *case.*

gerund A verbal ending in *-ing* that functions as a noun. The form of the gerund is the same as that of the present participle. Gerunds may have objects, complements, or modifiers. *Cigarette smoking is dangerous to your health.* [The gerund *smoking* is the subject of the sentence. *Cigarette* modifies the gerund. *Dangerous* is a predicate adjective complementing the gerund.] See also *verbal;* 67e.

gerund phrase See *phrase.*

helping verb A verb used with a main verb to form a verb phrase: *Sarah was living in San Francisco at that time.* See also Chapter 32 and 66c.

imperative tense See *mood.*

indefinite pronoun See *pronoun.*

independent clause Same as main clause. See *clause.*

indicative See *mood.*

indirect discourse See *direct discourse.*

indirect object See *object.*

infinitive The plain form of a verb, as listed in the dictionary; it usually appears in combination with *to* to form a verbal that functions as a noun, an adjective, or an adverb. Infinitives may have objects, complements, or modifiers. *He promised to mow the lawn.* [The infinitive phrase *to mow the lawn* functions as a noun, the direct object of the verb *promised. Lawn* is the direct object of the infinitive *to mow.*] See also *verbal;* 68c.

infinitive phrase See *phrase.*

intensive pronoun See *pronoun.*

interjection A word expressing surprise or strong emotion: *Oh, here he comes!* See also 66h.

interrogative pronoun See *pronoun.*

intransitive verb See *verb.*

irregular verb A verb that does not form its past and past participle by adding *-d* or *-ed* to the infinitive form: *fly, flew, flown; sink, sank, sunk.* See also Chapter 32.

linking verb See *verb.*

main clause See *clause.*

misplaced modifier A modifier positioned incorrectly in a sentence. See also Chapter 20.

modifier An adjective, an adverb, or a word, phrase, or clause used as an adjective or adverb to limit or qualify another word or group of words.

mood The form of a verb indicating a writer's (or speaker's) intent in a sentence. The **indicative mood** is used for questions and statements of fact or opinion: *John is a good student.* The **imperative mood** indicates a command or direction: *Be a good student.* The **subjunctive mood** expresses doubt, a condition contrary to fact, or a wish: *I wish I were a good student.* See also Chapter 33.

nominative case Same as subjective case. See *case.*

nonrestrictive element A modifier that is not essential to the meaning of a main clause. Nonrestrictive elements are set off by commas: *Mr. Perkins, who retired from the grocery business last summer, is a noted rose grower.* See also 36c.

noun A word that names a person, place, thing, or idea. **Proper nouns** name particular people, places, or things: *James Joyce, Chicago, Fenway Park.* **Common nouns** name general classes: *athlete, singer, hotel.* **Abstract nouns** name intangible qualities: *loyalty, grace, devotion.* **Concrete nouns** name tangible things: *desk, snow, glasses.* **Collective nouns** name groups: *team, squad, committee.* See also 66a.

noun clause A dependent clause that functions as a subject, an object, or a complement. See *clause.*

number The indication of singular or plural in the forms of nouns (*toy, toys*), pronouns (*I, we*), demonstrative adjectives (*this, these*), and verbs (*eats, eat*). See also *agreement;* Chapters 28, 29.

object A word, phrase, or clause that receives the action of or is affected by a transitive verb, a verbal, or a preposition. A **direct object** receives the action of a transitive verb or verbal and answers the question What? or Whom?: *Stan made money tutoring neighborhood children.* [*Money* is the direct object of the transitive verb *make,* answering the question What? *Children* is the direct object of the verbal *tutoring,* answering the question Whom?] An **indirect object** indicates to whom or for whom an action is done: *I gave David five dollars.* [*David* is the indirect object of the verb *gave. Dollars* is the direct object.] An **object of a preposition** is the noun that a preposition relates to the rest of a sentence: *Joan sat by the door of the church.* [*Door* is the object of the preposition *by; church* is the object of the preposition *of.*] See also 67c, 67f, 68a.

objective case See *case.*

parenthetical expression A word, phrase, or clause that interrupts the thought of a sentence. See also 23b, 41a, 43a.

participial phrase See *phrase.*

participle A verbal that functions as an adjective, an adverb, or a part of a verb phrase. **Present participles** end in *-ing.* **Past participles** of regular verbs end in *-d* or *-ed: The light from the floating candles created grotesque shapes on the dark walls.* [The present participle *floating* is used as an adjective modifying *candles.*] *He ran screaming down the street.* [The present participle *screaming* is used as an adverb modifying *ran.*] *The thief had taken her favorite bracelet.* [The past participle *taken* is used as part of the verb phrase *had taken.*] See also *verbal;* 68d.

particle Another name for the preposition or adverb portion of a phrasal verb. See *phrasal verb.*

parts of speech The classification of words on the basis of their use in a sentence. The parts of speech are nouns, pronouns, verbs, adjectives, adverbs, prepositions, conjunctions, and interjections. Each part of speech is defined in a separate entry in the glossary. See also Chapter 66.

passive voice See *voice.*

past participle See *participle.*

past perfect tense See *tense.*

past tense See *tense.*

perfect tenses See *tense.*

person The form of pronouns and verbs used to indicate the speaker (first person—*I am*), the one spoken to (second person—*you are*), or the one spoken about (third person—*she is*). See also *agreement;* Chapters 28, 29.

personal pronoun See *pronoun.*

phrasal verb Two-word or three-word verb consisting of a verb form plus a preposition or adverb (e.g., *look over, put up with*).

phrase A group of words lacking a subject or a predicate or both and used as a single part of speech. A **verb phrase** consists of more than one verb: *had been talking, was swimming.* It functions as a predicate for clauses and sentences: *The professor has been lecturing for more than an hour.* A **prepositional phrase** consists of a preposition, its object, and any modifiers: *under the house, after the party.* It functions as an adjective, adverb, or noun: *She wandered to the elm grove beyond the fence.* [*To the elm grove* is used as an adverb modifying *wandered; beyond the fence* is used as an adjective modifying *grove.*] An **infinitive phrase** consists of an infinitive, its object, and any modifiers: *to hear the peaceful music, to learn I had been selected.* It functions as a noun, adjective, or adverb: *To see her again was a pleasure.* [*To see her again* is used as a noun, the subject of the sentence.] A **participial phrase** consists of a participle, its object, and any modifiers: *studying all night, glancing through the album.* It functions as an adjective or adverb: *The man jogging around the track is my brother.* [*Jogging around the track* is used as an adjective modifying *man.*] A **gerund phrase** consists of a gerund, its object, and any modifiers. Like participial phrases, gerund phrases use the *-ing* ending of the verb: *watching the birds, hoping for rain.* Therefore, they can be distinguished from participial phrases only in the context of a sentence. Gerund phrases function as nouns. *Jogging around the track is good exercise.* [*Jogging around the track* is used as a noun, the subject of the sentence.] An **absolute phrase** consists of a noun and usually a participle. It modifies a whole clause or sentence. *The election being over, the loser pledged support to the winner.* See also Chapter 68.

positive degree See *comparison.*

possessive case See *case.*

predicate The part of a sentence that tells what the subject did or how it was acted on. A predicate must have a finite verb. The **simple predicate** is the verb and its helping verb(s). The **complete predicate** is the simple predicate plus any modifiers, objects, and complements. *This play should set an attendance record in New York.* [*Should set* is the simple predicate.] See *finite verb;* also 67b.

predicate adjective See *adjective; complement.*

predicate nominative See *complement.*

preposition A word that shows the relation of a noun or a pronoun (the object of the preposition) to some other word in the sentence. See also *object; phrase;* 66f.

prepositional phrase See *phrase.*

present participle See *participle.*

present perfect tense See *tense.*

present tense See *tense.*

principal parts The present, present participle, past, and past participle of a verb: *look, looking, looked, looked.* See also Chapter 33.

progressive tense See *tense.*

pronoun A word that takes the place of a noun. Words that function as pronouns are classified as follows. **Personal pronouns:** *I, you, he, she, it, we, they* and their possessive forms, *my, mine, your, yours, his, her, hers, its, our, ours, their, theirs.* **Reflexive pronouns:** *myself, yourself, himself, herself, itself, ourselves, yourselves, themselves,* which are also sometimes used as **intensive pronouns,** as in *I myself saw it.* **Relative pronouns:** *who, whom, that, which, whose.* **Interrogative pronouns:** *who, which, whom, whose, what.* **Demonstrative pronouns:** *this, that, these, those.* **Indefinite pronouns:** *all, both, few, several, nobody,* and so on. See also 66b.

proper adjective An adjective derived from a proper noun: *French perfume, Orwellian nightmare.* See also 47f.

proper noun See *noun.*

quotation See *direct discourse.*

reflexive pronoun See *pronoun.*

regular verb A verb that forms its past and past participle by adding *-d* or *-ed* to the infinitive form: *wander, wandered, wandered; scheme, schemed, schemed.* See also Chapter 32.

relative pronoun See *pronoun.*

restrictive element A modifier that defines or identifies the noun it modifies and is therefore essential to the meaning of the main clause. Restrictive elements are not set off by commas. *All students who have successfully completed sixty units may apply for upper-division standing.* See also 36c and 37f.

run-on sentence See *fused sentence.*

sentence A group of words that contains a subject and a predicate and is not introduced by a subordinating conjunction. Sentences are classified according to their structure. A **simple sentence** has one main clause: *Maria fell asleep.* A **compound sentence** has two or more clauses: *Maria tried to stay awake, but she fell asleep.* A **complex sentence** has one main clause and at least one dependent clause: *When Maria lay down to rest, she fell asleep.* A **compound-complex sentence** has two or more main clauses and at least one dependent clause: *Maria tried to stay awake because she wanted to study, but she fell asleep.* Sentences may also be classified according to their purpose. A **declarative sentence** makes a statement: *I am going home.* An **imperative sentence** gives a command or makes a request: *Go home now.* An **interrogative sentence** asks a question: *Are you going home?* An **explanatory sentence** expresses strong feeling: *We're going home!* See also Chapter 70.

sentence fragment A portion of a sentence punctuated as though it were a sentence: *Suddenly appearing on the horizon.* See also Chapter 26.

simple predicate See *predicate.*

simple sentence See *sentence.*

simple subject See *subject.*

simple tenses See *tense.*

squinting modifier A modifier placed so it may refer to either a word preceding it or a word following it. See also 20b.

subject The part of a sentence that acts, is acted upon, or is described. The **simple subject** is the essential word or group of words of the **complete subject.** The complete subject is the simple subject plus its modifiers. *A tall, stately gentleman appeared at the door.* [*Gentleman* is the simple subject. *A tall, stately gentleman* is the complete subject.] See also 67a.

subject complement See *complement.*

subjective case See *case.*

subjunctive See *mood.*

subordinate clause Same as dependent clause. See *clause.*

subordinating conjunction See *conjunction.*

superlative degree See *comparison.*

tense The form of a verb and its helping verbs that expresses the verb's relation to time. The **simple tenses** are **present** (*I laugh, you choose*), **past** (*I laughed, you chose*), and **future** (*I will laugh, you will choose*). The **perfect tenses** indicate completed action: **present perfect** (*I have laughed, you have chosen*), **past perfect** (*I had laughed, you had chosen*), and **future perfect** (*I will have laughed, you will have chosen*). The **progressive tense** indicates continuing action (*I am laughing, you are choosing*). See also Chapter 32.

transitive verb See *verb.*

verb A word or group of words expressing action or a state of being. A **transitive verb** expresses action that has an object: *She painted a picture.* An **intransitive verb** expresses action that does not have an **object:** *The artist failed.* A **linking verb** expresses a state of being or a condition. It links the subject of a sentence with a complement that identifies or describes the subject: *Their laughter was maddening.* A verb may be transitive **in one sentence** and intransitive in another: *She paints pictures* [transitive]; *She paints well* [intransitive]. See also 66c; tense, Chapter 32; mood, Chapter 33; voice, Chapter 34.

verbal Also called *nonfinite verb.* A form of a verb used as a noun, an adjective, or an adverb. Gerunds, infinitives, and participles are verbals. Verbals may take objects, complements, and modifiers. A verbal cannot function as the main verb of a sentence. See also *gerund; infinitive; participle; phrase,* 68c, 68d, 68e.

verb phrase See *phrase.*

voice The form of a transitive verb that indicates whether the subject acts (**active voice**) or is acted upon (**passive voice**). Active voice: *Donita wrote a fine research paper.* Passive voice: *A fine research paper was written by Donita.* See also Chapter 34.

Index

A

B

D

E

H

I

N

O

P

Q

T

U

V

W

Y

Correction Symbols

Numbers refer to chapters or sections of the book

ab	Faulty abbreviation, **49**
adj/adv	Misuse of adjective or adverb, **35**
agr	Error in subject-verb agreement, **28**
appr	Inappropriate language, **23**
awk	Awkward construction, **17**
cap	Use capital letter, **47**
case	Error in pronoun case, **31**
con	Be concise, **24**
cons	Be consistent, **21**
coord	Faulty coordination, **17b**
cs	Comma splice, **27**
dev	Inadequate development, **12, 14, 15, 16**
div	Incorrect word division, **51a**
dm	Dangling modifier, **20f**
doc	Error in documentation, **59**
emp	Revise for emphasis, **17**
exact	Inexact word, **25**
frag	Sentence fragment, **26**
fs	Fused (run-on) sentence, **27**
gl/gr	See glossary of grammatical terms
gl/us	See glossary of usage
gr	Grammar, **66–70**
hyph	Hyphen, **51**
inc	Incomplete construction, **22**
ital	Italicize (underline), **50**
lc	Use lower case letter, **47h**
log	Faulty logic, **2, 3, 54g**
mm	Misplaced modifier, **20**
mng	Meaning unclear
mood	Faulty use of subjunctive, **33**
ms	Fix manuscript form, **9**
no,	Comma not needed, **37**
no ¶	No new paragraph
num	Error in use of numbers, **52**
par, ¶	Start new paragraph
¶ coh	Paragraph not coherent, **13**
¶ unity	Paragraph not unified, **12**
pass	Ineffective passive voice, **34**
pron agr	Error in pronoun-antecedent agreement, **29**
punct	Error in punctuation
	! Exclamation point, **46**
	. Period, **46**
	? Question mark, **46**
	, Comma, **36, 37**
	; Semicolon, **38**
	’ Apostrophe, **48**
	“ ” Quotation marks, **39**
	: Colon, **40**
	– Dash, **41**
	. . . Ellipsis mark, **42**
	( ) Parentheses, **43**
	[ ] Brackets, **44**
	/ Slash, **45**
ref	Pronoun reference error, **30**
run-on	Run-on (fused) sentence, **27**
sp	Misspelled word, **53**
sub	Faulty subordination, **17b**
tense	Error in verb tense, **32**
trans	Better transition needed, **13**
var	Vary sentence structure, **19**
vb form	Error in verb form, **32**
//	Faulty parallelism, **18**
#	Separate with space
⁀	Close up the space
x	Obvious error
^	Insert, something missing
w	Revise wordy sentences, **24**